The Klondike Stampede

The Klondike Stampede

*As It Appeared to One
of the Thousands of Cheechacos
Who Participated in the Mad
Rush of 1898–1899*

WALLIS R. SANBORN
Edited by WALLIS R. SANBORN, III

McFarland & Company, Inc., Publishers
Jefferson, North Carolina

All illustrations are by the author, Wallis R. Sanborn.

ISBN (print) 978-0-7864-9651-8
ISBN (ebook) 978-1-4766-2812-7

LIBRARY OF CONGRESS CATALOGUING DATA ARE AVAILABLE

BRITISH LIBRARY CATALOGUING DATA ARE AVAILABLE

© 2017 Emma H. Hanshaw. All rights reserved

No part of this book may be reproduced or transmitted in any form or by any means, electronic or mechanical, including photocopying or recording, or by any information storage and retrieval system, without permission in writing from the publisher.

Front cover: *inset* Wallis Sanborn with gold nugget tie-pin; *background* of large group of prospectors bound for the Klondike gold fields, Chilcoot Pass, Alaska, 1898 (Library of Congress)

Printed in the United States of America

*McFarland & Company, Inc., Publishers
Box 611, Jefferson, North Carolina 28640
www.mcfarlandpub.com*

To my grandson
Armand Alan Hanshaw,
who expresses his appreciation of each
story that I tell him by saying,
"I'll be satisfied, Granddaddy, if you'll
tell me just one more story."
—Wallis R. Sanborn

Table of Contents

Editor's Acknowledgments   ix
Editor's Preface   1
Editor's Introduction   3
AUTHOR'S INTRODUCTION   9

Part I. Rockford to Dawson City, 3943 Miles, February 26 to July 1, 1898

1. ROCKFORD TO SEATTLE   14
2. SEATTLE   18
   Loading Our Outfit on the *City of Seattle* 22 • Outfit 24 • Personal Outfit for W.R. Sanborn 25 • Expense Per Man 26
3. SEATTLE TO DYEA   27
   Dyea 32
4. SHEEP CAMP AND CHILKOOT PASS   36
   Moving from Dyea to Sheep Camp 36 • Sheep Camp 38 • Sheep Camp to the Scales 41 • Chilkoot Pass 45 • Lake Lindeman, White's Cove 48 • Two Close Shaves 50 • Leaving Lake Lindeman 56
5. LAKE BENNETT   59
   Our Temporary Camp 59 • Aristocrats of the Trail 61 • Our Permanent Camp on Lake Bennett 62 • Our Ten by Twelve Home 63 • Cooking 64 • Our Neighbors and Ourselves 64 • Whip-sawing Lumber and Building Our Boats 65 • Letters To and From Home 68 • Tragedy 70 • Our Recreation 73 • Leaving Lake Bennett 75
6. THE BOAT TRIP TO INDIAN RIVER   77
   Caribou Crossing to Lake Marsh, June 4 and 5 77 • White Horse Rapids, June 6 80 • Lake Laberge and Thirty Mile River, June 7 and 8 83 • Down the Lewes and the Yukon, June 9–12 85 • The Stewart River Stampede, June 13–24 87
7. SUMMER IN THE KLONDIKE   92
   Dawson City, June 27 and 28 92 • Answering Questions from Home 94 • Bonanza and Eldorado Creeks, June 29–July 1 96

Part II. Prospecting Indian River, July 1, 1898, to February 21, 1899

8. EXPLORING INDIAN RIVER   102
   Arena Gulch Stampede 106 • The Indian River Bars 107 • Our Party Splits 109

9. Autumn in the Klondike 111
   Opportunity Knocks 111 • Back to Indian River 112 • Autumn Life on Indian River 115

10. Getting Ready for Winter 119
    Selecting Neighbors for the Winter 119 • The Story of Ben Butler 121 • Building Our Cabin 123

11. Winter on Indian River 130
    Hauling Our Outfit to Bedrock City 130 • Getting Acquainted with Winter Weather 131 • Daily Routine 136 • Thanksgiving Day Celebration 139

12. Winter at Dawson 144
    Coming Events Cast Their Shadows Before Them 144 • A Winter Trip to Dawson 145 • The Hunker Creek Stampede, December 21, 1898 150 • The Shortest Day of the Year 151 • How One Klondike Expedition Went Wrong 154 • Restless Days at Bedrock City 155 • Tobacco 158 • December and January Weather 159 • Thompson Goes to Dawson 160

13. Dawson's Social Life and Business Section 165
    Churches 166 • Breaking into Society 168 • Women and Dance Halls 169

14. Stampeding with Thompson 173
    Our Bonanza Stampede, February 1899 173 • Our Big Stampede, February 8–11 174 • The Old-Timer as a Gold-Digger 179 • 56 Degrees Below Zero 179 • Goodbye Thompson 182

Part III. Our Second Spring and Summer, February 22–August 16, 1899

15. Mysterious Creek 186
    How It All Started 186 • Mushing to Mysterious Creek 189 • The Klondiker's Soliloquy 193 • Prospecting 196 • At Last I Stake and Record a Claim 198 • Revealing the Secret of Mysterious Creek 203

16. Spring 206
    Getting Back to Bedrock City 206 • Spring Activities at Bedrock 213

17. Our Second Summer 219
    June 219 • Outfit for Sale 223 • Goodbye Dawson 226

18. Down the Yukon River 230

19. St. Michael to Seattle 242
    St. Michael 242 • Bering Sea 243 • The Pacific 246

20. Author's Conclusion 254

Index 257

Editor's Acknowledgments

When one is tasked with editing and publishing a work, rather than writing one, the purpose is different, the job is different. The editor must remain true to the extant text—in this case, a unique historical artifact—while the author must remain true to the authorial intentions that drive the filling of the blank page. Nonetheless, the editor and the author, who often work on the manuscript in solitude, do not work alone. As such, it is my honor and my duty to offer thanks and acknowledgment to those who have aided in the publication of this book.

A number of students at Our Lady of the Lake University, Angelo State University, and Texas Tech University helped with the transcription of this manuscript from its original format—a single, 450-page typed manuscript that had been copied multiple times—to its editable digital format. This process was labor-intensive, and without the help of my students would have taken much longer. So, a thank you, very much, goes out to Luis Forestier (a former student and also the manager of Personal Computing Support at Our Lady of the Lake), Walter Garcia, Dexter Gilford, Amber Gonzalez, Sonya Groves, Javier Medina, Corrigan Moran, Victoria Ohara, Ricky Saldaña, and Hannah Walker.

One student merits special mention: Lupe Hernandez was instrumental in editing the photographs, drawings, and other graphic documents included in the work.

To my partner of 14 years, Amanda, to my children Thomas and Mia, I owe you a debt of gratitude that I cannot repay. Thank you for your patience with me.

To my parents, Wallis and Judy, thank you for introducing me to this manuscript and thank you for the photograph of Wallis Remsen Sanborn—my great grandfather, Wallis Remsen Sanborn II—my father, and myself, Wallis Remsen Sanborn III (below).

To my dear cousin Andrea Lynch, you have been an unwavering pillar of support, and were it not for your comprehensive knowledge of family history and your exceptional motivation in seeing this project through, I might not have been able to complete this effort.

Next, I must thank the Hanshaw family. David and Aunt Emma have been wonderful to work with, and I treasure our kinship and our partnership in seeing this project to its completion. Further, David was instrumental in getting me access to the original sketches, maps, and photographs.

A special thank you goes out to A. Alan Hanshaw, the dedicatee of the original 1932 manuscript. Uncle Al was six years old when his grandfather, Wallis Remsen Sanborn, drafted the manuscript, which was culled from memory, letters, and a diary written during Wallis' time as a Klondike Stampeder in 1898–1899. Even as a young child, Uncle Al was fascinated by Wallis' stories of the Klondike, so in a way, Al is the impetus behind the drafting of the manuscript. Alan, Wallis' eldest grandchild, faithfully kept the manuscript, which he distributed to his children in 1998, the centennial of Wallis' stampede, with the following letter:

> With this note, I am sending each of you a copy of a family treasure, a book entitled *The Klondike Stampede*, written by my Grandfather, Wallis Remsen Sanborn, your Great Grandfather.
>
> Your Great Grandfather was born in Rockford, Illinois and graduated in the early 1890s with a Master's Degree in Civil Engineering from what is now the Rose-Hulman Institute of Technology—formerly Rose Polytechnic Institute. His first jobs found him working for several railroads in the Chicago area as a right-of-way engineer. His mission was to establish a plan for railroad tracks and bridges.
>
> After several years in this career, your Great Grandfather heard stories of gold in the "Klondike" of Alaska and Canada. He and two of his friends from Rockford began the long journey there together, and in 1898 they stepped off a ship in Dyea, Alaska to begin fulfilling their golden dreams. They soon discovered that the very rich gold field was spread over a large, very rugged area which they laboriously traversed both on foot and in a hand-made boat, carrying their required year's supply of food, equipment, and clothing with them. The conditions were anything but ideal. This wonderful book details the adventures of their journey inland and the two years two of them spent prospecting along the Yukon River. They found a little gold, but not the bonanza of their dreams.
>
> After returning from Alaska, your Great Grandfather went back to working for the railroads that ran through Kankakee, Illinois. He and a co-worker decided to start their own business quarrying the limestone that was prevalent in that area. Limestone was used as track ballast and for the making of concrete. The railroads were their best customers. Your Great Grandfather's perseverance and dedication of purpose allowed him to continue this business from its beginning in 1906 until it was sold after his

Left to right: **Wallis R. Sanborn III, Wallis R. Sanborn II, Wallis R. Sanborn, September 1966** (courtesy Judy Sanborn).

death at age 92. He was an honored and respected businessman in his community and the industry. The quarry remains in operation to this day.

W.R. Sanborn was intelligent and had great fortitude and judgement. His education and Alaskan experience helped mold him into an extraordinarily goal driven person as well as a great writer and map maker. On top of all this, he was a kind, warm, and friendly person with his primary interests being his family and his church as well as his business. He was a man of many interests and he built a wonderful life for himself and others.

My Grandfather and I had a very close relationship throughout his life, both in Illinois and in Florida and we spent a lot of good times together. I tried to emulate him. My hope and belief is that W.R. Sanborn left his mark on all of you, his Great Grandchildren, and your children. It is my great pleasure to share his wonderful story with you as I believe you will enjoy it as much as I have. It's a "whale of a tale."

Dad [A. Alan Hanshaw, 1998]

Finally, of course, I must thank the author of this work, Wallis Remsen Sanborn, my great grandfather. As Uncle Al notes, Wallis wrote quite a tale. What makes this work unique among other Klondike Stampede narratives is his engineer's eye and skill as a draughtsman. The drawings of the natural world, in the Klondike, at sea, on the Yukon River, are heretofore unpublished. And while the letters and diary have been lost to time, the sketches remain and are incorporated into the manuscript.

In closing, thank you to those who will read this book.

Editor's Preface

When editing an historical document for publication, there are certain responsibilities involved, the first of which is featly to the text. The editor is the caretaker of the work as it exists, and must draw from the manuscript the wishes of the author. I have attempted to do so, so as to remain true to my great grandfather's literary, stylistic, and rhetorical goals.

The manuscript was drafted from May to December 1932, culled from Wallis Sanborn's memory, his letters home from the Klondike during 1898 and 1899, and the diary that he kept while a stampeder. The letters and the diary have been lost to time, but thanks to my uncle, A. Alan Hanshaw, the manuscript has always been in the family's possession. It was written at the impetus of Alan, Wallis Sanborn's eldest grandchild, who as a young boy was enthralled by Wallis' tales of the Klondike Stampede. Wallis, motivated to narrate his participation in the Klondike Gold Rush, dedicated the manuscript to six-year-old Alan. Alan (1926–2004) always wanted to see the manuscript published but sadly did not live to see it. My father and mother gave me a copy, and in 2013 I made it my mission to see the manuscript published.

As faithfulness to the text was and is my primary goal, I must mention some formal elements that remain unchanged in the published text as well as some elements that were standardized for readability. As the manuscript was drafted from memory and letter and diary excerpts and includes liberal passages from both preceding document types, there are passages that incorporate present and past tense nearly concurrently. I have left these shifts in place. Thus, there remain passages that contain narration in both tenses, the past drawn from the 19th century documents and the present drawn from Wallis' memory. The flow of the narrative is not so abrupt, though, as to warrant synchronizing the tense throughout the manuscript. Doing so, I argue, would bastardize authorial intent and creation. It is far more important in 2017 to reproduce the document as drafted in 1932. Also, there are passages that the author clearly identifies as cited excerpts from the letters. When warranted, these passages are introduced by the author in the narrative and are set off as block quotations per house style.

I have tried to standardize names, numbers, distances, capitalization, punctuation, fractions of measurement and distance, times of day, legal tender, boat and ship names, geographic locations, et cetera, without hampering the design of the original typed document. I have left commas in place that my inner grammarian said to remove, but I have placed missing possessive apostrophes when appropriate and perhaps accidentally left out. Regarding numbers, distances, use of capitalization for common and proper nouns, I have chosen standardization over 21st century normative rules, and any failure at standardization of such, numerically or textually, is the entirely the fault of the editor, that is, me.

I have included as many of Wallis' sketches, maps, and photographs as possible. Some, because of a lack of contrast or clarity, could not be included. That said, I have placed those that are included per Wallis' placement in the original manuscript. Again, it is the drawings that make this work so unique, an artifact rather than a mere narrative.

The work, as published, is as close to the original as I could make it.

Editor's Introduction

"Must have experience you know, that's one of the things I am after." So writes the author of the account at hand, in Chapter 3. By all evidence contained in the narrative, experience and adventure, rather than riches of the golden sort, were what Wallis and his partner, Dan Dever, gained on their stampede to the Klondike, which began in the late spring of 1898 and lasted until the late summer of 1899.

On August 16, 1896, George Washington Carmack, his wife Kate, her brother Skookum Jim Mason, and their nephew Tagish Dawson Charlie struck gold at Rabbit Creek (later renamed Bonanza Creek for obvious reasons) and by the summer of 1897 the first wave of "fully 25,000 argonauts" (London 70) had set forth for the Klondike, driven by the lure of gold. By the spring of 1898, more than 100,000 souls were on the trail to the Klondike. About 30,000 made it, but only a few got rich, as the best claims were already staked, and most of those who gained wealth did so in Dawson City's "service industries" ("The End of the Trail" 32–33)—the saloons, hotels, supply houses, road houses, lumberyards, restaurants that littered Dawson City and the surrounding area. According to Pierre Berton, author of the seminal and comprehensive history of the Klondike Gold Rush, *The Klondike Fever* (1958), of the 100,000 people who set out on the trail, and the 30,000 to 40,000 who reached Dawson City, only 15,000 to 20,000 actually prospected for gold. Of those, only 3,000 to 4,000 found gold. Of those, only a few hundred "got rich," and of those, only a handful maintained their wealth (417).

Thus it is not surprising to read, late in the adventure, that Wallis took from the Klondike only $60 in gold, for the easy gold, if there was such, was long gone by the time word of the discovery got out to the public in July of 1897. And depending on the route one's party took—the Canadian Route, over sea from Seattle to St. Michael and up the Yukon River, from Seattle to Dyea or Skagway to Lake Bennett and down the Yukon River—it might take a year to get to the Klondike, and this length of time is relative to those stampeders coming from the continental United States. Thus, while gold was the goal of the stampeders, just getting to the Klondike was an arduous, often life-threatening endeavor. Arrival guaranteed nothing but more hard work. And, as the prime mining land had been staked and claimed and worked long before the mass arrivals of spring and summer 1898, stampeding the Klondike in the hopes of striking it rich was a fool's errand. Nonetheless, fools and adventurers headed north.

Wallis Sanborn and his party, initially consisting of Dan Dever and Clarence Reynolds, a.k.a. Pop, left Rockford, Illinois, on February 26, 1898, and arrived back in Rockford on August 16, 1899. In the course of 18 months, the party of three (which became a party of two as Pop left in July of the first year) worked and mushed and mined and sweated and experienced that sort of affirmation of adventure born of near absolute self-reliance for survival.

In the Klondike of 1898–1899, one survived upon what one had packed into the Klondike, and upon one's wit and work and guile. In Dawson City, where meals and supplies could be purchased—at a premium, of course—most miners had little or no discretionary income and had to make do with what they brought with them. To prevent the mass starvation of those unfamiliar with the brutal conditions of the North, the Canadian government, through North-West Mounted Police Superintendent Sam Steele's order, required stampeders to pack one year's worth of supplies when entering the Yukon Territory (Gray 291). So just packing for the Yukon meant spending hundreds of dollars on a miner's outfit of between 1,500 and 2,000 pounds of food and supplies.

With outfit ready, the party or prospector would take a steamer from Seattle to Dyea or Skagway, Alaska—a distance of some 1,100 nautical miles. From Skagway or Dyea, the party would have to pack its outfit up the Chilkoot or White Pass trails, in fifty pound loads, up the 1,000-plus feet of inclines and switchbacks, to the summit of the trail, and thence into Canada and down to lakes Lindeman and Bennett. Reaching Lake Bennett, the party still faced more than 500 miles of passage along the Yukon River—but only after felling trees and milling boards for handcrafted boats.

Assuming the party survived the river trip to Dawson City—many, ill-prepared to navigate the rapids died on the river—they were ready to stampede the Klondike. According to Wallis, after travelling 3,943 miles, the party from Rockford, Illinois, arrived on site. This distance was not uncommon but many American stampeders travelled farther still. Yet they came. The trip from Rockford to Dawson City took Wallis' party four months—a fairly efficient trek, no doubt.

Once on site, miner's had to purchase a "free" miner's certificate for ten dollars, and off the party went, into the Klondike wilderness. Generally speaking, a stampede consisted of going to an unstaked, unclaimed area, usually near a water source—a creek or a river—and digging prospect holes in the ground, down to the permafrost, past that, and down to the bedrock. At the point of the permafrost, the miners would have to build fires to melt the frozen gravel and muck, which was removed in buckets and kept for separating at a later, warmer time. Weeks would be spent digging prospect holes and hauling hundreds or thousands of pounds of gravel and muck to the surface. Once the bedrock was reached, color, i.e., gold, was sought, and more often than not, at least with Wallis and his party, very little if any was found. Miners who sought to separate color from the gravel and muck would, in the spring and summer months, use rocker boxes and sluices to wash the gold from the aggregate. Any gold located was then placed in the miner's poke, his bag for holding gold dust or nuggets. As Wallis notes, he and Dan Dever, and the other parties present in the narrative, dug plenty of prospect holes but found very little color.

As an engineer with an eye for detail, Wallis offers an in-depth and detailed narrative of the daily activities of a stampeder—the work, the travel, the conversation, the petty and major squabbles, the food, the other stampeders, the weather, the intricacies of the mining processes, as well as the ethos and pathos of the era. Present in the text, as evidence of the world-wide draw of the gold stampede, are many non–Americans who sailed and trekked to the Klondike.

He describes prospectors and support personnel who hail from or have been through

South America, Scotland, Australia, New Zealand, Ireland, Sweden, England, Denmark, Norway, Germany, France, Russia, the Pacific Islands, Armenia, Japan, China. There are some ethnocentric references present in the narrative, along with some use of what is now appropriately considered racist language—"long cadaverous Jew," "Colored man," "nigger," "thieving Japs," "Chinamen," phrenological-seeming descriptions of "Indians"—but context must be considered. Among the many nationalities and ethnicities, all types of people relocate to the Yukon—the rich, the poor, the lucky, the hard-luck, pragmatists and dreamers, the educated and the uneducated. There are miners, sailors, engineers, surveyors, painted women, grafters and grifters and gamblers, thieves, scam artists, capitalists, the strong, the weak, the lazy, the sick, the stupid, the righteous and the less so. There are men and some women who stampede, but, interestingly, no children of the stampede, no children of the stampeders. The work is framed by the presence of children, in the train out of Rockford and in indigenous villages viewed when steaming from Dawson to St. Michael, but there are none in the peri-stampede narrative.

With people come food, and food is a major motif in the text. In addition to providing sustenance, food was a commodity to be bartered—sugar was especially valuable. Food was used to maintain health; Wallis and Dan Dever had plenty of dried fruit, so scurvy was not an issue, as it was with many others. In fact, scurvy was such an issue that scurvy camps were created to house—isolate?—those suffering from the disease. (Jack London, of course, suffered greatly from scurvy, in the Klondike, initially, and then for the length of his short life.) Food had to be carried into the Klondike; it had to be thawed; it had to be cooked; it had to be re-thawed to be consumed after re-freezing. And as previously noted, a party or a Cheechaco (tenderfoot) had to pack a year's worth of food to enter the Yukon, and Wallis includes a rations list while he describes food, food preparation, and food items on a regular basis—bacon is mentioned more than forty times in the narrative, and Wallis notes they ate "bacon three times a day and seven days a week." Also, popular are beans, mentioned more than forty times. Wallis bakes bread and Johnnie Cake on a regular basis, and rice is loved by Australians. Essentials such as oatmeal, coffee, tea, salt, dried eggs, and butter are routinely mentioned, and occasionally moose is consumed. Wallis and Dan Dever were well prepared in their food supply, and as such, neither suffered any ill-effects from malnourishment while in the Klondike; however, meals purchased at "road houses" are frequently referred to, and the quality of such is a continual source of complaint.

Other aspects of the Klondike and of the stampede commonly in the text are the weather, death, the mail, reading material, movement, animals, miner's honor codes, and Dawson City. Weather is a constant in the text, and it affects every aspect of life in the Klondike, so Wallis keeps track of the daily high and low temperatures and keeps a table of such (see Chapter 12). Among the coldest days are a number in the fifty degrees below zero range, a point at which getting one's feet wet while mushing can mean death, à la London's "To Build a Fire." Death, while not mentioned as often as the food or the weather, is common enough, and men die by gunshot, disease, drowning, hypothermia, and avalanche. In the Klondike, men do not die of old age.

Mail is always a ready topic in the text—how to retrieve it, how to send it, whether to mush to town to check on its arrival. Much consternation is suffered waiting for mail, and much joy is experienced receiving and reading mail. Generally, the prospectors are always in search of reading material—books, newspapers, magazines. Reading is nearly the only form of intellectual stimulation in the Klondike, and at the time of course, the dissemination of news comes only in print, and as the magazines and newspapers of the day had to be packed in to Dawson City from the outside world, the news is slow to arrive when it arrives at all. Nonetheless, the stampeders are constantly on the lookout for books and for recent or even not-so-recent news.

Geographic and physical movement, from stampede to stampede, from Bedrock City to Dawson City, from camp to camp, is a perpetual aspect of the narrative, for Wallis and Dan Dever and their peers must move through the wilderness, often pulling sleds that weigh hundreds of pounds, to stampede and prospect, to retrieve and send mail, to seek resupply and respite in Dawson City, to seek or gain anything physical or material, and to get in and out of the Klondike. That which cannot be made through sheer ingenuity and effort, and from raw supplies at hand, must be sought, bought, or bartered for, and one must travel through the snow and the wilderness to the site of the desired object(s). And, while animals of all sorts are omnipresent in the text, for there are birds, rabbits, mice, vermin, moose, caribou, wolves referred to and seen, and there are horses, mules, and dogs in labor to man, the sled-pulling dog team is a fictional fallacy rather than an historical fact. And as evidenced repeatedly in the text, when men mushed hither and yon, it was with man in the sled yoke. Dogs were very expensive to feed and maintain, and the cost of feeding a pack of sled dogs was cost prohibitive for most stampeders. Horses and mules did serve as pack animals, especially on the White Pass trail, AKA, Dead Horse Trail. Miner's honor codes are implicit in the text, notably in reference to miner's food caches. One does not touch another's food cache; it is sacrosanct, as taking another's food could lead to that Klondiker's death. Also, equipment, boats, cabins are left lying around or unlocked, and for the most part, one does not take that which was left, be it equipment or a boat or anything else of use. That said, precisely when something could be determined to be "abandoned" was a matter of subjectivity. In one episode, Wallis and Dan Dever's dry docked small boat was taken, but their food cache, left at the same locale, remained unmolested. Finally, with Wallis' eye for detail, when on trips to Dawson City, he includes detailed descriptions of its saloons, gambling houses, churches, and atmosphere, and his geographic descriptions of the town and its architecture add a three dimensionality to the Yukon burg. And of course, as previously mentioned in the other front matter, Wallis' drawings and maps, his "sketches," as he humbly identifies them, are archival artifacts and are that which make this document historically unique, even and especially when measured against other narratives of the Klondike Gold rush. These sketches are invaluable, pictures of another time, another era, and they add richness and texture to the prose that other Klondike narratives do not possess.

Closing this brief introduction, four texts and a film of note are especially worthy of mention for further investigation into the Klondike Gold rush. Pierre Berton's works *The Klondike Fever: The Life and Death of the Last Great Gold rush* and *The Klondike Quest: A Photographic Essay 1897–1899,* Charlotte Gray's *Gold Diggers: Striking It Rich in the Klondike,* Kathryn Morse's *The Nature of Gold: An Environmental History of the Klondike Gold Rush,* and Colin Low and Wolf Koenig's *City of Gold* are each interesting and enlightening efforts that expand on the day-to-day activities explicated by Wallis Sanborn—see bibliographic information below. The four book-length studies are accessible to popular readers, and

Berton, of course, is highly respected as the preeminent 20th Century authority on the Klondike Gold Rush, while Charlotte Gray and Kathryn Morse are respected contemporary historians. Low and Koenig's film is a brief look back at the gold rush a half century after the stampede. What is interesting contextually is that, as the stampede was geographically proximal to Dawson City and occurred in a very small chronological window—primarily from the spring of 1898 to the late summer of 1899, each of the works are intertextually linked to one another and to Wallis' narrative. Many of the same names, locations, events, endeavors, issues, concerns, and people are found in each of the texts, which is evidence, paradoxically, that a world-wide event, an attraction that drew stampeders from every populated continent, could be so limited in temporal span and geographical scope.

Interesting, as well, is the fact that the Klondike Gold rush is still an ongoing topic of study and conversation—academic and popular—more than a century after the happening. Perhaps it is the gold that is timeless, or perhaps it is the adventure involved in the travel and stampede. Perhaps it is the theme of man versus wilderness or man versus nature or man overcoming great obstacles through will and perseverance. Perhaps it is a romanticized idealism about the past. Whatever the cause of the ongoing popularity of the Rush, as a scholarly editor, and as the namesake of the author, I must say I am pleased and honored that I was allowed to guide this project as the caretaker of this singular historical artifact.

Works Cited

Berton, Pierre. *The Klondike Fever: The Life and Death of the Last Great Gold Rush*. 1958. New York: Carroll & Graff, 1997. Six decades after first publication, still the most comprehensive account of the Klondike Stampede.

"The End of the Trail." *History Today* 47 (August 1997): 32–33. Brief narrative celebrates the centenary of the Klondike Gold Rush.

Gray, Charlotte. *Gold Diggers: Striking it Rich in the Klondike*. Berkeley: Counterpoint, 2010. Account chronicles the Klondike experiences of six well known—to Klondike historians—stampeders: Miner and author Bill Haskell; Father William Judge; businesswoman Belinda Mulrooney; miner and author Jack London; journalist Flora Shaw; and North-West Mounted Police Superintendent Sam Steele.

London, Jack. "The Economics of the Klondike." *The American Monthly Review of Reviews* 21 (January 1900): 70–74. Marxist/Capitalist reading of the Klondike Gold Rush by its preeminent author.

Texts for Further Study

Allen, Douglas W. "Information Sharing During the Klondike Gold Rush." *Journal of Economic History* 67.4 (2007): 1–24. Article shows how exceptionally harsh living and working conditions in the Klondike affected the security of mining claims and personal property, so much so that claim-jumping and personal property theft in the wilderness were quite rare.

Berton, Pierre. *The Klondike Quest: A Photographic Essay 1897–1899*. 1983. Erin, Ontario: Boston Mills Press, 2005. Rich photographic history of the Klondike Gold Rush with more than 200 photographs of the adventure and era.

City of Gold. Directed by Colin Low and Wolf Koenig. Narrated by Pierre Berton. National Film Board of Canada, 1957. Well honored, well regarded documentary that records the Klondike Stampede through the optic of 1898 and 1957 Dawson City, Yukon.

London, Jack. *The Call of the Wild*. 1903. *The Call of the Wild, White Fang & To Build a Fire*. Intro. E.L. Doctorow. New York: The Modern Library, 1998. 1–75. Classic telling of the life of Buck, a pampered pet until dognapped and sent to the Yukon.

_____. "To Build a Fire." 1902, revised 1908. *The Call of the Wild, White Fang & To Build a Fire*. Intro. E.L. Doctorow. New York: The Modern Library, 1998. 255–71. Naturalist masterwork about nature's brutal indifference towards the needs of man. In its presentation of the lethal dangers of the Artic weather, it is truest of the London works here and comes closest to Wallis Sanborn's narrative.

_____. *White Fang*. 1906. *The Call of the Wild, White Fang & To Build a Fire*. Intro. E.L. Doctorow. New York: The Modern Library, 1998. 77–254. The inverse of *Call of the Wild*, a wild wolf-dog is enslaved by man and forced to fight for survival.

Morse, Kathryn. *The Nature of Gold: An Environmental History of the Klondike Gold Rush*. Seattle: U of Washington P, 2003. Scholarly study of Klondike Gold Rush examines late 19th century monetary policy and nexus of transport, industry, and the natural world that led to the possibility and practice of the Rush.

Newell, Dianne. "The Importance of Information and Misinformation in the Making of the Klondike Gold Rush." *Journal of Canadian Studies* 21.4 (1986): 95–111. Examination of the effects of mass communication and its influences upon the Klondike Gold Rush; contains a useful pre-Rush history of the late 19th-century exploration of the Canadian Yukon.

Tarzlaff, Wayne A. "From Storekeeper to Prospector: The Experience of a Klondike Gold Rush Party from Emporia, Kansas." *Journal of the West* 38.4 (1999): 75–82. Brief but interesting account of five-man party's harrowing journey to the Yukon and back.

Tibbetts, John. "All That Glitters." *Film Comment* March 1995. 52–55. A brief history of the making of *City of Gold* with commentary on the 1949 discovery of Eric A. Hegg's glass-plate negatives in Dawson City, which were then developed and published and exist now as iconographic photographs of the Klondike Gold rush.

Author's Introduction

Gold has always had an unexplainable attraction to men, which is independent of the commodities which gold will buy. The adventures of gold-seekers have been told in innumerable books and stories, which have been widely read.

There is no thought in my mind of adding another book to the overcrowded book shelves of the country, but I feel that my children and grandchildren may read, with some interest, an account of my adventures in that wild country which in 1898 was popularly known as "The Klondike."

There are people who have been on some big adventure, who persistently inject it into every conversation, contrasting every present episode with something that occurred on that adventure. In the thirty-three years since my return, I have carefully avoided falling into that habit, and perhaps I have leaned too far in the other direction. During these years I have been so busily occupied with business and family, that I cannot presume to recall from my memory, all the incidents which I record in these pages. To refresh my memory I have all the letters which I wrote to my Mother and the other home folks. These letters provide the material for my story from Rockford, Illinois, to Sheep Camp, Alaska. From that point, I also have the diary which I kept at irregular intervals during the year and a half I spent in Alaska. I have omitted many parts of these letters which I feel would be of no interest, or which refer to persons and places not connected with my story, but in a general way I have quoted verbatim from the letters and the diary, thereby hoping to paint a true picture of what I saw and what I thought, and trying to preserve the conditions and atmosphere that prevailed at that time.

I only wish that I might preface my story with numerous pages from the daily papers of 1897–1898 so that you might realize what a gold-fever epidemic swept over the country at that time. Every paper and magazine carried front page stories about the Klondike, the Golden North, Dawson City, Eldorado Creek, the Bonanza Mines, Skagway, Chilkoot Pass, and the fortunes made by everybody who could get there. Thousands made the trip, and for everyone who really went, there were hundreds who would have gone if they could have found the price of transportation, or if they could have provided for their families during their absence. The mere fact that a man had a good business or a steady job was of no consequence. Men quit their jobs or sold their businesses and started for the Klondike.

I had graduated as a civil engineer in 1896 and for about a year worked on railroad construction on what is now the Indiana Harbor Belt Railroad, with headquarters at Hammond, Indiana, and LaGrange, Illinois. In the autumn of 1897, I got a job as

Instrument-Man on some double-track and grade-revision work the Chicago and North Western Railway was doing between Janesville and Madison, Wisconsin. I was there when the gold-storm struck the country. We talked about the Klondike as did everybody else. I frequently got back to Rockford for the weekend and there found everyone talking gold.

About New Years the Chief of our Engineering party was promoted to another division of the Chicago and North Western, and I might have been numbered with the multitude who talked Klondike and stayed at home, if I had been promoted to the position of Chief-of-Party. When a new engineer took charge, that settled it. I gave two weeks' notice and returned to Rockford.

When I was a small boy, one of the big boys who lived up the street a block or two was Dan Dever. He is Irish and proud of it, and Ireland may well be proud of him. When I was twenty-four the difference in our ages had ceased to be of any importance. We both were unmarried and lived with our parents. He had always worked in a meat market, and had a good job at that time. He had the gold-fever, and was looking for a partner. We soon came to an understanding.

As you read, you will observe that the eternal triangle doesn't always include a woman. Due to our inexperience, we did not know when we started out that two men can get along very well in double-harness, but that it is almost impossible for three men to live together and preserve harmony. In our ignorance Dan and I added a third member to our party, the son of an old friend of my father's named Clarence Reynolds. As he was married and older than either of us, Dan nicknamed him "Pop" and the name stuck to him. He was a farmer, and quite naturally his family and his farm occupied a major place in his mind. My letters and my diary handle him rather roughly at times, but now that I have a family and a business, I have a much greater sympathy for "Pop" than I had at that time. If I were to soft-pedal the incidents which led to the breakup of our three-man partnership, it would distort the picture of our experiences, so I have explained here in some detail, that I am sure that "Pop" was really much better than the "Pop" in my story.

I didn't have money enough to finance the trip. I had started on my first railroad job at $40.00 per month, and was getting about $100.00 when I left the Chicago and North Western. My Grandmother Wallis had always been my financial angel, and in this case she did not fail me. She didn't want to spoil me by giving me the money, but she loaned me $300.00 and I started on my adventure with a total capital of something less than $800.00, and I have always been rather proud of the fact that I arrived home a year and a half later, without sending home for money to get home.

One more word of explanation before starting the story. Many people start out with a predetermined policy, and change their policy when they encounter unexpected conditions. Probably our party had many ideas which never carried beyond St. Paul, but there was one idea that influenced us to the very end of the trip, and which explains in some measure why we did certain things or failed to do others. We were unanimously agreed that we were going to Alaska for the Big Money, and that it was to be whole hog or none, and as a part of such a program, we agreed that we should not permit our attention to be diverted from the main chance. Therefore, we were not to accept employment working for other people, regardless of how attractive such offers might be. I sometimes feel that Fortune might not have slipped past us, if we had sought employment for wages in the very heart of the active mining operations.

But this is the story of what really happened, and not what it might have been. So, let us proceed.

Wallis R. Sanborn
Kankakee, Illinois
May 20, 1932

Part I.

Rockford to Dawson City, 3943 Miles, February 26 to July 1, 1898

1

ROCKFORD TO SEATTLE

A description of the trip to Seattle might be omitted, if we had ridden in the luxurious Pullmans of 1932, which are no novelty to my children and grandchildren. However, the Tourist Sleepers of 1898 are an experience that needs reciting. Furthermore, as I had never been too far away from Chicago, my impressions of our trip may prove of interest.

We left Rockford on Saturday, February 26, 1898. Dan's sister and sweetheart went with us as far as Harvard. Dan's brother went also to get the girls back to Rockford. At Harvard, where we had to wait for a through train, we piled on board the Chicago and North Western train with about forty baskets full of grub and what not and our shotgun. We soon located our booth and piled our stuff up all around it. We ourselves had to go to the washroom to find a seat.

Then we felt that we had made a fair start on the trip we had been planning for months. We turned in and got a pretty good night's rest, considering that it was the first night.

When we awoke Sunday morning, we were within an hour of St. Paul. To get into St. Paul they pulled us way around the city and brought us into the Union Depot. It looked as though all the trains entering St. Paul use this depot and all enter it from the same direction. We ate our breakfast in the waiting room, checked our parcels and took a stroll about the town. We were rather disappointed in the place. Everything looked dirty and gloomy. We looked in at several Klondike outfitting places but didn't buy anything: "We bought our outfits before leaving home. We live in Chicago." That generally settled them. They let us out. We wanted a tin pot for making tea on board the train, and almost everything was closed on Sunday, we tried a second hand Hebrew establishment. He had no teapot but took us across the street to a clothing man. He hunted around among his clothes for a little and then took us up a block to another Jew. He had a two quart pail that he used to rush beer. "You can have him for 25 cents." We told him we didn't want him that badly and went back to the depot.

We went across the street to get some fruit and there found a whole shelf full of one quart tin coffee pots at 15 cents each. We got one, also some tea and sugar. We changed our tickets purchased at Rockford for three fresh tickets and for tourist sleeper tickets, boarded our train and left St. Paul at 1:30 P.M. Our train consisted of ten coaches, two of them tourist sleepers, and of the two we think we have the best of it. There is a party of 17 Klondikers in the other car, and about half of them are three fourths full. There is one girl in there and she must enjoy the trip. I guess she has a man along, but even then it can't be very pleasant. Our car is inhabited mostly by babies and children with a few older folks. Most of the kids are up in the other end of the car. Swede kids who bawl continuously. The two in our end are very well behaved. Just ahead of us is a little wrinkled old woman who wants to talk. Told us all about how much it costs to travel and how many people were travelling now, about the 1600 Klondikers who are coming on the train tomorrow and several more very interesting things. I quite enjoyed her and jollied her along, but she would get pretty stale in four days. Luckily for us, a man and his wife have the other berth in her section.

As soon as the train started we got our dinner from our many baskets. Menu, roast beef, bread and butter, tarts (with the stuffing all on the outside), mustard pickles, tea and fruit. It was a mighty good dinner. The paraffin paper is no good. The stuff leaks like a sieve.

During the evening we met a man named Seline who says he has been in Alaska for six years. We asked all kinds of questions and got all kinds of answers. He warned us against taking in too much clothing. Says that it is no trick to keep warm if you have grub enough. But he does say take grub, any amount of it. I don't know as he told us anything that was so very new, except about the clothes. But he convinced me that my estimates are not so very far off. We turned in about ten and got an extra hours' sleep for nothing, changing time in the night.

We awoke on Monday in the middle of Dakota and at first I was rather pleased with the country. All nice rolling prairie. At 8:20 or 7:20 we entered the "Bad Lands" and bad they are too. They must have been perfectly flat once, but creeks going through have cut the country all up. The railroad goes along the creek bank, so that we can look up and see just what the ground is made of. It is so dry now that the stuff stands up very straight and it looks almost like stone. We came to the Yellowstone River at Glen Dive and there I understood the Bad Lands are supposed to end, but the land is not good by any means even along the river. In the evening we played whist with the Klondiker, Seline, as the fourth man.

This tourist sleeper business is a circus. If a man is longer than 5' 10¼" he is going to get into trouble. Pop did. He had the upper berth all to himself and then could not quite get in without tying himself in a bow knot. Dan and I made out a bit better in the lower, but if we were each a bit fatter we might have had trouble. In the morning what looking women. The experience is rather enjoyable to one who has no kids to bother him. We have an awful load of kids but now they are behaving first rate.

The Yellowstone along here runs between yellow clay banks about ten feet high. Away off about a mile or so other layers of clay pile up.

We got ourselves another good dinner and here I would like to say a word or two about gooseberry tarts. When we first opened our box for lunch, each of the four tarts had doubled up and turned completely inside out. We ate one and packed the others more carefully than at the start. Suppertime came, each of the three tarts had turned back again, but in turning had left all the syrup on the outside. Part of the syrup had dripped off and mixed with the ginger snaps. We ate another to get rid of it and packed the other two most carefully. We went to bed and in the morning sat down to breakfast. One tart had divided itself into quarters and each quarter was playing tag with the other quarters, running here, there and all over among the grub. We grabbed one quarter and ate it and then sat out to find the other three quarters. Finally after getting most of them wound around our fingers we succeeded in getting outside of the balance of that third tart. Ever since we started we have eaten tarts to keep them from spoiling the other grub.

After dinner I began to look at the scenery. It began to get better, the clay of the bad lands began to solidify into yellow stone. Then the sandstone predominated and I went out on the platform and soaked up the scenery. I did just soak it up. I sat out on the platform until the boys called me in to supper. The rocks got more solid and piled up to 200 feet. The road follows closely up the left bank of the Yellowstone, does not cross it for some three hundred miles and of course in places the road becomes a bit cramped for room. Then the track runs along under a high wall or loose stone that looks as if it might fall any minute. There were a number of section gangs breaking up stones, so evidently sometimes stones do come down. During the afternoon we went through a short tunnel. Toward night the rooks receded and the country seemed to get a bit smoother. Every little while we passed a little station, and such towns you never saw. Mighty glad I did not live there.

We reached Livingstone about 10:30 P.M. and there the porter called us out to see the first real mountain. He showed us a little hill over to our left about a mile or so and told us it was a mountain and that it was 25 miles away. I did not believe it then, and now that I have seen real mountains, I don't believe it. Livingstone is the station where they turn off to go to Yellowstone Park.

We wanted to stay up and see the rest of the mountain that night and see the Great Divide but we were all so sleepy that we just had to turn in and miss a whole lot of the best part of the trip. At supper time we put on a second engine and began a hard uphill pull and the porter told us that near midnight we should have two more engines to help push us over the Divide. I was very sorry to miss seeing the roughest part of the journey.

Tuesday, March 1, we were up bright and early and the scene had changed entirely. We were in the region of quartz and other dark rough stones. I had an awful time getting breakfast. Had to run outside to look at something or other every mouthful. The weather was simply perfect. In fact from St. Paul to Seattle we have had May weather all the way, and I sat on the platform a good part of the time with no overcoat. During breakfast we went over two high trestles, one 145 feet high and the other 225 feet. I stood on the platform eating a boiled egg and tried to comprehend what a big thing 225 feet is when turned on end. The tall pine trees seem to grow anywhere, makes no difference whether there is any soil or not. We only passed a few places where the rock was so hard that trees could not catch hold.

We set our watches back another hour at the little town of Hope, Idaho. Here we had to wait a little and we all had to get off and stretch our legs. What a difference between a three day through train and a train going from Rockford to Chicago. I always used to get into a train, sit down and get out when I got to my destination. But on this journey the whole train load got off and stretched their legs at every stop. As soon as we heard the whistle blow we all started for the platform and fell off before the train came to a standstill. We always found the whole town out to meet us. We would look around, walk a bit, and then as the train moved off, would get back on again.

We got off at Hope while the engine took water, and I was so impressed with the town that I attempted to make a sketch of the place. Here the track runs next to a lake and above the track is the town. All the houses front the lake and every house looks over the house in front. The houses are all right on top of each other, all look of a size and there is still room at the top. Though I am poking fun at Hope, it is the place I intend to spend my summers when I get my pile. Hope is situated over Lake Pend Oreille. I never saw such a body of water. It is my ideal of a nice summer outing place. The lake has 60 miles of shore line, is dotted with islands, fringed with mountains and swamps, both covered with pines and cedars. It is at the top of the divide and empties into the Columbia River. On the short side of the lake the mountains come down so abruptly that the railroad has to skirt three-fourths of the way around it to get by it and over the divide. As we got near the foot of the lake the little old woman who liked to talk put on her bonnet and came out on the platform. She told me her brother lived out there at the next spur, that she had been there once for a month, had tramped all over that part of the woods, that her old woman was buried there, and that like as not her brother would be out somewhere when we went by. And when I saw a man chopping wood and asked her if that were he, you should have seen her jump up and down and shout and nearly fall off the platform, waving at him. Then she went in and told everyone in the car about it, and in about an hour we came to Spokane and she got off.

For some five miles out of Spokane we went up a good stiff grade through the prettiest piece of picnic ground I ever saw. A clear swift creek ran zigzag down the valley. The valley was only a quarter mile wide and was all green grass and pine trees growing just thick enough for a nice picnic ground. On either side the hills rose up some steep and some rolling, mostly green and nicely covered with pine trees. Here and there the sides were dotted with out cropping rocks, big chunks of granite, with a tree or two growing out of them. When we reached the top of the hill, we rolled out on a plain or table land and the scenery ended abruptly. Then I began to realize that a three days' journey is hard work, and began to wish for Seattle. I was dead tired all in a minute, turned in early and got up next morning at 5:00 A.M., changed cars and started on the home stretch for Seattle. On the way I saw one mountain which I take to be Mount Rainier. It was certainly a long way off for I could not see a bit of timber, only green and white.

Then we travelled a lot of low wet country until I sighted my first salt water, a small branch of the sound. Then about a mile over trestle work, among shops and houses and streets and railroads, all on trestles over the sound, and then into a ratty old depot and we had finally landed at Seattle, on Wednesday, March 2.

Such is our journey and if I had nothing else to do I'd buy a ticket back again just to see the same things over again. I would even buy a half dozen trips for there is some 500 or 1000 miles of the trip that I would like to see about a dozen more times. I would like to ride from station to station and stop off everywhere and spend a week. I would like to walk up some of those valleys for a three day's walk and then walk back again. I'd like to climb to the top of some or those peaks and take a view or the surrounding country. If the hills, valleys, mountains and rivers of the Yukon are anything like those of Montana and Idaho, I think I'll let the other boys dig the gold and I'll roam about and look for a quartz mine, if I don't spend all the time sitting down gazing at a bunch of trees or rocks. And to think that I have been cooped up for 24 years and never had a sight of these before. If I make a million in Klondike, I'll blow it all in railroad tickets and see what else the world contains.

2

SEATTLE

Our stay in Seattle has been too much like a nightmare to be reviewed with pleasure, quite a contrast to the trip out here. It is a chapter of business, hustle, delay and bother and I fear it will be a grand nightmare Monday, when we attempt to get our goods loaded on the boat. Before we tackled this out-fitting business, I said I would rather go over Chilkoot twice, and now that we have finished outfitting, I am sure I would prefer Chilkoot. This has been a mighty hard job.

As soon as we got off the train, we checked what stuff we had, and begun to "Rubberneck," and we have been rubbernecking ever since. We began to look at windows and the people, and see what we could learn. The streets looked like Chicago on a bargain day, only it is all men, most of them dressed in some sort of Alaskan garb. Our party looks less like Klondikers than any of them. Lots of people strut about in yellow mackinaws and top shoes. If they come from the east they wear corduroy.

A place to stay being essential, we came to this hotel (The Hotel Diller) which had been recommended to Reynolds. We took two rooms and are very well satisfied with the accommodations. No bugs, and good beds. We sleep like tops, because we are always dead tired by night. We don't eat at the Hotel Diller. We go out and skirmish about for our meals and our success has been varied. We have not patronized the same place more than once, except at the Stevens House. We go there once a day, and not being entirely satisfied, go on a tour of exploration for the next two meals and then back to the Stevens again.

I can't say much about the town of Seattle, as we hardly had time to look at anything but the stores and outfits. Once it must have all been a high bluff or hill running back from the sound. Part of the sound is filled in and the hills have been cut enough so that teams and street cars can get up and down. Beyond the low part of town, there is not a block of level street anywhere. The street cars are mostly cable lines, patronized, as Dan says, chiefly by the grip man and conductor. The track is in awful shape and nobody seems to care to fix it. The street cars and furniture stores are the only real dead things in town.

The wharfs run approximately north and south and the business streets are parallel with them. Next the wharf comes Western Avenue, looks very much like South Water Street, Chicago, then upon the hill, about a four story jump, is 1st St., a good business and hotel street. Up another four story jump is 2nd St., a retail business street with more restaurants, shops and the like. I have never climbed the next Chilkoot that leads to 3rd St., but I am told that business up there is slack, mostly boarding houses.

We spent most of Wednesday afternoon looking at hardware. Then we looked at groceries. A party of three also bound for Alaska recommended Winship Brothers. They said the house was a good one and had treated them very nicely. So we looked them over and

Hotel Diller flyer.

decided to buy there. That was Thursday morning. That afternoon we placed our hardware order and got a pile of stuff too, cost $124.00 for the party.

After supper I was ready to rest so I stayed in and squared the accounts of the party. As usual I am the treasurer and secretary of this company. I pay all the bills, take the receipts and have everything shipped in my name, and to a great extent buy whatever I think is necessary for the party.

Buying things for the other boys reminds me of Dan. He is a daisy and better than any Irishman that you ever read about. I never supposed that he was so witty. But he is, just full of it. I insisted that we all get compasses to find our way in Alaska, so did Reynolds, but Dan didn't want one. He had no idea whatever about how to use it. He knows that it is good to tell something, but don't know what. He had hardly had his an hour before he hauled it out of his pocket and wanted to know "If this would tell the number of my room." For him that compass can do anything. When we are hunting for a new restaurant for dinner he hauls it out and wonders "If we could get a good meal in here." He also uses it to find out whether he is hungry. In fact he can use that compass for everything and anything *except* to tell direction.

When we were packing our clothes at the place we bought them, Dan kept the clerk grinning all the time. For example we had been getting one thing and another and the clerk was very obliging. Then says Dan: "Say couldn't you …," and the clerk chipped in "Oh, certainly," and Dan continued "let us have this on monthly payments?"

Thursday afternoon we also placed our order for groceries with Winship Brothers for $187.00. They packed our stuff for us and brought the pork up from the depot, which we had carried all the way from Rockford. They held our hardware and clothes until we are ready to take them all to the wharf. Then they deliver them and ship them and we pay the shipping bill. Everybody we meet, whether we buy or not, treats us very nicely. They are all very accommodating, tell us all they know about all we ask and all are ready to pack our stuff and store it for us without charge. The town is just one great big outfitting establishment and if one picks the first class places there is little or no choice between them. Of course, there are dozens of second class joints, ready to skin us alive, but we have no trouble in steering clear of such places.

Friday morning we spent at the store of the Seattle Woolen Mill Company selecting our clothes. They make their own blankets and Mackinaws. We had been looking into a dozen places for clothes, were despairing of ever being suited and were glad to find this place, so placed a big part of our order with them. There were several things however which we had to get elsewhere. I got some $40.00 worth outside, but they were very nice about it, stored the stuff we got outside until we were ready to pack. We spent Friday afternoon and all Saturday in hurrying up the packing of the hardware and groceries and getting everything down to the grocery house. There were also 40 little odds and ends that we had to go out and find, and our clothes to pack. I had trouble in getting a pair of loggers (heavy shoes) to fit me. I had to chase around to nearly all the stores in town. Where I could get a good fit, the shoe was too heavy or too light, too high or too low, too one thing or another. And when I liked the shoe I could not find a size small enough. But I finally got what I wanted.

We are now all ready to take our outfit to the wharf on Monday. This morning we repacked our big grips with things that we don't want to use. In the smaller bags we put the things that we expect to use on the boat.

Our outfit is packed as follows: The salt pork and bacon (which we bought in Rockford for 8 cents per pound) is still in the boxes and will stay there until we get on the trail. Most of the clothing we brought from home is in the grips, useless, but going in just the same. (Dan's mother put in all the old underclothes Dan had, some too small for me even.) The clothes we got here are in canvass bags. The long hardware is packed with the tent and rope and such stuff in our sleds, which are lashed together in a very solid bundle. The small hardware is boxed now and is to be bagged when we get on the trail. The small groceries are boxed. Bags are put in the boxes, to be used when on the trail. The bulk of the groceries are in 50- and 25-pound sacks marked name, destination and contents. In fact everything is marked so that we can readily find our stuff.

"Pop" met a 45th cousin by marriage Friday night, who is selling a patent gold washer, weight 300 pounds, cost $100.00. The cousin hunted him up and was "going along with us to Alaska as soon as he could get out of his entanglement with the machine company. But there was one thing sure, we should take at least a machine each when we started, because it is the only machine on earth that will extract fine gold and this was just the kind of party he had been looking for to go along with, but his machine was a daisy, and he would advise that our party go to Kotzebye Sound, up 300 miles north of St. Michaels on the Arctic Ocean, there was a boat going in about a week, they had started to take only ten men but had concluded finally to take on ten more, and he thought he could get us passage, and we could all four of us carry 3000 pounds each free freight, and with four of his machines...."

I got up and walked away. Pop and Dan worked him for several drinks. As he was a relation of his, Pop had to be civil to him and Dan liked to jolly him. Pop and Dan got back an hour later none the worse for the washing machine, and the relation paid all the bills.

One evening we met our friends of the Tourist Sleeper and took a walk about town. We also tried to take in the show at a cheap theater, but it was too bum, we could not stick it out.

This morning while I wrote letters, Pop and Dan called on Henry Waldo's brother-in-law. Don't know what they did or saw, nothing I guess from all accounts. I'm glad I have no letters to Seattle people that I don't know. It takes time to call and then you wish you hadn't. I helped call on a lawyer to whom Pop had a letter and he was the most stuck up, smooth, self-satisfied article I expect to see in some weeks.

The people we see here are of three classes. (A) Natives selling Klondike outfits. (B) A bunch of idiots who have bought outfits and appear to be wearing on their backs all they have bought, folks who think they will get to Klondike but don't know whether it is a lake or a mountain, suckers who want to know when the next train starts for Dawson. (C) The third class is a husky looking a lot of men as I have met anywhere. Substantial looking fellows in white shirts, blue shirts or sweaters. They show unmistakable signs or really being bound for the Klondike.

You'll be interested in what happened to us at Seattle when we wanted some money. Dan had four $100.00 bills which he had brought with him and had no occasion to use. He wanted to change a couple of them to use on the trip so when I cashed one of my certificates of deposit at the bank he braced up to the window and asked to have a $100.00 bill changed. The teller smiled and hemmed and hawed and was very sorry but the bank had for two weeks past been refusing $100.00 bills on all occasions. The plates had been stolen from Washington some time last fall and a lot of genuine bills made on bogus paper. It was discovered during the winter and now nobody can tell the good from the bad except the paper experts at Washington where they must be boiled before even they can tell. The bills have all been called in and while 1000 of them are genuine the next one may be bogus so banks refuse to take them as they have to stand the loss if sent to Washington. Dan felt rather dazed, he had all kinds of money but could not spend any of it. Pop thought he didn't have much but he was richer than Dan because he could spend his. Dan tried the next two banks. No go. Then he tried to buy some stamps at the Post Office The man hauled in his stamps and pushed back the bill. We had paid all our bills for outfits and freight so there was no merchant on whom we could put the bill. We had started for the hotel to write Jim Joslin a scorching letter, calling him down for giving Dan bills that were not acceptable. We passed another bank on the way and went back: to try once more and pretty nearly fell over when the teller said "certainly" and passed out five twenties. We shoved him a second one and he changed it too. We didn't dare try a third but it gave us encouragement so we hunted up some more banks and cashed a third. That was all we wanted, so now we are rich and can pass the fourth up in Dawson I guess and if we can't we have money enough anyway.

I hope I don't have as much trouble cashing my certificates of deposit.

The Northern Pacific pulls hard for Tacoma (sort of pet town of theirs) and so the agent made out our steamboat tickets from Tacoma instead of Seattle. So the second day at Seattle we went down to have our tickets fixed up. We changed our one party ticket for individual tickets, but the agent would not give us any stateroom numbers. He said such things were all kept track of at Tacoma and that we would have no trouble when we got aboard for the purser would have our names and staterooms. It fortunately happened to come out all right, for us but next time I'll see to it that my ticket starts from the place I do.

Loading Our Outfit on the City of Seattle

The grocery firm had sent a man down with us to ship our freight on Monday morning. He has done the job dozens of times before and so is supposed to know the ropes. There were two big divisions of Dyea freight and due to either his ignorance or to just simple chance he made a mistake in the pile in which he put our stuff. But he did one good thing about it, he put the stuff right out on the outer edge of the pile.

At about 8:00 P.M. they began to load freight and began taking only the boxes and bags, leaving the sleds. They carried the Dyea stuff to the gangway in the middle, down to the lower deck and stored it back in the hold, while they took the Skagway stuff way to the other end and stowed it in the forehold. When they had about half finished one Dyea pile they went over to the other pile of Dyea goods where our stuff was and began to take some stuff right back of ours. We expected they would keep at it and take all our bags and boxes but they didn't. They took that one man's outfit and then went back to the first pile. That scared us so Pop set out to find and buy some of the head bosses and so get our stuff loaded. The grocery house had told us that every trip the boat left some stuff behind so Pop calculated to buy up some one and get our stuff on and then we could go to bed feeling all right. He gave one man a bill and found out what to do about our baggage. We could have done just as well with the baggage if we had waited until 10 or 11 for then everyone was checked and there was no hurry about baggage. Pop's dollar did not help our freight any, so he found another man who very readily accepted a dollar and said he would do all he could for us but he did not do anything. All this time the stuff had been disappearing down into the hold. About 11 it began to stick a bit at the hatch of the lower deck and go in slower; they seemed to be running short of space and all the time they were digging away at the first Dyea pile, and from the way they dug here and there it was evident that Pop was not the only one that was tipping the boss. Up till then I had not been bothered about our stuff, but when I saw people from the back end of our pile shaking hands with Pop's man I began to get anxious about our stuff. So I told a trucker I would make it worthwhile if he would take our stuff. I didn't go for the boss, but for one of the hands who were doing the work. He said that he couldn't for the life of him touch it, but he'd show me the man to talk to and whatever he said would go. So he waited a bit and he pointed out a tough looking Irishman, named Dan Conners, with a sort of railroad boss air and told me that he was the man that could fix us up and the only man. I approached him, showed him our pile and told him I wanted to get it aboard and do it pretty soon too, told him I'd make it all right with him, he asked how much and I said I'd give him two dollars. We shook on it and I gave him one on account. Then, I dogged his steps trying to keep the other crowds from getting to him. He could not get at our stuff at once for he had one job he had promised and had to finish that. (I expect he had about 20 such.) But as soon as he got that little pile done he would tackle ours. He got away from us once and some other party got to him, and so he didn't get to our pile at once. So I got him again and told him if he started in right there and didn't wait another minute I'd add another dollar when we were all aboard. That fixed it. He put three trucks to work at our pile but before he got one bag loaded on a truck the president of the steamship company nailed him for not finishing up a job he had started before. He went over and showed the president how he was "saving this stuff to pack in on top with" as it would pack to better advantage and how they had to be most careful of space and not waste any of it. So the president let him go and he went at ours with a will. As the middle of the vessel was almost full he put our stuff up in front. When he had stowed all of our bags and some or our boxes he came around and wanted his two dollars. I said "Nit." That when he was done I would pay him but not a bit sooner. He had to be satisfied but said that he sometimes did a job and they didn't pay him when done. But he kept on putting in the stuff. Put one sled up in front and the other two at the top of the gang way where they stood the best chance of being taken aboard. Then I paid him his two dollars.

Meanwhile I met a man who used to work at LaGrange last summer. His party had their outfit piled in the same row just back of ours. I told him whom to tip and he got his stuff on board for $2.00. While the boys were getting our stuff on board the president came round again. A big party with goods way in back somewhere had raised an awful howl to the president. Their stuff was in our row but way in back. The president gave orders to take everything in that row and to take nothing else until that was done. The boss took ours and the next party's and stopped right there, and went where he was getting a tip tor his work. He is only a sort of straw boss but he outweighs the presidents nine times out of ten.

Tuesday I met a man who had to pay $7.00 for a similar job, but he did not start until 4:00 A.M. and his stuff set right next row to ours too. He was one of the last ones loaded and was up nearly all night. He says that he don't think that they took more than half of the sleds. And as all the sleds are packed with hardware that means a lot of the hardware was left behind. The baggage all came aboard so this man says and he was up late enough to know.

After our stuff was all aboard I began to wonder if it was not all a put up job, to make the people think that their stuff was to be left and so work us for tips when in reality our stuff was all to be taken aboard. I had begun to kick myself and think that I was an easy fish to catch and I remained in that frame of mind until I met man who had seen the last stuff put aboard and a lot left behind. Since then I've been congratulating myself that all our stuff is aboard while others were not so fortunate.

When they began to take stuff from one end of the pile, the people who had stuff piled there thought they were all right. So feeling happy and content they turned in for a good rest. Our friend says that about 4:00 A.M. word began to go around some way or another and the fellows who had turned in began to roll out in pants and shoes and rubbed their eyes and wondered where they were at. Some who had a big pile of stuff still on the dock, made a grab for clothes and baggage and got off the boat and stuck to their outfit and if they didn't get it aboard stayed behind with it. I don't know what the fellows did who had part loaded and part left. And there are a lot of complacent fellows (perhaps we are) who think all their stuff is loaded, who will come up short when they reach Dyea. We turned in at 1:00 A.M. feeling that we were really on our way.

Note: After such a scramble to get our outfit safely loaded on the boat, you may wonder just what comprised our outfit and what it cost us, in the first instance, and how the cost piled up as we advanced on our journey. I have therefore, picked those items from the pages of my old diary or account book and have set them down in the tabulation which immediately follows.

The greater part of our company expense is covered by the tabulation. We had to supplement our outfit from time to time, but we really spent very little after leaving Lake Bennett, so it will be seen that less than $600.00 outfitted one man for a year or more and got him from Rockford to Dawson City.

Outfit

1. Food

Bought in Rockford

400 pounds bacon	$32.00
68 pounds ham	6.12
68 pounds salt pork	3.40

Bought in Seattle

300 pounds Whole Wheat Flour	6.00
600 pounds White Flour	12.75
150 pounds Corn Meal	2.25
120 pounds Rolled Oats	3.00
150 pounds Rice	8.25
225 pounds Navy Beans	4.50
75 pounds Lima Beans	2.70
270 pounds Sugar	16.20
20 pounds C. Sugar	1.00
75 pounds Dried Apricots	6.00
50 pounds Dried Peaches	4.00
50 pounds Dried Plums	4.00
45 pounds Dried Apples	3.60
20 pounds Raisins	1.20
20 pounds Figs	1.00
3 Doz. Pkg. Yeast	1.50
3 Boxes Candles	4.50
30 pounds Butter	8.40
30 pounds Baking Powder	12.00
3 pounds Soda	.18
1 pound Mustard	.25
1 pound Ginger	.25
30 pounds Coffee	10.50
35 pounds Tea	14.50
6 Doz. Soup	2.00
Jamaica Ginger	.40
20 pounds Pilot Bread	.70
½ pound Celery Seed	.20
1 pound Cream Tartar	.35
1 pound Cinnamon	.35
75 pounds Split Peas	2.25
75 pounds Evap. Potatoes	9.00
30 pounds Evap. Onions	15.00
4½ pounds Beef Extract	11.25
60 pounds Salt	.60
2 pounds Pepper	.50
2 Doz. Lemon Ext.	.40
6 Doz. Canned Milk	6.75
15 Bars Ivory	1.05
15 Bars Wonder Soap	1.20
2 Tins Matches	1.30
2 Qts. Evap. Vinegar	1.50
6 pounds Dried Eggs	6.00
Nutmeg	.20
Lime Juice	1.00
10 pounds Tallow	.50
46 Canvas Sacks	4.60

Bought at Lake Bennett

30 pounds Butter	15.00
Total	**$251.65**
Per man	**$83.88**

2. Hardware
   Shotgun

12 Bore-6 Shell	$10.00
200 Shells	3.70
Brakes for Sleds	1.75
Raw Hide Lacing	.50
50 pounds Scales	.40
Canvas Eyes	.20
Fish Tackle	1.30
Steel Tent Pins	2.00
Rubber Patching	1.00
Lanterns	2.00
Shoe Plates	.75
Mosquito Cloth	1.70
10 yds. 6-ft Canvas	8.00
Total	**$33.30**

3 All Steel Picks and Handles
3 Half Spring Long Shovels
2–3½ pounds Axes
2 Extra Ax Handles
1 Whipsaw
1–4' Cross Cut Saw
1 Ripsaw
1 Handsaw
2 Hand Axes in Sheathes
1 Axe Stone
1 Claw Hammer
1 Sharpening Hammer
2 Prospecting Picks
1 Jack Plane
1 Draw Knife
1 Caulking Iron
1 Brace and Extension Bit
1 each ¼" & ⅜" Bit
1½" Chisel
1 Cold Chisel

1 8" Monkey Wrench
15 pounds 8d Nails
15 pounds 10d Nails
150' 3/8" Rope
400' 5/8" Rope
1 7½" Block
1 Pr. 6½-ft Oars
1 Pr. Oarlocks
1 Chalk Line
30 pounds Pitch
15 pounds Oakum
2 pounds Candle Wick
4 Saw Tooth Files
1 Pit Saw File
2 Flat Files
3 Balls Twine
6 Prs. Leather Soles
6 Pkg. Hob Nails
1 Pkg. Shoe Nails
3 Pkg. Tacks
1 Pkg. Asst. Rivets
1 Spool 22 pounds Wire
1 Spool 16 pounds Wire
1 Spool 12 pounds Wire
1 Pr. Plyers
1 Pr. Hinges
2 Doz. Asst. Bolts
1 Long Box Stove
1 Frying Pan
1 Coffee Pot
3 Granite Cups
3 Knifes & Forks
3 Tablespoons
3 Teaspoons
2 Basting Spoons
1 Washbowl
3 Granite Pails
1 Pancake Turner
1 Galvanized Pail
1 Emery Stone
3 Gold Pans
1 Pr. Gold Scales
2 Compasses
1 Magnifying Glass
1 6" Magnet
5 pounds Mercury
3 Sleds
6 Prs. Snow Glasses
3 Packstraps
250 Cartridges 32 & 38

1 Tube Gun Grease
1 10 oz. 10' × 12' Tent
1 Canopener
1 Wire Fork
1 Rocker Plate

Total	$114.00

On the Trail
   12 Assorted Pans $2.50
   1 Dish Pan   1.25
   10 pounds 10d Nails   3.00
   200' ⅛" Rope   .50

Sub-totals	$7.25
	33.30
	<u>114.00</u>
Total	$154.55
Per Man	$51.52

Medical Kit
   100 3 Gr. Quinine Pills
   100 Cathartic Pills
   100 5 Gr. Dover's Powder
   100 ¼ Gr. Morphine
   50 5 Gr. Acetantilid
   10 2" × 5 Yd. Bandages
   10 Yds 1" Adhesive
   1 Oz. Zinc Ointment
   1 Oz. Vaseline
   ½ Oz. Iodiform and Bismuth
   ¼ pound Absorbent Cotton

Sub-Total	$6.45

   Foot Ease
   Cobb's Pills
   Petits Eyesalve
   Boric Acid
   Raw Quinine
   Perons Plasters
   Radway's Ready Relief
   Spirits of Nature
   1 Pt. Listerine
   1 Qt. Brandy
   Carter's Liver Pills
   Citric Acid
   Talcum Powder

Sub-Total	$8.55
	<u>$6.45</u>
Total	$15.00
Per Man	$5.00

Personal Outfit for W.R. Sanborn

Clothing
   1 Mackinaw Suit $12.50
   1 Rubberlined Canvas

   Coat   3.75
   2 Pairs Overalls   1.00
   2 Jumpers   1.00

½ Doz. Heavy Socks	2.50	6 Towels	
1 Pair Rubber Shoes	2.25	10 Handkerchiefs	
3 Pair Boot Socks	1.00	1 Souwester Hat	
1 Fur Cap	3.00	**Net Price**	**$24.80**
1 Clothes Bag	1.20		
1 Sombrero	2.50	8 Prs. Nappa Gloves	
2 Prs. 10 pounds Mac. Blankets	18.00	4 Prs. Pontiac Mittens	
		4 Prs. Hogskin Mittens	
Net Price	**$47.25**	2 Prs. Sheep Mittens	
			$5.00
2 Prs. Canvas Overalls	1.50	2 Prs. Drawers	
1 Pr. Heavy Shoes	5.00	2 Prs. Socks	
1 Pr. Ice Creepers	1.25		**$5.00**
2 Pr. German Socks	2.25	**Total**	**$82.05**
1 Pr. Seal Muckalucks	4.00	Fire Arms	
1 Pr. Heavy. Suspenders	.50	44 Colts Revolver	
1 Sleeping Cap	.50	200 Cartridges	
1 Pr. Gold Seal Hip Boots	6.50	1 Holster	
Tooth Soap	.25	1 Belt	
⅓ of Extra Clothes Bag	2.05		**$16.55**
⅓ of Canvas Sleeping Bag		Engineering & Assaying Kit	
2 Suits Underwear		Surveying Compass	11.85
1 Reefer Jacket		50 Ft. Steel Tape	6.00
2 Sweaters		2 Ft. Rule	.25
4 Pr. Light Wool Socks		Pocket Compass	3.15
		Hand Level	7.00
		Agate Mortar	2.75
		20 Sundry Articles	
			$30.35

Expense Per Man (Based upon My Own Expenses)

The Outfit		Transportation	
Clothing	$82.05	Fare Rockford to Seattle	$27.00
Fire Arms	16.65	⅓ Sleeper	
Engineering Kit	30.35	to St. Paul	1.33
Food	83.88	⅓ Tourist Sleeper to Seattle	3.33
Hardware	51.52	Fare Seattle to Dyea	50.00
Medicine	5.00	⅓ Freight to Dyea, 4435 pounds	17.82
Miners Certificate	10.00	⅓ Freight Dyea to Sheep Camp	37.50
Duty on Outfit	29.67	⅓ Freight Sheep Camp to Summit	44.35
Sundry Expenses en Route	72.00	⅓ Freight Summit to Lindeman	14.33
Sub-Total	**$381.12**	**Total**	**$195.66**
Transportation	**195.66**		
Total	**$576.78**		

3

SEATTLE TO DYEA

Our berth and seat at table on the steamer *City of Seattle* were more a piece of luck than anything else. I was a little late in getting to the purser, didn't know where to look for him and no one could tell me but after we got our baggage fixed I found him in the main cabin at a little table right at the head of the stairs. I gave him my tickets in exchange for our stateroom. I told him we had reserved our room from St. Paul, Room 92. I had nothing to show for it and he complained about not having the number of my room on my ticket but he finally got reasonable and gave me our proper room, and got out three charts and proceeded to give us our seats at table. Here's where my greenness played the old harry. I didn't know what I wanted or what I was getting so he poked off "third sitting" grub tickets on us and I took them without a murmur.

We never knew when the boat started, only woke up when the gong sounded at seven o'clock, Tuesday, March 8. Land was in sight on either side and the water was as smooth as a mill pond. It was just like going up a big river. We soon came up to Port Townsend and stayed about an hour. That is the last American town. Breakfast served at 8. We have to wait until the tables are cleaned and set twice then the third sitting goes to work and by that time we are hungry enough. There is a Jew at our table who raises a howl every meal about being as good as anybody and how he'll eat at first table tomorrow or someone will suffer for it. I don't find any great objection to the third sitting. I have eaten four meals there and am now ready for the fifth. Every time I go down there I eat and eat and when I can't hold any more I go up on deck and wait for the next eating time. The grub is mighty good, and there is any amount of it and all kinds of it. The waiter just chucks it at us, but I just keep cool and keep on ordering everything on the bill. The tables are all set over again and as near as I can tell all our stuff is served up fresh. (Leavings go to the steerage.) We eat,

Purser's Exchange Check, *S.S City of Seattle*, from Seattle, Washington to Dyea, Alaska.

eat, eat, and can't get full. I've always been told that eating too much was a bad thing as it would surely make you sea sick. But here's the way we look at it. It we are to be sick, we shall be, so, while we are well and can eat we are going to eat all we can for there is no knowing how soon we shall be unable to eat.

Pop has one on me. He sleeps in the upper berth and Dan and I sleep below. We all expected to be sick the first night out so I told Pop to be careful and to wake me up before

"Free" miner's certificate, March 8, 1898.

he got too sick for I lie right below him on the outside where I'd be in a bad fix if he threw up. About 3:00 A.M. Pop waked up. I was sound asleep. Pop called out "Look out Wall! Here she goes!" I woke up and Pop says that he never saw me make such a quick move. Before he had time to say "Here she goes!" I had rolled up on top of Dan out of harm's way. When I found it all a fake, I cussed him a bit, rolled back and was asleep at once. And here it is Wednesday noon and not a sign of sea sickness anywhere on the boat. The water has been smooth and the channel narrow. Mountains on each side, and no snow in sight except on the tops of some of the more distant ones.

At 11:00 A.M. Tuesday we docked at Victoria, B.C. Everyone got off at Victoria and the boat tied up until 4:00 P.M. so that all could go up town and get "Free Miner's Certificates." We went to the Custom House and stood in line for half an hour before we got in and became Free Miners at $10.00 a head.

At Victoria any kind of money goes. They just mix them up and go by size. I rather think they use U.S. nickels and dimes for want of their own. I got $5.00 in change and only one Canada ten cent piece; the fifty cent pieces seem to be more plentiful.

We left Victoria at 4:00 P.M. and enjoyed the scenery until after dark. There is a good deal of sameness to it, but interesting to look at just the same. I'd like to take the trip some summer in a little 2 by 4 boat and stop off whenever I felt so disposed. Slept soundly again and got up when the first breakfast bell rang. All the morning and until 3:00 P.M. we went through channels about a mile wide with heavily wooded mountains on each side. At 3:00 P.M. we came to the top end of Vancouver Island, out into Queen Charlotte's Sound. Here we got the full benefit of the open ocean, with no islands to protect us. A great many people were so struck by the ocean scenery that they went to the rail and left their lunch outside. And the poor dogs, were sicker than dogs. It didn't seem to hurt Dan any but poor Pop and I thought it might be a good thing to take a little after dinner nap. So we lay down on our backs and felt O.K. We didn't lose a bit of our lunch but might have if we had not turned in. At 5:30 we got under cover of the islands again, then we got up good as new.

During the morning one of the dogs who was untied jumped over, and swam to the island about half a mile away. We have about 100 dogs aboard. The top of the cabin and the foredeck are just covered with them tied all over. At night Pop says they wake him up and he wonders what's coming through the roof.

Wednesday night at bed time we got out in the open sea again for about an hour then we went into a very narrow channel (hardly visible on the map) and there we are on Thursday morning.

We have passed a dozen or more boats on our way up here. Evidently we are the fastest thing afloat.

We are getting acquainted with the fellow who paid $7.00 to get his freight aboard. His name is Lou Gorham. He is only 24 years old and his wife about 22. Both are very pleasant. He comes from Pennsylvania and West Virginia oil regions. Has been boring oil for all his life and has a pretty good thing of it, but is going to Alaska, to see what luck he will have. I guess we'll rather go along together. His idea is as ours, to prospect Stewart. He has a partner with a wife. The partner has a bad cold and keeps his room.

Thursday I initiated a new idea. I began to sketch, and up to date have about half a dozen choice etchings. I enclose two to illustrate the letter. To have the etching look right you must hold it off two feet and shut your eyes then they all look just like the originals.

Thursday at 12:00 A.M. we hit some more open ocean. Pop turned in pretty quickly and I followed as fast as I could. I fell asleep and woke about 5:00 P.M. We were just nearing Ketchikan, and the water was all quiet again. After sleeping five hours it was impossible for me to sleep at night. I woke up while the boat was docked at Fort Wrangell. I got up, dressed and went to see what it was. All the stuff had been unloaded, the people off, and the wharf was about 1000 feet long. So I didn't dare go ashore and see the town for fear of being left.

Looking west, Ketchikan, Alaska, March 10, 1898.

The first snow capped mountains, 50 miles beyond Fort Wrangell, Alaska, March 10, 1898.

An old Klondiker, his wife and boy got on here and after the boat started I sat up an hour hearing from him and a California hydraulic miner talk of Chilkoot, Dyea, etc. Then at 5:45 we came to Wrangell Narrows and I went out in front to see the fun. For an hour and a half we ran at one-quarter and one-half speed and the captain himself stood out in front and gave the wheelman orders to steer by. It was great, in places the water was only 200 or 300 feet wide. We would bump up against a mountain, get into a blind pocket, then we would turn a sharp corner and steam through a little hole into another mountain or into a swamp. They just kept the wheel hot. Part of the time, as it was not yet light, they used a search light to show them the whirls and rocks. The channel was smooth as glass except where a reef showed up and except for the tide. The tide just ran like a mountain brook with cakes of ice floating about. We ran up within 50 feet of shore at times and once between two buoys scarcely far enough apart to let us through. I have the greatest respect for the pilot but he has to have a pile of buoys and targets to run by.

The boat stopped at Juneau long enough for us to get a pretty good view of the place. Opposite Juneau on the other side of the channel about a mile south are the great Treadwell mines.

Juneau is not a very well located town, all up and down and wet. Streets are just about wide enough for teams to pass. After supper we went out shopping and bought us southeastern hats. Also took in the town by electric light. They have one good tough joint there, everything free and easy with theater attached. We stopped in and watched the faro game for a while. As I had gotten up at 3:30 A.M. I turned in early and at 11:00 P.M. the boat started out again.

When we awoke Saturday we were just coming into Skagway. Had breakfast and a horrible meal it was. The company and the waiter both knew that it was our last meal and soaked it to us accordingly. They knew we were down on them and so at the last meal they didn't care what they did. Dan and I got off at Skagway. From the town four wharves run out for nearly a mile to deep water.

The tide was out so the piers seemed to be on dry land. When we got to the end of the pier we dropped off into the mud and walked up to see the town. It was just one big mud hole with logs dropped down here and there to float you above water. Streets and lots are all laid out right and the stores and houses are planted on piles or down in the mud. We didn't think much of the town.

When we got back to the boat, all the people and all the checked baggage had been put off into a big scow and in about an hour, when the tide got right, it was to be towed around to Dyea, three miles. We got on the scow and waited. While waiting we had various diversions. One party with stuff for Skagway had had it on the scow for a week past, going back and forth and unable to get it off. Finally they had the chance and took the stuff off.

A team way up above us on the wharf was loading hay. A tug boat whistled, the team ran away. They were making for the town when a dog began to bark. That made the mules shy and over the pier they went. The wagon stuck, the mules hung by their necks for a second, then the harness broke and they fell down into the soft sand 25' below. Neither was hurt but the excitement drew a big crowd.

What liars there are in this world. Skagway is not a nice looking town, but I saw no dead horses in the streets and no people fall dead, nor did I see any bandits lined up in the muddy streets. I believe that Dyea people sling mud at Skagway and Skagway slings mud at Dyea. The general public gets more of the mudslinging but never a word of the truth of the matter. You have read wild tales of 40 people per day dying at Skagway. Fact is not 40 have died since last summer.

Dyea

Finally our scow set out, towed by a tug, for Dyea, loaded with all the passengers and baggage. As I get it, Skagway is on the south side of a mountainous point of land, and Dyea is on the north side. Probably my directions are in error a few degrees. The mountains reach up steeply from the water, but the water is not deep. Seems as if the cracks have carried so much material down to the water, that the water has become very shallow, for a long way from the shore line.

The tug pushed our scow in as far as it could, while the tide was high, and left it there where teams can drive right up to it, when the tide is low. Of course, they had no accommodations for keeping the passengers overnight on the scow, so little skiffs came out to get us and our hand baggage. We were so crazy to get off the boat that we probably would have waded ashore if the skiffs had not come to our rescue.

As the Post Office system is bad, you may or may not hear from me regularly, so I'll just say for the sake of easing your mind that Dyea is all right, not a bit tough, and as clean and tidy a place as one could ever wish for. I have been thoroughly surprised at every turn. The lies that have been told of this place are something awful. The hotel is good and cheap too, $2.00 a day for grub as good as I expected and better rooms than most summer resorts. Located high and dry on sand and gravel, that at some time must have been washed out of the canyon back of the town by a glacial freshet.

The hotel is built of rough boards, the partitions between the rooms are made of boards, that run up about eight feet high and open above. So in one end of the hotel it's easy enough to hear a man snore three or four rooms away.

I don't want to stay at this hotel forever, yet it is not bad for $2.00 per day. Since we got here I've almost died for want of water. I don't know that the water is bad, but have been told so and have drunk tea and eaten lemons. If there had been any beer in town I'd have used that, but this is part of Indian Territory, and so beer can be brought in here, and whiskey has to be smuggled. They make some beer here but it is rank and costs twenty-five cents per glass, too much for such stuff, made of that same water that I try to avoid.

Being cooped up on the boat rather knocked me out, from the lack of exercise and too much food but as soon as I landed I was all right and have felt fine.

The main street of Dyea is a very good looking street considering. It is pretty well lined with unpainted frame stores, boarded with dressed siding. The sand has drifted around very generally. Out of each side of the town is the Dyea River either branch of which could be filled as the town grows. Then the mountains rise up just about straight. We were taken off the scow that brought us over in little skiffs and went up to the Brunswick House, which had been recommended to Gorham by the Seattle hotel keeper. As we are travelling pretty close to this party perhaps you would like to know who they are.

There is Dan Wallace and his wife. He is an oil driller from West Virginia. Dan got an awful cold at Seattle and was laid up all the time on the boat. There is Lou Gorham and his wife. They were married in 1896. I am very keen about both of them. He is a right, jolly fellow and she is mighty nice even if she is red headed. They are evidently very well bred people, even if they are bound for Yukon. Then there is Jim Forsyth who comes from their town and who will probably stick close to their party. He bought some $150.00 worth of grub for himself alone. He fell in with a Montana miner named Jack Stere here at Dyea and has taken Jack along and grubstakes him in exchange for his experience.

Jim, or in other words Jas. A. Forsyth, is 47 years old, has been interested in oil all his life. His wife died about a year ago which may have something to do with his being here. He has a daughter of whom he thinks a lot and two sons. He bought his clothing of a Jew establishment in Seattle and says that "I haven't a damned thing that is fit for this country." He is like a lot of the people going in. Had no idea of what he wanted so he bought everything at top prices.

Jack Stere is an experienced prospector and miner. He has been following gold mining for years. He is about thirty-five or forty years old. He can work Norwegian Skis and I intend to learn if I break my neck at it. He can cook and do a bit of most anything.

Saturday afternoon we started out to look around Dyea and walked way back to the far end of town, just about one and a half miles, then up the trail a mile more. The town is strung along the trail just about one house deep. U.S. troops are camped right across the trail, about a half mile beyond out hotel, so that the town is rather out in two. The street was pretty muddy up above their camp.

We got back just at supper time and afterwards Dan and I set out to see how they run things after dark. Went to a joint where five or six games were going on, looked on a bit, invested $1.00 in a game and came away. Must have experience you know, that's one of the things I am after. The town was very quiet and well behaved even after dark, quite a surprise to us, for we had heard such awful tales about it. But the town is not perfect even yet. The same night about 2:00 A.M. when our gambling house shut up, the gamblers started for their quarters and two men held up the faro dealer. He resisted and they shot him dead. Even then he did not have the money. The murderers escaped, but I heard today that they had caught them.

Sunday at 8:00 A.M. we went down for our baggage and carried it some three blocks to the hotel. It was all there, but we could not get Dan's grip and mine. The custom officer wished to see the inside. And when he saw the inside he confiscated all our liquor except a bottle each and said that he was not doing right to leave that. When you come don't pack all your liquor in one grip; if you have forty bottles, put one bottle in each grip, then you can pass it in. We had a pretty good supply, as nearly everyone who came to the train at Rockford to see us off, had a bottle of liquor for us to keep us warm on cold winter nights.

Sunday morning when the tide permitted they began to haul up the freight from the scows to the store yard and the owners began to sort out their stuff. Pop stayed there to look after ours and Dan and I put on our heavy shoes, waded across Dyea River and climbed half way up to the snow line on one of the mountains between here and Skagway. Great climb we had over the rocks as big as a house, hanging onto pines and small bushes, digging our toes into solid granite or ice. Great sport and hard work but we got a great view of the valley and the town.

As it was near dinner time we took a slip and a slide and a fall and got to the bottom in less than no time but with marked effect on our clothes and shoes. When we got back to Pop we found a few of our bags with one bag of dry fruit torn square in two and the other smaller bags falling out of it. We stacked it with the others and this morning put it in a fresh bag.

When the tide came up about 4:00 P.M., the freight quit coming. Monday, March 14 we worked like niggers all day. At 8 the freight began to come up. About 200 men crowded around to receive it, pick out their own stuff and pile it up. We had two of our newly made friends down at the scow, where they held onto all our freight and sent it up in cart loads instead of one piece in each load. Three of us stayed around the storeyard to catch any stray bag or box that might be overlooked. We dined one at a time and at 2:00 P.M. checked up to see how we stood. Our party had everything but one sack of flour. Wallace and Gorham were short a can of coffee and Forsyth had all his stuff.

From the time we landed we have been on the lookout for someone to take our stuff to Sheep Camp. When our stuff was rounded up, we set out to let the job of hauling us to Sheep Camp. We found a dozen parties who would take the stuff at two and a half cents per pound and have let the job at that figure, to three separate parties. We have contracted with a man named Smithfield. We have about 4500 pounds. Wallace and Gorham 6000 pounds and Forsythe 2500 pounds. We checked up short one bag of flour but that was not worth crying about. The teamsters loaded up two wagons with our stuff about supper time. Then at 7:00 P.M. we had a good square meal, with the satisfaction of knowing that all our outfit except the clothes we wear has started up the trail as far as the freighters' barn.

Then we all wrote letters to our families before we took to the trail ourselves. To get our letters out promptly we paid a man a quarter apiece to take them to Skagway.

Dyea had a Post Office but Uncle Sam only paid a hundred or two per year to the Post Master so the Post Master would not send or deliver any mail unless we tipped him two bits. That's the only way he had of keeping up to the times and making something.

We heard that they never get any mail out from Sheep Camp and the interior but we had nailed so many fish stories by that time that we felt that the mail service might not be too good, but was probably better than reported.

4

SHEEP CAMP AND CHILKOOT PASS

Moving from Dyea to Sheep Camp

We all set out at 7:00 A.M. Tuesday, March 15, and had a nice little pleasure jaunt to Sheep Camp. Dan Wallace and wife stayed at Dyea until Dan should entirely recover from his cold. Mrs. Gorham held up well and would have made the trip all right, but Lou Gorham was not so well off. Monday he had worked hard all day running and throwing bags and boxes in spite of our warnings. He caught a bad cold and Tuesday he was also sore from his hard work. After four or five miles out he gave up, hailed a passing sled and he and his wife got on and rode to Sheep Camp. With the woman and the sick man off our hands we were able to push on at a much faster gait. About 11:00 A.M. We stopped at Canyon City for lunch, paid 45 cents for a big thick ham sandwich and two pieces of apple pie, best apple pie I've tasted since leaving home. We also got good water here, water from a creek that comes down the mountainside. The water at Dyea was not very good and all of us were very careful about drinking it. The Dyea River runs through the town but they bore wells and don't drink the river water. It looks clear and nice but there are too many dead horses upstream.

We saw a glacier today, the first on the trip. The only way to tell a glacier from a common snow drift is by the color. The glacier is blue, an opalescent blue, the prettiest light summer dress color. Snow drifts look yellow beside it. Then when the sun shines on the ice it shows every color one ever imagined.

The canyon was about a mile wide from Dyea to Canyon City and all covered over with 4 to 10-inch niggerheads. Teamsters have rolled the big fellows out to one side of the roadway and so the road was pretty good being covered over with snow. There are small clumps of trees here and there. Once we went through woods for half a mile. The river winds about anywhere in the canyon and is covered with ice and snow so that it is hard to tell were the river really is. The mountains are rather steep on each side, covered with trees half way up and snow and rocks the balance of the way.

After we ate at Canyon City which is only a little collection of log shanties, where the canyon begins, we struck off up the canyon proper. Here the canyon is only about 20 to 50 feet wide and runs straight up on each side. In the morning we saw a lot of people tugging along at their sleds but as the wagon trail and river do not run together we only saw them once in a while. When we got to the canyon proper we began to realize that there were some people going to Klondike. Men, dogs, and horses all hauled and pulled at sleds loaded with goods. We caught up with our teamsters at Canyon City. From Dyea to Canyon our goods came up in two box wagons each drawn by a pair of good horses. At Canyon City they took everything out of the wagons, put one box on bob runners, piled the outfit on the one wagon-box sled and put the four horses to it.

Dan and I stayed with the wagon to see how the teamsters earned their money. Pop and Jim went on ahead to find a camping place. The horses certainly earned their feed and perhaps the men earned their money. Every ten feet or so there was a hole, and down went the front bob and down came the hind bob, the greatest wonder the whole thing did not go to pieces. Our load measured 10 feet by 5 feet-6 inches by 3 feet-6 inches piled good and high and tied fast to the bob runners. The trail was not very steep but was very narrow and crooked and it seemed as if the steepest places the trail was the narrowest and crookedest. Then there were lots of people coming down and a whole crowd going up. The fellows coming down had to pull out to one side and wait for the loads. And a nice time they had to get to one side. The trail is hard and five feet wide, then each side of that the snow looks all right but it will not hold up very well. The water flows through the canyon all the time, under the ice and snow and does not freeze. The trail is made in a rather strange way. A heavy snow-fall fills up the canyon and freezes while the water runs under it. The teams drive on this crust of snow from 6 to 20 feet thick.

When they break a hole in this roadway they cut trees up on the mountainside, fill

Looking ahead, north of Dyea. X marks the entrance to the canyon, Canyon City, March 15, 1898.

the hole with wood, cover with snow, and go at it again. The packers are always afraid the canyon is going to go out, then they would have to pack up over the mountains. Jack says that a place like that is very slow to go out, and I guess he is right. Jack is the experienced miner who is with the Forsyth party.

Towards the upper end of the canyon it broadened out and the road got worse. There was no snow crust over the creek and the trail wound through the timber, everywhere and anywhere, between stumps and over rocks, into a slump hole every other step, with gullies and gutters and all kinds of obstacles for a team and pair of bobsleds. The small sleds and dog teams had smoother going, but even they earned their money. We were very well satisfied to pay $112.00 to get our stuff over that 14 miles at so little trouble to ourselves.

Sheep Camp

The canyon broadened out, good and wide and fairly level. It is known as Sheep Camp. This name applies to a piece of the trail about two or three miles long. Throughout this area people camp in the snow and make Sheep Camp their headquarters while they get their outfits over Chilkoot. The valley is about half a mile wide and was once wooded but now nearly cut bare. The snow averages some three feet deep. Some people camp on the snow, and some dig down and pitch their tents under the snow, that is with the sides of the

Looking ahead from Sheep Camp, March 16, 1898.

tent under it. When we got up to the place where the log houses are thickest we had arrived at Sheep Camp proper, paid off our freighters and unloaded our goods.

As we advanced on the trail we were offered all kinds of bargains in the way of hauling to the Scales, which is this side of Chilkoot and the Summit, which is the short name for the top of Chilkoot. Men offered to take our stuff to the Scales for four cents a pound (seeing that it was us), then a bit farther they wanted three cents (very low price). As we got on farther men offered to take the stuff at two and a half cents and at two cents. While we are unloading at least six men wanted to take our stuff at prices ranging from one and a half cents to three cents according to how green we looked to them. We sent them all off as we intended to take a look at the trail before we did anything toward letting the contract.

Lou and wife went to the Woodlawn Hotel where he was laid up with a bad throat. He was mighty uncomfortable and it must have been worse for her. They have one of the four private rooms in the hotel. The rooms are just partitioned off from one big bunk room so that whenever Mrs. G. has to go after anything or up and down stairs she has to go through the bunk room. Here the bunks run up three high and are as close together as people can walk. Pleasant for a woman; but she is game and gritty as sandpaper. To make it more unpleasant for them, there is a man next door who has spinal meningitis and is like to die any time. We tended to their goods as well as our own. We hauled ours out to the far side of the river some 500 feet from the main trail and pitched our ten by twelve foot tent on three feet of snow and nobody knows how much ice. We set things up in a hurry as it was getting late and we had to get our goods all over there, and piled and covered over with canvas. We were rather stumped for water. We couldn't forget the stories of the thousand or more dead horses that mingle with the nice clear sparkling water that flows under the ice of the river. The water question solved itself very early and satisfactorily. A woman in pants, who tents opposite us, told us that there was a spring up the mountain two or more hundred feet that was pure and had no chance at the horses. So we got our water up there and it is very good. We go up a stiff climb and then get down in the snow and ice in a hole that has been kept open, some six feet deep, and dip the water with a tin can tied to the end of a long stick. As it is no more trouble than going to the river for water, we use the spring water to drink, wash dishes and wash ourselves.

For supper, this first night of camping, we had bread, butter, bacon, tea and coffee and it tasted mighty good, only we felt a bit blue about Lou, who was pretty sick, and this is not a nice place to be sick. The hotel people were very kind, but the accommodations were limited.

Dan and I cut a lot of pine branches off a fallen tree, spread a canvas over the pine, a robe and ten pairs of blankets over the canvas and turned in pretty well tired out. We had covered a good piece of uphill country with all our goods, had a fair camp and plenty of good water for the first time since leaving home. We actually felt a bit at home, and who had a better right, as we must live in this way for some time to come.

Tuesday night we were too tired to notice things, but Wednesday night we all noticed that the brush and pine boughs were full of sticks and that the sticks all stuck straight up in the air. We did not rest well at all so on Thursday Dan tore up our bed, tramped the snow floor down harder, cut out the sticks we had slept on, and made a fine bed which has pleased us ever since.

We stayed at Sheep Camp long enough to observe a lot of interesting things, none of which in themselves seemed to have any direct bearing on our own adventures, but they all help to paint the picture as we saw it. I shall try to describe some of the things before continuing our own journey on the trail.

From St. Paul to Sheep Camp, the weather was far different than we had expected. We had regular summer weather all the way; even at Sheep Camp water didn't freeze, except at night. The snow seems to stay on the ground because of the cold in the earth below. All I wear is the outfit in which I left home, without the overcoat, and with a pair of German socks and rubbers in place of the shoes. Don't even know where my gloves are. I wonder what I shall ever do with all my heavy clothing.

Sheep Camp is full of men who have tried to get over Chilkoot but have got stranded in one way or another. They are packing from here to the Summit at wages way below what anybody can do the job for. They take the job at anything they can get, so that packing prices from here to the Scales and the Summit are very low.

But from Dyea to Sheep Camp things are different. The supply is too small for the demand. Boat after boat gets to Dyea and everyone wants to hire the first stage down, as we did, and then pack their stuff from Sheep Camp. So the packers at Dyea set their price and we have to pay it. They make money hauling to Sheep Camp, but I don't see how they make anything from here up.

Dogs, dogs, dogs. On the *Seattle* there must have been 100 dogs on the roof alone, above the passengers, keeping them awake. At Dyea dogs are thick. All along the trail, as many dogs as men. Here there are all kinds of dogs. None of our party have dogs and I'm not a bit sorry. There are a lot of mangy stray dogs belonging to no one. They will eat anything that we leave out so we leave nothing out.

Whiskers are the style in this country. We can measure miles from Seattle just by the whiskers. We can tell how much of his goods the man has over the summit by the length of his whiskers.

Our stove is a daisy. It has a three foot fire box with a hole in the back end of the top. Either the oven or the stove pipe fits into this hole and the pipe again fits over the top of the oven. So the heat and smoke goes around the oven. We have a can that hangs on the back side of the stove for a water heater. The oven bakes better at the front than at the back but it is the best stove in camp.

"Mush on." We hear that everywhere and all the time. It is the term used to make the dogs get up and go. We hear "mush on" so much that we all take up with it. When a stray dog comes up to nose around our pile of grub we throw a chunk of ice at him and tell him to "mush on." When all five of us are trying to get into the tent door at once the last one tells the others to "mush on." If we have rested on the trail, when rested, one of us says, "well boys, let's mush on."

There is a Dr. Howe and party from Indiana camped next to us at Sheep Camp. He has a partner and a young fellow named Homer with him. Homer's father has lots of money and Homer is helping him to spend it at a lively rate, so Homer's papa sent Homer out in the doctor's care and told the doctor that he would pay all the bills for Homer if the doctor would take him along. Homer seems to be a very nice kind of kid about 18 years old. He got cold feet and headed for home, before our party left Sheep Camp. Plenty of others do the same thing. The common excuse is that they didn't bring enough grub and are going back to get a bigger outfit. There is a rumor that U.S. declared war on Spain on March 16. That is now being used as a reason for going back. The war rumor was immediately branded as a fake.

Bunko men of all kinds have tackled us ever since we left St. Paul. At Seattle everyone tried to bunko us into going to a friend who sold fine outfits for nothing. On the boat our waiter tried to bunko us into eating in three seconds so he could clear off and loaf. At Dyea and Sheep Camp, it is the freighters who do the bunko act. When Lou Gorham got up here he had his load tipped off on a lot that some freighter had located. The freighter wanted to bunko him into a four cent rate to the Scales. Lou was sick and an easy mark. But Pop and Jim sent the freighter off about his business, and we piled Lou's stuff off the lot and on the river. That made the freighter hot. So this morning he came to Lou and wanted to collect storage; claimed the stuff had stood there overnight, and either he would pack it to the Scales or Lou must pay storage, Lou brought him over to see Jim about it. Jim and the freighter had a fine squabble and the freighter refused the fifty scents Lou offered, and threatened to call a "miner's meeting" which would square things, He thought he could bunko Lou out of $5.00 or more.

Gambling here is very much of the tin horn variety. There are four or five places going every night. The men running them are a cheap lot and don't know much more about their games than the players. The players are mostly packers between here and the Summit. They come in, win or lose a dollar or two and go out. The games are not even interesting to the spectator.

Sheep Camp to the Scales

Wednesday morning, March 16, we all got up feeling good, prepared to find out something about the trail from Sheep Camp to the summit of Chilkoot Pass.

After breakfast Jack, Pop, Dan and I put on our ice creepers and started for the trail. We are camped near the end of the double horse trail. Beyond here it is either one horse or a string of them or dogs or men. When we set out without loads, it did not seem very rough or steep, but some of the people with sleds behind them seemed to carry a very heavy load. The limit of a pack on a man's back is about 160 pounds, and lots of them carry less. Dog teams carried about the same and pack mules from 250 pounds to 300 pounds. There are two trails from here almost all the way. Two simply by chance because the country is such they could make a dozen if they choose. The valley is wide but the trails wind about a good bit avoiding rocks and taking easy grades. The grade is not very heavy from here to the Scales. It is just a good up-hill grade with occasional short steep spots. From here to the Scales is about three miles but it is quite a climb for a morning's jaunt. We stopped frequently and the view was worth stopping for. The things we saw could fill a book. The trail itself is full of strange sights. A team of one man and one dog tandem is very common.

I saw two little old women dragging up a sack of flour on a small sled, also a man and wife about 60, he pulling and she pushing behind. There are quite a few women going over, some in pants and some in skirts, most of them with their husbands. Babies and children are entirely missing. There is one woman with a mule packing up the hill and sometimes you see a man and woman hitched to 100 pounds of grub on a sled. The trail was pretty well crowded. There were hundreds going up and dozens coming down. They meet on the trail and someone has to pull to one side. Coming down is great fun, going up is just a steady pull.

Some two miles from Sheep Camp is a bend in the valley called Stone House for some unknown reason. Just opposite Stone House and visible from both directions is the small end of a glacier. It is rather high above us, and sparkles in the sunlight like an immense opal. We hear all kinds of tales about how far back in the mountains the glacier runs but here only a small patch is to be seen. I don't know as I ever saw such a color as this glacier shows. It is blue, a light summery blue and every crack and crevice in the glacier seems to be stuffed full and be bulging out with a blue opalescent vapor. It looks as if it might be something on fire rather than a mountain of ice. I said it was a small glacier, it looks small compared with the rest of the mountain, but really it is plenty big.

Between Stone House and the Scales the road is steep and the people who haul 200 pounds up on a sled either take it all off and pack 50 pounds sacks on their backs or they drag up a 30 pound sled with a 50 pound sack or maybe two sacks. There is where a dog or a mule comes in handy. But how they abuse the dogs. Men seem to think that dog can drag 100 pounds in places where a man can't.

The "Scales" is a place some three quarters a mile long and means almost any place this side the final climb to the Summit. It is so called because they weigh the freight at the Scales before packing it up the real Chilkoot. This is known as Hammond's Tram. It can handle about 30 tons a day. There are two stationary cables hanging from the summit which is way up above this big rock. On the cables are swung two pairs of buckets holding 600 pounds each. These are connected with a smaller cable that is moved from the power house. The middle of the tram must be some 200 to 400 feet above ground.

We only went as far as Hammond's power house, then turned and came back. Going up had been no snap because our ice creepers were no good and the trail was as slick as grease. Coming down was even worse. We just took a run and jump and slide in the snow and stopped and did it again. Where the sleds and people and mules go down they have worn a deep icy groove in the snow sometimes three feet deep and it is full of bumps like a switch back. The sleds bumped along on what was once smooth snow and rutted out these places. They serve to break the speed of the sled and make it possible to coast down the hill. After we had walked and slid down hill about a mile on our feet, etc., we asked a man for a sled ride. He was green at it and soon ran us off a smooth path into a deep rut. Then we walked a bit and got a ride with another man. He took me nearly to camp without an upset.

Thursday we arranged to have someone take our stuff up from here to the Scales. We let the job to a pack train of mules for one and a half cents. We also thought it would be best to have it taken from the Scales to the top and gave the contract to the Hammond tram at one and a half cents.

We take our full time about everything and don't accomplish anything in a day besides eating and cooking and discussing things about which we are all entirely ignorant and all have opinions. Friday and Saturday we spent repacking our pork and hardware, also that of the Wallace-Gorham party and seeing it started up to the Scales. Jack went up there each day to see it properly weighed and piled up. Lou Gorham was able to stand around and

Looking back from the Scales toward Stone House.

talk but no good for work. I made some Johnnie Cake and some biscuits but the oven is a terror and I burned both of them, but we ate them up clean just the same. When we wanted to exercise we either took a turn at dishwashing or wood cutting or going for water. We loafed pretty hard during those two days, all but Jack who had to go up to the Scales.

Saturday Dan Wallace telephoned to Lou (rate $1. 50) and announced that he was going back to the States. We all rejoiced because if he is going to be sick all the time we don't want him; and if he is weak-kneed we surely don't. That, however changes the outlook of things somewhat. It leaves us with 3000 pounds of stuff to dispose of. Lou is around again and so this morning (Sunday, March 20) he and Pop went down to Dyea to see Dan Wallace and arrange what is to be done.

Dan and I felt need of exercise, so we put on our creepers and set out for the Summit. Up at the turn I stopped and took off my creepers and drew a sketch of the valley below. We had just started out again when Jack caught up. He was bound for the Scales to see how our stuff was being handled. When we got there the tram people had just finished putting our outfit across and piled it on top of the summit. So now our supply of grub is higher than it will ever be again. Dan went on and up to explore the Summit and consequently got back to camp about an hour after we did. He didn't attempt to find our stuff.

When Jack and I started back for camp, we saw a man with a horse and sled going down. We told him we could take his sled down for him if he wanted us to. Of course he was glad to have us take it for him as his horse was enough for him to handle. So Jack and I got on and started down a hill about a half mile long and steep enough to give us plenty of speed. You have seen the pictures of the Yukon sleds, seven feet long, sixteen inches wide and covered with slats. Jack sat in front and steered with his heels. I sat back and we both had stout poles about four feet long. These we shoved down and braced against the arches of the sled and so broke our speed. Without them we would have broken our necks. The sled itself steered down this hill for it was in a deep gully so that sometimes I could not see over the sides. And the bumps would shoot me up in the air and down I'd come on

Looking back toward Sheep Camp.

the sled usually but once in a while I missed the sled. Then Jack had to stop and wait for me. We had to stop when we met a horse and sled. On the more even ground we let the sled slide as fast as it pleased. Then we got to another steep hill and drove in the gully again. Then we came to a long easy grade, just right to let her go her best and how she did go, never a stop except when someone got in the way. Then we had to use our sticks and pass them slowly. The ripples and bumps running across the trail shook us up aplenty but I could hang to all of them, except where we turned to one side and hit a bump at the same time. When I saw sailing up in the air the rear of the sled would slew out and let me down on the trail. It is a wonder I didn't tear all my clothes. I don't know when I've found any such sport. It is worth walking up hill all the morning. And that is not the best of it. We will have a whole week of it beginning Monday. We will have to slide our outfit down the far side of the pass. Just think of it. We'll slide downhill for a week.

We have had things very easy so far at a cost of five and a half cents per pound, but even if we had to pack it all ourselves, I believe we could have done it. Lots of people get sick of the trip every day but we have not, and I don't think we shall.

Chilkoot Pass

We didn't leave Sheep Camp on Monday as we had expected. We had to wait until Thursday, March 24. Sunday night the wind came from the south and brought snow. That meant that the top of the Summit was a regular blizzard. Very few people packed stuff on Monday. Tuesday was the same. We could have gone Wednesday, but we were not sure of the weather at the Summit. Got up at 6, had breakfast at the Woodlawn Hotel and started on sleds, tent and clothing ahead of us. We walked to the Scales with nothing to carry except ourselves, saw part of our bedding and baggage over the tram, left Dan and Jack to see to the rest of it, while Pop and I climbed the icy stairway to the Summit, and paid the duty on our outfit.

Chilkoot Pass is one of the places on the trail to the Klondike that got a tremendous lot of newspaper publicity. White Pass and White Horse Rapids are the other over-advertised obstacles that the Klondiker has to overcome. We had the choice of going in front from the coast either by the White Pass or by Chilkoot Pass. Chilkoot was undoubtedly the more popular route, especially for the small independent parties of prospectors such as ours.

All the trail from Dyea to Lake Bennett might properly be described as the Chilkoot Pass from the ocean to the interior, but the name "Chilkoot" means in everybody's mind that steep climb that leads to "The Summit." I am told that in the summer time it is the roughest kind of tumbled mass of giant boulders. In the winter the deep snow smooths out all that rough topography, and the problem becomes greatly simplified. Just an endless climb, step after step, with all a man can carry strapped to his back; other men in front of him and other men behind him, often so close together that they tread on each other's heals.

On such a climb 50 pounds on one's back gets mighty heavy, in a very short distance, and it weighs a ton long before the top is reached. There are steps either cut or worn in the icy snow. Some good angel installed a heavy rope along the left side of this series of steps. It doesn't help to pull us up the hill, but it keeps a man from falling over backwards, and when a blizzard breaks, it serves as a guide to keep us on the trail, and it helps to keep the string of men in line. When a man must rest, he drops out of line at one of the many little flat places at the side of the stairway. At 50 pounds per trip, if he has an outfit of 1500 pounds, he must make the trip some 30 times.

The sketch gives an excellent idea of Chilkoot on a nice day. At the right of the endless procession, various interests have installed all kinds of primitive devices for getting their own outfits up, or for hoisting for profit, the big idea being to avoid packing on the owner's back. A device consisting of a long rope and a pulley is rather popular. There must be 150 such contrivances between Stone House and the Summit. At the right hand going up the Summit there is a regular tangle of these things. The owners stand around and call out like hack drivers asking people to get on their sleds and ride down and so help pull up their

Chilkoot Pass from the Scales.

loads. Men also have climbed the cut-out stairs, ride down on these sleds and help those fellows, but I never saw where the other fellows helped them.

It is interesting to see the stuff that is being taken up over the pass. Boats 30 feet long, boilers for various kinds of engines, ribs for big barges to be built over on Bennett, big cog wheels, coils of wire, new-fangled prospecting machines that will take the prospector weeks to move.

When I first climbed the stairs, not having a pack on my back, I could make better time than the average, so I stepped out of line, to the right, and made pretty fair time, but about a quarter of the way up the slope, I had to get back into the slow line, because I could make no further progress without the help of the steps which were worn on the regular trail. I was wearing my ice creepers, but even then, I preferred the steps.

When Pop and I reached the top, the first thing we did was to find where the Tram had piled our outfit. We had to turn to the right of the main trail, and then rather downhill for aways to the high anchor of the tram. Our outfit was piled up nicely, at the north end of a big rock, fairly well protected, and in a place which can be described as being not so terribly difficult to reach. The tram management had not done as they had agreed, which was to pile our outfit 200 yards beyond the end of the tram, but here it was, so why go all the way back to the Scales to kick about it.

The top of the Summit is a fairly flat valley, between two mountains. It's about a half mile long, and wide enough to hold the mountains of stuff that have been brought up here. Nobody seems to know just where the U.S.-Canada line lies, but the Canadian Custom House is up here on the Summit. It was quite aways beyond where our outfit was stored.

While Jim stood around and swore at the tram people, Doc and Will loaded up some of their stuff and started for Lake Lindeman. Pop and I hunted up the Custom House and tried to pay our duty. One of the British officers told us that we had to go to a broker and have a bill made out. So we went next door and gave our grocery and hardware bills to the broker. He filled out a blank, charged us $3.00 and then the Custom House would accept $86.00 duty on our outfit. We paid 30 percent on hardware, 25 percent on groceries. Clothing for one year is free. Tobacco fifty cents a pound. The custom officer wrote a pass on a piece of foolscap and daubed a cheap rubber stamp on it, and that's all we have to show for our money. When we passed the Custom House with our stuff we had to show that paper. The second time we got by without showing it. When we got back to the outfit, we found that Jack and Dan had arrived and loaded a sled with the stuff we would need most in starting a new camp. Pop and I loaded another sled. Jack and Dan had a load of about 400 pounds. Pop and I took about as much. We took tents, blankets and cooking stuff and stove. Between our pile and the custom house there were a few places so steep that all four had to get hold of one sled and pull. The whole 300 yards was packed with sleds and backpackers and on each side of the trail goods were piled up and snowed under. The pass is about 300 feet wide and just filled with goods and snow mixed. We had lunch at a place run by an Indian. It surely was dirty. For 300 yards beyond the custom house there was more goods and snow, and a slight downgrade. Then we came to a steep pitch dropping down about 1500 feet to Crater Lake. Part way it was steeper than 45 degrees, and all the way it was cut with ruts about two to four feet deep. To get down we steer the sled into a rut. One man holds the side of the load and the other goes ahead and hangs on to the pole that sticks out ahead of the sled. Then it is a tussle to keep the sled from going too fast or running over you, even with ice creepers to help hold back. The load shoots you along for a few feet and then sticks in a hole. You pull it out and away you go for another 20 or 40 feet.

The bottom of the rut gets filled with loose snow and that stops the sled. Otherwise there is no knowing when or where the sled would stop. Sometimes a sled gets away and how does it go. Just like dropping it off a shot tower but they are strongly built and I have not seen a broken one or heard of anyone being hurt here. When we looked at the hill from the bottom it looked as steep as the other side.

Crater Lake is all covered with snow and drifted so one can't tell where the lake is. The trail goes rather up hill, if anything. Then we went around some rocks and up hill for sure, just a perceptible grade but no smooth sailing. Then came a downhill shallow canyon for a couple of miles. The sleds would not go themselves and the trail was high in the middle so the sleds slowed off to one side all the time. At places the trail was cut with slump holes that we had to pull out of. There are two short steep hills, but no sliding here for they are just wavy and bumpy, a sure tip over. About one and a half hours from the foot of the Summit is another lake, Deep Lake. And a mile farther on is Long Lake. This is about two miles long and connects over a short hill with Mud Lake, a mile long. Between the two there are a couple of hotels or lunch counters, I was pretty near played out for lack of food. It was a long time since 6:00 A. M. And the Indian lunch counter didn't do me much good. But Pop wanted to push on, he said Lindeman could not be far off, we should be there in a little while and get some good grub. So we went on and entered the deep canyon leading down to Lake Lindeman. We got in the canyon and there we stuck. It is about two miles long and the first mile is just one mass of jumps and sharp turns and little crooked slides with slump holes at the bottom of each. And this mile was just jammed and packed with people trying to get through. The trail up to this point had not seemed packed, because we could go around if the man ahead was too slow, but here there is but one place to go and so we have to wait for the slow people with heavy loads. I nearly froze waiting there. First time I have been cold since leaving home. Had been all sweaty and then to stop in that hole with the sun just gone down. We must have been an hour and a half on that first mile. On the other mile we pulled along in the dark not knowing where we went, but the trail was good and we could not help but go right. Finally we got out of the canyon and came to the lake.

Lake Lindeman, White's Cove

We asked our way to the Lindeman Hotel, for it was too late to think of putting up a tent and getting grub. After a half hour's walking here and there we got to the hotel, and found Jim, Doc, and Will there ahead of us. They had taken a mountain trail in place of the canyon and so had got ahead of us. Dan and Jack came in after we had eaten supper.

Such a supper and such a hotel. It is a big affair made of logs set up on end. Sawdust floor, and the supper was a blank, the hotel had been eaten clean. All we had was bull steak and molasses. The bread gave out while I was at supper. There never had been much more I guess. And it cost $1.00. The price held out firmer than the grub. I steered Dan and Jack to a place I had seen while hunting for the Lindeman Hotel and they got a good meal for fifty cents. We slept on mats thrown on the sawdust floor, in front of the bar with our feet to the stove. We used our own blankets and paid fifty cents for such lodging. Some men slept on the bar. Some on the dinner table. Upstairs was full before we got there. I was dead tired. I didn't get much rest after my hard days' work but was thankful to get any.

At breakfast the meat gave out. So we ate hot bread and molasses, for another dollar, then we got our sleds together and went to look for a good camping place. We went up the Lake about a mile and a half and located at a nice sheltered cove just off the trail on the east side of the Lake. The place is called White's Cove. We set up on top of ice and snow and carpeted the whole tent and part of the doorway with pine boughs. They kept the snow from melting. Fixed the tent up real nice and cozy, bed behind and stove and dining room in front. We roll back the bed to make a sitting room.

Saturday, March 26, just one month from Rockford, went to the Summit for our clothes and more grub. Jim did his best to keep us from going. Then, when we started he would go also. He went a mile, growling all the way or quarreling over something. We started at 7:30 and reached the Summit at 11:30. The distance is about twelve miles each way; we were back at 8:00 P. M. with some 250 pounds of grub on our sled. Not any choice between the canyon and the hill. Dan says if we should do such a stunt at Rockford, half the town and all the papers would wait to see us come in. We got in about as tired as it was possible to be.

Sunday we were all stiff and tired. So we chopped wood and I cooked and we put up Lou Gorham's tent. He has fully recovered and he and his wife came in tired and hungry about 5:30. Jack went to the summit to meet them and help them down. Jack can't get along with Jim any better than I can, Jim fires him every ten minutes and takes him back again.

Monday Pop, Dan and I were up at 5, went after more goods and brought about 750 pounds. We got back at 7:30 P. M. and were in good shape ready for another day Tuesday. We began to get hardened to a little thing like a 25 mile tramp. But we didn't go again Tuesday. It was too stormy. All the way since we set up at Sheep Camp, Jim and Jack have been living in our tent, using our stuff and letting us supply and cook most of the grub. Pop and Dan appointed me a committee of one to correct the situation. So today when he made no move to get into his tent, which we put up for him yesterday I asked him when he was going to bunk in his own tent. He said at once, so then we moved his stuff into his own tent for him. I cooked all day but could not cook as fast as Jim and Jack could eat it. Wednesday was the same. So after dinner I asked Jim how soon he was going to do his own cooking, sorted out his cooking tools and took them over to his tent. Then for supper our three set down for our first peaceful meal.

It is the first time since we began tenting that we have really owned our tent and grub. After supper we had lots of grub left. We all felt relieved. Pop and Dan get along with Jim but I don't. He's too old and cranky and set in his ways. Now that he lives in his own tent I expect we will get on better.

This is great weather, just like the first of May at home. I took cold from cooking with my coat on. So now I cook in my shirt sleeves and go around camp anywhere in my shirt sleeves. That's the only way to keep from getting in a big sweat. How did we sweat hauling the sled of grub. We got wringing wet. Our socks would catch it all and when we got in our rubbers would be full of sweat. Yet it seems to agree with us. I weigh 162 in my rubbers, when they are dry.

Two Close Shaves

When Jim and Jack went to housekeeping in their own tent that set up a train of circumstances that involved me in two adventures, either one of which might have brought my story to a quick finish. I never mentioned the first adventure in any of my letters, and my diary alludes to it in this very unintelligible sentence; "came to the conclusion that Blackjack is not my game."

The second adventure was in connection with the snow slide of April 3rd in which some 60 persons were killed. I took it rather calmly, but imagine the folks back home ...

Some events are so deeply engraved upon the memory that all the little details are available at any time. So after the lapse of 34 years, I am able to relate these adventures with little or no help from the letters and diary.

When we divided the cooking equipment and gave Jim his own, we found that we were short of some very important cooking tools. We borrowed some pans from Mrs. Gorham and we had also lost some things at Sheep Camp. So on the morning of Thursday, March 31, Dan and Pop set out early for the Summit, to bring back a load, and to find a man to haul the balance of our outfit from the Summit to Lake Lindeman. After I had straightened up the camp and cooked food for their supper, I set out for Sheep Camp to buy pans and cups and to mail some letters for Dan and Pop. It was not really necessary to mail letters at Sheep Camp as there was a Post Office at Lindeman but we felt that Sheep Camp was fairly sure. I arrived at the Summit at noon and there met Pop and Dan coming back. They had arranged with a man who owned a dog team, that I would meet him at the Summit Friday, on my return from Sheep Camp, and show him where our outfit was, and he was to take what was there to our camp at Lindeman.

I would have been glad to pack all our stuff down to Lindeman, and save the $35.00 that it cost us but Pop had begun to feel that it was horse work and we were moving too slowly. So he insisted that we have the rest of the outfit hauled to Lindeman. I thoroughly enjoyed the trip up and down Chilkoot on that fifteen mile trip, as I was getting well hardened to work on the trail.

When I reached Sheep Camp in the middle of the afternoon, I bought a leg of mutton, a considerable quantity of tin and granite pans, a damper for our stove, and some dry goods for Mrs. Gorham. Then having several hours idle time, I wrote letters to Mother and to Grandmother Wallis and posted those I brought over for Dan and Pop.

After supper, time began to hang rather heavy. Periodically, between boat arrivals at Dyea, the crowd would thin out, so that Sheep Camp would be nearly deserted for a day or two, except for the packers and hangers-on, who made it a regular business to exploit the would-be Klondikers. I wandered around, trying to find some of our old acquaintances, and noticing how the population had shrunk in a few days. There were very few real wooden buildings. There were lots of gambling games, generally conducted in a combination affair, consisting of wooden floor and side walls, surmounted by a canvas tent. I went into one of these places where a game of Blackjack was in progress.

In playing Blackjack, the dealer plays against all who care to play, deals two cards each to everyone, including himself. Aces count one or eleven, as the player elects. Face cards count ten, and other cards their face value. The object is to get cards that add to a total of 21. The dealer accepts bets from all players and when the cards are shown, the dealer pays his losses to the players when a hand counts more than the dealer's hand. If a player finds that his first two cards only add up to ten or eleven, he calls for a third card or possibly a fourth card, trying to make his hand total 21. If one of the cards he draws makes a total of more than 21 that breaks his hand and the dealer rakes in the player's money. If a player's two cards total 19 or 20 he gambles that the dealer will have a smaller amount, and if the dealer feels that his hand is so small that he must pay everybody, he draws more cards, which either improves his hand or breaks it.

If two cards total 18, there are only the ace, deuce and trey that will improve it, all other cards break it, so the probability of breaking is in the ratio of 10 to 3. If the players just ahead of me have drawn several cards all bigger than 3, it improves that chance that I can draw 3 or less.

The real professional gamblers didn't waste any time at Sheep Camp. They stayed at Skagway and Dyea, or travelled day and night to reach Dawson.

The dealer in this place was just an amateur and I noticed that he was rather too venturesome when he drew additional cards. However, he seemed to be making it pay, because the players were even more reckless in drawing cards.

When I saw how the land lay, I bet a dollar and drew cards and won. Next game I left my two dollars ride and won again. Then my four dollars became eight dollars, and next hand I had sixteen silver dollars piled up in front of me, one of them was my original entry and the others I had won from the dealer. There were no chairs, we all stood around a long table made of matched pine boards. The dealer was in the middle of our side, and I happened to be across the table and a little to the dealer's left. I figured to beat the dealer about once more and take my $31.00 profit back to the Woodlawn Hotel, and call it a day.

The two cards he dealt me were a ten and a nine, total nineteen. Unless the dealer had 20 or 21 I was sure he would draw cards until his hand broke, so when I peeped at the corners of my two cards I laid them quietly down on the table, face down of course, while he dealt cards to the players on my right, who were due to draw cards ahead of me.

As the dealer dealt cards to the man on my right, I noticed that he wasn't looking either at that player or at the cards he was dealing him. Instead, the dealer's eyes were directed to a point somewhat to the left of where I stood and slightly higher than my head. I don't know why I didn't turn my head completely around to see what so interested him. Possibly I felt that if I did, someone might pick up my stack of dollars. However, I did turn my head just a little, and that enabled me to see out of the tail of my eye the point at which the dealer directed his eyes, without appearing to take my eyes off my stack of dollars.

A few feet back of me, and a little to my left, was a great big ugly brute of a man. I've seen such men before and since and realize that they are not always as mean as they look, but this fellow carried a rather oversized hunting knife in a sheath attached to his belt, and his hand on the knife handle. His head was directed squarely toward me while his eyes met those of the dealer. He nodded his rather perceptibly in my direction and was answered by an almost imperceptible bowing of the dealer's head.

It takes time to relate all this in detail, but I caught it all in just one look. I realized instantly, that there wasn't a man in that tent who had even the slightest friendly interest in me. They addressed each other as Tom, Dick and Harry, and all they knew about me was that I was taking their money away from the dealer about as fast as he was able to take it away from them, and money talks. I certainly put my mind to work on that problem. I knew that he could have stabbed me in the back at any time he might have chosen. The dealer's nod was altogether too plainly a signal that he was to get busy if and when I should be winner in my gamble with the dealer.

The man on my right had drawn one card too many and the dealer raked in his wager. The dealer looked at me, expecting me to indicate whether I was satisfied with my cards or whether I wished to draw another. It flashed through my mind that although he was a poor hand at cards, he had eyes as hard and cold as tool steel.

I felt that if I indicated in any way that I knew what was going on, that in itself would be a signal for an attack, and there was no possible chance for me to rush the door. Under such circumstances, I've often wondered how I was able to think with a clear head.

My two cards totaled 19 … I had fully intended to play those cards … The chances that I could improve it by drawing a card were only 2 out of 13. It was my turn to pass or draw … There was no question in my mind … I indicated that I wanted another card … If it turned out to be an ace or a deuce, my hand would almost certainly be better than the dealer's hand … and the ruffian behind me had his hand on his knife … The card I drew was a three spot … just enough to break my hand … I threw my three cards face up on the table … the dealer raked in his $150 and my dollar, and asked the player on my left if he wanted another card.

I wondered what next, whether I would be allowed to get out, even though the dealer had recovered his losses, and what would be my proper method of making a getaway. I put my hand down into the pocket of my pants, where I knew I had no money, as though looking for another dollar, pulled my hand out empty, and turned away from the table. The man with the knife had disappeared. I walked to the door, expecting him to jump on me when I stepped out. He wasn't there. At the corner of every tent or building that I had to pass, I was ready to jump and run. When I reached the Woodlawn Hotel it was the one and only time that that old board shack looked good to me.

And the only report I ever made of that evening is the one little line in my diary "came to the conclusion that Blackjack is not my game."

Since that time I have wondered many times whether those fellows meant business, or whether they were putting up a real man sized bluff. I've never been able to answer the question to my own satisfaction. I have never felt that the circumstances were such as would have warranted me in finding out whether it was a bluff. There were too many open holes in the ice on the Dyea River, into which they could have dropped me, and nobody be the wiser. Thursday had been so bright and warm, that I was greatly surprised on getting up rather early on Friday morning to find it snowing hard. Our plans had not given consideration to the possibility of snow. I had told the boys that I would be back at Lindeman Friday afternoon, and that I would guide the packers to what remained of our scale on Chilkoot, and I was due to reach the Summit about 9 or 10.

Everyone in the Woodlawn Hotel was talking about how stormy it would be at the Summit, and how dangerous it would be to climb the pass under those conditions. I didn't really relish the prospect of such a trip, but it might not be so bad at the Summit, and I had agreed to meet those packers. If I failed to meet them, there would probably be an additional charge. And now, I'll even admit that I didn't want to stay over another day and take a chance on meeting the big fellow with the knife at some lonesome dark corner. He might have decided to finish his job. He doesn't know it, but I have always had a soft spot in my heart for that big ruffian. He didn't earn any such consideration, but all unknown to him, he really was a factor in my decision to start out for the Summit in that storm.

So I set out from Sheep Camp with a 30-pound pack on my back, not such a heavy load, but the dishpan, etc., made it an awkward load. It might be stormy on top but the trail was well marked. I had been over the trail often enough so that I didn't feel that it was particularly dangerous. The storm was not really bad until after I had passed Stone House. Then halfway between Stone House and the Scales I encountered a most peculiar freak of the weather. The snow had suddenly stopped falling where I sat and rested and all below me was clear. I was just on the underside of a big snowstorm blanket. The mountains rose up on either side until they were lost in the storm, so that I looked out of a sort of tunnel with a snowstorm roof. Below in the lower valley the storm had also cleared and from somewhere the sun shone down and lighted the valley below. The center of the scene was a bright yellow color which reflected back to where I sat and made patches of lighter yellow that contrasted with the bluish white of the snowstorm above and behind me. Black, white and light yellow would paint the whole picture. Then the sunlight vanished and it began to snow harder than before. Of course, there was not a sound in all that deep valley, except my own heavy breathing.

There were very few people on the trail beyond the Scales. That was far enough for most of them. At the Scales it snowed so hard that it was difficult to find the right path that

A stormy morning near the Scales looking west from the underside of a snowstorm.

led to the steps up the summit. I found it, and began the long climb up Chilkoot. The hand rope was most welcome. I hung onto the rope and dug my toes into the little drifts that had collected on the steps that had been cut in the ice. I counted five men on the steps where on nice days men were strung out two feet apart. Two of these had joined in with me in finding the path that led to the steps. At the top of the first long stairway was a level place some 200 feet long. Here thrifty merchants had set up a few tents and dug some caves in the snow. There was one place where a man had dug out a little shop in a snow bank and made a bar of snow and here he sold hot and cold lemonade on nice days. He cut the snow from the roof and melted it over a gasoline stove to provide water for his lemonade. After our hard climb the three of us went into this place to rest and escape the storm. The owner was absent and a dog lay there curled up in the snow. He was slowly freezing to death and would not stir when spoken to.

After a little rest I went on and climbed the last steps and reached the top in such a snowstorm that I could not see my hand at arm's length. I had never seen the like of it, but it was interesting to have a chance to see a storm on Chilkoot. The snow was fine, just like flour. The air was warm and I had on only the suit that I wore from home. I wore a sweater which Mother had equipped with a hood that left only my face unprotected. I was just covered with snow all up and down my back. The drifts too are made that way. There was no wind, so the snow stuck wherever it fell instead of curling over in the strange shapes I had seen at home. The three-quarter inch tramway cables strung up overhead were covered with snow until they were about six inches thick. There were only about a dozen people at the Summit who had come up from Lindeman and were loading their sleds or starting back with goods. It was such a contrast from the day before. On Thursday the place had been crowded.

I went across the Summit and down the hill feeling certain that our packer would not brave the storm. The snowfall was lighter after I left the Summit and the snow was deep enough so I could dig in my heels and walk down easily. At Crater Lake I found a number of people just going up and just coming in from Lindeman. There I met the man we had hired to take the rest of our goods to Lindeman so I turned around and went back with him, up the hill to the Summit.

On top of the Summit there is a sort of saddle between the mountains about a third of a mile long and 300 or 400 feet wide. Six months before people had begun to pile outfits up there, and day by day more people piled up more outfits. Of course many had been taken away but many lacked money to pay the Canadian duty. Many had turned back after getting part of their goods on top. As it snows there every little while, the snow had drifted over many outfits and buried them. The owners had to go down in what looked like caves to get in their tents. The whole saddle was quite completely covered with piles of goods and I expect that in places fresh piles were made on top of piles which had been snowed under months before.

The trail followed the natural center of the saddle. On each side were rude lunch counters and the Custom House and a few venturesome merchants housed in tents.

Our outfit had been piled with innumerable others near the end of the tramway, out near the end of a rather bold promontory, to the right of the icy stairs we used when we climbed Chilkoot. To reach our outfit, the packer and I had to travel entirely across the summit and zigzag out way out to the point on which our outfit was piled.

4. Sheep Camp and Chilkoot Pass

All the way up to Chilkoot and down to Crater Lake, the storm had been at my back. Now it was squarely in our faces, and how it did cut. I had to shut my eyes, button the hood of my sweater, duck my head and go ahead blindly, trusting principally my sense of location, in leading the packer and his dog team to our outfit. While we were on the main trail, it was fairly easy to find our way, because of the tents and outfits piled each side of the trail. To get to our outfit we had to make several right angle turns first to the left as we approached the icy steps, then to the right, and then several more turns, and finally out on the projecting shelf of rock where our goods were piled. It was snowing so hard that no landmarks could be seen, but I remembered that the path to the outfit followed a ridge, the crest of the projecting rock. Consequently as I broke a brand new trail to the outfit, if I found that my next step would require a downward step for my right foot, I would turn to the left a sufficient amount to avoid such a downward step. If my next step tended to be down to the left, then I turned slightly to the right.

Some of the photographs which I later saw of that point indicate that if I had missed our outfit entirely and gone about one or two hundred feet beyond it, I could easily have gone over the side of a precipice that dropped off fifty or one hundred feet into snow drifts of unknown depths. Needless to say that the packer trailed after me and his dogs followed him.

I turned the corners all right and found the outfit in due time, the first one who had been out there that morning. We loaded about half of our goods and followed the trail I had made back to the custom house. There the dog driver hired two men with hand sleds to bring what he had left. Then I went back again to show those men our stuff and to see that they took everything. The storm had let up enough so I could see the trail we had made earlier in the morning and as we were loading the storm suddenly cleared and in five minutes the sun was shining brightly again and I could see way off down the valley, past the Scales and almost to Stone House. It is one of the beautiful pictures that still imprints itself upon my memory after these many years.

It was also the scene of the fatal snow slide that quite likely would have engulfed me if I had waited at Sheep Camp until the snowstorm cleared.

On my trip back to Lindeman that afternoon men on the trail were few and far between and the trail was hard walking, but I made the 12 miles in about three hours with my 30-pound pack. When I arrived at our camp, I wrote a long letter to the folks at home, describing my trip. That letter ends with these prophetic words: "There is Chilkoot, pleasant and stormy, and we are done with it for a year or two at least. It will doubtless be dangerous in a week or two, but for me it has been all pleasure, and hard exercise."

A postscript to that letter, written just before I posted it, was very short and to the point. Here it is:

Lindeman, April 4, 6:00 P.M.

Dear Grandma and the Folks,

It is reported here that there was a snow slide yesterday down near Stone House and that anywhere from 16 to 50 were killed. I don't know how true it is, only I write to say that we are all right, and past all chances of snow slides.

Wallis

Next morning, when we had more detailed news about the snow slide, I wrote another letter, which was most welcome to the folks at home. It begins as follows:

Lindeman, April 5, '98.

Dear Mama:

I wrote you last from Sheep Camp, last Thursday. Nothing much has happened since then to write about, but you'll doubtless welcome this letter for if I'm lucky I'll get it to you about the time the news of the snow slide gets to the U.S.

I got my tinware and some mutton at Sheep Camp and returned to Lindeman in a snowstorm. I wrote to Grandma and told her about my trip over Chilkoot in a storm so will not repeat it here. I suppose you will be very glad now to know that we are now in flatter country, safe from snow slides.

Lou Gorham went to the Summit for goods yesterday, and failed to get in at 6. When news came of a snow slide on the other side of the Summit, Mrs. Gorham nearly collapsed. Lou had a tough day of it and got in at 10:20 P.M. The snow had drifted and covered the Summit some 10 to 20 feet deep, buried outfits, tents and horses, just drifting. The trail from here up was all snowed over which made it so hard to pull empty sleds that they only reached the Summit at 4:00 P. M.

The woman in pants who has camped near us again nearly worried to death about her husband too. A woman is a woman even if she does wear pants.

Wallis

Leaving Lake Lindeman

Before I made my special trip to Sheep Camp, Pop rigged a sail on one of our sleds. All day long we could see sleds sailing past our camp carrying loads of 1000 to 3000 pounds.

While I fought the snowstorm on the Summit, the weather was bright and clear at Lindeman. Pop and Dan loaded 1000 pounds on one sled and sailed it down to Bennett about 6 miles. Saturday the wind was not so good but we three got away with another good big 1200 pounds.

Sunday we loafed around, because it was snowing too hard to go to Bennett. Pop and Dan went for firewood while I was getting dinner. We had mutton chops, pea soup, rice pudding and biscuits. The pudding was made with condensed milk which doesn't seem to work like cow's milk, but the pudding tasted all right. I've not tried bread yet, never had time to set it and let it rise.

Monday, we took all the balance of our stuff except our tent, stove, blankets and some grub. Left just enough for one good load when we pull stakes and move our camp to some place on Bennett.

I got a touch of snowblind Saturday and didn't realize it. Monday I got plenty of it, although the day was partly cloudy. When I got in at night the heat in the tent burned my eyes, as if they were filled with sand. I cured it by keeping in the tent most of Tuesday and Wednesday. Thursday when I got out on the trail again, I took the precaution to get some crinoline and make a blind of it. Snow glasses that we have are no good at all, just worry the life out of us and do no good. Many people blacken their cheeks under the eyes, some simply shade their eyes, but the crinoline does a good job. We make a heavy or light veil of it, depending on the brightness of the sun and it is just as transparent as a screen door.

Our first camping place on Lake Bennett which we call "Camp Number 3" is situated about nine or ten miles from the head of Lake Bennett. We moved down here from Lindeman without hiring a thing done for us, and we did a great job. From our camp on Lindeman to the head of Bennett is about six miles. The first load Pop and Dan took down, they sailed on the icy snow. We had a sled fixed up with a mast, that we can put up when there is a breeze. Then a square sail hangs to the mast, and we load bags of grub around the mast to keep it in place.

Our sleds are great play things. They are seven feet long and sixteen inches wide, and six or eight inches high. In front, on the right side, there are two iron rings about two and a half and one and a half inches in diameter. Into these rings we fit a pole about six feet long called a "gee pole." That serves to guide the sled. When a sled is pulled by a rope, it goes about where it pleases. The gee pole is to keep a sled where we put it. Where the trail is all bumpy and full of side slips we must have a positive way to guide it.

So while I was upon Chilkoot, Pop and Dan took advantage of a fine breeze. The loaded the sail sled with 700 pounds of grub and put 500 pounds on another sled, and hitched it on behind. Pop took the gee pole of the front sled and Dan got behind his sled and the wind did the rest. Dan rode most of the way, while Pop slid along and steered the sled, keeping it headed in the right direction. The lake is covered with a couple of feet of snow and there is a hard beaten path across the lake. The snow drifts around outside the path, but the breeze generally keeps the path clean. The path has built itself up higher than the snow each side, and the side snow is soft. When we get off of the path and into that stuff, we are in a bad box and have to tug and pull to get the sled on the path again. Every little while we see a fellow pulling and tugging in that way.

The hard packed snow is slippery and our feet would slip, were it not for our ice-creepers. Creepers are contrivances we put on our feet, studded with sharp spikes which dig into the snow as we walk. I've seen a dozen varieties of creepers but very few are any good. My first pair was no good at all.

Then I got a pair of creepers that fit in the hollow, in front of the heel of my rubbers. Strap buckles them over the foot and another strap around the heel holds them from slipping forward. They work all right and I have no trouble with them, except that the strap at the heel sometimes chafes my heel.

From our Lake Lindeman camp to the end of the lake was about five miles. Then comes a canyon about a mile long. You've seen pictures of this passage, taken after the ice goes out. It was not half as bad as those pictures, where we travelled it. The stream has frozen over so that there is a nice flat place to run our sled. There are some stones to go around and some to pull over. That first day was the only time on Lindeman that our sail really worked right. The other times the breeze helped, but we had to drag the sled more than we sailed. Doc and his partner, and Jim and Jack generally work along with us so that we have lots of power to handle the loads when occasion arises.

You may have noticed that we follow a very definite plan in moving our outfit. While we were at Sheep Camp we pushed our outfit ahead to the Summit. Then we jumped the camp to Lindeman, while we moved the bulk of the outfit from the Summit to a rocky point on the edge of Lake Bennett. Then we pushed our camp some ten miles ahead of where out outfit was cached, preparatory to pushing out outfit farther ahead.

You may feel that we are very careless, the way we leave all the grub we have for a year and a half behind anywhere, quite unguarded. Everybody does it, and as far as we can learn, nobody has anything stolen. The type of men who would resort to petty thievery, evidently don't care to exert themselves as they would have to on the trail.

It may seem that we are doing a lot of hard work that could be done better with a team of dogs. We are rather glad, however, that we are not bothered with dogs. It takes a lot of grub to feed them, and a lot of time to prepare their food. Corn meal mush is one of the standard foods. It has to be well cooked or it makes them sick. After cooking it must be cooled to a normal temperature before they can eat it.

Dan picked up a story about an Irishman who says: "They are all such liars in this country that they lie to everybody and even lie to the dogs. They say 'Mush on ye devils' but devil a bit of mush do the poor dogs get."

Between Sheep Camp and the Scales the dogs could take care of themselves, by digging in the snow and uncovering a part of some of the many dead horses that had broken their legs on the rough trail, before snow and ice helped to make it smoother going. We frequently saw the bare bones of a horse sticking out of the ice.

5

Lake Bennett

Our Temporary Camp

Wednesday morning we broke camp at Lindeman and Wednesday evening (April 8) we ate supper and slept on Lake Bennett, 15 miles from our Lindeman camp. We got up at 6:30 and while I got grub the boys fixed our gee poles and got our hardware together. We packed our bedding in the canvas bags and our dishes and grub in one of the boxes which once contained our bacon. We took down the tent, and last of all packed little odds and ends into one of the three big telescopes. It made a fair load on our three sleds. We set out at 9:30. At the far end of the canyon and at the head of Lake Bennett, is the town of Bennett, great town too, tents and log houses, bigger than Lindeman and the seat of Canadian Law. There are four post offices at Bennett. I went the rounds looking for letters but didn't find any. Anybody can run a post office up here. After a twenty five cent lunch of coffee and pie we set out on Lake Bennett. We had about 300 pounds each on our sleds and after we were on the lake we wished we had taken heavier loads. The going got bad about 4:00 P.M. and as we were then about 9 or 10 miles from Bennett we stopped, pulled in a quarter of a mile to shore, and set up our tent.

Jim Forsyth and Doc got tired before they got as far as we did, and pitched their camp about 4 miles from Bennett.

We only intended to stay at this place a little while, so we didn't want to dig down to bare ground. Found a level place on the ice about ten feet above the lake. The lake freezes in the fall and the water keeps running out at the far end all winter, so when spring comes the water is way down and ice way up on the banks. We cut a couple of trees and trimmed them to make posts and ridge poles. Didn't join them at all, simply set the posts under the ridge poles, raised the tent, and staked the corners. We drove steel pins in the ice at the four corners and laid a heavy log on either side for the side guys. The bottom of the tent we packed with snow, to keep out the wind. While I put the stove together and cooked supper, the other boys cut some trees and trimmed off the "feathers" to carpet the tent. It turned out that we didn't have quite enough feathers. We slept soundly until the ice began to cool us off about 4:00 A.M. So next afternoon we put in more feathers and since then have been warm and snug. Thursday morning, when we got to Bennett, we each put 500 pounds on our sleds and started back. Well we got back but Dan and I decided that we prefer to drag lighter loads. That's my record, 500 pounds, nine miles in three and a half hours. Friday I put a new gee pole in my sled to replace the one I broke the day before. We only took 400 pounds loads Friday, and Saturday. We finished the outfit by taking 350 pounds each.

Lou Gorham is sore at Doc for some reason or other. So when Jim and Doc bought four dogs to haul their outfit, Lou went them one better and hired a mule to haul his outfit.

Friday, because of my late start, I was some distance back of Pop and Dan on our way back to camp. As I was leaving Bennett I met a man who had just come in with a lot of new Seattle papers dated April 1. There was a lot of war news in them. I bought them all at twenty-one cents each and sold them on my way back to camp, for fifty cents each. He had only 24 papers, and I kept one of each kind to read and two big New York papers. I sold the others before I was half way home and made $4.00. I only wish I had papers of April 4, with the account of the snowslide. Both Dan and Pop got a touch of snowblind today.

Sunday being a day of rest, Dan and I refuse to work, and so Pop has to lay off. I've made up my mind we can do more work in six days than we can in seven. This particular Sunday was no day of rest for me. I had set bread Saturday afternoon. Saturday night I sat up with the bread and kept the fire going until 11:00 P.M. Sunday morning the bread had hardly begun to rise. All day Sunday I cooked and kept my eye on that bread. I added yeast to make it rise and added flour so it might stay up after it got up. Finally when I came to bake it filled the oven plumb full. The top pan of bread reached the top of the oven and the bottom pan pushed up the top pan. But the bread was eatable, so I am happy. I also made pie Sunday. I made crust enough for a dozen pies, and had soaked only enough apricots for half a pie. Sunday night we had scrambled evaporated eggs to celebrate Easter.

Monday, it blew a hurricane, so we took two sleds and hoisted the sails, Pop took the one with the small sail and a load of 1000 pounds. Dan and I took 1200 pounds on our sled with the bigger sail and we ran up the lake eight miles in one and a half hours. We had to run in front and hold the gee pole to steer the sled. First Dan would ride on the load and I'd get in front and run, or rather have the gee pole run me, until I was winded, then I rested on the load and Dan ran. We had to keep on the path for about three miles, until we got around the point. Then we had ice with only an inch of snow on it. There is where ice creepers are necessary. After we had gone some eight miles we took in the sails, and went along the shore, looking for a good camping ground. Pop and I had a quarrel about the better place to make our camp. We unloaded our sleds, where Pop wanted to camp and came back to camp in two and a half hours and had dinner. After dinner Pop and Dan loaded up all the outfit there was left, except, tent, etc., and made the trip a second time. I stayed in camp to cook grub for today and pack our camp stuff, so we could move today. But today it is snowing, just about as wet as water, so we shall not move until tomorrow. Yesterday morning with 1200 pounds on our sled, we kicked ourselves because we had not broken camp and taken our whole 4500 pounds on the three sleds. Could have done it easily if we had only known how much the wind would carry.

We are all getting on nicely and don't even know what our medicine chest contains. We work like dogs, eat like hogs, and sleep like logs, and are feeling fine all the time. Catch a bit of a cold now and then from running around in our shirt sleeves, but a good sweat in front of sleds cures it better than all the quinine in Alaska.

Pop begins to appreciate what a job it would be to move our outfit down below White Horse Rapids, so we have decided to build a permanent camp up near where our goods are now cached and there build our boat and wait for the ice to go out.

How we do get away with the dried fruit. It is the nicest stuff in our outfit. The peaches swell up to be bigger than fresh California fruit and the apricots are even nicer than the fresh fruit. The plums are bigger than the apricots and the figs make a fine sauce. The apples go all right but I don't like them as well. You should get a tin of those evaporated onions. They dry to perfection and you never ate such fried potatoes as our granulated potatoes produce. The evaporated eggs are all right too, only it takes about two hours to get them dissolved. The vinegar is rank, nothing but colored acetic acid, but it goes and I'm getting used to it.

The cookbook you wrote out for us never says a word about how to bake anything so I have to guess whether to use a hot or a cool oven. Our stove is a scorcher. When I bake anything I have to hang on the oven door ready to jerk it open and jerk the pan out. But I am getting the hang of it.

Aristocrats of the Trail

Women didn't vote in those days. Mrs. Gorham and Mrs. Hubbell are the only women thus far noted in my story. There are no women mentioned in the story of our life on Lake Bennett, but the picture of the Klondike trail cannot be accurate without a word or two more about the women on the trail.

There was a scattering of dutiful wives such as Mrs. Gorham and Mrs. Hubbell, who wielded the frying pan, while their husbands built boats, but none of the other women that we saw during out stay at Sheep Camp and Lake Bennett had any interest in boat building. They were on their way to Dawson, and "Speed" was their password. Speed, so that they might reach Dawson before the ice on the lakes and rivers became impassable.

We would see a splendid team of dogs on the trail, headed north, and trotting along as fast as dogs can trot. The front end of the sled would be piled high with baggage, not grub such as we were transporting. A comfortable back, resembling the top of an arm chair, occupied the rear half of the sled, and the chair was occupied by a woman all bundled in furs. Sometimes there would be a second sled occupied by some soft specimen of a man, who it was plain to see, had never done a day's work in his life. We, on the trail, heartily despised such an outfit.

Frequently, instead of the second sled for the man, there would be a stalwart, husky chap running at the rear of the sled, guiding it, with poles attached to the rear and keeping pace with the dogs. We admired these men, beyond measure. Some of them were men who had made a fortune in the Klondike the summer before, and had been back to the States. Some of them were big gamblers, saloon proprietors, or other substantial business men returning from a business trip to the States.

Not all of these men who hurried past with dog teams had women with them, and neither did all the women have men with them. There were places where they could put up at night, and secure feed for the dogs. They knew their trail, and neither asked nor answered questions, while on the trail. They had no part in our adventure, but the picture of the trail would be incomplete without their casual reference to these aristocrats of the trail.

The various stories that I have read about the Klondike would lead one to believe that everybody rode in such state, instead of just those favored few.

Our Permanent Camp on Lake Bennett

On Wednesday, April 13, we were up at 5:00 A.M., loaded our camp outfit, and sailed to the place we picked for a permanent camp, while we built our boat, and waited for the ice to break up so that we could use the boat. The sailing was grand. I had no rope on the sled, just used the gee pole on the front sled with two sleds tied behind, and Pop and Dan riding on the load. When the sail had run me ragged, Dan would take the gee pole and I would ride. Somewhere between the two camps, we cursed the invisible line that is supposed to the boundary between British Columbia and Northwest Territory (later named Yukon Territory).

A little sketch map in one of my letters will be helpful in understanding relative relation of various points on Lake Bennett. Our permanent camp was about a mile beyond the larger islands shown on the map. The temporary camp was really about halfway back to Bennett.

We remained at the permanent camp until June 3. It is easier to relate our experience there by topics rather than the daily routine. Therefore, days may jump back and forth in the story as I have edited it.

We made a real job of setting up our tent. Dug down through the snow to earth, built a level platform of poles, which served as the floor, with two steps in front. We put up the tent temporarily that afternoon, and next day we put it up to stay. Then we collected all our outfit that we had cached on the edge of the lake, and stored it in good shape under the guy ropes of the tent.

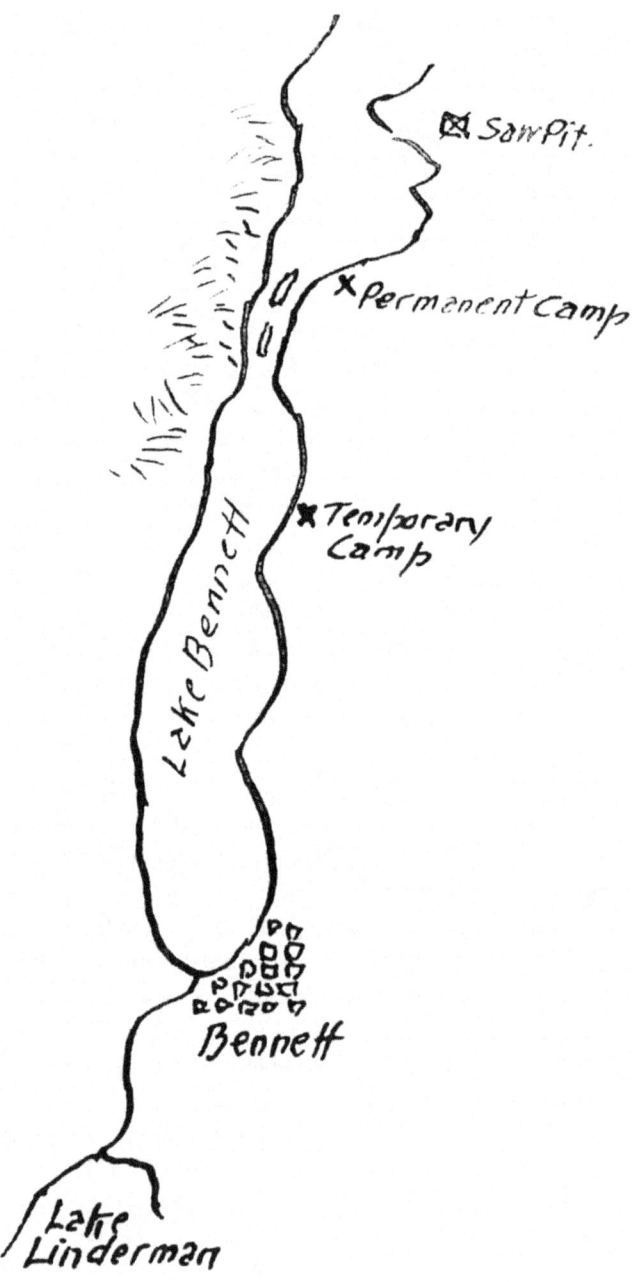

Various points on Lake Bennett.

Our Ten by Twelve Home

The location we had selected was well above the lake, back among some spruce trees, facing north. We had lots of neighbors, and plenty of room between us and our neighbors. The trees sheltered us from wind, rain, possible snow slides, and freshets. There were real mountains somewhere back of us, but just back of us was a gentle sloping hill, that would be classed as a mountain in almost any other country, but in comparison with the mountains on the west side of the lake, and away off to the north of us, it could only be called a hill.

Our carpet consisted of smaller poles, laid in the hollow between the platform logs, then pine feathers and pine needles, and finally a layer of moss. We selected two live trees for tent poles, nothing less than a cyclone would blow us down.

We all took pride in keeping things shipshape. Some of our neighbors had tents that were too sloppy for words. There was no effective way that we could prevent the little red wood mice from running around in the tent. Sometimes they would run around our faces at night, but they were harmless and did no appreciable damage to the outfit.

I note in my diary that on Sunday, April 17, "Pop bathed this A.M. Dan washed his neck this P.M.; and I'll wash my face in the morning." It was our first chance in many days. We used one of our big shallow prospector's pans when we bathed.

Lake Bennett looking south toward permanent camp.

Cooking

We serve anything you care to eat. Have made pie twice and doughnuts are common fare. Bread is no trick at all. Set it at 5:00 P.M. let it rise until 10:00. Then let it cool off until a thin skin of ice forms on top (i.e., 5:00 A.M.) Then build a fire, thaw the ice and let the bread rise until 11:00 A.M., mold, let rise, shape, let rise, bake, eat. It's fine too, only sometimes it gets too light. Rice is fine but the others don't like it cold. I cook two quarts, they eat it hot and I eat it cold. Beans baked in a tin pan make might good filling. We have 225 pounds of dried fruit and eat it all the time. Breakfast or supper, Johnnie Cake and biscuits (when we have no bread) and fried cornmeal mush go great with syrup.

Some of our neighbors are obliged to fry their Johnnie Cake and biscuits before they can eat them, but we are not. Fried ham, boiled ham, baked sliced ham, or salt pork, pork and beans, take your choice, or beef tea if you prefer. Since we put my Sheep Camp damper in the stove pipe it bakes much better, no burnt bottoms to things if we use the damper right. We have tea and coffee and the best ice water you ever drank, pure snow melted off of bold granite mountains and stored in a big lake.

Our Neighbors and Ourselves

We made a lot of new acquaintances at Lake Bennett, and some of our old friends dropped out of the picture.

Lou Gorham and his wife, with the help of almost everybody except Lou, got his camp outfit to our camp on April 20. Then everybody had to get busy and set up Lou's tent for him. Pop insisted that Lou locate right next to us, and of course that was just what Lou wanted. They were lucky to have a place to sleep when supper time came. So we had a big feed in our tent and invited them to supper.

Jim Forsyth and Doc Howe, having camped temporarily closer to Bennett than we had, pushed their permanent camp rather farther ahead than we had done. At times, while we were building our boat, we could hear Jim with his team of dogs out on the trail, urging his dog team along "Go on Fox, mush on Fox."

Jack Stere left Jim and got the job of distributing mail up and down the trail. When the Postal Service finally got organized we had frequent visits from Jack, and he was always a welcome visitor.

On my last trip over Chilkoot I fell in with a blacksmith named Alex Henderson, a Scotchman. He and his partner, Chas. Woodruff, a real estate dealer and architect, were from Riverside, Illinois. We felt that they were almost neighbors from home. They have a third partner named Avery.

There were Charlie and Phil Wigston and their partners, Dad Sorrell, and Painter. They were building a big scow for their outfit. Hawthorne and Curry were also building a scow. There was Duggan, from Australia, and his partner Russel, from Belfast, a regular Irishman, who counts his money by shillings. Gander and his partner Wilson are from Ontario, Canada. We lived close enough to all these people so that we all became quite well acquainted, and very friendly. Then out on the west edge of the camp were three Swiss, whose names we never did know. They kept somewhat to themselves, but were friendly when our paths crossed.

One of the Swiss had a single track accordion, or rather he only played one tune on his accordion. He played the tune every evening, way into the night. Night after night, it was the last thing on my consciousness as I fell asleep. It was only natural that I should memorize it. When the Swiss came to the end of the piece, he started right in again at the beginning, and repeated that one little refrain, hour after hour. The camp would not have stood for it, had he been an American.

The secret of the cordial relations maintained by this rather mixed group, was that we were very much occupied in building our boats, until the last ten days of May. Then everyone in our cove had finished work except Avery, Woodruff, and Henderson. Everyone else was loafing and some had been for two weeks. Two weeks more of idleness would have resulted in a pitched battle. Avery and Henderson were both fighting Woodruff even though they had work to do. Nobody in camp hand any use for Lou Gorham but most of us were too polite to show it. He and Curry didn't speak. Dad Sorrell broke off with his partners, the Wigston Brothers. Phil Wigston and Hawthorne came near having a fist fight when Wigston told Hawthorn he "needn't mind coming into his tent." The three Swiss minded their own business (except for the accordion) and didn't quarrel with anyone. Russel, the real Irishmen from Belfast, and his partner, the Australian miner, and Gander and Wilson from Ontario, were on good terms with everyone, but they were all loafing and might have taken sides in another week.

Monday, May 30, half of the citizens of our cove left for Cariboo Crossing (known as Carcross when the railroad was finally built). Lou Gorham was among them, and had it not been for his wife, there would have been some plain talk to Lou. The verdict of everyone who had anything to do with him was that he had worked us all to and beyond the limit.

One of the letters that I wrote to the folks at home indicates how our own party of three was getting along together. It reads:

> I have been very fortunate in my party, don't see how it could be better. We all have our faults and we have a little squabble now and then and we get into a discussion a dozen times a day, but it does not amount to anything. I believe it is all quite different from what Pop expected it to be, Dan never knew or cared what it would be. Pop is a hard worker, and if he would only put as much head into his work as he does muscle, he'd never have needed to come to Alaska. That's the only fault I have to find with him. He has one of those nervous, hurry-up-and-lets-get-started-and-done-with-it dispositions. It should be very useful when we stampeded to a new strike, or anywhere that things go with a slam and a bang, but it is not of much use in sawing lumber or making a boat. Dan says we'll quarrel all the time when we come to build the boat and I expect we shall. I generally let Pop do things his way unless I am positive he is going wrong. He is a pretty good mechanic if he just wouldn't cut a board in two before he knows why he cuts it.
>
> Dan is the wit and songster of the party. When asked to settle an argument he says: "I don't care a bit, you fellows just scrap it out." He's the happy kind, who might drop his rubber boots in the water bucket or the frying pan, without noticing what he had done. He's always ready and willing to work hard but it doesn't worry him if we are not at work at 7:00 A.M. sharp. He'll work or he'll loaf and make himself agreeable, useful or entertaining.
>
> A description of the third member of our party is not necessary. He has not changed materially in these two months. His hair is longer, his face and hands are as brown as an Indian.

Whip-sawing Lumber and Building Our Boats

Our main occupation for five weeks after we built our camp, was to whip-saw lumber from solid trees, and build our boat big enough to take our outfit down river to Dawson, and a small boat to serve as tender for the big boat.

Our daily routine has been to get up at 5:00, saw wood from 7:00 A.M. to 6:00 P.M. and turn in at 9:00. We lay off on Sunday, get up late, and load, or do what we please. That sounds rather humdrum and tame but I don't find it so at all. For me the days are not half long enough and one Sunday rolls around before we realize that another week is ended.

When we had been whip-sawing for a week, we thought we had something to show for it, but most of our boards were sawed in such fantastic shapes, that we had to reorganize our industry, and proceed in a more businesslike way.

Whip-sawing, like a great many other hardships, is not half as hard as it is reputed to be. It's far easier than dragging a sled but requires more skill. First we select and cut down a tree, peel off the bark and trim the knots. Some people square the tree with an ax before sawing into boards. That wastes considerable lumber but gives uniform sized boards. The saw pit consists of three wooden bents to carry the log above the under sawman's head. That is the standard method. Our first log was 28 feet long and 8 inches at the small end and 19 inches at the big end. It was too big to handle easily, so instead of a standard pit we pried the big end up 6 inches at a time and built up a square pier of short logs, 8 feet from the end. The little end was easy to lift, and we built another pier. Then we sawed the log resting on the two cribbed-up piers. Pop generally ran the top of the saw and Dan and I changed off on the underside. We snapped a chalk line over the top of the log and sawed to the line, more or less. I say that we sawed to the line, but some of the first boards show places one and a half inches too thick. Finally we quit the line altogether and just sawed parallel lines to make inch boards and those boards look as well as the others. With our second log we kept to the line much better. When the top man knows his job and the saw is in good condition, it is hardly any work to run the underside of the saw. I stand erect and scarcely bend my back. I never push up on the handles, simply raise my hands when the top man lifts the saw, and then pull down on the saw. Don't pull hard or the saw digs in and jumps. The weight of the saw helps greatly and the top man is bound to push a little in following the handles down. The under man simply stands still, raises his arms and leans on the handle until the saw gets down. The top man has more work but even that is not bad if he does it right. He can bend over and straighten up at every out, but that nearly breaks his back in a short time. Some people saw that way, but the day Pop had a sick headache, I took the top of the saw and soon discovered the easiest way of running it. Just lean over a little bit, plant myself that way and keep my back fairly stiff. The underman pulls the saw down as far as he can without bending. Then the top man raises the saw until his hands are six inches above his head, and rests while the underman pulls down. The saw does not cut out on the up stroke, so it is not as hard as it sounds. On a regulation pit they lay logs to stand on each side of the log being sawed, but we sawed our first log standing on the log itself.

When we noted that most of our neighbors were turning out much more uniform lumber than we made, we built a standard pit, cut smaller, better and more uniformly shaped trees, and much better lumber and much better time was made.

After we had completed our big boat, Pop and Dan sawed the lumber for a little 15 foot boat in one and a half days and I built the boat complete in three and a half days. She was a beauty compared to the other boat. Held three nicely and room for 500 pounds of outfit.

We finished sawing what we thought would be enough lumber for our big boat about

5. Lake Bennett

Building boats on Lake Bennett.

May 14, and dragged the lumber on the ice across the cove to our camp, about as fast as we could saw it.

My father was travelling for a glove and mitten concern at that time, so he selected what he figured were the most suitable gloves and mittens for our trip. I expressed my appreciation of his good judgment in a letter written to him on Aril 28:

> Thus far our mittens have fitted every need. First we wore the Pontiac mittens without covers. Then we wore the hog skins without the inner mitten for our rough work, as a protection from pitch, ice and dead branches, rather than for warmth. Now the hogs are getting too warm, and we use the Napas while we whip-saw. I've not seen anything in any other outfit or in the outfitting stores that can compare with ours in price or in mitts themselves.
>
> The pants that I have worn ever since starting have two awful holes in the seat, due to dead branches of fallen trees and to pitch, nails, etc. So now I wear a pair of brown riveted canvas overalls for pants. I got out my patent leather shoes to wear around camp, which gives both my feet and my heavy shoes a rest.

We spend Wednesday and Thursday (May 4 and 5) fixing up our ship yard. We had to shovel out a location where the snow was three feet deep. In another week most of the snow had melted. We set up our horses about twenty feet in front of our tent and our work bench between the tent and the boat. The boat is 26 feet long, 30 inches deep, 7 foot beam, and 5 feet wide at the stern. Friday I laid out the frame, and we got busy. There was not much resemblance to a boat, for she only had her bow post and two sets of ribs. That gave her her shape. Then we put in the stern board. At first we nailed on only the top and bottom side boards. Then we put ribs two feet apart, and filled in the remaining side boards. Then we turned her over, trimmed the bottom edges and put on the bottom boards. Then we caulked and pitched all the seams.

We didn't do all this in a minute. I did a good part of the boat building and cooked at the same time. Pop and Dan got out trees for oars and sawed more lumber as we didn't have quite enough. On May 17 we put in seats and the top rails and guards to strengthen and protect her top edge. Queen Victoria didn't collect any tax from us for building our boat, because we are in N.W.T. and the mounted police from Bennett don't bother us. Below the island is British Columbia and there the police sometimes make people take out a logger's license at $1000.00 We launched the big boat on my birthday, May 20, and began work on our little 15 foot boat.

Letters To and From Home

Until April 24, none of us have heard from home, and we all wonder whether our letters ever reach home. Anybody can run a post office and handle mail. So we never know whether our letters are really posted. There may also be men chasing around with letters for us who can't find us. Or who don't care whether they do. We pay twenty-five cents each to have letters taken from here and posted at Dyea. There is the only real U.S. Post Office.

The night of April 24, Pop got two letters from home, mailed March 23 and 24 and marked "Dyea, April 2." Where have they been since then nobody knows. Now maybe we'll all get some. Friday, May 13, Jack Stere, who is now carrying mail to and from Bennett, brought Dan two letters and brought me mother's letter of March 30. Six weeks in transit, but most welcome.

We are better supplied with general news than people at home realize. Sunday, May 15, we read the Seattle paper of May 10. They cost four bits each and we get one about every other day. Magazines have been very scarce all along the trail. Nobody seems to make the effort to get them in here. Woodruff's friends sent him an article from the *Century*. We all wish that we had brought more reading matter. We got hold of a March *Review of Reviews* with Klondike article in it. The pictures are interesting.

We didn't get so many letters, but we made it a point to start our letters back home very regularly. Because we lacked confidence in the men who offered to post our letters, we made several trips from our camp back to the city of Bennett.

About the last snowstorm we encountered was on April 12, the day we had picked to move from our temporary to our permanent camp. It was too stormy to move camp, but it gave me a chance to walk the 16 miles to Bennett to post letters and inquire for mail at the various Bennett post offices.

Again on May 2, after Woodruff had promised to post our letters, he went without them. So I took our letters and started bright and early for Bennett, 16 miles away. I had the good fortune to get a ride all the way down after walking about four miles. Bennett was growing. A real new post office had just been opened. They didn't have any mail and only about $100.00 worth of stamps. Would only sell twenty-five cents worth to anyone person. There are lots of stores there now, that is tents where they sell stuff. Nails are thirty-five cents per pound, other things in proportion.

Walking back after dinner was tough work. For twelve miles the ice on the lake was solid and good, but on top of the ice there was melted snow. I waded, literally waded up to my ankles in water or slush for that whole twelve miles. It was far from being a pleasant walk, hard work physically, and rather nerve wracking. I wore my heavy prospecting shoes with high tops and when I got back my feet were practically dry. Pretty good shoes. At the narrows the water and slush ended, and so for the remaining four miles to camp I had good walking. The snow and even water on top of the ice seems to preserve it. The last four miles at some places was not really safe for a horse and heavy load but all right for men but there were lots of horses on it. I made up my mind then that it was time for me to stop going on the ice. When I told the boys around camp that the ice was getting bad they laughed at me, but next day they begun to realized I was right. So Dan and Pop quit the ice and walked the shore lines to and from the saw pit. We brought our last lumber over the ice on Tuesday and none of us have been on it since.

Thursday, May 26, was warmer than any day we have yet seen, 82 degrees in the shade. Dan and I had intended to row down to Bennett after mail and to post letters and to buy a few things, but the lake was too rough to attempt a 16 mile pull against the wind. Friday was more favorable. Up at 2:30 A.M. just as the sun was crawling out, and at 5:30 A.M. we were out on the lake, just opposite our old camp. I would row for an hour and then Dan would relive me. We made the 16 miles in seven hours and it was no picnic. We rowed to within six miles of Bennett and there we encountered ice. So we beached our boat and walked. For two miles we walked over rocks and big boulders along the lake shore. Then we found a trail that led us up over a point for half a mile. Then more lake shore but the rocks got bigger. At one place we had to pay ten cents to be ferried around a steep cliff where otherwise we would have had to climb up 200 feet to get past the place. Farther along we did have to climb the side of the mountain, and finally arrive at Bennett. At the new post office I got mother's letters of April 15 and 21.

The Canadian officials require each boat and its passengers to be registered, so they may guess who is where in the Klondike. I got in line, and drew number 1739 for our boat.

One of our principal reasons for that trip to Bennett was to get some butter. Will you believe it, 32 miles of such travel, for butter. We ran out and tried it two days without butter. Then we borrowed two pounds until we could get some.

There were no more stamps at the post office, so I wrapped my letter and a dime in a piece of paper; the postmaster takes seven cents and sends the other three and the letter to Victoria, B.C. to be stamped and really posted. Postage is getting cheap.

There was open water for about three miles from Bennett, so we engaged a boat to take us half way back to our own boat. He took us four miles, and then we had to scramble over the rocks again. It was 6:30 before we got to our boat and got started and then how we did go. We only had 12 square feet of canvas for a sail but that was enough. When we reached the island we thought it was best not to attempt sailing around the island, so we beached the boat south of the point, and walked another mile. The little boat is a daisy. She rides like a duck but having no keel she will only sail with the wind. We got to camp at 9:00 P.M., 18 hours for one day's work. I had not been so tired since the first night that we pulled our sled into the Lindeman Hotel.

Lake Bennett at night.

Tragedy

The most popular topic of conversation anywhere on Lake Bennett concerned the question of when the ice was going out of the lake. On May 3 while we were bringing the last of our lumber across the ice from the saw pit, a horse broke through the ice near our camp, but the camp rescued him with the aid of some ropes. Next day another horse had to be pulled out.

On May 7, everyone conceded that the ice on the lake was very dangerous, in fact impassable. Everybody travelled along the shore line, unless it was very early in the morning.

On Tuesday May 10 we had overslept, so it was 6:30 before we were up and getting breakfast. Way out in the middle of the lake and considerably north of us, we were all rather startled to see a dog team and four men mushing along toward Bennett. The regular method had been to travel on the lake very early in the morning, while the night cold kept it frozen, but this was some four hours after sunrise.

While we were eating breakfast in our tent, we heard a great shouting over west of the point that separated our camp from the next camp of boat builders. Of course, we knew that the camp existed and occasionally met men from that camp but we had no particular acquaintances as we had in our own camp. Everyone in our camp had seen the dog team and had commented upon the danger of such a trip, so when we heard the shouting, we left our meal and rushed over to the other camp. Directly in front of this other camp (which for convenience I might call the West Camp) there was a long high rocky island, about a quarter mile out in the lake. About 100 yards from shore we saw two men lying flat on the ice, and a little way in front of them a hole through the ice, about 10 feet in diameter. On our side of this hole, we could see the head and shoulders of a man, with his arms resting on the ice. A little to his left the head dog of the team had his head and front paws on the ice, and was struggling valiantly to overcome the weight of sled or harness that was pulling him down. The dog didn't last long.

I don't remember that I ever saw a crowd collect so quickly, and be so totally unprepared to meet the emergency when assembled. We couldn't rush out on the ice and throw ropes to these men, because we knew how impossible it would be to reach them by such methods.

The ice on the lake was some two feet thick, but the sun and the warm air had crystallized the ice, so that it was very much like a vast area of hexagonal lead pencils, 24 inches long, floating on end and held from falling sideways only by the pressure of other pencils touching on all sides. Out in the middle of the lake there was much more cohesion between these long ice crystals, than there was to the ice between our shore and the rocky island.

As the men approached the narrow part of the lake, west of the island they began to realize their danger, changed their direction and headed straight for the West Camp. The ice got worse at every step. Finally two men lagged some distance back of the sled, to avoid a concentrated load on the ice. Then suddenly without the slightest warning crack, the sled sank through the ice, carrying one man with it, who was drowned immediately.

The two men on the ice lay spread out to the greatest possible extent, to distribute their weight as widely as possible. They showed splendid nerve all the way through. The man in the water was a most pitiful sight. The water was ice cold, and it was only natural that he should have tried to lift himself out of the water and onto firmer ice, but because of the big hole in the ice, the side pressure was removed that had held the long ice crystals upright. Therefore, every time he tried to crawl out, of the water, the long ice crystals which he hoped would support his weight, fell away from the main body of ice, and he was just where he started, only weaker and colder.

Don't image that we men stood there and did nothing. Some boat builders in the West Camp had a considerable pile of lumber piled near the shore. Everybody got a board and started to build a board path to the unfortunate man. We built a double path, as the boards were not wide enough to support the weight of a man going and another man returning. The man in the water never wasted a bit of breath by talking, and I shall never forget the look of agony in his eyes as we approached him. We were only about four board lengths from him when we found that we had no more boards and so must take up boards from one path to finish the other. When the man in the water saw the steady run of boards stop, he lost his head completely, and struggled repeatedly to climb out on the ice, and went down. We couldn't push a board out on the ice to him, as the ice crystals held the board like so much glue. We had worked with far greater speed than my written words seem to indicate, and had shouted our encouragement to him as we worked, but all to no purpose.

Then we had to change the lay of our board walk to avoid the hole in the ice, and reach the two men beyond the hole. They fully realized their danger, and the danger incurred by all of us who were trying to help them. We didn't have boards enough to reach them, and then the hero of the day approached; a man who said his name was Jones, tied a long rope to the tail of a sled, carried it to the end of the board path, picked up three boards, and worked these three boards alternately closer to the men on the ice, pushing the sled ahead all the while. Even this daredevil hero didn't dare get within 30 feet of the men on the ice. He gathered some slack on the rope, and threw the sled and one board within the reach of one of the two men. That man got the other end of his board to his partner, then while Jones re-laid his two boards to reach the shore, the men on shore slowly and steadily pulled the two men with the sled and the board to shore. Their weight left a channel in the ice that would afloat a board, but we got them safely ashore. They were soaking wet and fearfully cold. One man was rather old. He was the head of a party of 39. They had intended to make this one more trip to Bennett.

After we warmed them and dried their clothes, they looked around for Jones, to express again their appreciation of his bravery and he was nowhere to be found. He didn't belong to either our camp or the West Camp. He had faded from the picture as suddenly and as silently as he had entered it. We know he reached shore all right. We finally decided he must have been a solitary musher following the shore of the lake. When his job was finished, he must have picked up his pack and gone on his way.

After we got him ashore, that old man was so rattled that he gave the dead men's names to a reporter for Seattle papers as being Tom Barnes and Louis Deshan. That news was probably advertised all over the United States. The second dead man's name was actually Luke Richards. Next day Louis Deshan came down to help find the bodies. Just think of what Deshan's friends at home must have suffered while he was safe and sound.

So much for that affair; it spoiled our appetite for any more breakfast, and we were no good for work all that day. However, that was far from being all that the day held for us.

It was never really dark when we went to bed. Dan and I were out near out boat that Tuesday evening looking at a particularly beautiful sunset, when we saw a man and a heavily loaded sled, all by himself out on the lake, just beyond the point. He had stopped and was testing the ice here and there in an effort to determine his surest course. He turned his sled and headed straight toward the place where the two had drowned in the morning. Dan and I shouted at him and ran way out to the far end of the point to warn him. Finally, he understood us, and then much against his will, he left his sled where it was, and returned to the west shore of the lake. About midnight when the ice had stiffened to some extent, he came back to his sled, and next morning we found him safely ashore at our camp.

The two bodies were rescued by using Hawthorne's boat and big scow. Men on board pushed them through the slush ice, two feet thick, with no very great effort. We buried the men on the island. In pine boxes, with flour sacks full of shavings for pillows.

Our Recreation

Thus far, this chapter might indicate that our stay at Lake Bennett was all hard work and tragedy, but that is far from being the case. Every Sunday we went on the most enjoyable excursions, in all directions from our camp, and the things we saw on these excursions and scenery from our front steps was a source of never ending pleasure.

Around Lake Lindeman and at the head of Lake Bennett the mountains seemed small after seeing Chilkoot, but after getting north of the island we found more real mountains. At the narrow place the mountains begin to rise up abruptly. From our camp we can see a whole row of high rocky peaks on the left or west shore of the lake. They have only a little tuft of trees at their bases. They stop at the little cape because there is an arm of the lake beyond the cape; and way back 10 to 12 miles we see other ranges with whole forests of pine between. Directly ahead of our camp is a big peak, so big that it interested me and I made many sketches of it, which I sent home. To the right in the background there are rough stone mountains. Then on our right, on our side of the lake, there is a series of mountains that run up like steps. They start off very flat at the lake shore and slope back steeper and steeper. They are covered here and there with trees way to the top and run down south of us to the narrow place. Between these mountains many points of gravel run out to the lake, all well wooded.

Lake Bennett view to the north of camp.

Lake Bennett view to the northeast of camp.

  We explored some of these mountains, they looked so low and smooth and easy climbing. There was one nice smooth round bald headed mountain, with big patches of clear snow, which Dan and I wanted to climb, so on Sunday, April 24, we started. Pop went along and took the shotgun. We went across the arm of the lake, past the point where we sawed our lumber and up through the woods. Then we struck out for the mountain. It was a whole lot like work, and we waded through soft snow up to our knees until we encountered a deep canyon looking for the world like a railroad cut. Pop and Dan had enough of snow wading and so they stopped and turned back but I kept on, for that canyon was too good a thing to miss.

  It lay between me and my mountain. My side was all forest and deep snow; the other side was all smooth and bare. So I crossed it. I scrambled down through the pine trees at a 45 degree slope, and when about 100 feet from the bottom I had to go almost straight down. Some others had come up the route that I followed down, so I had a clear path to follow. I crossed the little creek on an ice bridge, and climbed up on the other side with the help of small trees and buses. It was hard work but well worth it. The nice smooth banks that looked so attractive were small hills of gravel piled up, each one higher than the other, until they reached the base of my mountain. Little blue wild flowers were in bloom on these gravel hills. Before I reached what seemed to be the real mountain I came to a flat place covered with pine trees, and snow up to my waist. That stopped me; my knees limit the wading depth of snow. To my right, the canyon kept on going up and forests of fine trees looked like nice patches of grass. To the left, gravel hills for a mile or more, and then mountains. Ahead of me beyond the woods was my bald mountain, a great big pile of gravel or granite. Behind me was the series of hills I had climbed and then the lake, and then the real mountains. We had started at 1:00 P.M., it was now 4:30, time to start back if I wanted my supper. I followed the right side of the canyon all the way down to the lake, for it was good clean walking all the way. There were a dozen or more others out for the same Sunday walk. I met some and saw tracks of others.

Dan and I went on our first gold stampede on Friday May 6. A week or so before Chas. Wigston had found some very small colors of gold up in the canyon which I have just described. He had been there several times and this particular Friday he and his partners set out early with some prospecting tools, and came back at noon for more. He talked to Lou Gorham very confidentially and after dinner Lou was nowhere to be found.

If there was anything there we intended to be in on it. So Dan and I knocked off after dinner and went after them. We found their location and claim stakes, but they had gone on, up the canyon. We met a young fellow who told us that we could find plenty of colors there almost anywhere. There is a 60 or 80 foot waterfall at that point of the canyon and bedrock is in plain sight all around. The stream had just cut its way down through it. The young fellow dug some gravel from the creek bed and washed out a weak speck of gold. I saw how he did it, got a shovel full myself and washed out my first color which I promptly mailed home. About that time the crowd came back and I got Wigston to wash a pan for me. He got a color and was so careful to take and keep it, that Dan and I concluded at once that they had not found any bonanza. So we went back home feeling that the gold would not fly away before Sunday.

Sunday we went at it right. We got up at 5:00 and were at the falls at 7:30. A hard piece of bedrock forms a dam over which the water once flowed. Part of the dam was broken out, this leaving a shoulder of rock behind which there was about a yard of gravel piled up. I dug into that and cleared it out to bedrock while Pop and Dan panned the gravel. We got colors in every pan, collected them and put them in a little pill bottle. They made quite a yellow spot in the bottle. Dan found the biggest flake. We had lunch with us and after lunch walked up the canyon a mile or so testing as we went. Colors everywhere and anywhere. There is no doubt of it, we are in the land of gold. I doubt whether there is enough up there to pay us to work it, but when someone gets a good big hydraulic apparatus there will be gold enough there to make it pay.

(About 30 years afterward, when Dan took his wife for a pleasure trip on the White Pass Railroad, he tried to find the canyon again, but was not able to find it. He always felt that we should have given the place more time.)

Leaving Lake Bennett

Our departure from Lake Bennett depended upon the weather, and the time when the lake and the Yukon River would be free of ice. So the weather and the climate were very important items to all of us who were camped on Lake Bennett.

The last snowstorm was on April 12. Toward the end of April the air seems so nice and spring-like that one could believe that the ice might go any night. A party hauling logs to build two 60 foot boats have worn a deep path through the snow in the woods. This path is a little creek at noon and ice in the morning. The ice on the lake is two feet thick or more and is covered with a good coat of snow. At night water pails freeze in the tent. In the early morning we walk on top of three feet of snow, at noon we must wade through it. At 8:00 P.M. there is plenty of daylight to see to write letters.

Early in May the ice on Lake Bennett had begun to melt. On Sunday afternoon (May 15) Pop and I took a boat ride in Charlie Wigston's little skiff. The ice had broken up for about 500 feet from shore. Evidently we are located where the ice first begins to go out. Nearer Bennett the ice has not broken up yet, but right around us it is going fast. Three days later the water was clear of ice for over half a mile from our shore and was open entirely across the lake and beyond the islands and up the narrows.

May 28, Lake Bennett is all open and dozens of boats are going every day. Some started five days before, but two boats got held up in the ice for a day as a result of being so impatient. Lake Tagish is not open yet, and from all reports we can hear it may not break up for another week.

May 30, about half the boats in our camp moved out, with the intention of going as far as Cariboo Crossing and waiting there until Lake Tagish would permit further progress.

Bright and early on June 2, that means (2:00 A.M.) we had intended to embark but the wind was too stiff for Pop. Pop is like an old hen, scared stiff at the sight of water and I believe that he will even kick against going in the boat, when the lake gets so calm that he can see his face in the water. Dan and I were willing enough to start out and I felt that there was no danger but Pop just set his foot down. We could go if we wished, but he would stay on shore. Woodruff, Curry and Henderson were in much the same fix. Painter kept Wigston on shore, and the three Swiss said they would wait until we go.

June 3 calmed down to just the prettiest sailing day man ever saw, just a little white crest on the lake and blowing straight up the lake, but it was a repetition of yesterday so far as Pop was concerned. Pop did get his nerve up enough at 10:00 A.M. so that we loaded our boat and the others did the same. Then we waited and at supper time, there we were, nowhere, with no place to eat or sleep and Pop wouldn't get off terra firma. I don't think he got much pleasure out of the lake and river trip.

We finally got started. After supper when the sun had gone down behind the mountain, the white caps were not so easy to see, so Pop said "All right, let's start," and we were off. We started at 8:15 P.M. Woodruff, Henderson, and Curry have a heavy scow. Painter, Nuhfer, and Wigston have a scow with somewhat better sailing qualities. The three Swiss have a tub of a boat but she can sail all right, fully as well as ours. They were not quite ready to start with the others, but caught up before midnight. Curry's scow fell way behind, and the hard wind was a big help for Wigston's scow. We reefed our sail as much as possible and so did Wigston, and that let Curry catch up. We sailed all night, never stopped for anything. About midnight, we were just opposite the mountain that appears in the center of many of my sketches. The east side of the same mountain is plainly visible all the way down Tagish. It was darker at 11:00 P.M. than at any other time and even then I could have read print although it was not a bright clear night. We saw the sun set in the north-northwest, and not long after the last blue color had faded out, the north-northeast began to get gray. Such is our parting memory of Lake Bennett. Now we felt that we were really on our way to the Klondike.

6

THE BOAT TRIP TO INDIAN RIVER

Caribou Crossing to Lake Marsh, June 4 and 5

At the outlet of Lake Bennett, there is a short stream that leads to Lake Tagish. The shores of this stream are low, look like meadows in prairie country. This narrow, shallow stream is called Caribou Crossing, probably because it has been a favorite crossing for caribou, when they migrate. When the White Pass and Yukon Railroad was built, it was located along the east shore of Lake Bennett, and crossed the outlet from Bennett at Caribou Crossing. Some punster named the place Carocross, which preserves the historical association, only when one knows the old name.

When our boat reached the end of Lake Bennett, it was quite light, even though it was midnight. The river which formed the outlet ran plainly enough ahead of us, so we guided our boat into the current. We had decided to run as long as running was good, so I rolled up in my blanket and slept from 1:00 until 2:00 A.M.

I awoke when we touched on a sandbar. We pushed away from it with little effort, and continued our way. The stream got wider, and the current almost disappeared. We had to get out the oars and row. We rowed steadily until 10:00 A.M., Dan meanwhile taking a nap. Pop would not think of sleeping until we should be safely through the awful "Windy Arm" of Tagish. He had heard such awful tales of this place and didn't know where or what it was.

I felt that we could handle our boat under all conditions short of a cyclone. She was nicely loaded, drew hardly a foot of water, which left 18 inches' protection against waves. We packed our clothes bags and some groceries ahead of the mast, and had a fancy homemade anchor loaded on the bow. We put two sleds upside down on the bottom and piled sacks of grub on them. We had dry firewood and other odds and ends in the stern, and more sacks between the stern and rear seat, then a clear space between the two main seats. In this space we set our stove on two boards, also some boxes to hold tableware and serve as a table.

Windy Arm was quite too tame. We had to row a long way across Lake Tagish. I got dinner about 10:00 A.M. when we were right opposite the middle of Windy Arm. There we caught a very light breeze which carried us lazily along until about noon. Then we caught a better breeze which carried us along nicely, and Pop slept for an hour.

The big, dazzling white stone mountain between Windy Arm and the main body of Lake Tagish was one of the wonderful sights that deserved more time than we gave it. It rose straight out of the water, with hardly a bit of vegetation, and very white.

The lake was dotted with innumerable boats of all kinds and speeds. There were no particular ties that bound us to stay with the boats of our Lake Bennett friends and neighbors, and as our boat appeared to have better speed than the others, we soon separated, and future meetings with our old friends were left for the future to decide. On leaving Lake Bennett, we developed a new friendship with the three Swiss who had the accordion. Their leader was named Joe. They copied every move we made from Bennett to Tagish Station.

After Pop had his little nap, I lay down and slept from 2:00 to 4:00 P.M. When I awoke we were approaching the far end of the lake. For a mile or so the water was very shallow, and full of boulders of all sizes. The sandy bottom was white, so the boulders showed plainly. We had to watch where we sailed. Then came a mile of the river which drains Tagish, and we arrived at Tagish House, as they called the Custom House and a Mounted Police station. We pulled our boats out of the swift current, and tied them on a muddy shore while we went to the post office. There was confusion at the post office. The man in charge thumbed through his entire pile of mail, each time anybody inquired for a letter. Pop and Dan each got a letter, but neither letter was from their family. I went to another office to have our passes stamped, and to report the progress of boat number 1739. I then had to find a policeman who signed our release without going down to inspect our boat as he was supposed to do.

The police had just brought in four Indians who had killed a man at McClintock River, up beyond Lake Marsh. That added to the general excitement.

After 7:00 P.M. the police would neither O.K. passes, nor permit any boats to pass the station. When I discovered that, I hunted up Pop and Dan and we sailed past the station, and tied up the boats at a point where we could continue our journey at will.

Then we walked back to see how our Swiss friend Joe who had sailed so close to us, was progressing. He had found a policeman too late to get his clearance paper signed, and was too late to get in the post office. So, as he had pitched his tent for the night, and could not proceed until 7:00 A.M. next morning, we left him hoping he would overtake us before we reached White Horse. We pushed our boats into the river again, and travelled the five miles of rather swift current that brought us to the head of Lake Marsh. This lake is very appropriately named. Of course there were plenty of mountains in the background, but the shores of the lake were low and marshy, and the land back of the shore had no apparent elevation above the water.

We figured that we had travelled about 37 miles in 24 hours, divided as follows:

Lake Bennett	12 Miles
The Narrows	3 Miles
Lake Tagish	17 Miles
Tagish River	5 Miles
Total	**37 Miles**

I show the sketch map of our route, which I made in my diary.

We beached our boat and turned in for a night's rest, Dan and I on the sacks of grub back of the mast, Pop in the stern seat, lengthened with sacks and boxes. Mosquitos had been so thick, and ambitious at Tagish Station, that they were one reason why we proceeded to Lake Marsh. There were even more mosquitos and more active mosquitos where we stopped on Lake Marsh. We wrapped ourselves quite completely in our canvas tarpaulins, and slept well. I awoke at 1:00 A.M. to observe the weather, and it was a dead calm. Pop

6. The Boat Trip to Indian River

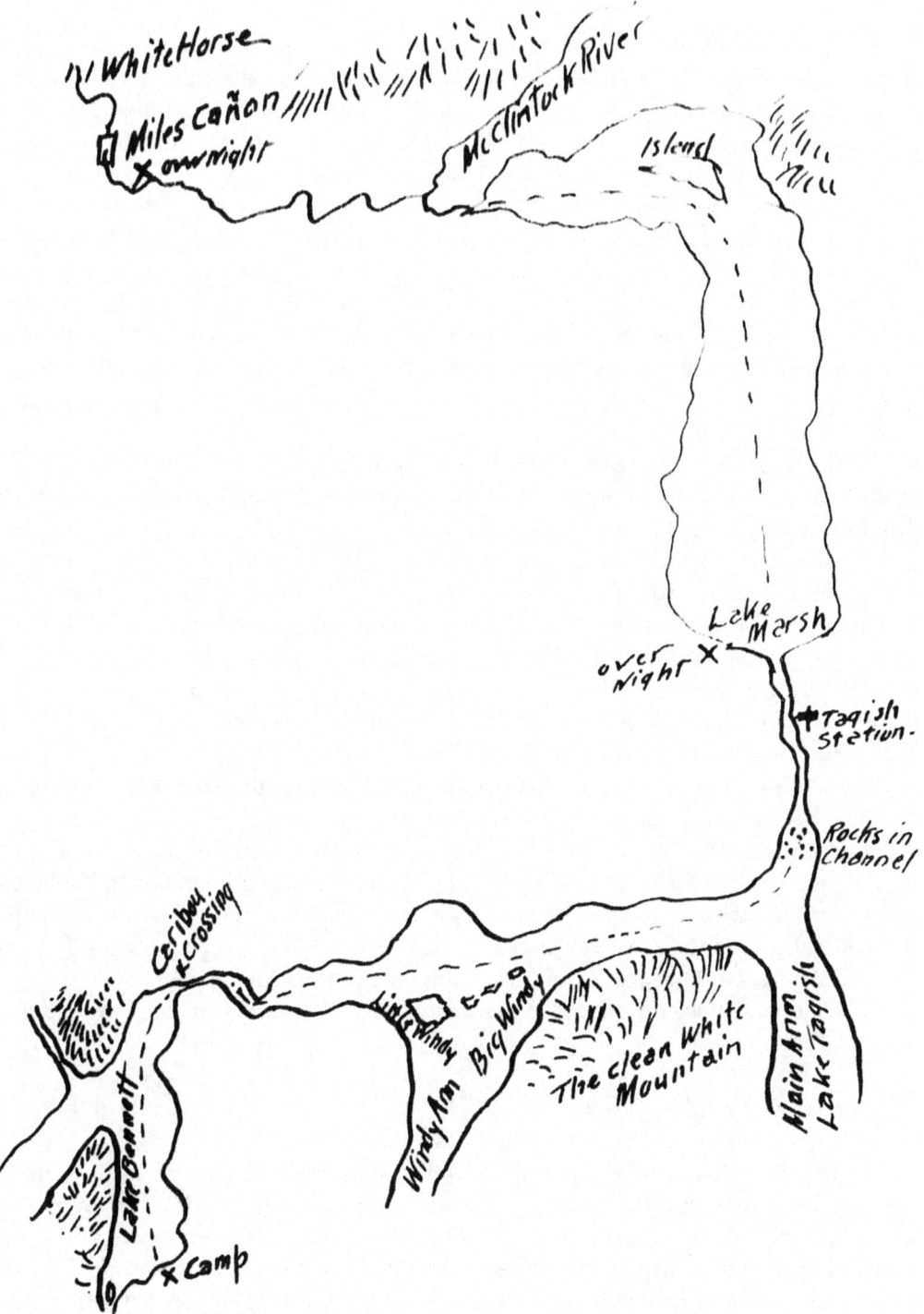

Water route from Lake Bennett to Tagish to White Horse.

awoke at 4:00 A.M. and as there was a slight breeze, we all turned out and started across Lake Marsh.

We ate breakfast on the boat, then had to row far enough out into the lake to find a breeze. When we at length did find the breeze, we slipped along at a merry pace. That gave us a chance to read the Seattle *Post-Intelligencer* of May 27 which I had found at Tagish. Pop threw a fish line out behind the boat, and to the surprise of all of us, he caught a salmon trout that weighed fully 3 pounds. It was a most welcome addition to our Sunday dinner.

As the breeze stiffened we reefed our sail. I took the steering oar, at the stern and headed toward the north end of the lake. It was fun until we passed a point, beyond which we encountered cross winds and little squalls. Then I had to hold her as close as possible to the wind to avoid getting in the lee of an island. Many boats could not avoid the island and had to drop sails while they pulled their boats into the breeze again. Our boat behaved well and we only dropped our sail when we reached the end of the lake. For a mile or two at the end of the lake, the water was less than three feet deep, but there were no boulders to complicate our navigation.

When we reached the river we beached the boat (among millions of mosquitos) and cooked our dinner. Fish, onions, biscuits and applesauce. It took us from 1:00 until 3:00 P.M. to prepare and eat that wonderful meal.

As we were eating Jim Forsyth, Doc Howe and Will came along in their big boat. They landed just below us and we had a most enjoyable visit. Jim had left Lake Bennett on Wednesday June 1 and had been obliged to lay up for two days at Windy Arm. Under these conditions they could not cut straight across Tagish as we had done. They had to go through Little Windy, wait a day and then went through Big Windy in the worst kind of weather. It took two hours of steady rowing, against wind and waves to cross Big Windy. The wind died sometime after, and that's why we got past so easily.

After our fish fry we started for White Horse, figuring to make that 15 miles, and call it a day. The river was rather narrow, and full of crooked turns. The current was good, but the wind was generally against us. For 10 miles the country continued to be low and flat, with a range of mountains off to the north. Then the river was bordered with the hills of sandy clay. One of these was dotted with thousands of holes, containing swallow's nests.

Jim pulled into the shore several miles above the rapids, just as we got there at 9:00 P.M. We slept in our boat again, but Jim went ashore to sleep and to cook.

We figured that we travelled 37 miles that day, 22 on Lake Marsh and 15 on the river.

White Horse Rapids, June 6

White Horse Rapids, the place on the trail that had shared publicity with Chilkoot. We were up and on our way at 6:00 A.M., with a fine current hurrying us toward this double-barreled obstacle. The river was very crooked and the current drove first to one bank and then to the other. At one place the river turned a square corner, around a sand-clay hill, and was joined there by a river coming in from the left. Beyond that the river was much wider and the current rather slower.

Another two miles, and we tied up our boats, on the north or right bank, about a mile above "The Canyon." Here the pilots solicit the job of taking boats through the canyon.

There is a big log saloon and hotel, the headquarters of the Canyon and Rapids Tramway Company. The tram is built of long poles laid like rails. It starts here but is not quite completed.

The right bank of the river was lined with boats, as closely as they could be packed, for more than a mile, and more boats arriving every minute. Every boat owner seemed to have the same thought. He went to look at the canyon before attempting to decide how he should negotiate it.

Pop, Dan and I walked along the top of the sand-clay hills to the head of the canyon. All along the route, we met people returning. Many of them carried cars over their shoulders. These were the pilots and steersmen returning from a trip just completed through the canyon.

For an hour we stood and looked down into the rushing water of the canyon watching the boats shoot through. They shot through the first part of it, into a round basin; they hesitated there for a moment or so, and then slow through the last half of the canyon out upon a rather broad swift river. The walls are of sandstone, and the water is piled up in the middle of the stream, several feet higher than it is along the sandstone walls. Boats must be guided along the high crest in midstream; if they slip off the crest, they are swamped when they strike the sandstone wall.

We watched boat after boat being guided through. Dan and I decided that we would like to take our boat through, and then go down and inspect White Horse Rapids. Pop sat down on that plan. He wanted to walk down to look at the rapids, and then have a pilot to take our boat all the way. The situation presented all the elements of a family quarrel. So we went back to the boat, had dinner, and talked it over calmly.

Dan was determined to ride the canyon and the rapids. Pop was equally determined that we hire an experienced pilot and his steersmen to handle our outfit. Billy Oakum the pilot whom we hired for $25.00 to take us clear through, said that I was only that much added weight, but accepted Dan, who could put double the weight on a steering oar that I could.

We shifted some of our load further toward the stern of the boat, took down the mast, and the stove, and put some of our firewood in the small boat. Then we covered the front half of the boat with canvas, nailed down, and ridged up in the middle, so it would shed water. We decided to let the little boat find its own way through both the canyon and the rapids.

When everything was ship shape, Pop and I hurried overland to the canyon, to see Dan and our outfit go through. We had no time to waste. We had hardly reached the edge of the canyon, when here they came. Dan and the steersmen McKay hanging to the steering car, which was secured to the stern board, the pilot looking ahead and giving his orders by the motion of his arms. The roar of the water made it impossible for the best-lunged man to make himself heard. Our boat behaved perfectly and in a few seconds, she shot out at the far end of the canyon and into the smoother waters beyond.

Then Pop and I set out for the rapids, which we had not yet seen. Below the canyon we saw two boats wrecked upon the same rock. The small boat had hung up there first, and then the larger boat had piled on top and crushed the smaller boat. The owners had arrived and were more than busy trying to salvage their outfit.

The canyon was a real thriller, but after the canyon, the real White Horse Rapids were only a side show. Boats could and did get into trouble at the rapids, but Miles Canyon is the place the newspapers really meant when they wrote column after column about White Horse Rapids.

Dan had enjoyed the whole trip greatly and when we arrived we found that he had our outfit safely secured below the rapids, and he was having the time of his life, watching the other boats shoot the rapids.

Just after a boat gets through the rapids, it jumps up and down three or four times, is caught by a swift even current, that will make the boat downstream a mile or more in a big hurry, unless the boat man promptly throws a line ashore and ties the boat.

Our boat was tied some 500 yards below the rapids. Dan was delighted with the rapids, just enjoyed sitting there and watching the boats shoot through, and they all shot through nicely.

Old Jim was tied up below the rapids, in easy reach of the White Horse Saloon. When Doc and Will appeared they embarked and resumed their journey.

We had let our little 15 foot boat shift for itself. We turned it loose above the canyon and expected to find it waiting for us at the rapids. We waited and it didn't appear. While we waited we picked up some of the hard luck stories in connection with White Horse.

Opposite our outfit, there was a big scow with a 10 ton outfit. She had hit a rock in the canyon which tore away half her bottom. The pilot couldn't stop, so he put the scow through the canyon, the two miles to the rapids and through the rapids and then hung up for repairs.

There was also the wreck of a house boat, which had hit a rock in the canyon and whirled along entirely helpless. The grub was all lost. Two men lost their heads and jumped off the boat as it approached the rapids and were drowned. The third man stuck to the boat, shot the rapids was saved. Anything that will float will shoot the rapids easily.

After supper at 8:00 P.M. when our small boat had not come down, Pop and I went back to hunt for her. Dan stayed with the big boat to catch the small boat if it got past Pop and me. We walked along where we could always see both shores, keeping a sharp lookout. There was a smooth path worn by the many others who had done much the same we were doing.

Our little boat was hung up across the river, just below the canyon. The owners of the scow had just finished getting her cargo up onto dry land. We shouted to them and they pushed our little boat into the stream. It stuck again on a bar some distance below. I walked up stream on our side of the river, and found another small boat whirling round and round in an eddy, rather close to shore. I got it out of the eddy, rather close to shore, got in and shot across the river to the bar that had stopped our boat. Then I pushed the other fellow's boat out into the stream, threw the firewood out of our boat, re-arranged the loading of the sled and poles, made rope rowlocks (as the others were smashed) got in and shot across the head of Squaw Rapids, landed and set her adrift again. Pop and I followed her downstream. She stuck again at the bend above the rapids. I went down the bank and shoved her off. Then she stuck on a big raft of drift wood. I had to crawl out on the drift wood and push her off with a long pole. Before I could regain the shore she had shot through the Rapids. Pop and Dan caught her, and when I arrived she was safely tied to the stern of the big boat.

Three scows were wrecked today. One got turned stern forward as it approached the rapids. The steersmen's oars was jerked from his hands and he was thrown into the water.

His partner grabbed him and pulled him aboard. The boat floated on downstream, with no damage except the broken oar.

My reassuring letter to Mother reads as follows:

> I didn't shoot White Horse just solely on your account and I've since been kicking myself that I did not. But I am following the plan of not taking any chances, so we hired the boat taken through.

Just another example of that popular Klondike proverb: "Don't believe anything you hear, and less than half of what you think you see."

Lake Laberge and Thirty Mile River, June 7 and 8

Tuesday morning we were up and on our way about 6:00 A.M. We were seven hours reaching the head of Lake Laberge, 28 miles from White Horse. I had a chance to turn in and sleep from 10:00 A.M. until noon. The current was very good part of the time, and at times we could use our sail.

Some three miles before we reached the lake, we encountered a peculiar puzzle. The river broadened to a regular lake. We sensed a joker being hidden in the pack when we saw two boats who had missed the right channel, pulling back towards us. Luck was with us, and we followed the current along the left bank of the river. It suddenly turned swiftly into a narrow channel, which brought us out again in another broad expanse of water, which led to several more channels. We guessed the right channel again and soon sighted the lake, but we were not there yet. The river was all choked with sandbars. The channel we had followed lay within 20 feet of the left bank, all the way until we finally reached the lake. Then for a mile or more the lake was less than three feet deep.

The early afternoon was rather uninteresting. The shores were low and flat. There was no wind. Only a cat's paw now and then. We took turns rowing and sleeping. Finally, late in the afternoon, we caught a fair breeze, and when we had time to look about, we found that we had entered a veritable fairy land, one of the scenic gems of the entire trip.

We ran to the left of the large island, shown on all maps, had a late supper and headed for a little cove about a mile beyond the island, and tied up for the night at 11:00 P.M. The entire left side of the lake seems to be cut up with numerous islands, of various shapes and sizes. Along the east side of the lake there is a range of clean white mountains.

That evening trip among the islands on Lake Laberge, supplies one of the beautiful pictures that have imprinted themselves up my memory. Everything in the picture seemed to be so clean, the shores so sharply defined, and the colors so enchanting.

We were up and away next morning at 4, and a fair breeze brought us to the north end of the lake about noon, and we entered Thirty Mile River.

The North is a land of violent contrasts. Laberge left a permanent memory of beautiful scenery. Thirty Mile River left a permanent memory of unforeseen menace and unexpected catastrophe, which is as real to me now as it was then, and which I greatly fear I shall be unable to describe in adequate words. I've never been quite able to understand why the papers gave such publicity to Chilkoot and White Horse, with never a word about the terrors of Thirty Mile River. We entered the river with the happy thought that there would be no more rowing on becalmed lakes.

The current was swift, but the water was clear and deep. It was my turn to get a few winks of sleep, so I turned in and slept peacefully for about an hour. Then the boys called me to give a hand at managing the boat. The boat was racing around sharp bends in the river like a runaway locomotive on a steep grade. The current at each bend of the river bore over to the steep river bank, and the boat would have been thrown against the bank at every turn, except the heroic efforts we made with our steering car.

The water was clear, but it was full of long submerged ropes of some white slimy stuff, which Pop declared were remnants of disintegrated dead men. The thought did not add any to our comfort. I've wondered many times what the stuff might have been.

The river was narrow and we could not see any distance ahead, so we knew nothing of what dangers might be awaiting us until we were right upon them. We may have passed a dozen big submerged rocks in the channel without suspecting their existence, but when we saw lumber floating along in the water, all too evidently parts of a boat that had gone bad, we began to realize that we were involved in another adventure.

It was high time we did. Just ahead of us there was a big scow, which had driven itself up, nearly out of water on a submerged rock, which was so sharp, that it had cut the bottom boards of the scow, and held the bow captive while the other end rapidly filled with water.

On our right was a boat that smashed into kindling wood. The outfit she once carried lying scattered along the shore or in the water, for 500 yards. The men of that party shouted to us to keep our boat so close to shore, if we would avoid their hard luck. We kept it there, regardless of the effort it required, and missed the jagged rock that lay just below the surface of the river, by only a very few feet.

A little farther below we passed more wrecks, some of them smashed beyond repair, and the poor fellows who owned them sorrowfully fishing for sacks of grub that lay plainly visible in the clear water as we passed over them. One boat was piled up on top of a raft that had climbed a hidden rock. We missed the same fate by less than 10 feet, and it took the utmost we had in us to do it. I presume that the 15 foot boat which we had trailing along behind the big boat made steering doubly difficult.

We soon realized that we had to organize our boat's crew. So one of us rode the bow and scanned the water ahead for hidden rocks, while the other two handled the steering oar. Pop and Dan elected me as the lookout. It didn't take much muscle, but it put all the responsibility on me. It is marvelous how rapidly we can learn when compelled to. I soon found that there are certain little dimples, or shadows, or colors on the surface of the water, which can be seen some distance away, which betray the existence of a submerged rock, which may be 10 or 12 inches below the surface.

It took us eight hours, in that swift current to navigate what was called Thirty Mile River. I have no idea what the scenery was like along the shore. We did note two camps of Indians. Every 10 or 20 minutes the boys would have to work to the limit to escape a shipwreck. We also saw signs posted along the shore which read "Keep to the Right" or to the left. I had more confidence in my own ability to read the water than I had in the signs, and there has always been a doubt in my mind as to whether all of those signs were honest warnings, or dastardly traps. In two instances, if we had followed the directions of the signs, we would most certainly have smashed up.

We saw about 15 wrecks, some of them complete smashups, and generally the greater part of the outfits were a total loss. When we afterwards talked about Thirty Mile with others who made the trip, they invariably said they would prefer White Horse thirty times rather than Thirty Mile once. Some of my subsequent experience leads me to believe, that we arrived at Thirty Mile at a most inopportune time, while the water was at its minimum stage, and the rocks most dangerous. Possibly boats that followed us a few days later found a higher stage of water, and had nothing to indicate how fortunate they were.

At 8:00 P.M. when we swept out into the broad smooth river, made by the junction of the Teslin River and Thirty Mile, it was a most welcome sight. At the junction there was a camp or a town called Hootalinqua. There were a lot of boats tied up there, but we didn't stop to explore it. We continued downstream until we found a convenient place to tie up, had a late supper and we glad of the chance to sleep, with no mosquitos to bother us.

Down the Lewes and the Yukon, June 9–12

The Thirty Mile excitement and loss of sleep gave Pop a headache, so he slept in Thursday morning while Dan and I ran the boat. The river was swift and we had to be watchful, but it was getting wider all the time, and there were no bars to trap us.

We arrived at the police station at Big Salmon River at 10:00 A.M., landed and showed our pass. There were only two police there. One sat in an arm chair under a tree and motioned to passing boats to come ashore; the other inspected our passes when we landed. Some boats paid no attention to the man in the chair and floated past unchallenged.

We found many boats tied up at Big Salmon, whose owners proposed to go up the Big Salmon River and prospect. We also noted a novel method of communication, on the trees near the station. These trees were hung full of men's names, and letters to partners, who followed, telling where the writers were going or what they had done.

Our small boat was rather bothersome in this nice current, it made steering hard, and retarded the speed of the larger boat.

As we passed the Little Salmon River Station, about 5:00 P.M. we shouted our number 1739 to the policeman on shore, and kept on going. We had considerable difficulty finding a suitable place to tie the boats for the night. Then the trouble began. Mosquitos by the millions, little bits of fellows, who were evidently all bill and appetite. Finally I rolled up right in canvas and slept until 6:00 A.M.

The scenery was changing, the mountains were now just high hills, heavily timbered, no bold rocks showing from our viewpoint on the river. The river was broader, but not swift enough to suit us. We tried to take the best possible advantage of the current. We had different ideas of the best way to make progress; Pop and I had a heated argument about it.

Our argument was cut short when we encountered Five Finger Rapids most unexpectedly. As we argued we noticed a lot of boats tied up on the right bank. I also noticed a small nicely constructed square board set on shore, but couldn't see what the sign read. Dan yelled to someone on shore, and asked what the sign said. Someone yelled back "Five Finger Rapids, One Half Mile."

Then we had to jump to the oars and guide the boat to the right shore. When we got the boat over near the shore, we were too far down stream to find any landing place, so we just kept on going. Maybe 50 feet from the right bank the first big rocky finger sticks up a big square block of yellow brown sandstone, with a swift straight current between it and the bank. We had time to see two boats shoot through the rapids and drop entirely out of sight for a moment, and then reappear farther downstream. We were sucked into the current, rather too close to the finger, turned sharply to the right, following the center of the current. First we felt a big drop, and the little boat tugged on its rope. Then we tossed up and down a few times, then another forward and downward chute, and then up and down in the eddies below the rapids. The little boat appeared to be quite delighted at having made the trip so nicely and in its enthusiasm, it smashed into our rear steering oar and then we had to row to get out of the way of other boats that followed.

We regretted not having a better view of the rapids. We were unable to find five fingers; there are two very prominent rocks that flanked well marked channels, and two smaller, less prominent rocks, which gave me the impression that there might be a lot of broken rock in the channels near them. There is an island and what looked to be rapids or shoals over near the left bank, below the fingers. We kept to the right, as everyone who built a boat on Bennett had been instructed to do.

About an hour below Five Fingers, we came to Rink Rapids. They are little advertised and don't amount to much, at the stage of water which we then had. We kept to the right again, could see the tossing white waves over on our left, and the big drop in the level of the water was easily noticeable.

For the first time, we tied up to eat dinner, and the mosquitos had all the best of that meal.

It's supposed to be 54 miles from Rink Rapids to Selkirk. We tied up at 10:00 P.M. about 4 miles from Selkirk, not knowing we were so near to it. We were up at 4:30 A.M. Saturday, and were much surprised to find Selkirk so near where we had camped.

Selkirk is an ancient fort, at the junction of the Lewes and Pelly Rivers. At that point the Yukon River begins. Evidently everybody tied up his boat at Selkirk, and explored the town, which consisted of about 20 small log houses. Strange Indian graves at the edge of the town indicate a sort of ancient permanence that we had not found anywhere since we left Juneau.

I relate my story as if there were only we three in all that vast country we had travelled. Of course there were boats and people everywhere. The crowds of Dyea, Sheep Camp and Chilkoot, were all on the water. We associated with a new crowd every day, generally people who had left Bennett before we did, which indicated that we were not lagging behind. The Yukon was wide and full of islands, we could often save miles by selecting the proper channel, rather than letting the current have its way. The Yukon had the appearance of being two separate streams, with a whole system of islands between the two main streams. Two parallel ranges of mountains some to lay some 5 or 10 miles apart, and the Yukon bounces back and forth across the flat between the two ranges.

Sunday, June 12, we were all excited. Up at 4:00 A.M. and passed the mouth of White River at 6:00 A.M. and arrived at the mouth of Stewart River at 8:00 A.M. just eight and a half days from our camp on Bennett. There is a big flat island in front of the mouth of Stewart River. We made the mistake of passing to the left of the island, but we had lots of company, even though we had missed being in the main camp.

We spent the day building a cache of poles, up off the ground, to hold our outfit while we went prospecting up Stewart River. I can't explain why we wanted to go up Stewart

River, nor why thousands of others greenhorns did the same thing. It must have been the result of some species of mob psychology, or possibly a result of the reaction that set in, when we realized that we were finally in the land of gold. My diary says: "I feel like a green boy, just landed in Chicago. We're here, and don't know where we're at." Those who read my story can never understand, because they lack the atmosphere in which we had lived since leaving home.

When our cache was completed, I rowed the little boat over to the main camp to post some letters and get what information I could about Stewart.

A party from Seattle with a 10-ton outfit built a cache near us and left a man named Guy Hedrun to look after the cache while they went up Stewart. He agreed to keep an eye on our cache for $2.50 per month.

Following is an extract from one of my letters. I hesitate about including it in my story, because in recent years I have had the reputation of being a more or less steady-going business man. Here it is, read it and weep:

> We know nothing about Stewart River, but we shall try it for a while anyway. Tomorrow we shall load our little boat with three months' supply of grub and start up Stewart River. I'll send letters if possible, but I have doubts about that. This place has no post office, no policy, no name, just a little bunch of camps. Only one boat in ten stops here, but that makes a formidable showing. Very few have gone up the river yet, as the water has been too high. It will be a tough job, but we can do it. Don't worry about me, even if you don't hear from me for three months. Then we will doubtless go to Dawson for mail and winter supplies if we strike it on Stewart, or will go on to American Territory if Stewart is no good. I have great faith Stewart and expect to stay there.

The Stewart River Stampede, June 13–24

It took us all of Monday to fix up our little boat, and select the outfit we needed, and get our main outfit nicely packed on the cache. When we loaded the boat we found it leaked badly in the upper seams that had been out of water all the way from Bennett. So we had to drag the boat up a steep bank and caulk it again.

We made a late start on Tuesday, the little boat was about level full of outfit. We had the biggest part of our footwear and heavy clothes, but were short of underwear and things that didn't weigh much. We had 175 pounds of flour, 40 pounds of rice, 50 pounds of beans, 50 pounds of sugar, 20 pounds of cornmeal, 20 pounds of oatmeal, 50 pounds of bacon and pork, 7 pounds of baking powder, and a lot of odds and ends. When we added some hardware and the stove, there wasn't room to get into the boat without piling things up high above the gunwale.

Our little boat was not worth the nails in it, for that kind of water. Stewart River requires a long narrow, double ended boat that can be poled against the stiff current. Our boat was anything else. While Pop and Dan did the shore work and pulled a 150 foot line with the boat attached, I sat in the boat and steered. It is not as hard as pulling but it is no snap. I sailed through all kinds of whirlpools and rapids and over and around snags and sandbars. Everywhere the current would try to swing the boat around broadside. Sometimes the boat tipped sideways and I had to counterbalance it. Every little way there would be a tree that had fallen over into the river. Then we all three had to work the boat around the tangle of driftwood that generally accumulated around the fallen tree. When our side of the river skirted a rocky cliff, we three all got in the boat and shot across to the other shore, generally losing some 300 yards in the process. I wore my rubber boots as I had to jump out and pull the boat off of bars, but Pop and Dan wore shoes. They had to wade often but water drains out of shoes easier than out of boots. So they were pretty damp all day. Life on the big boat was one long vacation compared with Stewart River. We ate any old way, mostly pancakes and tea, and washed when we happened to think of it. We had a hard time distinguishing between dish towel and the one company face towel, but as we didn't wash the dishes much, that didn't matter.

The first night we camped on a gravel bar that had been under water a short time before. We all rolled up in canvas when we went to sleep. We had made crinoline veils, so that we could get some air when in the canvas, but it was difficult to ensure a mosquito-proof fit, between the canvas and the veil. I didn't sleep any too well. Pop and Dan declared that they only got 10 minutes sleep during the entire night. The gravel under the canvas wasn't any too smooth either.

Wednesday, you may well imagine, we made a rather late start. The same old grind all day. We rescued a box of candles marked "Dr. E. J. Hill, Skagway," which we found floating on the river, and were not able to rescue some other stuff that floated past. We left the candles on a pine log. About a quarter mile beyond we found a man who claimed to be the owner, Dr. E. J. Hill. He said his boat had collided with another and he had upset in the swift current.

I have always felt that in that little incident we were scratching the surface of some criminal episode. I could never put the puzzle together. There was a series of wide channels all connected with the main river, but somewhat secluded. I don't know just how we came to be pulling up on these channels. The going was rather easier than the average. There was something about the man who claimed to be Dr. Hill that gave us all the impression that he was telling us the truth. The boat with which he claimed to have collided was nowhere in sight. It was not natural for a man who had collided, to leave the upset craft, without making an effort to helping recover the outfit. The man refused our offer of assistance, in a rather ungracious manner. One man could not have pulled that boat where it was. There were no other men around. I've often wondered if the body of the real Dr. Hill might have been somewhere close by, or whether it was only a case of thievery. Just another mystery of the North.

We came to a rapids, seemed to be a fall of three or four feet in 100 yards. We took part of our load out and left it at the foot of the rapids, until after we got the boat pulled up above. Then we did a real job of putting up the tent, with the side walls, laid on the sand as a floor, and our canvas over that. That night we really rested and forgot mosquitos.

Thursday was just as hard as the preceding days, but Friday morning we had really decent going, much like it would be pulling up a river in Illinois, with a well-defined gravel shore for a path. It was so nice, that we stopped a while, and got out our prospector's pans, and tested the gravel along the river bank. We found color, as the little gold flakes are called, in every shovel full that we panned. This greatly helped Pop's morale.

We got acquainted with an outfit who called themselves "The Buckskins," and also with some French Canadians, whose names we never knew. We camped with them that night, and spent a rather pleasant evening.

Saturday was more of the same kind of hard work. Sunday we slept late, and it was 10:00 A.M. before we got started. The gently sloping hills on each side of us were thickly carpeted with bright yellow poppies and wild roses.

Monday, June 20, my diary reads as follows:

> Got a good start and made good distance. Crawled almost to the end of a wall, and lost our grip, and had to swing back and try it again. Failed to make it that time, so we crossed the river, in the rapids, and then had a hard mile of rapids, with a narrow channel, and only a fair foot path. While we ate dinner, we saw the first steamboat of the season come up the river. The *Victoria of St. Michael* bound for McQuesten. Saw very few people on the trail today. Two boats passed us, and we saw two boats who had turned back and were going down stream.

Tuesday was just another round of hard work, crawling through deadwood, or hanging to stone cliffs by our fingernails, or lifting the boat up the rapids. That day the *Victoria* went down river from McQuesten. Wednesday, was the longest day of the year, and maybe the hardest. We were making progress and the tow path was getting better, but it was evident to me that we were not going much farther. Saturday, Pop was good and ready to go back and was pumping Dan. Monday we stopped to rest frequently; Tuesday, more frequently; Wednesday, most frequently and Thursday we turned tail and went back. We had gone up river 60 miles, and undid in one day what it took eight and a half days to perform.

How we did go, down the river. It was most enjoyable trip. We started down at 11:00 A.M. and at dinner where we had camped a day and a half before. We met an old time miner who was going up to work on the McQuesten bars all summer. We met Swiss Joe and his party pulling up on the many rapids. Of course we landed and had a visit with Joe.

By supper time we had passed fully 500 people going up river, including two women.

The river wasn't as high near the mouth as it had been when we started. We met a party who made as much progress up river in one and a half days as we had made in three. Consequently our boat travelled more slowly as we neared the Yukon. At midnight we tied up, set up the tent, had a big sleep, and a big breakfast.

We had hardly got the boat loaded in the morning when along came Woodruff, Henderson, Phil and Charlie Wigston with their two little boats. They had left Lou Gorham at Laberge. Curry was watching their cache at Stewart.

They went on up river, and we stopped at Stewart to have dinner with Curry and swap stories with him. Everybody in camp tried to ask us all kinds of questions, all at the same time.

That was our Stewart River fiasco. I didn't want to turn back so soon, and I don't believe that Dan did, but Pop insisted and as I was not doing the pulling, I had to surrender, and maybe it was all right. I didn't expect to pick up a fortune in 20 minutes. I felt we must learn the country and how to mine before we could expect to find gold.

So there was the end of our second stampede, hardly a prospecting trip for we didn't really prospect. Pop was so dead anxious to hurry up and get there that we could hardly stop to prospect on the way up, and when we came back we were in such a rush to get to Dawson, that we could not stop.

When we got up thirty miles we began to prospect some of the bars. It was comical, but it always hurt me to see Pop turn over a big rock expecting to find a nugget as big as his fist under it. He began to realize that gold goes not grow on bushes even in Alaska. We found color everywhere and I sent home a sample of the dust from Stewart River bars. At one place we found some fair color, where I am sure a man could get $5.00 a day if he would work for it, but beyond that there was nothing as good. Everyone was just as green as we were, most of them greener.

I am now on my way to Dawson but the outfit is not going to Dawson if I have anything about it. Dan says Pop is anxious to get to Dawson so that he can get down to St. Michael and get home this fall. Pop is disappointed, but I don't think he's a quitter. But maybe he is. He dropped a good ways, and hit pretty hard when he found that the bar digging of the Stewart didn't yield nuggets as big as hen's eggs.

So we loaded up the big boat, and started down the Yukon again on Saturday, June 25. We passed Rosebud and Reindeer Creeks and saw people poling up the Yukon to them. At Ogilvie we stopped and found that it was only a trading post, no mail, so soldiers, no people, just a big log store and a keeper waiting for Indians to come and trade. Here we met Jack Stere and his partner Smith. They had also been up Stewart River. They were now going up Sixty Mile River to hunt moose, which sells at $12.00 per pound at Dawson. Many people are cutting logs and rafting them to Dawson where they sell at $50.00 a 1000-footboard measure. It's against the law to cut without a logger's license, so greenhorns don't try it. The police may confiscate the raft and its load. I notice that most of the loggers who have poled up from Dawson have been there long enough to know what they are about.

We pulled up on an island at the mouth of Indian River and camped for the night in an empty boat. On Sunday morning June 26, I went over to the mainland while the boys cut some wood. We were headed for Dawson but I wanted to find out something about

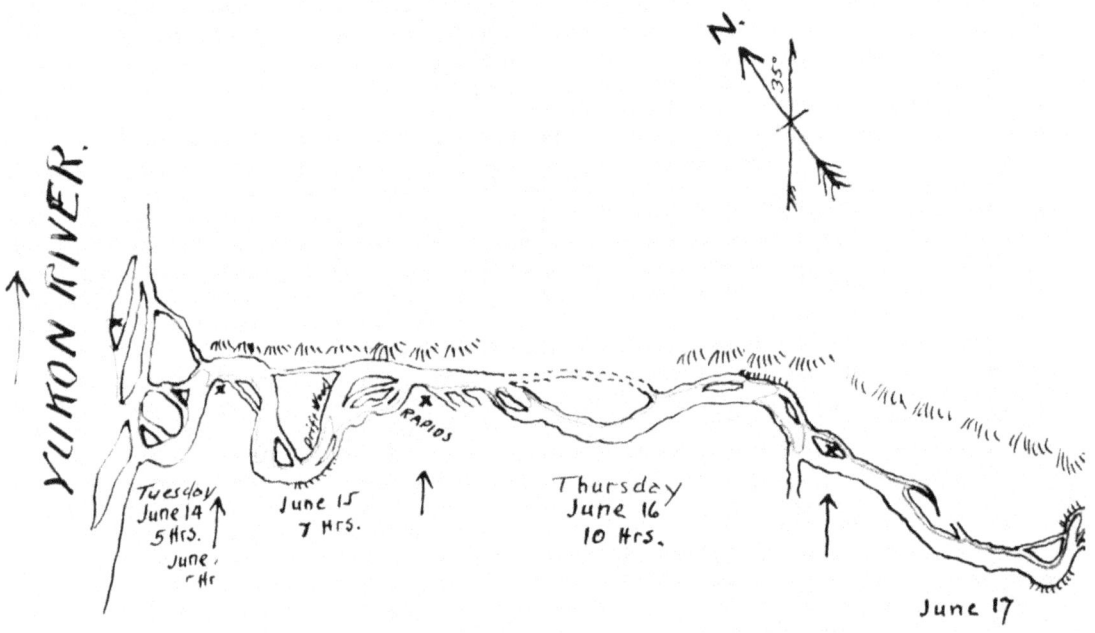

Map of Stewart River Stampede, June 13–24, 1898.

6. The Boat Trip to Indian River

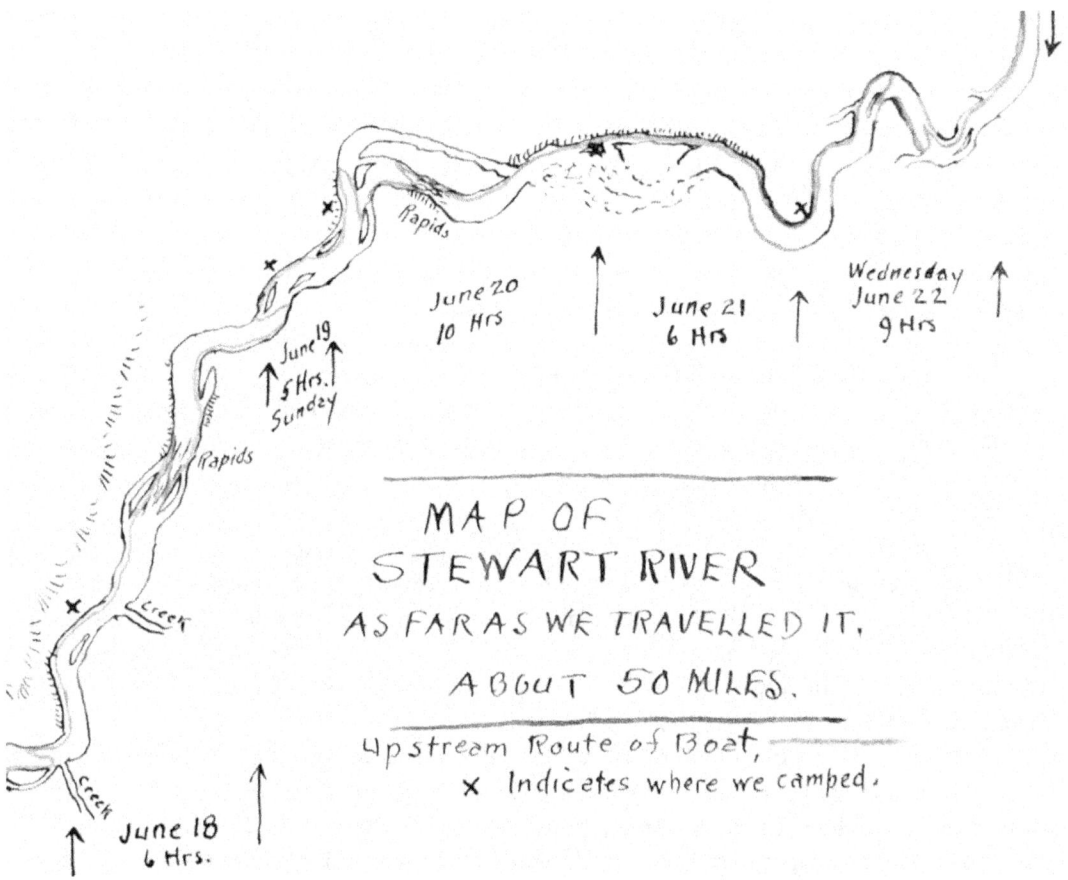

Map of Stewart River Stampede, June 13–24, 1898.

Indian River. I talked with a young fellow who had just come from Dawson. He walked up Bonanza, Eldorado and over to Indian and down to the mouth. I went back, and Pop and Dan went over to look around, and the result of it all was we concluded to cache our stuff there. So we rowed our boat over to the mainland and set up our tent. We had concluded to take six weeks grub and prospect Indian River.

7

Summer in the Klondike

Dawson City, June 27 and 28

We decided that Pop and Dan would build a cache at the mouth of Indian River, while I went to Dawson for the mail. Then I would go up the Klondike, Bonanza and Eldorado Creeks, over the divide to Indian River, and find the boys there. The plan pleased me greatly. I wanted to see the creeks that really produced gold, even if they were all staked out, and no chance for anybody except their owners to get gold from them.

I was lucky enough to get a ride from Indian River to Dawson, with a party of Australians, O'Neill and Company. There were two Norwegians, Peterson and Brink, who got a ride with another boat load of Australians. I had a tough time at dinner. Australians don't think beans are fit to eat, and that rice is the stuff of life, and I wasn't so very keen about a meal consisting entirely of boiled rice with no trimmings. But as I was their company, I made the best of it.

We reached Klondike City in the middle of the afternoon and the Australians tied up there, rather than to get in to the mob on the Dawson water front. Klondike City is on the east side of the Yukon. The tents and log houses are perched on top of each other. For every tent, there is a cache, made of somebody's boat, cut in two, and stuck up in the air.

When we set out for Dawson, we soon reached the limit of Klondike City; we came to the Klondike River and a toll bridge over it. I paid fifty cents to walk across the bridge. Then I was in the suburbs of Dawson. Dawson is built on a great flat plain, only 10 or 15 feet above the Yukon. At the southern edge it is a city of tent campers and cheap merchants. No streets nor attempts at streets. I didn't think much of the town then, but the town grew better as I advanced. I had just reached the main part of town when I ran into Con Duggan, the Australian miner who camped near us at Bennett. He invited me to stay with him while in town, so there's my headquarters. Wilson has sold his outfit and gone back. Gender, Hawthorne, Sorrell, Russel and Duggan are camped here, trying to learn something of the country and trying to get into the swim. All the boys except Hawthorne and Duggan had just gone twenty miles downriver to stake something or other.

Then I started up town to see the town. The main street runs along the water front, right on the edge of the higher, solid ground. Down by the water is a city of stranded boats and tents. On the river side of the main street there are as yet few stores or buildings, but the tents are springing up fast, and this will soon be a solid line of tent stores. They support the front end on the street and support the rear of these places on piling. I noticed a number of places made of the sides and bottoms of old scows. Lumber is scarce here, but a greenhorn coming is glad to get $50.00 for a big scow.

The other side, the east side of the street is pretty well lined with substantial log buildings, many of them two stories high. First comes a big stockade around the police headquarters. North of that comes a long line of hotels with saloon and gambling tables, the most conspicuous part of them. There are a number of mining exchanges and a lot of doctor's signs. Jewelers are very much in evidence. No mosquitos in Dawson. Farther up the street they are putting up bigger frame buildings, saloons of course, but it looks more like a town up there. Finally come the stores of the North American Transportation and Trading Company (NAT & T Co.) and the Alaska Commercial Company (AC Co.) and the North-West Mounted Police (N.W.M.P.) The river comes close to the bank there, which makes it easy to land goods.

There is gold here but you must get out and hunt for it. When someone finds any within 100 miles of Dawson he creates a rush and the creek is staked in 24 hours. They keep making such finds every little while. Montana Creek was the last and you will hear of another before many months.

Meals here have come down from $2.50 to $1.50, effective today. Lots of people are selling out and going out, fare to Seattle $160.00. So many outfits for sale and the great mob of new restaurant keepers knocked the price of grub. Flour is only $4.00 per sack. I met a man who brought in a horse, got here about three weeks ago, and sold it for $400.00.

I think there are three newspapers here. Every building is plastered with signs, little pen written notices of this, that and everything. Dogs everywhere and all look hungry.

There is lots of work for engineers here; not now, but the longer they let it run, the bigger the job will be when they try to unsnarl the tangle. The streets have been straightened once, making Second Street run partly through a swamp. First Street is crossed every few hundred feet by deep gullies, out through to drain the back country and hastily bridged. Every store has a dust weigher and every saloon a half dozen of them, but there are now so many "Cheechacos" in here that Cheechaco money is beginning to replace gold dust in many places. All the old timers or "Sourdoughs" have their gold sacks full of gold dust and would be insulted if you offered them round money. It doesn't take much dust to make a dollar. The $620.00 that I saw weighed and poured into a sack didn't make much more than a teacup full.

The second day in Dawson I felt that I was still a Cheechaco or tenderfoot but I had learned a thing or two since yesterday. I stood in line in front of the post office from 7:00 until 9:15, then I got in. They let in about ten at a time and three men at the counter attend to us. I asked one man for my mail and got it rather promptly. Mother's letter, of May 2 and Grandma's of May 11. Then, against the rules, I crossed over to another clerk who stood at the other end of the counter and got Dan's mail. He got a lot. Then I went to the middle clerk and tried to get Pop's mail, but the clerks had my measure by that time and fired me out with orders to stand in line again if I wanted anyone's mail. I had letters to mail so I left and went a quarter mile away down to the barracks and there bought stamps at one cabin and posted the letters at another. Notices posted about town said the mail left at 10:00 A.M. and I wanted mine to go.

I went back and ate a late breakfast with Duggan, helped him and Hawthorne get started on a prospecting trip up Swede Creek and then took a nap and read my letters.

Answering Questions from Home

You and Grandma both keep writing that I must enjoy life from what I write, but that I don't say anything of my hardships. Hardship is a relative term. A man's definition of hardship depends entirely upon his temperament. When someone gulled Pop into believing it was 14 degrees below at Lindeman, that was a hardship to Pop. My trip over Chilkoot before the slide would have been a hardship to him, to me it was enjoyable. To eat a meal without hot coffee is a hardship to Pop, to me it is the ordinary. The trip from Bennett to Stewart was a hardship to Pop, to me it was pleasure. Thirty Mile River was extreme hardship to Pop, and he sweat and worried and stewed so much during the eight hours that it took to make it that Dan and I were almost persuaded that it was a hardship. We have had lots of hard work but never any hardships until we went up Stewart River. We always had a good bed, and the best meals that our outfit would provide. But if I am to be considered sane, I'll have to class our Stewart River trip as a hardship. Loss of sleep was the greatest hardship for me. Five hours was not enough and very frequently that was all I got. We often traveled until 8:00 P.M. then I got supper while the boys put up the tent and about 10:00 or 11:00 we went to bed, with two layers of canvas and two blankets between us and the ground. The ground didn't always fit my shape, so when we got up at 6:00 A.M. I frequently felt that more of that same bumpy bed would be better than no bed at all.

The grub never bothered me. I like anything and everything that can be used for filling and just as soon have it hot as cold. I'd rather have yeast bread than biscuit, but it is no hardship to do without both. Cold rice or oatmeal will do just as well. I baked biscuits once a day, enough for the day. Both Pop and Dan feel that a meal without bread is as bad as not eating at all.

Why didn't I get a sleeping bag? Well I don't know why we didn't, but now we are glad that we didn't. Blankets are much more serviceable. We can use them all or separately and they are far less bulky and bulk is a great factor at times. In winter I shall sew my blankets into a bag and sew a canvas bag around the blankets and there you are.

This morning I bought two good heavy pairs of drawers and two socks of a party going out for $5.00. As I look the city over I find any amount of people selling out and going back. They are the people who have encountered hardships at every turn, people who expected to find gold blowing in their eyes when they got to Dawson. Even though there is not a boat coming up river this summer, there will be more than enough grub here next winter. Thousands are selling out and getting out. They have never been out of their boats to look for gold but as the gold has not hunted them up they are disgusted. You'll read some great tales in the newspapers when this crowd gets back. The town is full of people who sit around and wear out their pants instead of their shoes and swear at the queen and the bad laws of the country. A far different class from those we met up Stewart River. In the States the cry is that there is no more room left for new doctors or lawyers or engineers. Here the cry is changed a bit. There is no room left for a Cheechaco to stake out a paying mine. If every greenhorn believed that and acted upon it as many are doing they would all quit and go out at once. Someone, who doubtless doesn't know any more about it than I do, informed me that of 15,000 claims recorded, only 150 were paying. I'll know more about that next year than I do now.

It's hard to tell whether there is as much money in circulation here as one would expect. All the gambling is done with chips so we don't see much gold dust. But across the street in the stores and restaurants there is always a crowd and they all seem to be busy buying and the prices are something awful. Meals are $2.50 at all but one place. I tried that $1.50 place last night. The waiter brought me a tin plate with some cold boiled evaporated potatoes, some cold canned beef and an egg with yolk and white well mixed. The man sitting next to me had a pretty fair layout but the waiter had spotted me as green and served me accordingly. I told him to eat his own stuff and I got up and went out paying twenty-five cents for the slice of bread and tainted butter that I had bitten into. I didn't feel like paying $2.50 for a meal so I went into a new place and got half a peach pie for fifty cents. The woman came from Illinois and the pie was fine. Then I went home to Duggan's tent and filled up with fried potatoes and biscuit.

I didn't tell you of the midnight sun did I? I had wanted to see it from the top of some mountain but I was disappointed. But here, Monday night, when I left town to go back and turn in at 11:30 it was lighter than I have seen it many times at home on a cloudy day. Lamps were used in the saloons just for form and not because they're necessary.

I wish you could see me and my crop of whiskers. Some are a good brown, but some look as if they had gone to seed and are drying out. My mustache is a killer. A sort of baseball mustache, with one on one side and nobody on the other. But whiskers have uses here, and so does a crop of long hair. They keep off mosquitos. Mighty handy out in the woods, though not stylish in Dawson. Here pretty nearly everyone is shaved, that is people who stay here all the time.

Never having seen a live mining town I can't well judge Dawson. One man says it is a good lively town and another says he never saw such a dead town. I'll have to stay here a year before I can find out whether it is a good country or not. A man can spend all the summer chasing around the country and planting stakes in every gulch and creek. He does not have to work his claim until it freezes. Then has either sold the claims or let them out on lays. In that way hundreds of worthless claims have been staked and a few good ones. The miners don't waste any time working any of them. They wait for some sucker to dig down in a claim near them and then sell on the reputation of his discovery. In this way a very few people have "staked everything near Dawson." Who knows whether they have or not. And if they have it's not legal. When the working season opens there will be lots of chances. One thing is sure. Lots and lots of men go out from Dawson with packs on their backs bound for somewhere, looking for something. They don't say much and you would not know that they went unless you happened to be down near the south end of town where they have to wade the river. At present very little work is being done at the mines. There is no water to sluice with. So they loaf until it freezes in October. Then they dig the pay dirt and sluice it in the spring when the water is high.

When I awoke this morning I heard one man telling another that he was just returning from a trip up country. Had been buying claims in Dominion and Sulphur. I heard him mention such figures as $3,000 and $4,500. Afterwards I learned that he was an agent of some English syndicate.

You've asked about the weather. Well it's been such an unobtrusive kind of weather that I've not taken any particular notice of it.

As long as they were whole and for a few weeks longer I wore the clothes which I wore when I left home, with the addition of German socks. Then when my pants got too bad, I changed them for a pair of brown canvas overalls and at the same time changed my footwear to heavy coarse woolen socks and a pair of heavy miner's shoes. I've not found it necessary to change my style of dress since then. For the past month I have not worn my coat and vest very much, only evenings or on cold days. And here it is, the last of June and I am wearing my winter underwear and a heavy sweater and heavy socks. If it ever gets warm enough I will change the sweater for a canvas jumper and then I'll be in hot weather attire. This afternoon I slept from 1 to 4 and for the first time I was uncomfortably warm. There was hardly a cloud in the sky and the sun beat through the canvas. But it is cold every morning, at about 2:00 A.M. Up Stewart if I went to bed under one blanket, I generally wanted two in the morning. So far the weather has been very nice. I've only seen rain twice since we landed at Dyea, and those two times were during the past week. I've been told by an old timer that rain sets in about the middle of August.

I'm very sorry your map is so used up. I would send you one of Wallace's maps of Klondike and Indian Rivers but I hate to spend the money. As one young fellow expressed it "A fellow who has earned his money in the States hates to spend it here where the ounce ($16.00) takes place of the dollar."

Bonanza and Eldorado Creeks, June 29–July 1

On Wednesday I got Pop's mail. Then I spent the afternoon sleeping, eating and writing letters. At 8:15 P.M. I set out on my journey, back to meet Pop and Dan, on Indian River. Everyone travels at night on long trips. Day time mushing is uncomfortable, but daytime is very comfortable for sleeping, so the regular order of things is reversed.

First I went down the long crooked row of tents set up in a lower Dawson, places where Cheechacos are camped, where every ten feet there was a sign of "Outfit for Sale." This part of town presented a sorry appearance. The people were all green. Just came to Dawson to empty their flower sacks and refill with gold dust. Some of them were waiting to hear news of some big strike, then they would rush to it, maybe. Some were just waiting for something to turn up.

Before reaching the end of this settlement I came to the bridge and crossed the Klondike River. As it enters the Yukon, the Klondike broadens and divides, going around a big island. A bridge company built a board walk across the island, and swung rope suspension bridges across the two channels. For fifty cents, I crossed the Klondike and landed in Klondike City, formerly known as Lousetown. This place was quite a town, a rather select suburb, not many saloons or stores, but many log huts and caches—queer, lopsided, irregular looking boxes, set on stilts. Lopsided boxes on stilts? When people landed, they cut their boats or scows in two, put the outfit in one half, turned the other half over it for a roof and boarded up the cut end. Thus, lopsided boxes on stilts.

Instead of going into Klondike City I turned to the left, taking the trail up the Klondike. The bridge company has cut a flair trail to the junction of Bonanza, some three miles. First it follows the Klondike near the river, on a stone quarry set on end, then rounding a bend, I went up the side of the mountain and down again, across a swamp and out again to the river bank. Here for a mile or more I followed the Klondike and then left it.

The river is about 70 feet wide, seems fairly deep and the water is as clear as crystal and ice cold. It is rapid in places, but I noticed several boats being hauled up, and saw a raft or two coming down. The new trail which I took meets the old trail at the ferry. Here the old trail which started from Dawson proper, comes to the other side of the Klondike, and people are ferried over and start up the Bonanza Valley. There is a saw mill here and to all appearances plenty of timber not far distant.

Up Bonanza there is a corduroy road built on top of the deep moss for a considerable distance. Then the mountains on either side close in, the claims begin, and the good road vanishes. Good road is a rather misleading term, for the corduroy road is not perfect. It is some five feet wide, built of small trees and brush, covered with moss or mud. Pack mules, generally pick the best road, and now the pack trail winds on either side or across the corduroy, first one side and then the other, worn down nearly to the woodwork where it crosses, with a high bank or unpacked moss, where the corduroy is not used. With all its faults, the corduroy is far better of any trail I found beyond it.

The trail went from bad to worse, and before I reached Indian River, I had become thoroughly accustomed to breaking my own trail through brushwood where I dare say nobody ever walked before. The claims begin where Bonanza Valley narrows from two or three miles wide, to about 600 yards. Downstream from Number 20 Below Discovery, the claims are not paying and very little work seems to have been done on them. The mountains are high at first, but as I progressed they began to slope back and resemble hills. In places the trail led over to where I could see what the outcropping wall of rock was like, and then began to lead down into the swampy bottom land again. The sides of the mountains were just full of springs and in places it was very swampy. At these swampy places the trail broadened, each succeeding man going further around, trying to find a dryer spot than the man who preceded him.

I fell in with a little man from Chicago and walked with him as far as Boulder Gulch, where he left me. He was going to work for someone up there.

About 1:00 A.M. I sat down by a stream and prepared my breakfast. My cooking outfit was a tin cup and a spoon. First course consisted of beef soup and bread (fifty cents per loaf at Dawson), second course boiled potatoes salted and washed down with water. Third course, beef tea to warm me after drinking the ice water. The trail was crowded with people going both ways. Quite a few had collected there to eat. I noted that my outfit was as compact as anybody's. When I started on again, it began to sprinkle. That was about 2:00 A.M. and it continued to sprinkle more or less until about 9:00 A.M.

I began to see signs of mining; long flumes and occasional piles of yellow muddy gravel; near them were black water filled dangerous looking holes with the moss falling in around their edges. About 5:00 A.M. I was so sleepy that I began to look for a sleeping place. Log huts were getting numerous, and I was not far from the mouth of Eldorado, but the huts all seemed to be occupied or were locked if vacant. Here the mines were being worked. I frequently saw crowds of men shoveling the dirty yellow gravel into the sluice boxes. One man was collecting the gold dust from his boxes. He had a gold pan piled up with gold just about as full as he could conveniently carry it and not spill it. He was not very talkative. If I had realized that he carried some $15,000.00 in that pan, I think I my eyes would have ceased to feel sleepy. About 6:00 A.M. I finally found a vacant cabin that was not padlocked, I went in, stretched my canvas on the floor, lay down, covered myself with the canvas and slept. But not for long. In about an hour I began to realize that I was most uncomfortable and cold and wet. I was also sleepy, so I curled up tighter and slept again. I did that until 10:00 A.M., curling up tighter and tighter each time, until I finally thought sleepiness preferable to chilliness. Then I got up, and started on my way. The sun warmed me.

I mushed along, reached the mouth of Eldorado, ascended it to the first nice spring, and there I cooked some grub, and rolled up and slept like a top on a nice sunny slope until 5:00 P.M. Then the sun got so hot that I could not sleep any more. I ate another meal and inspected Eldorado Creek.

Near the mouth of Eldorado, above the valley, there are a few bench claims that are paying well. They are high and dry above the creek, so they have to haul water, and wash the gravel in a rocker. Some of these claims are low enough on the side hill, so that they get water by leading long flumes back up Eldorado. All around this locality the mines are rich and are worked intensively.

There is but little work going on now. The holes which produced the muddy gravel are full of water, and all that is being done is to finish washing last winter's dump. The whole valley looks as if it had been turned inside out. The gravel is on top and the muck has gone down somewhere below. The creek has gone too. It has been caged up in sluice boxes and had its course changed so many times that there is no knowing where it originally ran. Wherever there are good mines in the creek beds, people are prospecting the bench claims, up on the hills, and once in a while they make rare finds. If the prospector is fortunate in finding gold, his troubles have just begun, for like as not someone has recorded his location last year sometime, and he has no way of knowing it until he tries to record the claim. Wood is getting to be rather scarce. All that was really handy has been used to thaw the holes, which yielded the pay dirt. They are now going up the gulches two or three miles for wood.

I have taken a fancy to these benches. I believe strikes will be made on these benches for two or three years to come. Where French Gulch comes into Eldorado, just above Berry's claim Number 16, there are several bench claims away up some 200 feet above the creek. These are dry digging, where the sun thaws the gravel all the way to bed rock, and they dig the gravel out as if it were a gravel pit. In winter those miners lay off. Now they are working their claims, and rocking out $1,000 per day on some of them, with little or no expense. French Gulch itself is barren, and the claim below Berry's does not pay expenses. In ten hours the Berry claim cleaned up 100 pounds of dust, about $25,000.00.

I examined some sluice boxes that were piled up for the summer, laid by until next year. Imagine my surprise at seeing gold flakes in the bottom of such boxes as were standing right side up. Gold wasn't a foot deep by any means, but there it was, the genuine stuff and I felt that the owner was very careless about it. Had all the boxes been right side up I might have thought that the owner intended to brush them out later, but as they were piled any and all ways, to get them in a compact piles, it was evident that the owner attached no value to what remained in the boxes. I gathered some $2.00 worth from the bottom of one box and went on my way feeling that the owner was very careless or that he was greatly in need of better foreman, if I could have paid him $5.00 per day for the privilege of dusting his boxes, I could have made a good thing out of it. I hurried past the famous Number 16 mine and didn't examine the French Gulch Benches, for I had to meet the boys on Indian River next morning and it was then 8:30 P.M.

I was nicely rested, had a full stomach, an important fact, and the end of my journey was just far enough ahead of me to make me work. I passed Little Eldorado and turned up Nugget Gulch. This is just a gulch between two mountains with a little two foot stream running down it, the water coming from melting ice and snow. It has been thoroughly staked off, but nobody has cared to do any work. There was an empty cabin or two, and a few old prospect holes, but no mines.

For two or three miles a good trail had been made by wood cutters. The trail was so good that I took the wrong fork and followed it up a steep mountain for half a mile, when I should have stuck to the water course. When I saw that I was off the trail, I went back down the mountain and had no more trouble about correct trails. The farther I went the steeper the trail became, the dimmer the trail, and the deeper the moss became. After a while, about a mile before reaching the divide, the water ceased and from there to the top, every man made his own trail. This Alaska moss, must appear to one of the mosquitos who lives in it, just like a dense pine forest looks to a man. It grows up nice and fluffy, like a mat of thick carpet. Each plant consists of a single long upright slender threat, with little feathers, about a quarter inch long growing out from the stem. In places it was knee deep, that is until I stepped on it, then it all matted down to nothing and I felt as if I had made an extra step above the top of a set of stairs. There were no real trees on the divide, but the whole hillside was a snarl of brushwood that looks quite like a willow. It was a lonely and depressing kind of place. It would have been better if I could have rested, but his majesty the skeeter said, "nit, nit, NIT, NIT," and then he would stick me. As long as I would mush on they left me alone, but the second I stopped the whole force was out for blood.

At precisely 12:00 midnight, I stood on top of the divide where I could look ahead down the valley of Nine Mile Creek, or could look behind me down Nugget Gulch, to its junction with Eldorado Creek. I could just make out the yellow dumps of gravel waiting to be washed. My underclothes and my vest were wet with sweat. The wind on the divide was chilly, and the mosquitos more vigorous as ever, but in spite of these discomforts, I took time enough to look back at the midnight sun, or more properly stated the combined midnight sunset and sunrise. Everything was a hazy gray, excepting a half eclipse in the north. That was a bright yellow. To the right I could see the reflection on the snow covered tops of a range of mountains countless miles away. I wanted to stop and make a sketch, but I had no appropriate paper and pencil. The scene was a bit beyond my ability, even if I had been properly equipped. But I can still see the picture in my memory.

Then I turned and started down the easy side of the divide, easy not because the exertion was any less, but because progress was greater. I set myself a merry pace for first two or three miles. Being a south slope, the moss was either short and springy, or was crowded out by grass. The tangled brush gave way to small cottonwoods, with an occasional clump of pines. I just ducked my head and tore along. The tearing process included the mosquito cloth on my hat, but I was learning how to protect myself without mosquito bar. There was no trail, but I could make time anywhere, and I was bound eventually to reach Nine Mile Creek, so called because it is supposed to be nine miles long. I soon found a trail, rather blind and little travelled, but better than none. The fall from there to Indian River was not steep enough to make a good trail; in places it was very boggy and the bunch grass very annoying.

I haven't mentioned firearms since making the list of our equipment. On this trip I carried on my hip that heavy unwieldy cannon called a Colts Revolver. I felt all the time that it was just so much excess baggage, and carried it only because I had felt that this trip over the divide would be so lonely, that I might need Colt for Company. I'm sure I don't know what would have become of me if I had really been attacked, but for once the Colt was very helpful to my morale. There were very few dangerous wild animals in the country, except wolves. I hadn't seen one of those big gray wolves at that time, so like the famous babes in the woods, I mushed along, happy in the thought that I carried a Colts Revolver, while on either side of me, I could, from time to time, hear the stealthy sounds of wolves and other wild things moving in the brush.

I expected to find the boys and grub and blankets at the mouth of the Nine Mile Creek. About 3:00 A.M. I was much disappointed to find that I had only reached the forks of Nine Mile, while I had thought for some miles back, that I had sighted the Indian River. So I stopped at the forks, cooked some grub and warmed some beef tea and pushed on again. Rain threatened, so I hurried and reached Indian River at 5:00 A.M. The boys were not there, but Peterson and Brink, who went to Dawson with me, had arrived at Indian River about two hours ahead of me, so we built a fire in an unfinished cabin. I ate again and talked to the two Swedes for a while. Then I rolled up in my canvas and slept until about 1:00 P.M.

There is little to be said about the rest of the trip. It was hard, for it was the last end of a long tramp, but the trail was fine. I travelled with Peterson and Brink, started about 3:00 P.M. and inquired of everybody I met for "a man with a thick head of curly red hair and short thick red whickers, who wore no hat but whose hair looked like a fur cap." I always got the same answer. They had not seen any such person, or they had seen him eight miles from the mouth of the Indian River. I expected to see the tent and boat at every bend of the river, but it was 10:00 P.M. before I found them. That ended my tramp of 60 miles in 50 hours, including time to sleep, eat and rest. Saturday, I did a good job of resting.

Part II

Prospecting Indian River, July 1, 1898, to February 21, 1899

8

Exploring Indian River

Indian River was such an important part of our Klondike experience that I must describe in some detail, the geography of that region, and some of the other influences that impelled us to explore Indian River, rather than go directly to Dawson or to the very heart of the mining regions at the junction of Eldorado and Bonanza Creeks.

If we had been back home, we would have lived in an atmosphere charged with Spanish War propaganda. We read of the war, about a week or so after things occurred, but to us the Battle of Manilla was only a news item. We were not unpatriotic. We were just living in a different atmosphere. For four months we had been on the gold trail; we had therefore, picked up every possible scrap of information bearing on Dawson and the gold fields surrounding Dawson. We absorbed facts, fairy tales or propaganda indiscriminately.

We knew the general geography of the country long before we reached it. We knew that the heart of this marvelous gold field was near the junction of Bonanza and Eldorado Creeks. We knew that Hunker Creek which emptied into the Klondike, to the east of Bonanza, had developed some excellent mines; that Sulphur and Dominion Creeks, which originate in the same mountain as Bonanza and Hunker and empty into the Indian River, had also developed some excellent mines.

We knew that Nine Mile Creek, which I traversed on my trip from Dawson to Indian River, had been staked from end to end in November 1897, and was all relocated in February 1898. There is no undeveloped creek any closer to the real center of things than Nine Mile.

We knew that all the gold that had been found up to that time was placer gold, i.e., gold which the glaciers, or some other natural process, had ground out of the gold bearing rocks, and deposited under the gravel, on top of or in the seams of the bedrock. We knew that in every other placer mining district in the world, the gold ore in the solid rock from which the placer gold was derived was sooner or later discovered, and that such ore usually developed mines of far greater value than the placer mines.

A high mountain, called the Dome, at the source of the creeks just enumerated, had looked to be a logical source of gold bearing ore, but no ore had been found there, after much diligent prospecting.

We knew a lot about the ins and outs of the Canadian Mining Laws, and Mining Customs.

It seems strange that it would be possible for 10,000 men to stake off every claim in 10,000 square miles, when the claims are only 250 feet long and the whole country is a network of streams and gulches. Charge that up against the Canadian Law. A man has ten days, after staking, to record his claim. Having recorded, he has one year to work on it. During the year he must be present on his claim and work on it for three months, but he is at liberty to loaf the first nine months and do his work in the last three, during which time he can't be away from it for 72 consecutive hours. Between May and the freeze-up, a man can stake off 500 claims in one place or another. He records none of them. A second man comes along and can't relocate any one of the 500 claims. If the claim he wants is on

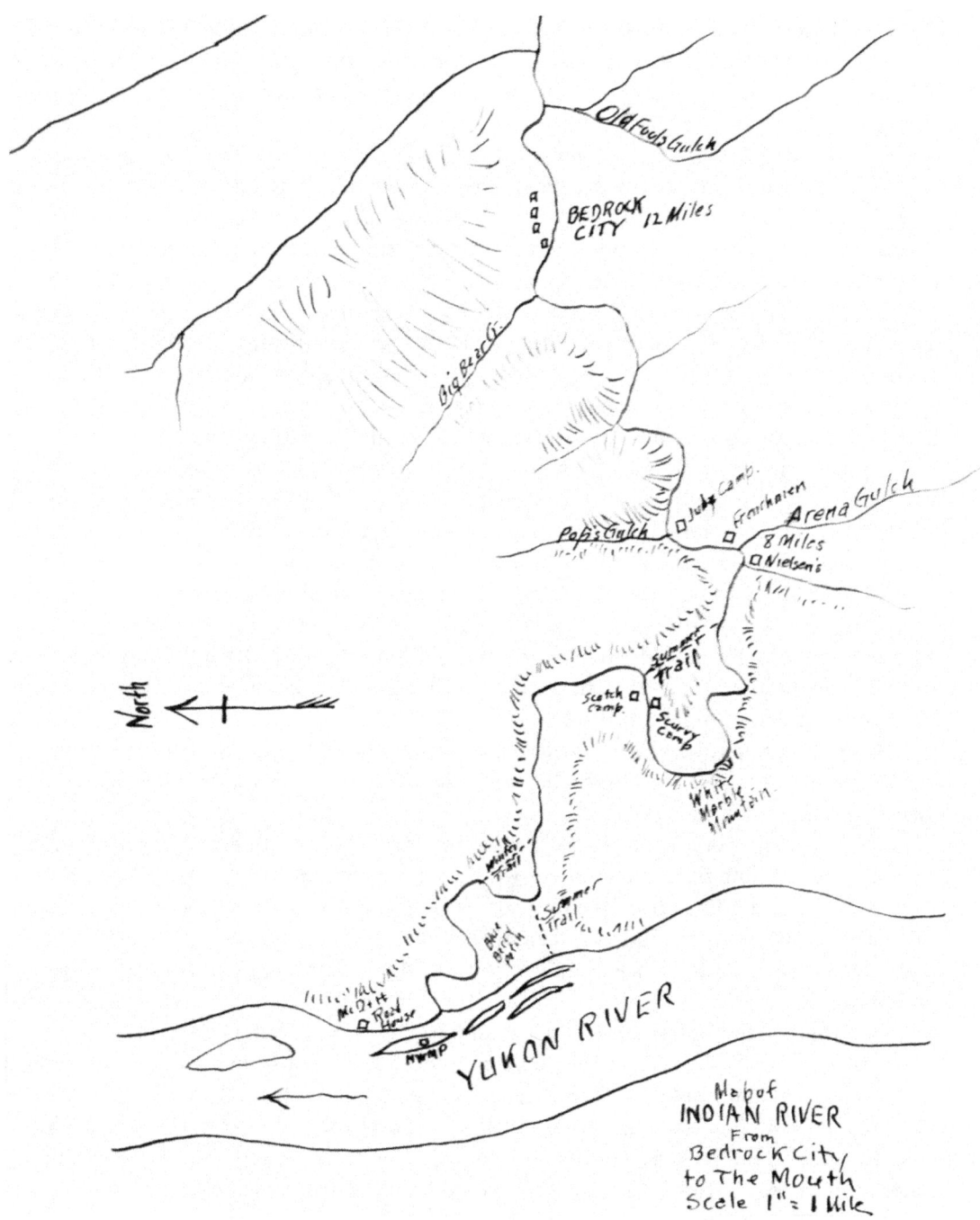

Map of Indian River.

a good creek, he naturally supposes it is recorded. If he goes to the recorder's office, they will not let him see the records. If the claim is good and not recorded it is current gossip that the recording officers tell friends about the snap. So a law intended to benefit the locator and give him plenty of time to do his three months' work, works to his disadvantage.

If I should set stakes on some perfectly barren creek, and go away and leave them, they will doubtless stay there until they rot, but for a year nobody will know whether I have recorded and intend to work the claim. That illustrates the case of an undeveloped claim or creek.

On the other hand, take Eldorado Creek or its bench claims. There are many rich bench claims. They were discovered in the six months preceding our arrival, and it was generally understood that all the claims of any value had been located. I heard of two Swedes who went prospecting benches on Eldorado and found what they thought was a good unlocated claim. They staked it, went to Dawson to record it and were told at the office that the claim they wanted was already recorded. Some people are so bold as to say that the recorder made out a record for that particular claim for some friend of his and set the date back a few days and the two Swedes got nothing. More conservative parties say the Swedes picked one of the claims held for the crown. Then someone is disloyal enough to remark that the crown does not reserve its bench claims until it is sure of good ones.

We know that even Eldorado was spotted. Some claims that sold for thousands in 1897 were worked at a big loss during the following winter. Bonanza is staked right to its mouth, but the lower seven miles of it does not appear to be worth developing.

We knew that we couldn't believe anything that anybody told us about anything. The man with the worst tale of woe who says he is going on out, may be on his way to record what he thinks is a good thing, going to tell his friends about it, and let them in before others know of it. The man who says the creek is all right and who tells of the biggest finds, may be booming a certain creek to help a friend sell a worthless claim, or he may be quitting the country and is ashamed to admit it.

At home, I might be able to make use of some other fellow's experience and profit thereby, study the problem and see wherein I might improve it. But here it seems that my own experience is all that counts.

All these angles of the gold mining situation, formed the main topic of conversation evening after evening from the moment we got off the train in Seattle. We talked almost daily with the gold miners from the four corners of the earth, and now and then we had a chance to talk to someone who had been in Dawson, or knew someone who had been. So it was not a casual circumstance when we "concluded to take six weeks grub, and prospect Indian River."

Whoever named Indian River did a good job. The water is red, not a faint pink but a bright ruby red and as clear as a ruby. In a cup, the color is not so marked, but in a pool six feet deep it is almost black rather than red. The color comes from the moss over which the water has flowed in coming from the little gulches. The water is not perfectly pure, but it tasted all right, and we generally drank tea or coffee. At the river mouth the white muddy water of the Yukon mixes with the red of the Indian, to make intricate patterns like little clouds. The river will not average more than 65 feet wide for the 25 miles I traversed, and in depth varies from nothing to four feet. Probably a bit less than nothing for in places the stones in the river are above the water. The river flows along with little or no current for 1,000 feet then goes down over a ripple of gravel. At low water the stones stick out at these ripples and in getting a boat up stream, its bottom is soon worn through. At times when the water happens to be rather higher, it is rather easy to pull a boat upstream, but impossible to row. We wanted our mail, so I made the trip to Dawson to get the mail, while Pop and Dan put the bulk of our outfit on a cache, and started up Indian River with a six weeks' supply of grub.

The mouth of Nine Mile Creek is about 25 miles up river, and they were to meet me there. Then we were going on to the Sulphur and Dominion Districts. I was disappointed when I did not find them at the mouth of Nine Mile, but when I finally found them, practically stalled, only eight miles up Indian River from the Yukon, I was mad all over and thoroughly disgusted.

I've thought many times since, that Pop and I must have been alike in many ways. Opposites attract, and like repels like. Dan and Pop were opposites and sometimes they united upon some plan which might be very distasteful to me. Dan and I were opposites and we frequently united in doing things that displeased Pop. Pop and I never got together on any plan which left Dan out. Pop lost all heart and hope in the country after we had gone up Stewart River a few miles. After that Dan and I just had to drag him along. And he dragged like a heavy boat with the bottom out of it.

He had worked hard and expended a lot of wind and muscle getting into the country, and then found that the hard work had just begun.

Just as soon as I had made a fair start on my trip to Dawson, Pop began to urge Dan to put the outfit in our big boat and follow me down to Dawson. Dan wouldn't listen to such a proposal, so finally they cached the outfit and started up Indian River with the small boat.

I've often noticed what a small world this really is. About eight miles up the Indian River, when they stopped to cook a meal, they fell in with three Irishmen who were also cooking where good drinking water was handy. Mike McGovern once ran a milk wagon in Chicago, and Pop had known him there. Jim Riley came from Pittsburgh and Jack Wamsley from Chicago. Jack was cook for the party, an engine wiper, boiler cleaner, "marine engineer," by profession. He had lost both forefingers and one thumb and was slightly lame. He described their boat as being "without mate nor shape," and began most of his sentences with "So God forgive me…." He was a fair cook but his lameness prevented him from getting around easily. When Pop found his long lost friend Mike McGovern, they all had to stop and talk over old times, and conditions as they found them in the Klondike. They had camped on the south bank of Indian River, and opposite them, there was a narrow gulch. It was the last place in the world for anyone to prospect for gold. The walls of the gulch showed rock and clay which results from the disintegration of rock. There were no signs of gravel anywhere, and it was evident even to a Cheechaco that the bed of the gulch consisted of a sandy silt, generally called muck, for lack of a better name.

However, we all were quite too familiar with the motto that "Gold is where you find it," and we had heard many of the most unbelievable talks about the unfavorable looking places that produced gold.

So, when I arrived at our Indian River camp where they were, Dan and Mike McGovern had started a prospect hole about a mile up Pop's Gulch, and Pop and Jim Riley had a hole somewhat close to camp.

I told everybody what I thought about the whole situation, and I was angry enough to phrase my sentences in words that were easily understood. They could work there just as long as they pleased, and I'd see that the meals were ready for them, but they could count me out, when it came to digging in such a location.

Dan had the best looking hole. Pop's hole got too much sun, so it thawed around the edges and slumped down into the bottom. They had to crib it around the top, and then did better. They found some six inches of moss, and right under the moss, the ice and frost began. They cut wood and split it and built a fire in the prospect hole. While the fire burned they cut more wood. After the fire had burned out, they threw out the ashes and dug out and picked out as much they could of the defrosted earth, and repeated the process. Old miners told us that this method was all right in winter but in summer it was better to heat stones and let them thaw the ground. That kept the sides of the hole in better shape. They tried the stones and liked the method better. Of course, Reynolds didn't finish his hole. When down 12 feet it got to caving so badly that they had to quit it. Dan and Mike kept at theirs until they got to the bottom, 24 feet through frozen muck to bedrock and never a color. Soon after they had started their holes, Pop soured on the job and wanted to go to Dawson but Dan would not hear it. He had made a good start on his hole and he proposed to see what was at the bottom. As July 4 found us in Queen Victoria's domains, I cooked all day, and carried grub to the boys, up the Gulch.

Arena Gulch Stampede

We had an agreement among the half dozen parties located within a mile of us, that if anyone found a good thing he was to tell all the other parties, and allow everybody to secure a good claim. Back of our camp about a mile, a creek runs into the Indian River. The creek is 15 to 20 miles long. It is a little stream some three feet wide, running in a wide, deep, gravel channel, and on either bank there is a broad stretch of flat moss covered bottom. Three of our friends were sinking a hole some three miles up this creek.

Wednesday night, July 6, just as we were turning in, about 11:00 P.M., one of these men rushed in with the news that their creek had been stampeded by a big party from Dawson. A couple of Swedes who had been in here four years, camped with them a week before. Unknown to anybody they had gone up the creek three-fourths of a mile beyond our friends, staked out discovery claims, gone to Dawson, recorded the discovery and started a big stampede for "Arena Gulch" as they had named it. Wednesday the crowd got there and began staking anything and everything.

We all got our boots on in a hurry, and off we went like a pack of dogs after a rabbit. When we reached the creek we found men everywhere, some friends, some strangers. From Number 4 Above to Number 43 Below Discovery, the creek had been staked. Some of us decided to push on up the creek. We knew that the Queen came in for every alternate ten claims. Someone had given her claims from Number 7 to Number 16 Below. So we gave the Queen a block of ten from Number 5 to Number 14 Above. I carried a measuring tape, but in that thick brush we only made a bluff at measuring. In return for my work of measuring the claims, the boys let me stake claim Number 15 Above and then I measured claims for the others. All the strangers had stayed below the Discovery Claim. All of us who were above Discovery knew each other and had no trouble nor disagreement. Dan got Number 20 and Pop Number 21 and when we got beyond Number 24 we gave Queen Victoria 10 more. We located 16 claims for ourselves and 20 for her.

Then we paused to see where we were. First we found that we were some seven miles from camp, then we discovered that we were tired and sleepy, then we began to figure the value of our claims, and unanimously concluded that we had been sold, and the claims were worthless, and we wished we had slept instead of stampeding.

The discovery hole was just a shallow shovel hole on a bar in the creek bed. Nobody could find colors anywhere on the creek except in that one particular place. We went on back to camp, slowly and sleepily and got there at 6:00 A.M. Anything eatable was devoured and we turned in and slept until noon.

When we began to make inquiries, we learned the facts about the Arena Stampede. Pete Jepson was already famous in Circle City for a big blind stampede he started there two years before. When he saw this creek, he salted a small piece of it, staked his discovery on July 3, and rushed to Dawson. He sent about 10 of his friends out immediately, and then after a little started every Tom, Dick and Harry in Dawson after them. Dawsonites were told that the creek was richer than Eldorado, dirt ran $3.00 to the pan and all such stories. Pete and his ten friends sold out to some poor fish, and the other suckers nearly killed themselves getting there, only to find themselves bunko-ed. Even as late as Friday night they came along carrying little or no baggage, very uncommunicative, but all wanting to know where Arena Gulch was located. Friday, Pop and an old miner prospected the creek, from its mouth to Number 21 Above and concluded that there was no gold at the surface. If there was any gold there, it was down at bedrock, which nobody had prospected.

Saturday, July 9, Mike McGovern met a friend named Kelly who gave him a hot tip, about Squaw Gulch, 10 miles upstream on the right side of Indian River. Up we went, Mike, Whitecap and I. We went up the gulch three miles, and evidently we were the only people who had ever set foot in it. We came to the conclusion that we were stung again. I rather think that Mike's friend Kelly was sending us up there for the "experience."

The Indian River Bars

In going up to Kelly's stampede, and on our return trip, we noticed a man panning gravel at a place where the river ran over bare bedrock for some 400 yards. Here is a typical cross section of valley of the Indian River.

The bedrock is, of course, rough and full of ridges, pockets and crevices, the pockets being filled with gravel. The man was scraping the gravel out of these pockets and seams and washing it. I could not see what pay he was getting, but I decided that I would go up and see what was there. Three days later he came down river. Of course, he stopped and talked to us as all travellers do. He and his partners had sunk a hole 18 feet deep on Australia Creek with no success. I asked if he was the party I saw scraping bedrock a day or two before. One of them answered yes and another pulled out a bottle containing about $3.00 in dust. I had the impression that he got it up there on Indian River. Jack got an impression that it came from the hole they dug on Australia Creek. That was a question that was never answered. I went up next day and found that it was easy to get fifteen to twenty cents per

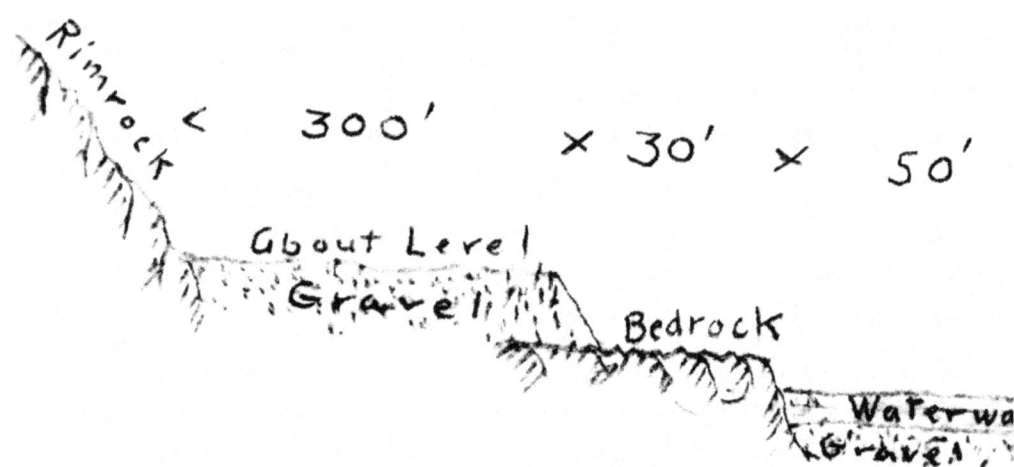

Cross section of Indian River bar.

pan by removing the top gravel from the pockets and washing the bottom gravel. I didn't get any pieces as big as peas like those fellows showed us. Jack Wamsley nearly convinced me that they got the stuff from Australia Creek. Then again I was certain that they got it from my bar.

On July 18 a forest fire, which started in Arena Creek, threatened our camp. We fought it, off and on for three days, but the wind favored our fight, and the fire made slow progress because of the damp moss, but it kept Pop from the prospect hole he and Jim had started on that side of the river.

On July 19, Pop announced to the camp that "the freeze-up would not find him in the Klondike, unless he found better prospects." This announcement was influenced in part by the fact that we had opened our last can of butter, just a day or two before.

Next day the fire broke out again; Pop and I were kept rather busy building a back fire, to protect our camp. On July 23, we had slowed down very noticeably, late in rising, slow to get to work, argument about almost everything; and my diary says: "Our butter is all gone, and unless we can find more, I think we will soon go." Pop had lived on the farm so long that he looked upon butter as one of life's necessary foods. We didn't know much about vitamins in those days, but we did know that bacon grease was a common substitute for butter and lard in the Klondike.

Next day being Sunday, there was no work in Dan's prospect, so he went up river with me to look at the bar that had interested me. We met two New Zealand miners, who told us that we were wasting time and effort, in washing gravel in a prospecting pan, that a rocker was much better.

Dan was delighted with the place and wanted to prospect it in earnest, rather than scratching around here and there as I had been doing. Monday Dan and I went up again and Reynolds came up after dinner. He didn't come because he wanted to or because he wanted to find any prospects. He came to be able to say he had been there and in his estimation the place was no good. He was very careful to select places where there were no colors, panned a couple of pans, found nothing and pronounced the place no good. My diary for that date says "Nothing impresses Pop favorably, except Dawson."

Our Party Splits

Tuesday Morning, July 26, just exactly five months from the day we left Rockford, the McGovern party announced that they were going to Dawson. Pop said he would like to see Dawson also, that he would take his clothes and some cooking utensils and go with Mike's party.

There was no formal announcement of the dissolution of our partnership, but Dan and I knew that Pop would never be back. Our triangle had gone the way of all other three cornered partnerships.

So Pop went to Dawson, and Dan and I moved our camp up river to the bar which interested us so greatly. We knew that we would soon have to go to Dawson and make some kind of settlement with Pop, but we didn't propose to follow right along at his heels.

A week or so earlier, I had found a very good gold rocker, on a raft that was drifting down stream. We soon learned that it is no snap to work a rocker, but after some experimenting we finally learned the best way of running the thing. Then we found that we could strip more ground in one day than we could rock in four. We started digging into the gravel bank above bedrock back toward the rim rock. There was some six feet of gravel to be dug off, then a pay streak six inches thick that averaged four or five dollars per square yard of bedrock surface.

Stop for a moment to consider the effect which this prospect had on us. We had come to the Klondike to find gold. We had found a few very light colors on the Stewart, and here just over the hill from Eldorado, we were finding substantial quantities of fairly coarse gold. We all know to what extremes men have gone to get money. The sight of bright flakes of yellow gold in the bottom of a pan or rocker produces a type of insanity that can never be understood by those who have not had the experience.

We were inoculated. I could see myself as I had seen the man on Eldorado, carrying a pan full of nuggets from our sluice boxes to our cabin, in the same matter of fact way that a farmer boy brings in the morning's supply of eggs.

We had some friends sinking holes about three miles further up river. They were Harry White, Brink the Swede (whose partner Old Petersen stayed at the Mouth), another Swede, a tanner called Little Peterson, (to distinguish from Old Petersen), and a man named Fred, whose last name seems to have escaped me. Fred was first mate on an ocean freighter, before coming to the Klondike. Little Petersen had relations in Rockford.

When they saw the coarse colors we found on our bar, they quit their holes, came down and staked claims above and below the place we were prospecting. Two of them were old miners, Harry White from Australia and Brink from California. Referring to our rocker the Australian said "Throw away the bloody buggar and make a sluice box. You can wash more dirt in a day in a box than you can in a fortnight in a cradle." Without even trying their claims they set to work whipsawing lumber for sluice boxes. We furnished the tools and helped saw and they made us a set of three or four boxes.

Dan and I had been there nearly a week. We were out of flour, sugar, oatmeal and bacon, and Reynolds was down at Dawson headed for home, so Dan and I had to go to the Mouth for more food, and figured that we might as well go to Dawson and settle with Reynolds. So we left our tent and camp equipment in care of Brink and Company and headed for Dawson.

Tuesday, August 2, Dan and I set out on foot for the Mouth. We got a late start as it rained most of the morning. Arrived at the Mouth at 6:15 P.M. and camped with Old Petersen who was keeping an eye on our cache. Found our cache in good shape, except that the little red mice had found and eaten every bit of our chocolate. There were very few boats tied up there at that time.

Next morning, we were fortunate in meeting an outfit known as Wood and Company, who had been 25 miles above the McQuesten, on Stewart River, and were on their way to Dawson. We soon landed at Lousetown, crossed the Klondike at the Free Ferry, and hunted up our old friends.

We had met a boiler maker named Raber out at the Mouth of Stewart River who had once worked in Rockford. When we met him in Dawson, he invited us to cook our meals on his stove, and use his frying pan. Then we found the Petersen party, whom we had known at Lake Bennett. They had an empty tent, which they offered us for sleeping quarters.

We found Pop living with Hawthorne (of Lake Bennett) on Hawthorne's scow, tied up on the water front. Hawthorne invited us to have supper with them, and afterwards we took in Dawson by lamplight, until about 1:00 A.M. Thursday and Friday we spent inspecting Dawson. Then Pop proposed that we should buy his share of the outfit. Saturday we offered Pop $200.00 for what he had left of his share of the outfit, which had originally cost him about $400.00. He insisted that unless we would pay him $300.00 everything must be divided in three parts, and he would take his third. We would cut four feet off one end of the tent; we would cut one-third of the barrel of the shotgun; we would cut the firebox off the stove.

When we saw him again on Monday, he had had more time to think it over and the $200.00 which we offered him looked mighty good to him. Dan and I felt like a couple of school boys who had suddenly been given an unexpected holiday. A load was lifted from our shoulders, and we laid our plans for the future. Dan had never said anything nor kicked about Pop until we had been on Indian River about two weeks. Then he told me what he thought about the case, everything.

After we had settled with Pop and he was on his way back to the States, Dan said: "Wouldn't it be awful to be caged up with Pop all winter, always sour and wishing he was home and damning the country and damning our folly for ever coming here."

9

Autumn in the Klondike

Opportunity Knocks

On Saturday, August 6, Dan and I did a hard day's work. A big batch of new mail had just arrived, and was to be distributed. We were in line at 8:30 A.M. and there were 300 or more ahead of us. We pushed and shoved, and were pushed and shoved, and got dry and hungry until 3:30 P.M. Then we got into the office and got our mail. We felt that we had earned a square meal, and invested $1.50 each. This was our fourth square meal in Dawson. We were most economical and never spent a cent, but in one way or another it always cost us something to stay in Dawson.

Sunday and Monday we saved money. We went up Bonanza to the Forks, on a wild goose chase, looking at a bench claim that had been offered us on a lay. "Working a Lay" is the miner's way of saying that the owner of the mine gets a miner to work his mine on shares. Of course, the owner does not give a fifty percent lay, if he knows he has a real gold mine, but if his mine (or what he thinks may be a mine) has never been worked, he frequently finds someone to work it for him for some agreed percentage of the gold that is taken out. The claim we went to look at did not amount to anything but we were glad that we inspected the creeks. We avoided two days of waiting for Pop to accept our offer, saw two famous creeks, got a small sample of gold from the same pile of boxes that I inspected on my previous trip, and fell in with and bunked with two mighty pleasant fellows from California. They were experienced miners, and had been in just a year and were working a lay on the fraction between Number 7 Above Bonanza and Number 1 Eldorado. They also had a bench above Number 2 Eldorado where they were then working, rocking everything from moss to bedrock.

We spent a most enjoyable evening with these two miners. They seemed to be veritable encyclopedias of mining information. Every little bit of mining news was at their tongue's end. They explained how gold is generally found under the creek beds, in the bottom of the valley, and how occasionally, it is found in bench claims, benches being the shoulders of the creek beds, where the mountain sides begin to rise up. They gave us the full history of the rich bench claims that had been staked out that spring before we arrived in the country. They encouraged us in our Indian River prospecting, when we showed them our samples, and told them how the land lay on Indian River. They told us a multitude of funny things that Cheechacos did in their search for gold.

They told us about a crazy Cheechaco who had gone way up on top of the hill, near the junction of Eldorado and Bonanza and was digging a prospect hole away up there. This poor fish evidently thought that he was on a bench, and didn't know the difference between a bench and the top of a mountain. He had a hole down almost one hundred feet, and was still going. When he started his hole, he had a lot of visitors, because it was such a novel stunt, even for a Cheechaco, but as time went on, people lost interest in this wildest example of what a greenhorn will attempt.

Next day Dan and I gave all the established mines a rather thorough inspection, thanked our hosts for their hospitality and returned to Dawson. On our way back, we heard a rumor of a very rich strike having been made on Indian River, by our friends the Nielsens, who were camped at the mouth of Arena Gulch. When we reached Dawson we found that some of our friends had followed the crowd who had gone up river to investigate the report. They were back in Dawson in another day or two, with the rumor exploded.

It was several weeks later, after Dan and I had returned to our Indian River prospect, and were building our cabin, that we learned that the "poor fish" in the deep hole above Eldorado reached bedrock the day we were inspecting the creek and found gold in such fabulous quantities, that the Canadian government promptly cut the size of claims to 100 feet square.

What a chance we had, and missed! If we had only had the curiosity to climb the hill and look into the 100 foot hole, the greenhorn was digging, we might have staked Number 1 next to Discovery! Fortune almost pushed us into a real gold mine, and we failed to see her guiding hand!

How we kicked ourselves, time and again, for being so blind, and yet as I see it now, there is a certain degree of satisfaction in the thought that it's better to have had a chance and lost, than never to have had a chance at all. "Gold is where you find it."

If when we had first come down river we had gone to Dawson, or to Eldorado, we might have been away over on Sulphur or Indian River, instead of right there where the strike was made. Because we had gone up Stewart, stopped at Indian, separated from Pop, found Dawson expensive, we eventually found ourselves right where the strike of the season was made, on the day it was made, and missed it!

Back to Indian River

When we got back to Dawson on Monday, we heard that there would be another big lot of mail distributed on Thursday, so we waited for the mail. Time hung a bit heavy on our hands in Dawson, so we wandered around among the saloons and dance halls, enjoying a lot of funny sights. That Monday evening I made $16.50 playing a dice game, the first game of chance for me since my Sheep Camp adventure. We spent the profits, taking in a prize fight, at $5.00 admission.

Tuesday evening, by careful play, I won $24.50 on one roulette wheel, and by more careful play lost $20.00 of it, on another wheel. Wednesday evening, I played the bird cage game, until 11:30 P.M. and lost $35.00. Then I made up my mind again that it's impossible to beat any of these gambling games.

Thursday, August 11, we stood in line again at the post office, all day without food or water, Dan got no mail, and I got letters dated June 19 and July 8. Dan wrote a long letter to the folks at home, which was so interesting that the Rockford paper printed it in full.

Some of my letters also found their way to the newspaper, but it would only be repetition to show my news articles here.

Thursday evening we attended a show at the Monte Carlo Theatre. The program is rather more interesting than the entertainment, which was a bit rough in spots.

Dan and I were both getting tired of Dawson and its crowd of long faces, blue inhabitants, and were very glad, after getting our mail, to set out for the tent in the woods, which to us was home. We thought we would not be very heavily loaded. Besides a pair of 10-pound blankets each we only had a few cooking utensils and bread, bacon and oatmeal enough to do us for two days and a 6 by 9 foot canvas to sleep under or on according to weather. We rolled the small stuff in the blankets and strapped them tightly in our pack straps, hitched the packs to our shoulders and left Dawson Friday.

It Will Be a Rattling Go! Boxing comes to the Klondike.

The bridge people charged fifty cents to cross the Klondike on their bridge. That was very nice for them while it lasted, but some public spirited Cheechacos donated several boats which the public used for nothing, rather than pay for the bridge. It was not easy to get into one of the boats. A sawmill company had a big boom full of saw logs in near the shore. With our packs we had to be careful in getting out to the edge of the boom, but finally accomplished it by running out on one log, taking a jump, landing on another log, that we had to jump off one instantly, to find better footing on another and then we were on the edge of the boom. The boom is made of a string of logs chained together, and is fairly good footing. The boat was on the other side, a crowd has just got out of her, and five or six others were ready to bring her back. Some of them used paddles and some poles and away they went down stream and nearly out onto the Yukon. The water means business in all of these Alaska Rivers, a stream doesn't take its time as it does at home. The boat finally made a landing at the lower end of the boom, and the passengers ran the logs to shore, the more impatient men getting wet to the middle, when they picked poor logs. We pulled the boat to the head of the boom, some 200 feet, and with a shove and a paddle and a push and a pull landed on the other shore. We walked across the island to the other channel and there made an easier crossing, that channel being only about 30 feet wide.

Klondike City is built on a little flat with a very steep hill behind it. Beyond it, on the Yukon, is an impassable vertical wall of rock. To get around that we had to climb the hill and get up to the flat above. There is a trail up the hill and a number of cabins on top. We

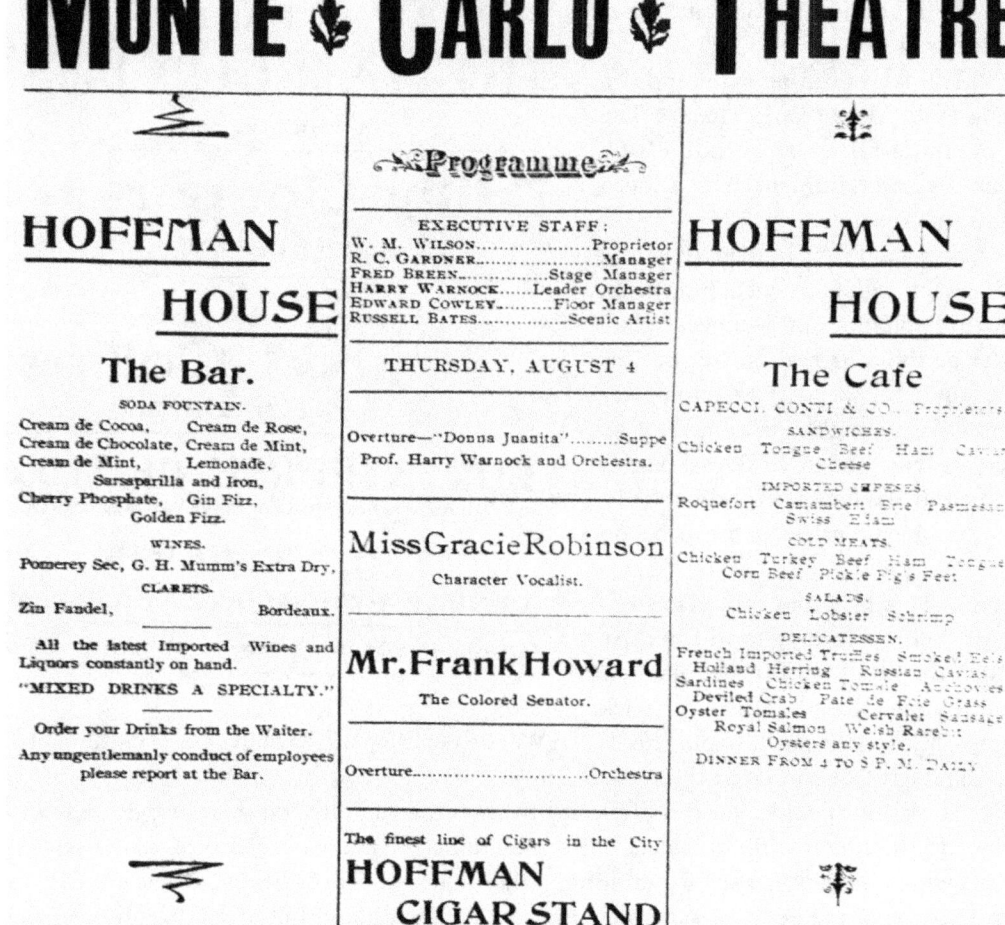

Monte Carlo theater handbill and menu.

kept on top of the hill for a mile and then down to the Yukon again. All the morning we walked along a nice, well beaten path close to the river. After our dinner of oatmeal, bacon, bread and bacon fat, we were feeling fine until we came to another stone wall. This wall was not so steep. The rock was very rough and jagged and gave lots of foothold. Our packs were in the way and threatened to pull us over backward into the Yukon, but we always found some crevice or jutting stone for a foothold or a handhold. But the wall got steeper and smoother and when within 100 feet of the end of this cliff, there seemed to be no place to get around, and no bottom to the river below us. Rather than go all the way back and then up and over, we decided to start there and go up and over the bad place. When we got up a few feet, the bare rock left off and we had grass and small brush and an occasional tree. We did some tall climbing and soon found ourselves about 150 feet above the river, with smooth slick grass under our feet and dry dead grass in our hands. I was ahead and Dan close behind. A short, stocky pine tree two feet ahead of me offered an inviting hand hold. I heard a slip and a slide, looked around and there was Dan vainly trying to dig his feet into the grass, only to have them steadily slip from under him. When he grabbed a hand-full of grass it was only to pull it out. There wasn't time to say anything. I grabbed the pine tree close to its roots, stretched out at full length and yelled to Dan to "Grab Hold." He caught my ankle, and as his weight stretched me out, my hat fell off and rested on my shoulder. I nearly let go my hold on the tree to save the hat, or rather to go sliding down 150 feet into the Yukon, which the hat did when Dan crawled up over me to a place of safety. Another hundred feet and we were past that bad place and a deep gulch forced us to go down to the river again. But we could not follow the river long. We were soon up against another wall, which we had to climb over.

We were about all in, when we found two Swedes in a boat who were having a tough time poling their boat past another vertical wall. With our added pushing power the boat performed nicely, and we all camped on the river bank for the night. Next morning we helped them all the way to Indian River. They were headed for Stewart.

Sunday we visited at the Mouth with Petersen, Old Petersen and Fred. Monday it rained, so we stayed there.

Tuesday we made up some rather heavy packs of grub, etc., and Old Petersen went with us to take grub to the Brink party. We stopped for two hours in a blueberry patch, and picked about three quarts. Rain added to the weight of our packs. We rested often, ate dinner, before wading the river at the White Marble Cliff and when we got near Arena Gulch we crossed the river in a boat belonging to a man named Kermis, made a short cut back of our old camp, and arrived at our tent about 7:00 P.M.

We were just unloading our packs, when two men came down river with more moose meat on their backs than they could conveniently carry. They had shot a bear and a bull moose way back from the river. They had to leave most of it, but brought out a big round of moose, and the bear's hide and ham. We bought about 15 pounds of moose for $5.00. Dan's knowledge of meat came handy. They gave him his choice and he cut off the insides of the round. If I had not known that it was moose, I should have thought it beef. It was a trifle dryer than beef, but was very nice and tender. We feasted on moose, three times a day for three days.

Autumn Life on Indian River

Our picture would be very imperfect, without some mention of the bugs, the flowers, and the animal life that we found on Indian River.

Game was not numerous. Every little while we heard of a bear or a moose being seen or shot but they were very timid and only experienced hunters knew where to look for them. The bears were small black fellows. Soon after arriving on Indian River, I met a bear and her two cubs in Pop's Gulch, but of course, I had no gun.

In some of my letters, I sent home flowers and seeds from Indian River. The dark blue flowers Dan called the "Old Woman's Bonnet." The prettiest thing I saw was a big purple mosquito shaped flower. It grew with the "Sweet Suzan." There was a flower almost like "Garden Heliotrope." And what a sorry specimen of a dandelion I saw along the river. It looked like a homesick tenderfoot. There was a big vigorous crop of asters that grow 5 inches high with a single flower at the end. It had light purple petals and yellow centers. I wanted to send home nice specimens of that all abounding moss that served many purposes. The stuff was soft for a bed, warm for chinking cabins, cool to make the cover for an ice box out in the frozen ground, and lastly this moss was a fine hideout for mosquitoes. When the moss was burned off, the skeets quit, and when the moss was stripped off clean, the sun readily thawed the gravel under it.

We became quite acclimated to the mosquitoes. It seemed as if they didn't like the flavor of us after we became completely inoculated with the poison they carry on the end of their bills.

Early in August we began to be fearfully annoyed by two little gnats, which the Indians called "No-see-em" because they were so small that they could not be seen until after they had bitten us. One is very much smaller than the other one. Both bite and fill up on blood. They just stand on their heads and bore in. And how their sting itches and keeps on itching. We would scratch until it bled and the sore spot would still itch. Mosquitoes were tame compared with those fellows when once they got action. When they first came they were so small that we didn't bother about them except to dig them out of our eyes. Next day I thought I had sunburned my ears and Dan's arms were in awful shape. Then we discovered the cause. They are devilish little creatures. They aim at your eyes or nose or mouth or ears and fly straight in. I began to wear a handkerchief around my neck and ears most of the time but had plenty of bites anyway.

The home newspapers of 1898 gave a lot of publicity to the "camp robber." He is a bird that steals grub out of the fry pan. He's nothing more than a blue jay faded in color and a bit rougher than his southern brother. They were very bold, and flew right under our feet to get a scrap of bacon or anything else that could be eaten. They may be good eating, but we never tried them.

One bird we did eat. We ran into a big flock of grouse or partridges back of our tent. We killed seven of them. They were perfect fools. If I walked right on top of one, he would up and fly away, but if I kept 100 feet away he would just turn tail and run along the ground. The black burned-over ground gave a good background to shoot against, and I killed five of the birds without wasting a shot. When they light on trees or bushes they are so near the color of the tree that it is difficult to see them.

I sent home a little paper of garnets that I washed out of our Indian River. The garnets being heavy, settle to the bottom of the sluice box, along with gold and black sand. They had no value.

Don't imagine that Dan and I spent our time collecting flowers and studying the habits of the camp robber. We worked long hours, every day except Sunday. Routine work doesn't make very entertaining reading, but as the work was a part of our life, I may as well record it.

The Brink Party who had worked while we were in Dawson had rather hard luck with their sluice boxes, as the river didn't have sufficient fall to give a good water head in the boxes. There was a bit more fall where we were working, and we built a wing dam to divert water to our boxes. Of course, that took work.

We had lots of visitors, all the time we were at work; men who were just hanging around, ready to stake a claim and rush to record it, the minute we might make a rich strike. We were surprised at the quantity of clay gravel that an apparently bare piece of bedrock could turn out.

Brink, White, and Little Petersen quit and went to Dawson on August 22. We found that the sluice boxes required a lot more labor than the rocker, because we only had a fall of 12 inches in our boxes. We always found some gold dust in our boxes, but some gold was not what we were seeking; we wanted cartloads of gold. That which we did get, kept us keenly interested, and we spent our evenings around the camp fire figuring from what we knew about that part of the bar which we had worked, which way we ought to go to find the "old river bed," the main deposit which had supplied our bar.

It seemed foolish for us to clean up that little bar for a return of only about $5.00 per day, when there might be another Eldorado somewhere within 1000 feet of it. So we began to dig two holes back of our tent between us and the tableland behind us and worked the sluice boxes on the bar while our fires were burning. There were no trees handy so we had to carry wood for our fires. The dead rotted moss was three or four feet deep, frozen of course, then came three feet or very fine mica and sand mud and then gravel. We picked our way down to the gravel, but frozen gravel was just like picking solid granite, so we had to thaw it.

On August 29, a party who had been camped near the Nielsens at Arena Creek came up to see what we were doing and pitched camp in a way that indicated they were interested. They went up on the bench about 150 feet above the river bottom and started to sink a hole there.

We had a lot of trouble with rain for about a week. We had such perfect weather ever since leaving Lake Bennett that we had difficulty in realizing that the rainy season had arrived. Rain delayed our work in more ways than one. Sometimes it put out the fire we had built in the hole, and the timber had to be taken out before we could prepare the hole for another fire. The rainwater added weight and reduced the solidity of the material we had to hoist out of our holes.

By September 1, all the foliage except the pines had turned yellow, with here and there a splash of red. Our flour, cornmeal and salt had all been used, and sugar, oatmeal and beans were getting low. It was getting dark much earlier, in fact at 8:00 P.M. it was night and black night too.

On September 2, it rained hard; the river came up and we had to pull out our sluice boxes to prevent the river from washing them away.

Then we decided that we would just have to stop work long enough to go down to our cache at the Mouth for a supply of grub. We borrowed a poling boat from one of the parties camped near us.

Got started at 5:20 A.M. on September 5, and arrived at the Mouth at 7:20 A.M. It was a pleasure to go downstream that way. I steered, and only hit rocks twice. The first time we hung suspended and balanced with a rock under the middle of the boat. Once I narrowly escaped being swept out of the boat when we shot under a fallen tree. We loaded up some 300 pounds of grub, hardware and all our clothing, left at 9:30 A.M. and got back to the tent at 7:00 P.M. The current was too swift to permit us to pole the boat upstream, so we had to tow it on the end of a rope as we did going up Stewart.

Both our prospect holes had barrels of water in them, which had to be bailed out before we could resume sinking. Saturday, September 10, we found bedrock in both holes, and colors not quite as good as we had been working on the bar. So we went back to the bar again, as the rainy weather more than doubled the work required in sinking prospect holes. I noted that we sluiced only $4.50 on September 15, and that we had our first little fall of snow on September 18. Then we suspended mining operations, and built our winter quarters.

10

Getting Ready for Winter

Selecting Neighbors for the Winter

My letters to the folks at home fully describe the log cabin which we built, and the neighbors who built cabins and lived near us throughout the winter. Following is my letter of September 27:

> I suppose that you never heard of Bedrock City. Bedrock City is the official name proposed by Dan and accepted by the whole party of 11, for our settlement here, 12 miles up the Indian River. Dan and I came back from Dawson, worked this piece of bare bedrock, sank two holes back from the river and two more way up on a high plateau, south of our tent.
>
> September 16, we settled the question of where we would spend the winter. Three parties came up the river, and settled near us proposing to build their cabins for winter here. Dan and I thought we might as well do the same. Here we are at the same old place, and here we shall be until spring. There being four parties consisting of eleven people, we thought we deserved a name, and at Dan's suggestion the name of Bedrock City has been adopted.
>
> We have sharpened our axes and are at work on our cabin. By tomorrow night, September 28, expect to have the walls completed.
>
> I suppose that you wish of all things to hear about is the weather. So here is a discourse on that much worn topic, although I have a million other things that I would rather write about. I know that you will imagine that I've had all my fingers and toes frozen by this time, unless I state very particularly that I haven't. The weather was fine all summer, but during the past month I've seen a whole year jammed into thirty days.
>
> The latter part of August, we ate out of doors and cooked there too, and after supper we would sit down and read the articles you sent us. To keep the No-See-Ems away we built a fire, and read by its light. The heat was of no use, it was too much of a good thing. Summer everywhere, but the asters going to seed warned us that it was almost over. Then for a few days we had spring. It rained hard for three or four days in short showers, and the rain was rather cool too. Then came a week of autumn. This whole valley was a picture. When I went up on the hills for firewood, I would rather loiter to look at the picture up the valley. As far as I could see, there was one mountain after another, all covered with dark green pines, white birch, and cottonwood whose leaves turned first red and then yellow. Here and there, the red river with its pink foam was visible, and the sky above was the clearest, most transparent blue. On mountains which I knew were 15 or 20 miles away, it seemed as if I could see the individual trees. During the rainy days we moved our stove and grub box into the tent, since then I have found it quite essential. The autumn was short; the leaves fell off before I could hardly realize that
>
> > 'The melancholy days have come,
> > The saddest of the year' (Wm. Cullen Bryant, "The Death of the Flowers," Line 1)
> > The summer's gone,
> > We have no gold,
> > And winter's nearly here.

On August 27, we found a film of ice on the water pail. Sunday, September 18, we awoke to find a cover of snow over everything. It soon melted, but snow is one of the signs of winter. September 22, we had a good snow, stayed all day and in some places there was a little left the next day. The water pail has frequently frozen when left out overnight, and on September 26, it had a half inch of ice inside our tent. It's the ground that's cold not the air. It is uncomfortable working in the sun. The river water is ice cold and our little rivulet from which we get our drinking water is a mass of icicles. It's nearly winter, yet we wear the same clothes that we did July 4 and feel comfortable. Twice in the past month I have noticed a slight breeze stirring. Usually the smoke from our fire rises and floats down the valley, filling it all the way across. Nearly winter, but it does not inconvenience us as we work on our cabin.

I fear you'll never want to come up here, the mice would not please you. At present we are boarding some six or eight of the cutest little auburn haired mice that you ever could imagine. They are getting so fat that I shall soon be able to catch them, as of yet they are too lively. They come within two feet of me to grab a crumb or a bean, but I can't manage to grab one of them. Our bacon hangs on a little tree, and the mice climb the bark and eat bacon, one fell on Dan as he came into the tent the other day. Our dinner table is a smooth high grocery box, but they climb it, eating any crumbs they find and leaving behind those they ate yesterday. We tried keeping our bread in one of our big telescopes, but the mice got in between the bottom and the cover and ate the bread. It's time we had a cabin to live in.

Let me introduce the other residents of Bedrock City. Farthest up the river, four hundred yards from our cabin, and back some three hundred feet from the river, at the head of First Avenue, is the 10 by 12 foot cabin of Stemple and Carr. They are foreigners of some kind, but hail from San Francisco.

Poole Stemple is a short man with a badly smashed or twisted nose, with a rather high voice, and a full beard. Like nearly everybody up here he is strongly individualistic, once he gets a notion in his head, it sticks there. It is a noticeable fact that nearly every man up here is of that type. If they were not so built, their friends would have talked them into staying home, or once in here someone with "cold feet" would have talked them into going out again.

Bert Carr, I believe, is a Pole, he has the features. He is tall, very rawboned and always wears a great big good natured smile. He has seven tow-colored hairs on each side of his chin, six on either chop, five on either side of his upper lip, all being about half an inch long. It's a long way from his eyes down to his mouth and the space is all filled up with nose.

At the head of Second Avenue, some 100 feet west of their cabin, is the 14 by 16 foot cabin of old Carl Jorgenson and two young fellows. Someday I'll write a book about old Jorgenson, but not now. He is a Scandinavian of some kind. He was raised in New Zealand, has lived in Hawaii and 14 years ago moved his numerous family to Humboldt County, California. By trade he is a carpenter. Has a broad flat face, with gray whiskers wherever they can find a place to grow, and gray hair. He wears a little Dutch cap perched on one side. He has grub enough for the winter with the exception of tobacco and sugar. He hasn't had a red cent to buy anymore, except some $3.00 or $4.00 which the boys have taken off Bedrock here. That will buy sugar and the boys are whip-sawing lumber for Thompson to earn money for tobacco. His son, Alfred Jorgenson is about 20, and has a habit of leaving the last half off of every word when talking; even if he added the last half of each word, his accent would be half Negro dialect, from Hawaii, and half English. Emil Gunderson, the other member of that party, is about half my age and looks to be a nice clean Swede. He has always lived across the street from Jorgenson no matter where Jorgenson went. The only difference in his speech is that he says the whole word.

Some 200 feet further west or down the river, and back in line with the other two cabins is the 16 by 20 foot cabin of the Thompson Party. The cabin is lacking a roof and many other essentials but when done will be the biggest house in town and the hardest to heat.

Jas. H. Thompson, age 51, has always been an honored citizen of Poughkeepsie, N.Y., a wholesale leaf tobacco dealer, a 32nd degree Mason, a Shriner, etc. He is quite gray, except a certain tobacco brown all over his hair and beard. His wife once told him that if he ever had his whiskers cut off again she'd quit him, for he was too hatchet faced to be endurable. He spent three years out west in Illinois and Kansas before the Civil War, going out in a schooner (unmarried I take it) and building some stage route through Kansas. He was in the war. Until Cleveland's last election he was doing a good tobacco business. Just before the exportation of Cuban tobacco was forbidden by Spain, he bought $15,000.00

worth. Then a man who held his notes for some $15,000 had to have money. Thompson asked his New York firm to cancel his purchase of $15,000 of Havana tobacco which they did willingly and thereby hangs Thompson's tale of woe. Exportation was soon after forbidden, and if Thompson had received that tobacco, the profit on that one shipment would have been far more than $15,000. It broke him and here he is, his business sold for half its value to pay his debts. But Thompson says that's nothing, when he thinks how he got only one vote, when he ran for re-election for some high office in the Masons that he had held for some time. So he organized this party of four and here he is looking for gold. They moved into Bedrock City on August 29.

George C. Trowbridge is 29 and enjoys a good time whenever he finds the opportunity. He is in the hardware and plumbing business with his father, and is up here to add a line of gold dust to their already big line of iron, brass, copper, and tin. He is a very sociable fellow, and can sing every song ever heard in a theater, in a rather poor voice. Has not attended college but last year he took a course in French and was studying German when he left home. He brought in a few of Dumas's books in French and I've read one of them.

Ford Cole is from some place near Poughkeepsie in Connecticut. He looks to be 35, but is nearly bald, his whiskers are very thin and no particular color to them. His false teeth are perfect. In playing poker he delights in bluffing when he holds nothing, and the other man has two pairs. He is a druggist by trade.

Frank Reed looks for the world like those campaign pictures of Benjamin Harrison, only a bit younger, his whiskers being brown. I've seen Harrison and Frank does not look anything like him, but looks as much like Harrison's picture as Harrison does. He is a carpenter, and the less he is required to talk, the better he is pleased. When we play poker, we would never know he was in the game, except for his growing pile of blue chips.

While they build their cabin, they are just across the river from our tent, in a big 14 by 16 foot tent. Two or three evenings a week Dan and I would go over and we'd play poker from 7:00 until 9:00, for chips only. Sometimes the Jorgenson boys drop in and we have a big game. When old Jorgenson joins in we have a jolly game.

Good water, good firewood, and a good game of cards are three things that come far cheaper in Bedrock than Dawson.

When the Indian River freezes we shall bring up the balance of our grub on sleds, and put in the winter looking for gold in the bottom of the river and in the country around us. Old miners who have dug bar gold will hardly believe us when we show them what we are getting from this bar. They say it is too coarse for bar gold. Bar gold is usually as fine as flour, and is called flour gold. We may find a $100.00 or so here yet, before winter stops us.

Of one thing you may be certain, we shall not feel the cold as much as you will feel it for us.

Write to Dawson for the next three or four months and remember that we like the country well enough to stay here, or we should not stay.

Wallis

The above letter was taken to Dawson and mailed by an old miner, named Ben Butler. On September 27, he came mushing along, leading a mule, and the mule carrying Ben's pack of grub and blankets. Ben was an old Colorado miner, who could take care of himself anywhere. He camped right in front of the cabin we were building, cooked over an open fire, and slept in Thompson's big tent. He stayed with us four days, and as we sat around the fire each evening he told an interesting yarn that I feel has a place in my story.

The Story of Ben Butler

Ben Butler was born in 1854, at Maple Grove, Kane County, Illinois. His father raised 14 children and his uncle 18, so he "must have had 150 cousins farming in Kane County." "The Butlers own Kane County," says he. Ben moved to Colorado when rather young. He started mining almost immediately, also studied at the Colorado School of Mines, where he learned assaying and a smattering of surveying. He had just purchased a nice new Surveyor's Compass, when a man offered him $50.00 to check what was probably a correct survey. The owner didn't like the first survey because the surveyor had used an old, weather-beaten instrument. Ben's new compass shone like the sun, but the people who sold it to him had forgotten to enclose one of its essential parts. Ben needed the money, so he looked through his instrument knowingly and made a lot of measurements with his steel tape and earned the $50.00.

In 1876 he was in South America, where he worked in nearly every kind of mine. He acquired a wonderful knowledge of geology and mineology, and handled big words in that connection that I couldn't duplicate, although I was only two years out of college.

I've always regretted that I was not able to set down in detail the masterly address he delivered one evening on the theme that "Economy is the Root of all Evil." He cited the profligate generosity in nature, the thousand blossoms on the apple tree for each apple that matures; he cited man's ability to raise and manufacture far more than his requirements and pointed out the dire results to be expected when a person failed to consume the product of their labor. "Show me a country that economizes, and I'll show you a country of paupers."

He had found, dug out, and spent any amount of gold and silver in the 24 years of his mining life, and had no regrets about what he had spent. "It is not what we have found that counts, it's what we are going to find."

He had been a government scout in the Apache wars, but didn't like the monotony of Indian warfare, and the restraint of government service.

He could make money, but never had a bit of luck investing what he made. Shortly after he bought a $60,000.00 horse ranch, somebody invested in electric street cars. That broke him and he lost his ranch.

At one time he owned a railroad "but there are 30 or 40 men in this country who hold all the rest of this in their palm, and they are always ready, willing and able to crush us if we get ambitious." The nearest he had been to his old home since he left it was when had been east to sell his railroad, but he went broke instead of making a fortune, so he just went right on through the old home town, without stopping.

"Dig your money from the ground. Bury it in the ground and dig it up again as you need it every month."

He was offered $2,500.00 for his place at Dyea on February 1; $1,200.00 for it on March 1; and tried his best to sell it for $100.00 on April 1. "Held on too long."

Brought a fine looking stock of goods down the river headed for Dawson and would have made a stake on that outfit, but when he was at Bennett he couldn't see that the straw hats were selling at $5.00 and up. Also sold a horse and wagon at Bennett after he got them safely over White Pass and could have sold them for $1,200.00 in Dawson.

On his way back up stream from Circle City to Dawson, he camped near an old Indian who had a bad attack of indigestion. He had fixed the old chief up, and the old Indian was so grateful that he offered Ben one of his daughters and a boatload of fish. Ben said he could have made some money on the fish, but didn't want the daughter, so he had to tell the old chief that he couldn't put any more load in his boat.

"If I may offer advice to a young man, never hurry and never wait."

"This country is one of the best places in the world to make a stake, stick to it, and there's only three things that can prevent you from getting rich—whiskey, women, and gambling."

He had two partners, who were down near Mouth cutting hay. He had come over Nine Mile with the mule, to haul logs for a raft to move the hay. He had left his mule near our camp while he walked to the mouth, where he found his partners had caught a ride on a big partly empty scow. So here he was on his way back to Dawson via Nine Mile and mighty glad that he had not dragged the mule over the rough trail to the Mouth and back again.

He may settle down on Dominion Creek at Number 6 Below Discovery and will always be glad to see us.

When a man talks so intelligently about chemistry, assaying and other rather technical subjects, who can say how much or how little of his story is true? I do know that he mailed our letters of September 27 as he promised he would.

Building Our Cabin

It was nearly a month before we had another chance to send letters to follow the folks at home. Following is my letter of October 23 to October 29:

I've done my best to write a full and complete account of our trip, and have never failed to find plenty to write about, but each time I've been obliged to leave out a lot of interesting events.

On October 1 my last letter started for Dawson in the hands of Ben Butler, old time Colorado miner, whose relatives own half of Kane County, Illinois. I hope you got the letter. Ben may have mailed it or if he failed to mail it and if it lay very long in the post office it would have been destroyed in the October 14 fire that destroyed the Dawson Post Office and Green Tree Hotel. I hear that the mail was all saved. I hope it was, for I must have a bushel of it there. Dan says getting a letter is like seeing folks from home. It's now two and one half months since we received mail.

Our cabin, per the master sketch:

Number 1:

The first sketch shows the cabin from across the river where we camped last summer. Our cache of bacon in the trees at the right, the steps to the river at the left. Back of the cabin a lot of dwarf pines 10 feet high. Dan's woodshed enclosure shows at the left front of the cabin, made of poles running from ground to roof.

Number 2:

An interior view from the front door. Clothes hanging thick on the left wall. The bunks back. At the left of the bunks a lot of sacks of grub, with clothes bags on top and up high a shelf full of my books and odds and ends. Most of our groceries, all of our footwear and our medicine case under the bunk. At the right of the bunks is a pile of grub sacks piled nearly as high as my bunk, the upper one. The small pile shown in the picture is the fault of the artist not the grub. Dan's grip full of clothes and mine full of dried fruit are prominent. Since the picture was made, these are partly hidden by a big cupboard made of a grocery box. The back shelf contains hardware, the two in front from the pantry. The window is just visible. And in the invisible corner between the window and door is the kitchen.

Number 3:

Just a little idea of what the place looked like during construction, looking down the river to where we cut our hay for beds.

Number 4:

As I have stated previously is a view looking up this river and I may add our future gold mine is somewhere in that picture, location not yet definite. Like one of those old time puzzle pictures. Turn it this way and that and see if you can find the gold mine. We haven't but hope to.

Master sketch of the cabin.

From September 19 to October 29 we directed all our effort to making ourselves comfortable for the winter. To fully cover my subject I shall have to drop back to September 19 and starting from there give you all a full account of

Our House,
        All it Contains,
                How we made things,
                        Whence they came.

10. Getting Ready for Winter

When Dan and I came up here we began to prospect on the south of the river and naturally pitched our tent on that side. We also staked a claim there, but the claim did not seem to be of enough value to warrant us in building our cabin on our claim. We preferred a nice handy spot for the cabin. Dan selected the location. It is directly across the river from our summer camp, where we did our prospecting. The little mark X at the left of the sketch marked Number 4 is about where the cabin stands. It is about 60 feet from the river, on a little knob of ground, some six or eight feet above high water mark, and also some two feet higher than the big flat across the river.

Sketch Number 4 shows pretty much what our cabin location looked like before we civilized it. By simply altering the title, this same sketch might serve for a thousand and one different landscapes between Lake Laberge and Dawson. Widen the river and add an island and it is a sketch of any part of the Yukon; widen the valley a bit more crooked and it is Bonanza or Eldorado or leave it as it is and it is the Klondike. The real scenes are all decidedly different, and each has its own distinct characteristics, but in the hands of an amateur artist with only a lead pencil, one picture serves them all. It's the color of the air, water, and trees that tell us whether we are on one creek or another. The air that hangs over the Yukon is that clear bright "glacier blue" I told you about when at Sheep Camp. Up here on Indian River I can see up the valley ten or fifteen miles and the air is absolutely colorless and without substance. Before the snow came, the mountains one mile away, and when the cottonwood trees turned yellow I could almost feel that I saw the leaves on the trees 10 miles away. (With the genuine "poet's license" I have wandered away from Our Cabin.)

Big pine trees grow in a narrow belt some 30 feet wide all along the river, wherever the bank is old enough to permit of such growth and is secure from floods. Behind this belt of big trees, there is generally a flat from 100 to 1,000 feet wide, covered with little stunted pines, some 10 feet high, and then back at the foot of the mountains, big trees grow again. This fringe of big trees along the river can only be explained by the fact that such trees are getting a full supply of moisture from the river, while the small trees growing on top of the hard frozen moss become stunted from the lack of moisture.

Our first job was cutting trees to make the walls of our cabin, which we did September 19. There were some 20 or 30 trees near our cabin site, but some were too big and heavy to handle, so we left them all standing and went up river about 200 feet, where we cut trees that just suited us. We tried to get logs that would average eight inches, and as we had several hundred trees to choose from, we got just what we wanted. I did most all the chopping that day. I felled and helped trim 17 trees; Dan fell one. I cut the tree so that it dropped over into the river. Then we trimmed the branches off that part of the tree that was on shore, and if the balance was too small to use we cut it off and let the top float downstream. Dan wore his hip boots and together we hauled the log into the river. Dan tied a rope around it and drove it down to the landing place in front of this campsite. While he was going and coming I cut and trimmed another tree and so on. It was no more trouble for us to bring a log 1,000 feet than it was to bring it 100 feet. Dan soon learned to drive two logs very well and kept me hustling. When I have a family and I tell Tommy that I cut four cords of wood in one day he will conclude that his dad can tell bigger woodpile stories than his grandad. Our 18 trees made 31 logs.

Getting the logs out of the river and up the rather steep bank to the site was no snap. We had an ideal landing space, and no work to get the log five feet out of water and that much up the bank. Then we pull a roller under the end and two skids under the roller. Then a rope around the log, and after a good bit of lifting and tugging, the log rolled up to the more gently sloping ground, and was pulled and rolled 40 feet more with comparatively little work.

We next prepared a location for the cabin. We had several six inch trees to cut out and any amount of three or four inch trees. The best building moss grows above high mark, where the pines are thick and high. Right where we wanted to build the cabin there was a patch of moss that was too good to lose. With only my hands I loosened it, and rolled it out in big patches three feet square, taking only the live top growth, about 6 inches deep. As it grows the moss just keeps on year after year growing out from the top. The old growth dies, rots, and freezes into black muck and once frozen the new moss in sight, we cleared a site in good earnest and the place looked quite like a park, for while we cleared away all the small stuff, we kept all the big trees and lots of the bright yellow green moss, which looked like a thick bed of ferns. Then we spoiled the beauty of the place by digging up and throwing out the moss we had left, and some dead black moss under it, and in spots a fine rich soil rotted moss. Then came that ever present blanket of ice. I'll bet our house never settles even though it is only a foot from the surface of the ground to the bottom of the foundation.

Next was the rather tedious job of laying up the logs to form a box 10 by 14 by 6.5 feet inside measurements. We hewed the top and bottom of each log and left the sides rough. Dan was the artist who did the hewing. Then we rolled it over to where we wanted it, and I finished the ends. The logs were all 18 feet long, which gave plenty of stub ends. Where the logs crossed, I had to hew them, top and bottom, so that they would dovetail into one another. Then I sawed and fitted the log into place. Having fitted it I rolled it out and placed a layer of moss about one inch thick on the log and rolled the new log back into place.

We built our walls 10 logs high, and had to cut all the suitable trees near the cabin, and even had to make another trip up river for 10 logs.

September 29 we had the walls done and began on the gable ends. We gave the roof a pitch of 30 inches in 14 feet and there is not a neater pair of gables in Bedrock than ours. I would figure the length and slant of each log, and Dan would hew the ends. Then we laid the log in place, and I bored holes in the end and pinned each log to the log under it and gave it its regular layer of moss. After we set the ridge pole, you could not jar the gables with a 50 ton locomotive. Besides the ridge pole we put in two purlins, all three of them being 8 inch logs 23 feet long, sticking out in front to form a porch, one of the necessary parts of a good cabin. I mortised these logs onto the gables and then we were ready for the roof.

That was October 1 and if you will consult the Bedrock City weather report you will see why we pushed things and soon had the roof on. It began to get chilly, and we wanted a more substantial roof than 10 oz. canvas. We laid a solid roof of rafters, poles from 2 to 4 inches through; straight or crooked, they all went. Then for the first time I used nails, common, wire nails and a small carpenter's saw in the place of a 4 foot cross-cut saw, in the construction of our rustic cottage. I had to saw a rafter in two for a stove pipe hole, and to keep the pieces from falling in I nailed cleats to the adjoining rafters, and there was a fine Klondike chimney 7 inches square. Meanwhile Dan had just cut some fine big sods from our supply of moss; the moss had just frozen enough to cut nicely with a shovel. We covered our roof and our front porch with these moss shingles 3 by 3 foot by 8 inches thick, and big as they looked, they were so light that Dan pitched them up on the roof to me and I shingled them on and made the roof nearly tight. That night after supper we built a big fire on the floor in the middle of the cabin and the Thompson party came over and visited us. The fire dried the moss on the roof and in the walls and even dried the logs a good bit. We repeated the fire three or four evenings, in fact we credit those fires for giving us the driest house in town. The last fire cooked the pitch of the wall logs and dried it so hard that it falls off and never sticks to anything. That fire scheme was Dan's idea and a mighty good one.

It was 4 degrees below zero on October 4. We dug sandy dirt rather fast that day, and put a layer 4 inches deep on the moss on our roof. We had to go down by the river for our sand. Up to date we have not seen any water leak through. Jorgenson has to shovel the snow off his roof after every storm as the heat in the cabin melts the snow on the top and it comes in. Thompson's leaks a little now and then.

Next we pitched in enough sand to cover our floor 4 inches deep. It is not every one who has a real floor such as we have. The others laid poles and some covered them with clean gravel. But we sport a board floor. Last summer when Brink, White and Fred Mack were up here, they made sluice boxes and had lots of lumber left over. They gave us all the boxes and lumber and this we converted into a good board floor. There are cracks in the floor, wide enough to drop a knife through, but the size and number of them makes a draft or cold floor impossible. We too banked up all around the cabin. The floor boards being only 12 feet long left a space 2 feet wide at the west side of the cabin, but that does not matter, we filled it in with poles. We moved in the minute the floor was laid. Thursday afternoon, October 6, there was not a thing in the cabin, only the floor, but that answered every purpose. We ate, slept, drank, cooked, or played cards on the floor or on hastily arranged boxes, until we could find time to make better arrangements, and even yet, October 30, two boxes serve for a table.

As it is easier to eat on the floor than it is to sleep on it, we first went to work on our bunks. Four posts, from a rectangle 3 by 7 feet. Two cleats are nailed head and floor and on those rest about a dozen poles not that much bigger than my thumb nailed at one end only. These poles make a spring that can't be duplicated back home. Of course we have a mattress to prevent any one particular hole from getting too prominent. For the mattress we crossed the river, went down 500 feet and out the fringe of tall dry

10. Getting Ready for Winter

grass that hung out over the river. We used the butcher knife to cut the grass, slashing it so that it fell out on the clear ice that had formed all along the edge of the river. At one place the river was frozen entirely across but not enough to hold us, but we threw our bundle of hay across on the ice and dragged it to the cabin. The other inhabitants of Bedrock went up a gulch some two miles for their hay and while they found lots of it, they had a time getting it home. How did we sleep that night! Only a hole for a window and a canvas door, but warm as toast even when one foot wandered out from under the blanket. First real bed since we left home.

Last summer, I found an old rocker; Dan and I fixed it and used it here, before we went to Dawson. Afterward I put a wheel and handles on it and it became a wheelbarrow. At present, that same aggregation of boards furnishes us with eight shelves, some board, some narrow, some short, some long, but the old rocker certainly served us well.

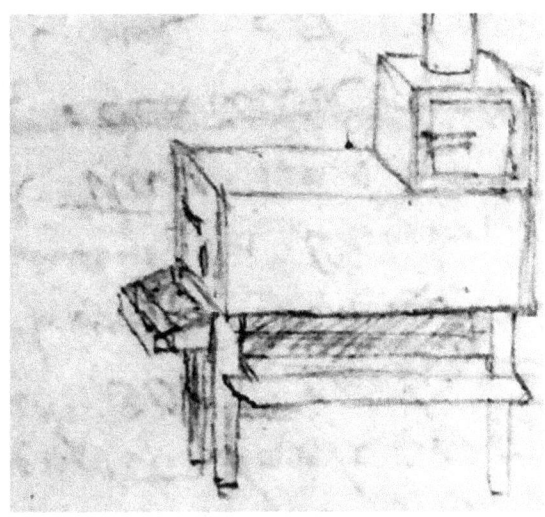

A Klondike stove.

While waiting for the river to freeze and become a public highway, I made our door casing and door, from what was left of the sluice box lumber. The door is no beauty, but all the cracks around the door are packed with moss. Moss is like charity, will keep out lots of cold if used properly.

Next I made a wooden frame to hold our stove, a spittoon, a water pail, and two chairs. The stove has four 2 inch round legs 18 inches high with a shelf 4 inches below, extending back of the stove and under it and in front of it, and a little box of sand to catch sparks from the firing door.

The spittoon is a simple but useful affair; details will be furnished if needed. The water pail, for river water, to be used for dishwashing, etc., was once a butter tub. The tub Dan and I packed on our backs, several miles up Lake Bennett. A little soap and hot water, together with a five-eighths inch rope handle, made a very good pail of it.

The works of art, and the envy of the whole town, are the two high back chairs that I made. They are made for use and comfort; when I sit in one I can just feel myself grow stronger. Until you have tried it, for eight months at a time, you don't know how impossible it is to find any kind of sitting posture that is comfortable, other than a chair with a back to it. To lie on the grass is comfortable enough, or to prop against a tree, but a three legged stool is torture, when you wish to get near a light and try to be comfortable. The pitch of the back makes the chair easy to tilt back against the wall, and be comfortable. The canvas seat of one chair reads "4 Peaches 1 Apricots."

A chair fashioned from Klondike wood and canvas sacks.

On the other is the inscription: "'From Winship Bros. Co. Wholesale Grocers & Outfitters, Seattle, Wash."

The canvas backs also have a certain hieroglyphics reminding me that they are dining chairs. These canvas sacks, that once protected our grub, are made to serve many purposes here, one of the most common being to patch pants. It is not uncommon to see a man wearing a pair of blue overalls, with a large white patch on the seat, bearing the inscription "HAMS." On the front of either leg, other patches extending from the pocket holes to below the knees (to cover all the many holes at one patch) one labeled "WHITE BEANS" and the other "ROLLED OATS."

But to return to the chairs (an ever pleasant return). They are made just like civilized chairs, with three quarter inch holes bored half way through the legs and rungs fitted tight in the holes. These are held by wooden pegs driven into one quarter inch holes bored through both legs and rungs. At the top of the left rear leg, a hole is bored of a size to hold a candle, and there is the lamp, a part of the chair. They beat anything in town, and consequently we have more company than chairs, but we only had room for two chairs in the house, so I made nine three legged stools and stored them outside until needed.

We couldn't make tables without lumber, and we hadn't a board. Dan got out the table legs three weeks ago, but now they will soon be under the table. We went up to Jorgenson's sawpit, cut a 13 inch tree, rolled a 16 foot log on the pit and cut off two slabs, which made two more shelves. Friday, we marked the log into 4 boards 1 inch thick, 8 inches wide, and 5 boards a half inch thick and 8 inches wide, and sawed part of it. Saturday, October 29 we finished the job, brought home the lumber and now it is seasoning up overhead in our cabin. When seasoned (three or four days) part of it becomes a table 2.5 feet by 4.5 feet with two drawers; part of it will be a washtub, square, but just as serviceable as a round one; part of it will be made into a good rocker to wash any dust we may find this winter. And the nine three legged stools will take some of it. I would like to add that Dan and I sawed that log without a swear word, or a jawing match, a feat which to my knowledge has never been equaled in the annals of whip-sawing. The lumber gives evidence of that fact, for it is as smooth and straight and true as if sawed by machinery.

Now I shall begin to mend my socks and patch my pants. We provided a space for a three cornered fireplace in the southwest corner of the cabin, but I don't ever expect to build it. Jorgenson has a fireplace, and also Thompson. Thompson's throws smoke into the room and smoke up the chimney. I think we'll call our cabin completed and furnished.

While I've been making furniture, Dan has kept equally busy; outside he cuts wood and brings water while I get the grub, and cutting wood is a real item, for we use lots of it, dry pine, which burns fast. Dan landscaped our front yard, and cut a trail to the spring, 200 feet northwest of the cabin, where we get our drinking water, and helped Ford build a roof of boughs over the spring to keep snow out. That spring comes right out of the side of the mountain, cold clear water, just like artesian water, and a big improvement over the red Indian River water.

Dan also closed in the west side of our front porch to make a wood shed and built a sawbuck about 8 feet long which we use to saw our firewood. He also built a rustic bower out back of the cabin, which though not beautiful is good, in its way.

He cut steps in the bank leading to the river, and to our wash water hole, and he built a cache in the three trees in front of the cabin to hold our bacon. (See sketch Number 1.) We have a towel rack and a lot of nails back of the stove, with a fancy candlestick for the table made of a stick with a hole in it, nailed to a section of a tree for a stand. Grocery boxes with the covers made into shelves, serve as cupboards when firmly nailed to the wall.

A large tin coffee can, picked up somewhere, serves as an excellent mousetrap, when set out on the wood pile. The first day I caught seven nice fat little red mice, with stubby tails and since that have one nearly every morning for breakfast. How surprised the mouse must be when for the first time he can't climb. None of them have come into the house yet, but the wood pile being within a foot of the door, I shall keep it clean of mice, and so the house.

So much for our cabin and its contents. This is a letter long. Please don't publish it broadcast, and invite Mrs. Tom, Dick and Harry to hear it read. I have written it to you and for you, and believing you would be interested in all the little ins and outs, I've put them all in. It should interest Will, for he likes to "make things," but I know Dad would rather have a letter saying "Have spent six weeks building cabin and furniture and a warmly housed for the winter." When he finishes reading this, if he ever gets through it all, he will wonder what it has to do with "gold prospects." Most people want to hear about million dollar nuggets and not "nasty stuffy little cabins." I believe Grandma would like to hear it read, but I'll bet she would not wade through it herself and Aunt Net will say "For Heaven's sake, why doesn't he write less, and spend more time looking for gold."

I imagine you prefer this letter weight for weight.

Wallis

11

Winter on Indian River

Hauling Our Outfit to Bedrock City

While we were most busily occupied in building our cabin, our bacon, tea and potatoes gave out all at once, and we had to make a trip to the Mouth for more grub. Luckily the river was frozen so that we could cross it in many places, and could walk on the ice along the edges almost anywhere.

It took only three hours to travel the 12 miles to the Mouth, and we decided long before arriving there that we would bring back a big load of grub on one of the sleds, which we had left in our big boat near our cache.

The Nielsens were nearly ready to move into their cabin at the mouth of Arena Gulch. About half a mile below them, we took the short cut over the mountain, then cut around the next mountain, followed the river for half a mile and then cut across to the Yukon.

Imagine our surprise when we found that our boat, oars, and sleds were gone, probably taken by someone who really believed they had been abandoned by their owners. Our cache of grub had not been disturbed. On inquiry at the headquarters of the Mounted Police, one of them remembered having seen the boat within a week. We really needed the sleds. One of the Police told me of another abandoned boat with sleds in it, but I couldn't find it, although I hunted for it for an hour or more.

So we started back up river with only 10 or 15 pounds of grub in each pack-strap, and it didn't take much time or effort to get back to Bedrock in time for supper.

Saturday, October 15, we went to the mouth again and brought back half our cache, each of us hauling some 450 pounds on his borrowed sled. That would be a big job back home but only a small job here. Our only hard work was to keep our feet on the glare ice. Snow had fallen a few days before but the river had overflowed and frozen and so was almost entirely covered with glare ice. How nicely the sled slipped along over it. And how we slipped on it in spite of our ice creepers. There were four or five places where we had to drag the loads over grass and stones on shore to get around an impassable place on the river, for the riffles were still open in places, although the water was not a foot deep anywhere.

I broke my left ice creeper at the last bad place, two miles below home, and slipped on the ice soon afterward, twisting my knee enough so that I could not make another trip on Monday, although I didn't notice anything the matter on Sunday. So Dan went alone on Monday and a tough time he had. It had snowed, just about 2 inches but that 2 inches ruined the nice sledding. The snow slipped on the ice when he stepped on it, and piled up in front of the sled runners like so much sand. He brought 350 pounds as far as Nielsen's that day and finished the trip on Tuesday.

Wednesday, October 19, we both went again and brought back everything; about 300 pounds each and we brought our good luck with us. The day was the warmest in October, going up to 48 degrees and there was a breeze blowing, a most rare occurrence. The result was that before we got started back the heat and the wind had softened the snow and made it slushy, so that it made walking easy, and the sled slipped along as smoothly as on glare ice. We felt so good at having all our goods safely stored in our cabin that we just loafed the balance of the week. And it was in that thankful, lazy good mood that I wrote that long letter, about building our cabin.

The Nielsen Party are such good friends of ours and the nearest neighbors to Bedrock City, so I must introduce them. We always stop to visit them when we travel the river, and we frequently exchange visits. Captain John Nielsen organized this party of four, brought them in, left them on Indian River and went back to the States in midsummer. Chris Nielsen, the younger brother of Captain Nielsen, who succeeded him as head of the party, is a Dane, who for most of his life, has been sailing with Captain John, recently his mate. Chris thinks that John is the greatest man on earth, and it's always "My Bruder this or that." Chris is all right, but he does like to argue. And he will yarn away indefinitely, as long as he can hold an audience.

Fred Melby, the most quiet of the party, is a Norwegian, has spent 20 years in California ranching and placer mining. Has a wife and three kids and does not say much, but is a very nice fellow.

John Mohlman is a Hanover German and a sailor from boyhood. Has been everywhere and done most all kinds of work. Tells a rather truthful appearing yarn, but I don't say his yarns are true. He has an innocent German air about him. For the past seven years he has sailed under Captain Nielsen in a sailing vessel. Gets drunk once in two years, says he never yet looked for a job, the job always found him out.

The Nielsen's are the only party of three that ever succeeded in sticking together and keeping friendly and I figure they stick because each of the three feels that he is the partner and personal representative of the absent Captain John. They all talk with a Scandinavian accent and are always ready to lend a hand wherever needed. I have referred to them frequently as the Nielsen Party. You will become better acquainted with them as the story develops.

Close to the Nielsen cabin, there was another, inhabited by a party who generally went by the name of "The Frenchmen." I remember that two of them were named Phil White and Achille Dubray. The third was Wallie Lambert. Possible we never knew the full names of the other. We made many friends whom we knew only as Tom, Dick, or Harry, which was all right at the time, but rather inconvenient later. Dubray was a real Frenchman, his address being 133 Rue Grand, Le Vallois Perret, France.

Getting Acquainted with Winter Weather

One rule of polite society says, "Talk of anything except the weather." There is one exception, the Klondiker has that privilege. So first I'll explain the official weather report, which consists entirely of cold facts. I never expected to bother myself about details of the weather. We brought a thermometer along because it was given to us. The thermometer is the only thing we got in Seattle that didn't cost us something. The hardware clerk made me a present of it, but he probably made it up somewhere else. It's a nice instrument, alcohol of course, and reads from minus 80 degrees to plus 120 degrees. In the alcohol column there is a little jigger shaped thusly: .___. and almost about that size. I learned at college (and forgot immediately) that such a jigger would record the minimum temperature. I had noticed it in my thermometer but had never tried to utilize it.

October 1, 2 and 3 were nice enough days. We were still living in our tent. We felt rather too chilly as we slept, but that was nothing. In the middle of July it had sometimes been rather chilly during the night. Dan and I began to get curious as to just what the temperature might be, so I got the thermometer, found how to get the minimum temperature and set it out overnight. Four below zero is what the little jigger registered. Then I thought how easy it would be to keep a record of the weather and how interesting it might be sometime. So I started my weather report and kept a copy of it on a piece of Profile Paper (see Chapter 12, December and January Weather, for example).

Each column represents a day of the month, numbered at the top. The horizontal lines are the same as on a thermometer. The ragged frosty lines show the ups and downs of the thermometer for each succeeding day. Every morning I note what the lowest point was during the night, as recorded by the jigger. Then after dinner I look again. That reading may not be the highest of the day but it is not very far wrong. The little rows of letters you will find explained on the diagram. You'll see two and sometimes three for each day. One is for the weather in the morning and the other for the afternoon. Then if there is a noticeable change before the next day I put in a third letter for the weather during the night.

Ten inches of snow fell on October 25 and 26. It came down perfectly straight, and not a breath of air. Next morning, every stump, every log, every branch of a tree, anything and everything was covered with 10 inches of snow, none more, none less. Little twigs as big around as a lead pencil, had snow piled on them, and it wasn't wet snow either. Woe to him who walks under one of these branches. A touch of the hat and down comes the load of snow. Pass by a tree, a small sapling, and hit it with your arm. Down comes a regular snowslide. A little tuft falls from the top, strikes a bigger bunch just below and together they go down, making a clean sweep. The breezy days of November 13–15 have been rather hard on these snow piles. Many have been blown down, but there are plenty left, as I find every day, when I go ducking through the brush looking after my rabbit snares (see below). That 10 inches of snow fall is the heaviest yet. The others are only one or two inches.

The first week in November was bright and cold all the time. Never a cloud in the sky, day or night. But on those brightest days it snowed half an inch to an inch several times. What little moisture there was in the air just froze out of it. This frozen air moisture about makes up for the settling of the regular snow. During the night of November 15 the wind drifted some of this snow onto the trail and next morning as I plowed my way through it, it was just like kicking up a dust on a country road in August. The heavier particles would fall at once, but the fine stuff rose in clouds.

Our front door, like all other Klondike doors, lets in quite a bit of daylight. That permits a draught, and draughts kill folks, but these Klondike draughts are easy to handle. We can see them, and avoid sitting in one, for each and every draft is painted white by Jack Frost.

As you look over the temperature curves, notice how the bright and the cloudy weather brings on cold or warm temperatures. See the sudden drop November 11 when the sky cleared for a few hours. As you view "those horrid cold snaps" on the diagram, I suppose you'll wonder "if the poor child managed to keep warm," and also if a drop of 10 degrees more will finish him. Well he has loafed around out of doors, in sweater and blue jean pants, with the alcohol at minus 50 degrees and is back inside, alive and ready to tell this tale.

On October 13 my diary states that that in going a quarter mile to Thompson's cabin to play cards, "The wind made a sweater and undershirt feel insufficient." But since that time, there being no wind, such wear has been comfortable.

The morning of October 29, zero and twenty below, looks cold on paper, but Dan and I didn't find it so. We were whipsawing, I in the same old shirt and sweater combination that I wore in the heat of summer, and a blue jean jumper to keep me warm when we stopped work, but, we did have to wear mittens that day. I remember having quite a time hunting for mine, had not needed them before. The log we sawed was just like oak or hard maple, frozen full of sap. By the third of November we were acclimated to 20 degrees below and no longer thought of it as cold weather. Nobody ever thought of covering ears or nose at 20 degrees below, unless it be old Thompson, and mittens were worn only for style.

November 6, rather takes your breath away, at 36 to 42 below. Well it surprised us to see the way the old thermometer bottom fell out the evening before. The town was at our cabin playing cards and they all expected to freeze before they could get back to their cabins, yet all survived. November 6 being Sunday, nobody worked. We just visited around, and wondered if it would ever get cold enough so that we could feel it. Well it did, next day.

Dan had started a prospect hole up above Stemple's cabin, about one-half mile from here. A half-mile beyond that, there is a flat just swarming with rabbits. On Sunday I made a box trap and laid half a dozen snares. Monday after diner, when it was some 30 degrees below, I put on my mackinaw hat, a pair of the big sheep skin mittens, and went up to my rabbit patch to bring home the bunnies. I didn't freeze my ears, but they would have felt better if I had worn a cap. My nose also got rather cold. On my feet I had a pair of woolen socks, a pair of nips and a pair of mucklucks. The nips are about like those rubber boot socks Dad sent me when I worked at Hammond. The mucklucks are shapeless affairs like boots made by the Eskimos. They are soft and pliable, the soles made of a single thickness of walrus hide, and the tops, coming up nearly to the knee are made of a paper like hide of the sea lion, with the hair removed. My feet were perfectly comfortable, queer too, as I never could keep them warm at home in freezing weather.

Placing rabbit snares is not the best kind of cold weather job. The rabbits run about in the snow, break a plain trail and then follow that trail in their later rambles. To set a snare, find two little saplings between which the rabbit trail runs, notch them both, cut a cross stick to fit, trim a small sapling standing nearby for a spring, tie the snare to the cross stick and the cross stick to the spring and bunny is yours. It's easy enough to tell about and easy to do, only it can't be done with a big clumsy pair of mittens on your hands. And it is a rather slow job if you never set one before. And with the thermometer down near minus 35 degrees, it is no small job to whittle green twigs. They resemble hickory in hardness and if you ever touched anything really cold, these pine twigs are even colder. I made two snares in two hours, counting the time I had to stop and beat my arms, after setting the first one.

Thinking so continually about my fingers, I quite forgot my nose and ears and paid no attention to the small avalanches of snow that I shook from every twig and branch down my neck, into my pockets and down the baggy front of my hand-me-down blue jean pants. And it was nearly dark then (3:00 P.M.). I only set two snares, beat my hands warm and came back.

I had made up my mind to have rabbit pie for Thanksgiving, so I went up there again next morning, but I wore my fur cap for my ears' sake. I carried the shotgun, and near my rabbit patch saw signs of some half dozen wolves that had come down river the night before and gone into my hunting grounds. It's impossible to get within half a mile of one wolf but I've heard that in larger numbers they are not so timid. So before going into the patch I took a look at my shotgun. Snow had got in around the trigger and hammer, the heat of my hand had melted some of it and the hammer was frozen hard and fast. I'd like a wolf skin, but would prefer shooting him rather than choking him, so I came home again and left the rabbits to the wolves.

That afternoon I took a bath, changed my clothes and dressed for the cold weather. I put a light wool shirt over my undershirt and put my sweater with the hood over that. It was the hood I was after. That's a great thing. There being no wind, it keeps head and ears perfectly warm and not a flake of snow can get inside it. I go to the rabbit patch every morning, leave the shotgun home and carry the six shooter instead, strapped under my coat where it keeps warm and no snow can get to it. I am sorry to say the wolves have all gone back to the mountains.

The warm spell starting November 10 put the rabbit business on a paying basis. I now have 50 snares at work, got 20 rabbits last Monday and every day I bring back from one to three rabbits, which when dressed will average 2 pounds each. As long as one man can work the hole Dan will keep on digging and I'll quit gold mining for a while and go at something more profitable, the meat and fur business. It requires the good part of a day to do the cooking and carpenter's work, look over and set the snares, skin and clean the rabbits and stretch the skins. These Klondike rabbits are not like the little gray bunnies we have in Illinois. They are much bigger, much like Belgian Hares, with great big hind paws built like snow shoes.

We now have nine rabbit carcasses hanging by our front door frozen hard as granite, also three grouse that I shot last Sunday afternoon, and inside we have nine of the prettiest white rabbit skins you ever saw. They are as soft as angora wool, and the hair long and thick. When the weather warms again, that is gets up to minus 20 degrees, I shall put out more snares and when I get a hundred or more, we shall go to Dawson to see what we can get for them.

Dryness is the great thing in cold weather. Dryness means comfort. Dan had an experience last night. We were cleaning rabbits. We have a big tin can for the refuse. Dan brought it in from outdoors, washed his hands, picked up the can in his wet hands to carry it out again and froze fast to it. And he was there for keeps. He could not get loose until the ends of his fingers froze dry. Then he had to get snow to thaw his fingers. It was a genuine freeze. It wasn't deep, and as soon as thawed ceased to bother him.

Dryness is also the secret to warm feet. Dryness does not necessarily mean forty pairs of socks on the feet. A shoe sole full of nails will draw frost, as a magnet does iron. A stiff sole is not much better. In German socks and rubbers Dan sweats his feet, the moisture works through to the rubber and then turns to ice or snow. When he came in tonight, the whole inside of his rubbers was coated. One of our friends from the Nielsen camp came up this way hunting moose today (no moose either). He had worn stiff hogskin shoe packs and when he got back here this afternoon his feet were cold. He had been out all day. He took off the shoe packs to warm his feet and there was enough frost in them so that he could empty it out like snow.

They are no beauties, but my mucklucks are just the thing for this kind of weather or any other kind that we have found. But for cold weather, after mucklucks, there is nothing like moccasins. They are just right for this country. But don't make the mistake of attempting to wear them in sloppy weather. When a man wears them in zero weather, they will not keep him warm with a single pair of cotton socks inside them. Two pairs of woolen socks may fix them, but one pair of woolen socks and one pair of German socks provide an insulation that will permit a man to wade in snow for an indefinite length of time.

On the evening of November 17 it was particularly still and cold. I took the candle and went out to see how cold it was; 9:10 P.M. and just 50 below zero. Dan and I got so interested in writing our letters that we let the fire go out, but these log cabins are warm if they are built right, and ours is. We never have to boom the stove. The fire is out 10 minutes after we get into bed and in the morning we get up in as comfortable a room as man could want. We go away after breakfast, let the fire go out and when we return at dinner time, we open the door, and feel the nice cozy warmth. I wondered at first what we would do for ventilation, but the hole around the stove pipe settles that. All the smoke from the cooking and our breath too goes up through that hole, and the place always smells as sweet as the air outdoors.

And how the bread does raise, on the little shelf behind the stove. Set it at night, 40 degrees below outside and bake it next day at 2:00 P.M.

I suppose you would like to hear something about "those long winter evenings." About Christmas time I can tell you all about them, but in the middle of November they are hardly long enough to write about, only six or seven hours of candle light. There is something very curious about the way daylight and moonlight and electric light are supplied us here. It gets light every morning about 7:00 A.M., but it gets dark earlier and earlier each day. Now it gets dark at 3:00 P.M. and at 4:00 P.M. the stars shine as brightly as they do at 10:00. And as for sunlight, none has touched the cabin in November. These three rather curious facts are not hard to explain. The river valley runs almost due east and west. Across the river, some 500 feet from our cabin is a big flat about 125 feet above us. It runs south for some two miles, getting very gradually higher and then running up into a mountain. The same flat runs up river about two miles before coming to another mountain. To the southeast the flat is cut by a gulch that runs back 10 or 15 miles. The flat to the east and gulch southeast gives us all the daylight there is in the morning. The sun is so low that it is not visible until nearly noon. And even then it is not high enough to peep over the flat opposite us, and down into the river valley where we are located. The sun shines brightly on the mountains back of us and in the morning we see it just brush the top of the mountain west of us, thus making plenty of daylight, but no sunlight. West of us about 1000 feet, a mountain rises up, and extends down to the south far enough so that at 2:00 P.M. we can see the shadow of this mountain cast upon another mountain behind us, and above the shadow the last bit of sunlight. Then in a little bit a higher mountain farther to the southwest shuts out the sun altogether.

We can make a pretty fair guess as to when and where we shall find the sun. The moon just runs wild. The seal of that quart of brandy has never been broken, but it is a fact that the moon supplied to Klondikers is not run on any schedule time. I've always been taught that all moons rose an hour later each evening, but I've been getting experience in moons. When the moon rose at 8:00 P.M. one day, 7:00 P.M. the next and 6:00 P.M. the third day, I was not much surprised that almost everything works backwards up here, or I might be mistaken; it might be that the moon ought to rise an hour earlier each succeeding day. So I waited patiently for a month to see whether it would do the same thing next time. One night about 9:00 P.M. up pops the moon, squarely to the south of us. He must have seen a surprised look on my face, for he only stayed up about 10 minutes and then ducked his head and disappeared. Next night, at 5:00, off to the east of us, the moon came up smiling, just as if nothing had happened, and sailed across the heavens just like a civilized moon. But next night he failed to show up until 8:00 P.M. and then in the northeast and I lost all confidence in Klondike moons. Perhaps you know what ails the Klondike moon. Perhaps it is the outline and elevation of the country.

You may wish to know about the Aurora Borealis. It has a trick on only appearing on bright nights and then the alcohol in the thermometer almost disappears. So about the best description I can give of it is the Englishman's summation: "It's deuced nice doncher know, but a body gets so bloody co-old." I suppose from the top of the mountain behind us we would have a grand view of it. And I'm sure that I don't care enough about it to climb a mountain at 50 below. We have a good display every night after our usual bedtime. Like the moon it is quite a bit irregular in its actions, but it never gets to the south of us. We would enjoy it more if we bundled up instead of running out to see it, with not even a vest over our sweater, and no hat or mittens. One evening it looked like a whole lot of rainbows, the whole north just filled with them. Another time it turned the stripes the other way and presented a half umbrella, bright streaks of fire running down in all directions north, east and west of the zenith. Then plaids becoming stylish, it combined the other two effects and that was a beauty. Sometimes just a bright hazy cloud of fire seems to drift across the sky, changing shape, direction and brightness as it goes. Then again there is a little stage sunrise off to the northeast. One night, when I went out to look at the thermometer, off in the northwest over the top of the mountains was what appeared to be a bright, hot furniture factory fire.

Daily Routine

Perhaps you would be interested in knowing how a day passes here, and why it seems to be so short to us. Yesterday, December 1, was a fair example.

I awake about 5:00 A.M. but we are not early risers, so I turned over for another nap. I just guessed it was 5:00, but it may not have been. Our muslin window was nice and light, but that is no sign, the darker the window the later the time, for the moon sets about 7:00 A.M.

At 7:00 I got up, lit a candle, looked at my watch, to be sure it was not midnight, and then started the fire. 7:00 is about an hour or an hour and a half earlier than we have been getting up, so Dan lay for a few minutes longer.

As usual I went out to see how the thermometer stood. It was 30 degrees below zero, evidently we were to have a nice comfortable day. The moon was just above the mountain over west of us, and in the east all was black, not the faintest sign of dawn. The stars were all working and helped the moon light things so that I could read the thermometer.

The fire having a fine start, I put on the coffee pot (used indiscriminately for tea or coffee) and the oatmeal dish, then mixed a Johnnie Cake, the egg for it having been soaked overnight. Very inconvenient for the cook, to be obliged to soak anything for a day or so, before it can be brought out of its evaporated state.

Dan thought he had slept enough and got up. He generally is up first and has the coffee pot on before I roll out. As soon as dressed he took the water pail and went back to our spring for water. These Yukon stoves are fast cookers, so the Johnnie Cake was ready soon after Dan returned from the spring with the water. The water in the coffee pot was boiling, so I dumped in the tea and set off the pot. I burned my fingers setting the oatmeal dish on the table. Dan sliced some bacon and I fried it. The milk can being empty, Dan filled it with water and flavored it with condensed milk. Our big quart pail of lima beans had warmed up on top of the oven, so we sat down to breakfast.

Dan rinsed out the teapot while I put away the salt, pepper, etc. The frying pan of bacon fat was very carefully emptied into our lard can. Bring lard with you when you make a trip up here. We have found by experience that it is difficult to get enough grease to fry doughnuts, even though we eat bacon three times a day and seven days a week.

Dish washing is a picnic, the dishes get a regular picnic wash. We used one of our gold pans, until one day Dan picked a dish pan out of the bottom of the river. We don't use many dishes so we only need a little water and it soon heats. If we are to have dish water clinging to the clean dishes we prefer it free from soap, so we don't use soap except on extra occasions, when things are very greasy.

With a good substantial foundation of lima beans and oatmeal, we were ready to go to work. Our everyday trousers are overalls, so we don't cover them, but when working we put on a jumper to keep our sweaters clean. Nobody wears a vest here, and a coat, a mackinaw-coat, only when walking or standing around out of doors. We put on our mackinaws, went out, down to the river and up river on a well beaten trail, for about a half mile to the place where we are sinking a prospect hole. The hole is 12 feet deep, just too deep to throw the dirt out, without killing ourselves. So we work it up in two throws. Dan throws it onto a little platform we built at one end, about 7 feet below the surface. I throw it from there to the surface, and then while Dan picks a fresh layer loose, I shovel the dirt back from the edge of the hole. The fire we had put in the day before was a good one and thawed down about 18 inches. The hole is about 4 feet by 7 feet and the gravel is now very course, with lots of rocks as big as my head and every now and then one than nearly gets away from me on the end of the rope. We worked as though we expected pay for it, until 11:30. Then having cleaned out all that had been thawed, we went home to a dinner very much like breakfast, but one that went right to the spot as all dinners should. It was 1:00 before we were through with the dishes and Dan's pipe of tobacco.

On my way home to dinner I had stopped at First Avenue to say hello to Stemple and

Karr, then stopped to chat with old Carl Jorgenson for five minutes. He was just taking up the ever present beans, expecting his two boys down from their hole on the hill, at any moment. Carl has started a hole just off Second Avenue and wishing to see how it was progressing I went down Second Avenue to the river. A little this side of Second Avenue and 50 feet from the river Thompson has started a hole. Hearing him picking away at it I looked in. He is a worn out old man, with no business up here, of all places. He is a little man and looks 82 instead of 52. The whole town is unanimous in declaring him an awful bore, but I felt mighty sorry for him as he straightened up to say hello. He had been picking and shoveling for two or three hours and didn't straighten up all at once. He took the kinks out of his back by degrees. I know how kinks feel that is, young half grown kinks, but I could imagine what is old full grown kinks were like. His white tobacco trimmed whiskers were filled with icicles of frozen breath mixed with the dirt that flies from the pick. He smiled a smile that showed several of those backachy kinks said, "By gosh, Wal, this is pretty darned hard work, ain't it. I guess I bit off a pretty big chunk. I think I won't try to do so much all at once. What's the weather last night?"

Everybody in town is keeping a weather report, I have the only thermometer, and it keeps me busy to keep in mind the temperature for a week back. The usual greeting from any of our neighbors is "Hello Wal, what was the weather last night? And say what was it last Sunday, I missed that?"

Thompson began his hole last Saturday. He is now a little over two feet deep, digging in frozen muck and clay and sand. Such stuff can be picked out much faster than it can be burned, but he has discovered that it is much easier to spend a half day getting wood enough to thaw out four inches of sand, than it is to pick out a foot of it in the same time it takes to get the wood. That is, it is easier on the back than so much picking. After getting to gravel it will be different. It is impossible to pick this frozen gravel. It is just as hard and tough as the granite rocks of which it's composed.

But I've wandered away from my text of yesterday's happenings. After dinner, Dan went up to our hole again, and cut wood for another fire that kept us shoveling until 1:00 P.M. today.

This afternoon, I planned to go up river to what I call my Rabbit Patch, a flat inhabited by thousands of rabbits, many of which are foolish enough to poke their heads through the snares set there, just to see how they work. Just as I was starting out, two of our suburban friends came up the river. One of them Chris Nielsen came from the camp four miles below us. He was followed by his dog Jumbo, dragging a sled with Nielsen's coat, blanket and gun on it. The other man was from Nine Mile Creek, some 12 miles above here. Nielsen also had some butter with him that he was taking to Nine Mile, to trade for meat at the rate of one pound of butter for two ribs of a steer. The steer was one that escaped from a drove pastured over on the Yukon and had wandered over to Nine Mile where he was promptly shot. I swapped news with these two on our way to my Rabbit Patch, then I dove into the bushes and snow, over bunch grass and under trees that are always looking for a chance to slip a small snowslide down one's neck. The result was two rabbits, with the snares frozen so fast in their fur that I had to bring home snare and all. It was 3:00 P.M. before I got back to the cabin, and the stars were shining.

I stopped again at First Avenue. Stemple and Karr have a hole on the bench across the river. They are down 30 feet and when I went in they were just washing some gravel they had brought from the whole. They got one color, as big around as a pin head and not so thick, but it's the best yet for that hole. George Trowbridge was there and Frank Reed soon came in. Having some cooking to do I soon left and came straight home. I set some yeast bread, which was cooked in time for supper tonight, in spite of the 27 degrees below. I chopped up some dried figs, expecting to experiment a little and convert it into a fig filling for a cake that I shall make tomorrow. Then I got supper and Dan came in when it was ready, he also having visited all along the line on his way.

After supper Stemple and Karr visited us and we played whist until 10:15. It was card games of one kind or another every evening after supper. Dan took off his shoes and smoked his pipe as usual before turning in. I fixed my diary and weather report in short order and was sound asleep before he had finished smoking.

So much for one day. The other days are not materially different. It's a very free-and-easy go-as-you-please kind of life, but to me is not at all unpleasant. We have become accustomed to not reading the newspapers and the controversy about the free coinage of silver does not worry us anymore. When we dig a new prospect hole now, we don't dig for gold, we dig to get to the bottom of the hole; that done, dig another. But if we should happen to find gold in the bottom of one of them, I fear we are just mercenary enough to stop and gather it.

Thanksgiving Day Celebration

There was a station of the Mounted Police at the mouth of the Indian River. This made it a convenient place for a road house, so a couple of men, Jack McDonald, and Arthur Hewitt saw the need and built a log cabin which soon became known as "McDonald's Road House."

Hewitt had graduated as a mining engineer from the University of California in 1894, and had been in the Klondike for two years, had some money and wanted more.

Besides the road house, they hauled freight up the Indian River to the mines on Dominion, Sulphur and Quartz Creeks.

On Tuesday, November 22, with the thermometer at 45 degrees below zero, we suddenly decided that we ought to make a trip to the Mouth to get some late newspapers for Thanksgiving Day.

Frank Reed and George Trowbridge felt that they should have a couple of bottles of McDonald's whiskey for Thanksgiving, so they accompanied us. We got started about 10:00 A.M. with the thermometer still at 45 degrees below zero. We travelled single file that being all that the width of trail would permit.

The trail was fair, but once we almost got our feet wet, at a place where the river ice had cracked, and the water had wet the snow that lay on the ice. We stopped at Nielsen's long enough to say hello, and mushed on.

Dan was leading the way, and without warning a big piece of ice that had been left, high and dry above a dry gravel bar, broke off and let him down. If there had been water enough to wet his feet we would have had to rush him back to Nielsen's cabin, but luckily there was no water under the broken ice bridge, to wet his feet.

When we reached the Mouth, we found that the Thompson Party's big boat had been crushed by the shifting ice jambs that continually occur upon the Yukon, while it is freezing for the winter. The boat had been badly crushed, filled with water, and was frozen in a sheet of ice of indefinite thickness. The Yukon River out in the middle had a nice coat of ice, fairly clear of snow, and the packers had made a fine horse trail and were putting lots of merchandise into Dawson.

McDonald and Hewitt's road house stood high up on a clay bank, well above the reach of the river. We climbed from the trail on the river, to the top of this clay bank, by the aid of a long knotted rope, anchored there for that purpose.

They had a big log house, with a lean-to, also a barn to the south of it, which at the time was piled full of merchandise. Inside the main building was a rough bar at the left, with shelves and four empty whiskey bottles back of the bar; also two open boxes of "Bedrock Bouquet" cigars, put out by the North American Trading and Transportation Company, commonly known as "N.A.T. Co." There were various other odds and ends on the shelves, and on the bar itself, a carpenter was constructing a gold dust scale box, containing the drawer for gold dust taken in payment for goods and services; while the scales were securely mounted on top of the box.

One window at the left of the door lighted the bar, another at the right, lighted a large round table. The sheet iron stove occupied the center of the room, directly in front of the door. A bench or two, a few stools, and some short pieces of tree trunks furnished seats.

A merchant bringing in supplies sat at the table writing a letter.

The entire back part of the main building was cut into six bunks, two high, boarded up on the side nearest the office, with the center left open for light.

The lean-to showed four bunks, and proved to be the kitchen, dining room and family bed room.

Hewitt was glad to see us and sorry that the whiskey was temporarily exhausted, but would we all have a cigar. As we visited we heard a great noise out on the ice, and found the cause of it to be some eight or ten mule teams dragging big sled loads on the ice to Dawson. The first load consisted entirely of cigars; the others consisted of insulated wire, and various boxes and barrels, such as electrical goods are generally packed in. It was in fact the major part of Dawson City's new electric light plant.

While we waited for lunch, two parties came into the road house. Two young fellows named Burns and McRay were going up Indian River to Nine Mile Creek. The other four with a fine dog team were going back to Skagway. (Burns appears later in the story.)

McDonald had gone to Dawson and would not be back for a couple of days, so we accepted Hewitt's hospitality, of a lunch consisting of bread, butter and coffee, (without sugar or cream) and started back for Bedrock at 3:00 P.M. just at dark, the moon full bright and the stars just beginning to shine.

Halfway back to Nielsen's there were two cabins, which we knew only as the "Scurvy Cabins." Scurvy we know is caused by a lack of vitamin C in the diet. We thought then that a lack of vegetables and fresh meat caused scurvy. The men at these cabins had scurvy, and we stopped to see how they were getting along. The Nielsens had been doctoring them and they were responding nicely to the treatment, but the cabins and furnishings were very crude. One cabin was built on a hillside, all open under the floor, requiring a fire kept day and night to be anywhere near comfortable.

At Nielsen's we had bread and coffee for supper and stayed to play a game of pinochle, while Dan visited the Frenchmen in the next cabin. We left about 8:00 and were back home by bedtime. George and Frank got no whiskey, and Dan and I got no papers, but we had all seen some new faces and discussed new topics.

Wednesday morning Thompson came over and woke us up at 10:30 and built our fire for us. While we were eating our breakfast Burns and McRay came up from the road house and ate with us. Then I got busy with preliminary cooking for Thanksgiving. I greatly enjoyed Thanksgiving Day and so did Dan. Thompson said, "I wonder what I have to be thankful for, to be alive, I suppose."

After a fairly early breakfast, I made a raisin pie. George Trowbridge brought over a can of St. Charles Evaporated Cream, to trade for a can of Eagle Brand Condensed Milk. We liked the cream on our pie, and they liked the sweetened milk for their coffee. I stuffed three grouse for roasting and Dan sawed wood to get up an appropriate appetite.

When Thompson dropped in, while I was cooking the grouse, Trowbridge promptly left. I couldn't get away, because of the grouse, so I had to wait patiently while Thompson wrote several days in his diary, and told me a few of his personal experiences for the fortieth time.

After Thompson left, Bert Karr came in with a live rabbit that he had rescued from one of my snares. It was fearfully frightened and hid in a dark corner, when Bert let him loose in the cabin.

When Bert left, Dan came in for dinner. We had baked grouse, stuffed with bread dressing flavored with wild sage which we found in the summer, growing very profusely. We also ate potatoes, but left the lima beans and evaporated carrots untasted on the stove. Dan ate a slice of bread and we forgot the apricot sauce cooling outdoors. One grouse, each, with stuffing and gravy and onion pickles, filled us completely. How nice the meat of that grouse. Tender and sweet and just enough flavor of pine, to tell us that it was a wild bird.

And then big sections of raisin pie, smothered in sugar and St. Charles evaporated cream, and we were just pleasantly uncomfortable. George dropped in to say hello and leave each of us one of his good cigars.

While we washed dishes, Frank came in and stayed until Dan and I finished the cigars. We smoked and watched the rabbit wash his face, always just one jump from his hiding place under Dan's bunk.

Then Dan and I went to visit our neighbors. We had never seen the Thompson cabin so cheery and comfortable. The fireplace was booming and not smoking. The stove was being used to get dinner. They took turns cooking. George and Ford cooked that week, so Thompson was taking a nap, while Frank watched George and Ford stuff rabbits, make gravy, etc. On one shelf was a nice chocolate cake that made my mouth water even though I had a full stomach. On the shelves were plates of potato balls and other odds and ends to be cooked at the last moment. A rice pudding came from the oven and rested on the window until needed. Then the rabbits went into the oven.

Dan and I left and went to Jorgenson's. The boys were out and old Carl sat reading and getting dinner. The rabbits were cooking in the Dutch oven, behind it a big pot of rice, a relic of Carl's New Zealand training. Three big cups of apricot sauce stood cooling on the table. Dan and I had supplied dried apricots but couldn't spare any sugar. I wondered at the time if I could be as jolly and contented and good natured as Carl, if I had to eat Thanksgiving dinner without sugar.

The boys arrived, and soon Emil was playing his mouth organ, Dan singing and I whistling. We spent a most enjoyable half hour, talking about our prospects, which was Carl's favorite topic.

While Carl added water to the boiling rice, every now and then, and rolled hard tack, with which to thicken the gravy, he told us a long yarn about his woman. I wish I could give his exact words and dialect.

Some sixteen years before he had failed in the general hard times in New Zealand, saving only his furniture from the house building business he had run, and the fancy goods business run by his "woman." They started for the United States, against her wishes, and landed in Honolulu with $1.80 and six children. He tried without any success to find a job as a carpenter and an overseer. One man to whom he applied asked if he could do anything else. "Yes, anything, work in the garden, milk—" "Milk!! Why didn't you say so before." So Carl got a job on the plantation, and was soon handling all the carpenter work too, and getting $125.00 per month and board. He built a house and moved the family out to the plantation and then the trouble started. She wouldn't stay on the plantation, so his boss gave him a job in Honolulu at the same pay. That didn't suit her either. She wanted him out in the country while she in turn drew all his pay each month. When Carl found how the land lay he announced that from that time, he would wear the pants. She had him arrested and as the prison door closed behind him, he swore never to let her have another cent. She sued for a divorce on the grounds of non-support, but couldn't prove a case. As Hawaiian law does everything for the woman, he kept entirely clear of her, until the night before he was to leave for San Francisco.

Then he went to her house to kiss his babies goodbye and she tried to have him arrested, but the Yankee captain of the boat hid him in a chest while the police inspector searched the boat. After she spent the money she had saved from his earnings, she followed him to California and got a divorce with $25.00 alimony. Carl was too quick for her. He deeded his homestead in trust to a friend and moved to Humboldt County and went house building again. One after another the children left the Mother and came to Carl. Then she came, trying to collect her $25.00. He left her in his house. He married again and built another house. He tried to settle wife Number 1 on his homestead, bought lumber and was to build her a house. She bought two mules and starved them. The mules died and as they had not been paid for, their owner attached the lumber Carl had bought and she moved back to town.

While Carl debated whether to leave for New Zealand or Denmark, the Klondike was discovered, so here he was with his favorite son, Alfred. When he left Wife Number 1 smiled as she said goodbye, "But not a damn cent do she ever get from me."

The fireplace burned cheerfully, the coffee pot boiled quietly on the back of the stove, and the low steady bubbling from the Dutch oven gave promise of a meal, for which Carl could be truly thankful … thankful too, that he had found a place where his woman would not follow him.

We found Stemple and Karr also cooking rabbit. There were no particular signs of Thanksgiving, unless it be that two candles burned on the table today. Dinner would soon be ready and the cabin was too small for two visitors, so we soon left, taking some of our borrowed books home with us.

Jorgenson's dinner was almost ready too, so we moved on to Thompson's.

There Thompson, George and Frank were seated for the first course and Ford was flying around as a cook and waiter is expected to do. It made Dan and me hungry to see them eat, so we went home, had one-half a cold grouse each, with dressing and gravy warmed up, with carrots on the side, and dessert of raisin pie and cream, cake and cream and apricot sauce.

After reading borrowed magazines for a while, we returned to Thompson's and the entire camp played stud poker until midnight, and when the party broke up we were unanimous in the thought that it had been a day of real enjoyment.

12

Winter at Dawson

Coming Events Cast Their Shadows Before Them

It is easy to see that Bedrock City was a comfortable little camp; life with us was pleasant and in due time we should have welcomed the spring time.

But the human element must always be considered. Dan and I got along perfectly, never a quarrel of any kind. We often had different ideas, but never any disagreement.

Jorgenson and his two boys got along nicely, because the boys never questioned the old man's right to be the boss. But everything was not happy there, because they were never more than a jump and a half ahead of starvation. The boys recovered some forty to fifty dollars' worth of gold dust on the bar above ours, where the Brink party had worked and they were very careful of it. It spelled tragedy for them when they reached bedrock in a prospect hole and failed to find a fortune buried there.

Stemple and Karr had always worked for a living. They got along well together, but by November 21 Stemple was considering moving to Dawson. What he could be certain of earning in Dawson appealed to him more than what he might find on Indian River.

The Thompson party was a queer outfit. Poor old Thompson, the supposed head of the party, didn't have a word to say in the party plans. The other three had no sympathy for him, and according to Thompson, they did about everything they could to annoy him. He told his troubles to Dan, by the hour, and Dan patiently listened to him.

We had jokingly elected Thompson as "Mayor of Bedrock" when we began building our cabins, and two months later it took a lot of electioneering by Dan and me to prevent Thompson from being deprived of the empty honor of being occasionally called "Mayor."

"Ford, Frank and George" is the entry that is repeatedly found in my diary. If they did something, or went somewhere, Thompson was not with them.

With such a combination of human factors, it is easy to see that our pleasant peaceful Thanksgiving was only that quiet calm that precedes one of nature's upheavals.

After Thanksgiving, Dan and I got busy again on the prospect hole we had started, and reached bedrock in our sixth hole at Bedrock City, on December 6 and were again disappointed. My diary says: "We washed out seven pails of bedrock and gravel, and no pay. Now let some of the others find bedrock and pay dirt, before we do any more."

December 6 the weather turned unusually warm, 25 degrees below at night and 30 above at noon. There was also a real old time Illinois breeze blowing, which completely changed the whole appearance of the landscape. The wind stripped every bit of snow from every tree and bush, and the flat pale picture to which we had become accustomed became a study in black, gray, dark green and white, with the sharp contrasts that are seen after a summer rain.

We couldn't be idle, so we tried a new method of prospecting. We had heard so much about Arctic rivers freezing solid all the way to the bottom that we thought that would be a fine time for us to explore bedrock under where the river ran in the summer. So we selected a place on the river, rather close to shore and dug a hole through the ice. Much to our surprise we found that the gravel under the ice had not frozen at all, and there was a considerable current of water in this gravel, which soon filled the hole we had made in the ice. Next day we picked another place which we knew had been above the water level when the river froze, and began to thaw a hole to bedrock.

We were interrupted by the arrival of two men from Bertha Creek. Chas. Fulker had come originally from Janesville, Wisconsin. Jim Johnston was from Idaho. They were the remnant of the Murphy Party, whom Mike McGovern and I had visited when we came up river in July on our eventful stampede, which had been such an influence in locating us permanently on Indian River.

There were many such visitors. A few days before a Mose Muldonald from Southern Illinois, and his partner, Wilson, from New Zealand, had stayed overnight with us. They were working a lay on Number 2 Above, on the left branch of Eureka Creek. Dan and I had met them back in September.

Sunday, December 11, was Dan's birthday, so we had a raisin pie, instead of a birthday cake. Phil and Archie Dubray, two of the Frenchmen who lived next to Nielsen's, came up to pay their respects. They stayed to dinner with us. We had liver and bacon, the accumulated livers from many rabbits that have been kept frozen for this special occasion.

A Winter Trip to Dawson

Starting December 10, the whole topic of conversation in Bedrock City suddenly centered on a trip to Dawson. It presented several problems. Everybody wanted to go, but nobody wanted to take Thompson along, and someone had to stay to look after our cabins. So I explained it in a nice way to Thompson and he agreed to stay and do police duty. Ford Cole decided to stay and watch Thompson, and Old Carl felt that the trip would be too much for him.

Monday, December 12, was a busy day of preparation. I went over to see Carl, and he cut my hair, which certainly needed attention. He cut it in the style adopted by the Norwegian Army when Carl was young and belonged to that army. He left it about an inch and a half long, everywhere, top, sides and back. When Dan saw it, he offered to improve upon it, so he trimmed it a bit more. My head would have been as smooth as an egg if I had let everybody improve it that offered to do so. I tried to help the situation by trimming off most of my beard.

Then we all had to select the clothing for our trip and protect our supplies from damage during our absence.

Alfred and Emil struck bedrock in their prospect hole that morning at a depth of 43 feet and that ended prospecting at Bedrock City for several weeks.

So on Tuesday, December 13, eight of the eleven inhabitants started on the trip to Dawson, about 40 miles. We were up at 5:00 and by 7:30 the procession started. First Dan and I with a sled, one pulling and the other pushing. On our sled we had all our bedding and about 50 pounds of grub and dishes, 18 nice fat rabbits, and a clothes bag with some extra footwear, underwear, etc. Alfred Jorgenson and Emil came next with a sled similarly loaded and our stove. Then came George Trowbridge and Frank Reed of the Thompson Party with a sled apiece, and not having much on either. They carried the tent. In the rear came Stemple and Karr with their sled.

It was so dark that we could not see the trail, but had to feel for it, easy enough, for it was hard and level and banked with snow on either side. We all felt good at starting, for our loads were light and the trail fine. At 8:45 we reach Arena Gulch where the Frenchmen and the Nielsen's were camped. It was 15 below but we were all steaming and after sitting around for a few minutes at each cabin we began to get chilled. But it was easy to get warm. Just get in the collar and mush for five minutes and nobody complained of cold.

We mushed along at a good gait and everything went very nicely, until about three miles from the Yukon. There we found trouble awaiting us. The Indian River had cracked its coat of ice and the water coming up on top of the ice had flooded the whole river, run through the snow and made slush a foot deep. The river does that, here and there, from time to time, then the slush freezes and forms a glassy top that later makes fine going for our sleds. But this place was of recent origin, and the steam rising from it showed that it was impossible to go through it dry shod. So we did the next best thing, hauled our sleds up, high and dry on shore and pulled them for 1000 feet through thick tangled willow brush, over stumps and logs and through snow 18 inches deep. Once more on the river, we had good going to the Yukon, and what a trail we found there, hard, broad and smooth, packed by the sleds of the people going up and out to civilization.

On the Yukon we got a glimpse of the sun which was a novelty to us. My shadow lay down in front of me, and I amused myself by pacing its length. It was about 105 or 110 feet long. We stopped at McDonald and Hewitt's road house to say hello and accept a free drink. Then we mushed on for about a mile, and being hungry, we stopped there for dinner. I would never have bothered with tea or coffee, but the others all had to have hot tea to make a meal. So we built a fire, melted bushels of snow to get one coffee pot of water, melted the handle and spout off George's tin coffee pot and finally got some tea. We had any amount of cooked beans with us, all frozen into hard bricks, and they thawed out just about as readily as a brick would melt. The bread was frozen as hard as the beans, but could be cut, when lots of power was applied, and soon thawed when held to the fire. This all took time. It was 10 degrees below zero and the longer we sat around, the colder our sweaty clothing became. Dan in particular was cold, for at the overflow on Indian River he had gotten one foot wet, that is, wet for this country where perfect dryness is so essential. I imagine the others got no more satisfaction from that meal than I did. The hot tea instantly changed to iced tea on being poured into the cups, the beans that were thawed on the outside of the brick, burned before the other beans began to thaw and the chunks of hard frozen beans cooled the hot burned beans wonderfully quick. Alfred gave me half a dozen hard tacks and I made a good meal on them as we mushed on after our so-called dinner.

Cold and sweaty and in anything but a pleasant after dinner humor, we packed our stuff and set out again after a delay of an hour and a half. We had come 12 miles and had 9 or 10 more to go before stopping for the night. The trail followed the east shore of the Yukon and wound in and out of the many sloughs, made by the many islands, in the Yukon. But the trail was fine and we soon thawed out, ducked our heads, said little and mushed on.

Ensley Creek was where we intended to camp. About two miles from Ensley the main channel of the Yukon hugs the East bank, so we had to quit the smooth sloughs and travel on the river proper. That was hard going. When the main channel freezes it makes a hard fight against it. The result is a surface that looks like a stone quarry. Cakes of ice stand on end, sometimes five feet high, but even the 12 inch and 18 inch points and blocks and hollows don't make the trail any too good. The man who first had to break the trail must have had slow going. It was bad enough for us, and the sharp corners had all been worn off and many of them cut away, but the ups and downs and short turns made hard going, especially at the end of a 20 mile tramp. But at 3:30 we came to the end of the bad trail and to Ensley Creek, and there we camped. It was dark, and the stars were all shining, so by their light we proceeded to pitch our camp.

Stemple cut four poles about 11 feet long while I unrolled our 10 by 12 foot tent. I tied the tops of two poles together, spread the poles to form an "A" and did the same with the other pair. The back end of the ridge rope I tied to a fallen tree, lying out over the river. We put a pole "A" front and back of the tent and tied the front end of the ridge rope to a sled weighted down with a log, tied the four corners guys of the tent to the four poles and our tent was set up on the level, frozen, snow-covered Yukon River.

The minute we stopped to camp, Dan tried to change his footwear, but it was all frozen together with his pants, so he took dry clothes and went to the little cabin of the Arctic Express Company, thawed out there and changed. The Arctic Express Company had cabins all the way out to Bennett. The North-West Mounted Police also had a line of cabins and beside those, there were road houses every 20 or 30 miles. This Arctic Express Agent was an old time ball player and knew all the old Rockford players, so he and Dan had a fine chat.

While we were putting up the tent, the other boys took the one ax we had brought along and cut firewood and Klondike feathers. The latter used to carpet the snow floor of the tent, and the former we crowded into the stove as fast as it would take it. But nobody in the party can ever get the nice bone dry firewood that Dan gets. When he got back, he got a stick that did great business, and Stemple and I began to get supper. George hadn't exerted himself to do anything, so to keep warm he brought in his roll of bedding and got as near the fire as he could and got warm. The other boys brought in their bedding and sat around more in the way than they would have been if the tent were larger. Some of the boys (neither George nor Emil) got water from the Arctic Express Company's water hole, so we didn't have to melt ice. I sat on our roll of bedding at the side of the stove and Stemple at the end, with all the grub within our reach and it didn't take long to knock out a good meal for eight hungry fellows.

We put the grub down by the stove and sat around it in a circle, and every man made a grab for what he wanted. Alfred and Emil and had forgotten to bring plates, cups or table ware, so we fitted them out with the tablespoons I had brought for cooking and an empty roast beef can. By 6:00 we were all fed, warm and good natured, and all felt tired and ready to roll in. A visitor named Freeman kept us up for an hour. He was camped near us for the night and came in and told bear stories for an hour. He was on his way out to bring goods into Dawson. As soon as he left we began to go to bed.

Stemple, Karr and George had sleeping bags, which they spread on top of some canvas and rubber cloth. Frank did the same, and so the four blocked the door of the tent. Alfred and Emil slept together with canvas and blankets. Dan and I had two canvasses that we lay upon with our blankets on the canvas. I had mine sewed into a bag so as not to get my legs out of doors. We also spread our mackinaws over us. Being the last one in bed, I blew out the candle and put it and some matches where I could get them when wanted. I slept nicely until about 1:00 A.M. Then I woke up feeling cold. I was not so cold, but the blankets were and whenever I touched my bare legs or feet to them I knew it. For about an hour I tried to curl up tightly enough to keep warm but it was no use. Then I got up and put on my drawers, pants and socks and got back again. That went better, and after I once got the socks and drawers warm they stayed warm. I got up at 4:00 A.M., lighted the fire in the stove and roused the other boys and the second day of our Winter Pleasure Trip began.

We had bacon, beans, bread, coffee and six quarts of oatmeal mush for breakfast. We ate the first three without trimmings, ornamented the coffee and oatmeal with sugar, price fifty cents per pound in Dawson. The water pail and coffee pot had stood in a little puddle of water, melted in the ice by the heat of the stove, when we retired. When we got up we had to spend some time digging them out of the icy prison. The big pail of oatmeal had taken a long time to cook, and after breakfast we had to roll up our bedding and pack our grub and knock down the stove and tent, so that even though we were up at 4:00 A.M., it was 7:30 before we got away.

There was a road house about a half mile ahead of us and we met three or four teams of dogs drawing heavy sled loads up river, always up river; we seemed to be the only ones going down. As we passed the road house a long string of dogs came down the incline to the river and we could hear men and dogs up at the house, getting ready to start. But we could not see anything, for the stars were covered by cloudy weather. From Ensley Creek to Dawson is 20 miles, but after crossing the Yukon several times and winding in and out among islands, I'll venture to say the sled trail measured several miles more.

We were all a little stiff at starting but that soon wore off as we got warmed up to work. That morning we met our old friend Hubble, of Lindeman and Sheep Camp, the husband of the woman who wore pants. He was on his way to Selkirk, leaving Mrs. Hubble in Dawson. We wished to get to Dawson before dark. So we mushed along, one step after another, passing mountain after mountain, and hoping at every new turn to see the big white scar on the mountain behind Dawson, which can first be seen some 6 or 8 miles above Dawson. That scar is the prominent feature of every picture of Dawson. We didn't see the scar when we should for just about that time a light flurry of snow limited our range of vision to a mile or less. But I knew as we rounded a long low point that Dawson ought to be in sight. We were then about 5 or 6 miles from Dawson, and seeing a nice pile of dry pine poles we cut up several, tied them to our loads and hauled them along for firewood while in Dawson.

Our lunch that second day was of hard tack and water, both taken as we walked. We had loaded our pockets with unfreezable hard tacks before starting, and for my part I found this far better than our hot lunch of the first day.

About four miles from Dawson, Karr, who had held his peace as long as he could, wanted to know if we were never going to stop to have some hot coffee. We didn't stop and he went on as mad as a March hare, and I was just boiling to think he should have the nerve to even suggest such a thing. A mile further and Stemple complained. "How did we know but what Dawson was 40 miles further on, hadn't we better stop and camp here." We didn't stop. We would have seen Dawson had it been clear. We were tired enough; my knees were stiff and it was comical to watch the stiff legged gait of some of the boys, but to stop there three miles from Dawson was nonsense. So we kept on. Then good fortune overtook us in the shape of a jackass hitched to a short heavy sled with two men riding. Dan helloed to the men and the driver told us to hitch on our sleds and you may be sure we did. If he thought we had made some rich strike and so by hailing our five sleds might learn something, he made a big mistake. The lift was a great help to us. Our benefactor claimed to be a dealer in firewood. His partner was a capper at a stud poker table. He hauled our string of sleds to Dawson and the full length of the Main Street from the Barracks to the Alaska Commercial Company's stores.

People would run up to one of our party and want to know where we came from, what was up and all sorts of crazy questions. We were the whole thing as long as it lasted, but at the Alaska Commercial Company corner, our man left us and we got into the collar again and mushed on like common mortals. We crossed to West Dawson on the ice, and there Alfred found two cabins owned by friends of his, into which we tumbled just as much at home as if we owned the earth, and mighty glad that we didn't have to pitch the tent.

It was just noon when we breakfasted on Thursday. Then we got our mail, the first in four months, and all went to the Northern Saloon to read our letters. Dawson was an old story to me, having been there on two other occasions, but we wandered around from saloon to saloon, like lost sheep. I won $5.00 at a roulette wheel, and that supplied the price of $1.50 suppers for Dan and me. After supper George and I made the mistake of trying to beat a dice game, while the others attended a show. The show was no better than the dice game, but it cost less.

Dan had been supplying the money to keep us going from time to time, so while in Dawson I cashed a $300.00 draft, at a cost of $9.00 and squared myself our accounts. With my last draft cashed, I began to get thrifty, and kept away from the dice games, but still continued to wander around with the others from one saloon to the next.

We sold our rabbits to a little man Dan had once met in Rockford. He came into Dawson with sixty head of cattle which he was selling at retail. We met him in the Oatley Sisters Dance Hall, where he was more than spending his income from the cattle, even at Dawson prices.

On Saturday I got acquainted with a Norwegian Civil Engineer, named Olaf Winningstad. He had rented an office and intended to work as an engineer, but hadn't found much of anything to do. He promised that if he got a real job, he would be glad to have me help him.

We met one of our acquaintances, W. H. Thomas of Truckee, California, who insisted that we go over to Lousetown and have supper with him. His cabin was up on the plateau, about 110 feet or more above the river, and when we left, after a rather indifferent meal, it was so dark that we never could explain why we didn't break our necks, getting down to the river level after supper.

Here is a very interesting extract from my diary of that day: "Went to the Monte Carlo Theatre after supper. Rotten of course, but the kinetoscope pictures helped to redeem it." So as nearly as I can figure it, I had to go to far off Alaska to see my first crude moving pictures.

West Dawson sprang up in a hurry after the river froze so that people could cross it easily. It was built on a rather wide plateau some 100 feet above the river. One cabin that we occupied was owned by Fred and Nels. I can't just place them, but I believe it was the same Fred, who is mentioned so often during our Summer on Indian River. I knew him so well that I always refer to him as Fred, and I wish I could recall his last name. The other cabin was owned by a crowd we knew as the Hansens.

Fred and Nels had a lay on one of the good creeks, so when they left that Saturday, all of our crowd except Alfred and Emil moved into their vacant cabin, used their bunks and anything else they had left, except their grub. It wasn't considered nice to eat other peoples' grub unless extended a special invitation.

Dawson was closed tight on Sunday, no booze could be bought and no dance halls were going. Men had to have some place to stay out of the cold, so the saloons and dance halls had their doors open and a good fire in the stoves, and were full of men. After supper, as we loafed around waiting for the "Family Show" to start, we overheard one man telling another about "a couple of parties sinking holes on Indian River. The dammed fools might as well get in the middle of the Yukon River." It interested us greatly. (We had heard the same remark made about the discoverer of Gold Hill, and still regretted that we had so readily accepted it at face value.)

The show was really very enjoyable, all in good taste, which couldn't be said of the week day shows. There were lantern views, Seattle to Forty Mile; illustrated songs by Fred Tracy; torch singing and Indian Club swinging; the Kinetoscope and popular songs. My diary says "The best thing for a show that I have seen in Dawson."

The popular songs of Dawson that winter were "She was Bred in Old Kentucky," "On the Banks of the Wabash" and "Pretty Swallow, Homeward Fly." There was another which told how "she left me all alone, in our once bright happy home, with nothing but a faint and broken heart." Those songs had to work overtime. The Wabash was changed to "on the banks of the Yukon far away" and went over in great style. All the audience invariably joined in the singing.

On Monday, Alfred and Emil arranged for a lay on Lombard Creek, and we all made preparation for starting back to Bedrock City early Tuesday morning. When we got up on Tuesday there was a stiff breeze blowing from the north, so when someone said, "Don't let's start until Wednesday" we promptly agreed.

The Hunker Creek Stampede, December 21, 1898

It is surprising what trivial incidents bring about the most unexpected adventures. That little breeze held us in Dawson a day longer than we had planned. Tuesday evening someone told the Hanson brothers about some bench claims on Hunker Creek that we could stake and record if we would give half to some grafters in the recording office. Hunker is a good creek and Stemple and I thought the claims worth looking into, so we decided to go and see them. That delayed our start back home for another day. Stemple and I started right after breakfast on Wednesday, December 21. We didn't know how far we were going, and only knew where by a little rough sketch that I had pocketed. We didn't take a thing with us except some hard tacks, intending to sleep at a road house or cabin.

We went up the Klondike, past the mouth of Bonanza, past Bear Creek and then came Hunker. That is the trail that goes over to Upper Dominion and is even better than the

Yukon trail. We walked along at a jolly good gait and were at the mouth of Hunker almost before we knew it. There we branched off and travelled a fine broad straight trail that crosses the creek about Number 100 Below. Our claims were near Number 79 Below. We reached the Last Chance Road House just four hours after leaving Dawson, distance 16 miles. Here we found two Hansons, who had agreed to meet us there, just finishing lunch. So Stemple and I had a fifty cent lunch, and the four of us went to hunt the four unrecorded bench claims. The numbering of claims was badly mixed and it took us an hour and a half to find our claims. The Last Chance Road House stood on one of them. Not a thing had been found within three or four miles of that locality and the ground was full of prospect holes too. I soon made up my mind that I didn't want any of it and the others felt as I did. Sold again.

It was then 3:00 P.M. and the moon was just rising big and bright. I wanted to go back to Dawson so that we might start home next day and get home for Christmas. Stemple intended to stay in Dawson for a week or so and look for a job. So I left him with the other two, and I set out for a quick trip to Dawson. And I made a quick trip too. At a road house, half way down, I stopped for a lunch of doughnuts and mince pie, and there met another man bound for Dawson. He was a long-legged fellow and how he did stretch my legs. But I didn't object to that. I wanted to get back and get a good rest for the next day's journey. When I got back to Dawson I was more than ready to sit down and rest. I stopped at the first saloon on the street and sat by the stove watching a whist game for half an hour. Then I hunted for the boys, to let them know that we could start in the morning. How I had stiffened, sitting by the fire for 30 minutes, I could hardly walk. Not finding any of the boys I went over to West Dawson, started a fire, got some grub and was about to turn in at 11:00 P.M. when the boys came in, and we decided to start back to Indian River early next day.

The Shortest Day of the Year

Thursday, December 22, the shortest day I ever set eyes upon, but I hope I never again experience a day as long as that one. Of course, we had to get up at 4:00 A.M. to get any kind of start. Our late nights and irregular living and scanty grub while in Dawson had not helped our sled pulling or walking powers. In addition to that I had but little rest after my 35 mile trip of the day before. I started only because I knew we would have to, if we were to get back to Bedrock before Christmas. We counted on three days for the return trip.

Dan did all the packing for our party and he pulled our sled the first four miles without my help. My sheep mittens were damp inside and I hadn't life enough in me to warm them, so my hands were cold all the morning. Frank and George each had a pretty good load of groceries purchased in Dawson, and Karr had nobody to help with his sled. They all sat down to rest every little way and while I was not a bit unwilling to rest, it always chilled me and stiffened my joints, so that I could hardly start again. The day was cloudy and stayed dark unusually late. I pulled the sled a half mile, while Dan pushed behind and then turned it over to him again. Then I discovered that I could push a little, and after I was so nearly played out that I could not get any more so, I began to limber up. Then I relieved Dan again and gave the sled a good long pull of several miles. And all this time my hands were like ice.

At 1:00 P.M. about 12 miles from Dawson, we came to a little tent with a stove in it and two men using the stove. I went in to warm my hands and found the men to be travelers, just finishing a lunch and about to go on to Dawson. So we took their place, kept the fire going, and had a lunch there in the little tent. There was nothing in the tent but the stove and it was a work of art, made of two 25 pound potato tins, telescoped together, the pipe loosely set over a hole in one end and a funny little home-made door in front. We smashed up a brick of beans and thawed them out in a frying pan and toasted slices of bread on the top and sides of the tin stove. We had a block of frozen stewed apricots, but not so hard that a knife would not cut it, so we ate beans and five loaves of store bread, and ate slices of apricot ice to quench our thirst.

It made new men of us. It warmed my hands, and greased my joints all around. After lunch I did my share at pulling our sled, and our old camp ground being only eight miles further on we decided to make it. The last four of the eight miles were rather longer than the first four, but we had a definite objective and that helps. Strange to say, I kept feeling better the farther we went. It was still cloudy, but the moon did us a little good, and by its rather faint light we made a new camp near the Ensley Creek Road House. The location was not quite as good as the other, but a half mile counts.

I had intended all day to sleep that night at the road house, but I felt so good when we got there that I didn't care for the road house bunk. So we pitched camp and got supper and turned in again. George and Emil, or course, didn't do anything but eat and rest and get warm. That's all they ever did on the trail. Karr, now and then did enough to save his reputation. Frank quietly did anything he was asked to do, I cooked, and Dan and Alfred got the wood and water. The water hole was nearly a half mile away and Karr and Alfred had a hard time finding it. But we soon managed to have a good square meal of potatoes and bacon and beans and lots of it.

The temperature during out stay at Dawson had been unusually warm, from 2 to 20 degrees below. It was about 30 below that night.

By 8:00 we were all sound asleep, but we slept too soundly. I learned afterwards that it was 30 below and there was a stiff wind blowing down the Yukon. Outside we had banked the tent with snow, but even then the wind got under and blew directly on our heads. I awoke in the middle of the night, chilled from shoulders to the top of my head. The hood of my sweater was over my head, but I afterwards found that my nose had been nipped by frost. I buried my head in the blankets and smothered there until Alfred woke me at 4:30. Alfred was the alarm clock of the party. He was always the first one to awake and roused the rest of us. I was sleepy and waited for someone else to get up and light the fire, but it soon became evident that if I didn't do it, nobody would. I guess everyone else felt as I had the morning before.

So I crawled out, put on all my clothes, fur cap and mittens and started the fire and the breakfast. Dan got the water and all the while I was getting breakfast, I took a delight in sitting down heavily on George's legs and feet, as he lay sleeping right in my way. Our grub was about gone. A little bread, a good meal of bacon, some potatoes and lots of oatmeal. That oatmeal was a fancy dish; when nearly done a nice long candle fell over into the pail and went out of sight. By the time I had fished it out on a spoon it wasn't much bigger than a lead pencil, but the mishap didn't hurt either the candle or the mush. We used them both.

It was 8:00 before we got started. Dan and I took the lead and I pulled while he pushed for the first hour and a half. I set them a jolly good pace, slow enough so nobody could kick or lag, and steady enough so that we covered lots of ground. That brought us to the mouth of the Indian River at 11:00 A.M. where we all rested and ate lunch with Hewitt at the road house. George, Frank and Karr wanted very much to stay there and make home the next day, but they didn't say so. They knew that Alfred, Emil, Dan and I were set on getting home and were going anyway. So we started up river for Nielsen's, eight miles. There we could decide about going further. We got a real work-out on Indian River. It had snowed eight inches while we were at Dawson and the trail up Indian River was covered with about four inches of loose snow that we had to plow through. Alfred and Emil having the lightest load, took the lead. Dan and I next, the single sleds behind. Dan was nearly played out, he said so and he looked it. I pulled the sled all the way to Nielsen's. We stopped to rest at the Scotchman's cabin. The rest stiffened the boys' joints so that they could hardly walk. But we finally pulled in at Nielsen's. It was way after dark, but the moon was shining brightly.

At Nielsen's we had a lunch of bread and tea and a good rest. George, Frank and Karr stayed there that night but Alfred, Emil, Dan and I went on again. Home was too close to stop anywhere else. So at 6:30 we got into the collar again, Dan pulling at first. All the way from Dawson we had not been bothered much with water. We encountered some little overflows that we easily got around, but we had hardly left Nielsen's before we ran into a wet place. It was not very big, but would be very hard to get around. So we went straight through it, wading in slush and water up to our ankles. We didn't get our feet wet, for the slush froze to our moccasins instantly and we had to knock the chunks of the ice off, with our pushing poles. Of course, wet feet or even stiff footwear are not the proper style up here, but we were less than four miles from home so we pushed on.

About a mile further I took the pulling rope, and Dan pushed and when within two miles of home, we encountered an overflow about a quarter mile long, slush a foot deep all over the river, and on the steep sloping bank two feet of loose snow. The four of us had all we could do to pull Alfred's sled through that snow on the river bank. Our sled was enough heavier so that it was no easier than the first even in the trail the first sled had made. Dan was all in. He had often lightened my loads, but this one time, I pulled while he rode the sled. We rested about every 500 feet for the next two miles, but by 9:00 P.M. Dan and I sat in front of a roaring fire in our own little cabin; and we sat until after midnight, wondering as we sat there if we should ever be more happy to return to our mothers' firesides than we were on our return to that dismal little log cabin up in Alaska.

It is interesting to note the physique that a young fellow develops as the result of ten months of outdoor life. I had walked some 75 miles in those three days, and the third day had been the most strenuous of all. I have not heretofore said much about the time I had in acquiring this knack of perpetual motion. There really was a knack to it, which cannot be appreciated by those who live in the flat prairie country of Illinois.

When I first began to climb Alaska mountains, I immediately found that it took more wind than I could pack into my lungs, and it also brought into use an entirely new set of muscles in my legs and body that had never been called upon to do much work, and consequently suffered greatly when used for mountain climbing. It didn't take so much wind to go down a mountain, but that brought into play a third set of muscles. Therefore, in hilly country, after I had developed enough lung power to do the work, I found that two complete sets of muscles rested, while the other did the particular work for which it was designed. So in hilly country, a man soon develops the ability to travel three times as far as he can in the flat country to which I had always been accustomed. So as a result of such training, I had become a 160 pound locomotive. Dan weighed about 200 pounds, consequently on the trail, he had more to carry, and more to lift when he climbed a mountain. He was as powerful as a steam shovel when it came to pulling a sled out of a hole, so between the two of us we had a team that could do almost anything and get almost anywhere.

So we were home and the three boys back at Nielsen's had an additional three inches of snow to pull through the next day. George was a chap who was always telling us what an athlete he was, but he seldom showed evidence of it. Dan and I never gave it a thought, but after the others got back, George showed at various times that he rather regretted that he had been compelled to drop out at Nielsen's.

Our cabin had become so thoroughly chilled in our absence that it didn't really warm up for several days. That circumstance and the wind on our heads the night before gave every one of us a cold, except Frank. It was the first cold that Dan and I had since starting on our trip. It struck me deep in my throat and it took a week to drive it out. We slept late on Saturday and celebrated Christmas on Sunday by sleeping late, eating whatever was easiest to cook, and reading again the many letters we brought back from Dawson.

How One Klondike Expedition Went Wrong

I heard a good story about a woman who wasn't much good, who stayed home and sent her husband to the Klondike.

Will had plenty of money and a pretty wife, but Will was a thin sickly specimen of a man, always in poor health, and finally it was decided that as they couldn't find anything definitely the matter with him that he must be coming down with consumption. Doc was a big husky chap, who made patent medicine for a living, and made eyes at Will's wife when Will wasn't looking.

Will's wife had it figured that Will wouldn't last very much longer, and as she didn't intend to be without a man, she already had Doc picked out as Will's successor. The papers reported that the Klondike was sure death for anyone with bad lungs, so Doc suggested that a trip to Alaska was just what Will needed and Doc offered to go along and see that things were made easy for Will. Of course, Mrs. Will supplied Doc with money for his share of the trip. Then they convinced Will that the trip to Klondike would be just the thing to help Will back to health.

Mrs. Will kissed Will goodbye. She had already kissed Doc goodbye and told him that if anything happened to Will, not to bother about the gold, but to hurry right back home to her.

In Doc's tender care Will went to the Klondike. He never saw a real bed after he left Dyea. Slept in a tent at Sheep Camp, climbed Chilkoot with all he could carry on his back, hauled a sled to Lake Bennett and helped build a boat and handle it to Dawson.

When they arrived at Dawson, Doc began to get so nasty about money matters that Will got a job at one of the Eldorado mines. As a result of all this fresh air and exercise,

Will picked up weight, muscle and spirit and got over his cough. Doc hung around the saloons of Dawson, and it wasn't long before his money was gone, and then Doc got sick.

When Will had earned enough to go back to the States, he got back to Dawson just in time to attend Doc's funeral, and caught the last boat going up river. Will wasn't as blind as Mrs. Will and Doc had thought he was, but he still loved Mrs. Will and so he headed home.

This is a rather unsatisfactory story, because we never knew how Will was received by Mrs. Will, but it if was a real he-man that she wanted, she had one when Will arrived home.

Restless Days at Bedrock City

Dan and I were delighted to get back to the little log cabin that we called home, but Bedrock City was never again the same as it had been before Thanksgiving. We had all the same ingredients for a delightful Christmas Day, but the day passed almost unnoticed.

Hope as to what the Future will provide for it, seems to be the main spring in the life of any community.

We had dug so many prospect holes at Bedrock City that we were convinced that it was wasted time to dig any more, and still we kept digging. We had heard many stories about big strikes that had been made by the persistent prospector who had kept on when all others dropped out. So on Monday Dan and I returned to the hole we had started on the edge of the river. In a few days we sank the hole to bedrock through frozen gravel. Then the water ran us out. It came up through the cracks of the bedrock and soon the hole had six feet of water in it. We only found one good color. All the others at Bedrock worked rather steadily at various kinds of prospect holes. Bert Karr and Thompson worked together. Ford and George got busy finishing holes that had been started and had not been sunk to bedrock. Dan and I worked our scheme of sinking holes right next to the river, where there was no heavy overburden of silt on the gravel. Every time we reached bedrock, we found very fair colors, and the water pressure in the seams in the bedrock promptly filled the holes as fast as we reached bedrock.

While we were at Dawson, the big topic of conversation, everywhere, all the time, was the fabulous wealth being dug out of the bench claims on Gold Hill, at the junction of Eldorado and Bonanza; the big chance that Dan and I had allowed to slip through our fingers in August. We had, of course, heard about that rich strike while we were building our cabin, but at the time it had seemed rather far away, and not directly connected with us. While we were at Dawson, we felt that every dollar taken from Gold Hill, was our own personal loss.

Knowing the old saying that "opportunity knocks but once" I had begun to feel that fate had decreed that I should not be the discoverer of some famous new Gold Field. All through the spring and summer I had treasured every little scrap of knowledge about prospecting. Now I turned my attention from the discovery of a new deposit, and began to figure how I might get title to something worthwhile in some of the creeks that were known to be good.

The claims staked out when gold was first discovered were permitted by the Canadian government to be 500 feet along the creek valley. The miners were not experienced surveyors, so some claims were staked less than 500 feet and the next miner might stake a claim much in excess of 500 feet, but the government would allow him to retain only 500 feet and there would result a "Fraction," consisting of all acreage over his 500 feet up to where the next man had staked his claim.

It is easy to see that there would be many such fractions, and they were legally open for anyone else to stake who would be satisfied with a small claim.

When it was discovered how rich the Klondike was, the government only permitted claims 250 feet long to be recorded. Until this was thoroughly understood many people staked 500 feet, and were only allowed a title to the 250 feet nearest to the Discovery Claim, and the other 250 feet was open to anyone else.

The first bench claims were 250 feet square, and Gold Hill was cut into claims 100 feet square, and that made many fractions. I discussed these things with everyone I met and studied how I might locate such a fraction on a real creek. The very first answer to that problem was that I'd have to be in Dawson if I expected to get any real information about such opportunities. Consequently as soon as I got back to Bedrock, I was ready to go right back to Dawson, the first time I had an opportunity.

When we got back to Bedrock we found Carl Jorgenson laid up with a bad knee. That and the condition of his teeth indicated that he had a touch of scurvy. So we all donated dried fruit and fresh rabbits to help put the old man back on his feet.

December 28 Alfred and Emil began hauling their outfit down as far as Nielsen's. Then they were to push it ahead to McDonald's and to Dawson, and then to Upper Dominion Creek, almost a month's hard mushing, without much show for gold when they finally reached their lay. But they were about broke, and had to do something.

December 31 Alfred and Emil put old Carl on the sled and took him down to Nielsen's. We were sorry to see them go and hoped they would prosper in the new venture. After supper we all assembled at the Thompson cabin and played black jack and poker until the arrival of the New Year (1899). Then we started the New Year by finishing the bottle of Hiram Walker that George had brought back for Christmas.

Glaciers are one of nature's most interesting phenomena. The hills of northern Illinois were made by glacial action. The glaciers to be seen on the Alaska coast are a source of never ending interest. At Bedrock City we had the questionable pleasure of getting acquainted with a glacier in the making. The little spring which supplied us all with fine drinking water, came bubbling out of the foot of a mountain, about 300 feet northwest of our cabin, and from it there flowed a little rivulet six or eight inches wide, in a direct line to Indian River. This little trickle of water froze, as was to be expected at the prevailing temperatures, but the water kept coming from the spring in its regular volume. Then this water ran on top of the ice which covered the rivulet and through the snow lying on that ice. This is turn froze, and so the process continued, and the top surface of the new ice gradually got so high that the water started to run down the path that led to our cabin. We promptly stopped that, by shoveling a lot of snow across the path near the spring, and building up a snow and ice levee which forced the miniature glacier over to the west of the ordinary course of the rivulet. While we were at Dawson the weather was rather warmer than the average, and that permitted the water to flow around in the loose snow without forming a very heavy crust of ice.

Ford Cole and Thompson had their own path to the spring, so they paid no attention to conditions on our path.

Right after we got back to Bedrock, the temperature dropped to about 50 degrees below very regularly every night. That froze a very heavy crust of ice, wherever the water lay in the snow. This crust of ice extended to Indian River, and out upon the river, and 200 feet or more along the river, all frozen into a solid mass, with a stream of warm water from the mountain spring somewhere under the ice.

In the middle of the night of January 2, Dan and I were awakened from a sound sleep by a roar such as a cannon makes, and a crashing like the rocks make in a big quarry blast. We had heard the river make such explosions and had seen the water run out all over the top of the ice, so we paid no attention to that extra loud explosion.

In the morning we found great cakes of ice from our glacier had been forced up from the fan of glacier ice that had spread out on the river and shot clear across to the other bank. Between the river and the spring the ice had also broken and the water under the ice had found its way under the snow, to our wood pile and saw brick, and started to inundate the steps that led from the river to our cabin. Dan and I put in a busy day building more snow levees to lead the water and the glacier away from our cabin.

On January 12 our pet glacier went on another spree that threatened to drive Dan and me out of our cabin. It overflowed one of our levees and came down the path right to the side of our cabin. So we spent that day digging channels to the river, and making better and higher levees. We stopped our work long enough to visit with Hewitt, who made the trip up to Nine Mile to buy a moose that Burns had killed. Next morning all the channel we had cut for the glacier water was filled with a slushy sort of ice, and the water going where it pleased again.

Saturday, January 14, Dan and I went to visit the Nielsens and the Frenchmen and to say goodbye again to the Jorgenson party, who were about to move old Carl ahead again. Phil and Archie Dubray had been to Dawson and brought back some new books, some of which they loaned us.

Next day, Burns' partner Conway came up from the Mouth with $120.00 which they had received for three fourths of the moose they sold to Hewitt.

Monday we had another battle with our pet glacier. When Thompson left us after a game of cards, about 10:00 P.M. he stepped into water right in front of our door. Then we discovered that there was also water under our board floor. So went with two candles at 30 degrees below zero, and dug a ditch along the side of the cabin. At midnight when we thought we had the matter under control, we went in the cabin, and there was a nice little trickle of water running into the cabin from between two of the logs in the wall. We worked until 4:30 A.M. before we finally had the water under control, draining away from the cabin in a series of ditches, and kept away by a new series of levees. At 8:00 A.M. we cleaned the ditches again and slept until 1:00 P.M. Then we found everything very much as we had left it at 8:00.

The cabin looked as if a cyclone had struck it, because at the first alarm we had piled all our grub and clothing and hardware a foot or more above the floor to ensure it against the water.

Next day with picks and shovels we made a real ditch, 10 feet wide, all around the cabin and led the glacier over toward the Thompson cabin and let it flow into the river some distance east of our cabin. That solved the problem and we had very little trouble with our glacier after that.

We reached a point where we only burned one candle per day about January 11 and that signified that the days were getting appreciably longer.

We knew that Bedrock was getting to be a rather dead town. Ford, Frank and George would come in and tell Dan and me what an old fool Thompson was. After they left, Thompson would drop in and talk about his three reprobate partners. Then Burt Karr would come in, and we would talk about the entire Thompson Party. As Dan expressed it, "what would we have to talk about if we didn't have the troubles of Thompson and his party." The Thompson party had a camera and several dozen films. They took pictures from time to time, and had had them developed while in Dawson. The only two snapshots that showed anything were two of their partly built cabin.

Poole Stemple returned from Dawson on January 23. He and Karr at once started moving their outfit to Nielsen's and thence to Dawson.

Tobacco

Any true account of the Klondike must give a considerable amount of space to the tobacco question. Tobacco didn't mean anything to me, so I can qualify as an unbiased spectator of how tobacco influenced the others.

Dan brought in a good supply of smoking and chewing tobacco and also some snuff. He smoked once after each meal and once before going to bed. So his supply held out far better than he ever admitted to anyone except me. Everybody traded rice for pork, or bacon for beans, but very little tobacco changed hands. Dan bought more chewing tobacco on our trip to Dawson. People didn't offer tobacco to everyone they met, and cigarettes were only smoked by those who came from California or Mexico. Before our trip to Dawson, Dan had been chewing a mixture of smoking tobacco and snuff.

The Nielsen Party were far less fortunate. Their smoking and chewing tobacco both gave out about the same time. They managed to get a little chewing tobacco in exchange for some sugar (which sold at a standard price of one dollar per pound everywhere) and some dried fruit. They could not get any smoking tobacco.

Fred Melby could do without chewing tobacco, but he couldn't get along without his smoke, so he had been smoking tea. Then he tried mixing tea and chewing tobacco, which smoked fairly well if it ever got lighted.

John and Chris just had to chew and didn't care about smoking. They wouldn't stand Fred's extravagance in burning chewing tobacco. So Chris and John chewed the tobacco and carefully saved and dried their chewed out cuds, and deposited them in a tin box. When Fred wanted to smoke that is what he smoked, and he found these dried out cuds much better than tea.

After their small supply of plug tobacco had been chewed and then smoked, and some of the cuds chewed a second time, they were in an awful fix. Then John and Chris had a bright idea. Fred had half a dozen corncob pipes which he had smoked until they were strong enough to drive a person out of the cabin. John and Chris mixed the rich black juice to be found in these pipes with tea leaves and various other dry leaves and chewed that. When the juice gave out, they cut up the corncobs and chewed them as if they had been plug tobacco.

Therefore, it is not surprising that a day or two after we got back from Dawson, Chris and John came up to Bedrock City "to hunt for moose." It was about 50 below, and we knew it was tobacco they were hunting. Dan didn't propose to divide the little supply he had bought at Dawson, and he knew that Ford Cole had lots of chewing tobacco. So Dan sent them over to see Ford, and it just happened that I went with them. It had snowed the night before and everything was covered with the purest coat of white.

On our way to Thompson's, Chris stopped suddenly. There on the pure white snow was a great big stain of tobacco juice. Chris stood and looked at it, heaved a big sigh and said "Mine Gott! What a damn goot shew dad feller must haf!"

Old Ben Butler handled his smoking tobacco in a way that made me wish that I smoked for my own pleasure, rather than to please whoever it was that gave me a cigar. Ben was just a duplicate of many old miners whose pipe smoking captured my admiration. After supper, as he sat by the fire, he would bring out a long plug of T. & B. smoking tobacco, and whittle away at the end of it in the most unconcerned way while he related some story. It might take him 10 or 20 minutes to cut enough for a smoke. Then for another 10 or 20 minutes, he rolled and crushed the tobacco in the palm of his hand, under the pressure of a powerful thumb, never delaying his story in any way. The process of packing it and tamping it almost solid in the bowl of his pipe took almost as much time. Then he had to interrupt his story. Our matches were made from little blocks of pine about two inches long and one inch square, split at one end into about 100 or more matches, but still connected as a single block at the other end. They were tipped with the old-fashioned sulphur heads, and one match wouldn't even light a handful of loose gun powder, so he would break off a little bunch of six or eight matches, and slowly and carefully apply the flame to his pipe. By repeating that process several times he had the tobacco nicely lighted, and that pipeful would last him all the rest of the evening. He really enjoyed a smoke.

December and January Weather

If I don't give the Klondike temperature a lot more publicity than I have so far, nobody will believe that I was ever there. So I have charted the weather from December 1 to March 7, so that it can be seen at a glance. In Illinois at 30 degrees below zero, street cars stop and everybody is late getting to the office, but from December 1 to 5 Dan and I worked regularly burning our prospect holes, and my diary doesn't mention the weather, except to record it. We considered it rather mild after that week in November where the temperature never got warmer than minus 40 and dropped to minus 50 every night.

On December 6, when the temperature rose to 34 degrees above zero, we felt as comfortable as the polar bear at the circus on a hot August day. You can see what nice weather we had while Dan and I were in Dawson.

Starting December 28 there was a week of minus 40 to minus 50 degree weather, and I do find in my diary on December 29, when it was 43 below at noon, the following reference to the weather: "it is too cold to do much outdoors, but nobody seems to be doing much inside either."

It was 50 below when Alfred and Emil loaded old Carl Jorgenson on a sled and hauled him to Nielsen's.

On January 2, at 44 degrees below I note that "Those of us who are left in Bedrock, began to work in earnest today. ... At night I felt that I had started the New Year with a good day's work."

It will be noted that January maintained a very even temperature throughout the month, never above minus 10 degrees and very generally dropping to minus 40.

Dan kept the report in February, while Thompson and I went to Dawson, but he only observed the minimum temperature recorded by the thermometer each night. It will be seen that February was usually very comfortable, and I shall describe the uncomfortable February weather in more detail, in its proper place.

Of course, our toes and fingers got cold, and noses and cheeks were frequently frost bitten. But as long as we kept feet and hands dry, and kept moving, these low temperatures never really bothered us, except on those rare occasions that I give in detail in the story.

Thompson Goes to Dawson

You may well imagine how restless we became after we had been back at Bedrock for a few weeks. After the Jorgensen's and Stemple and Karr pulled out that left only the Thomp-

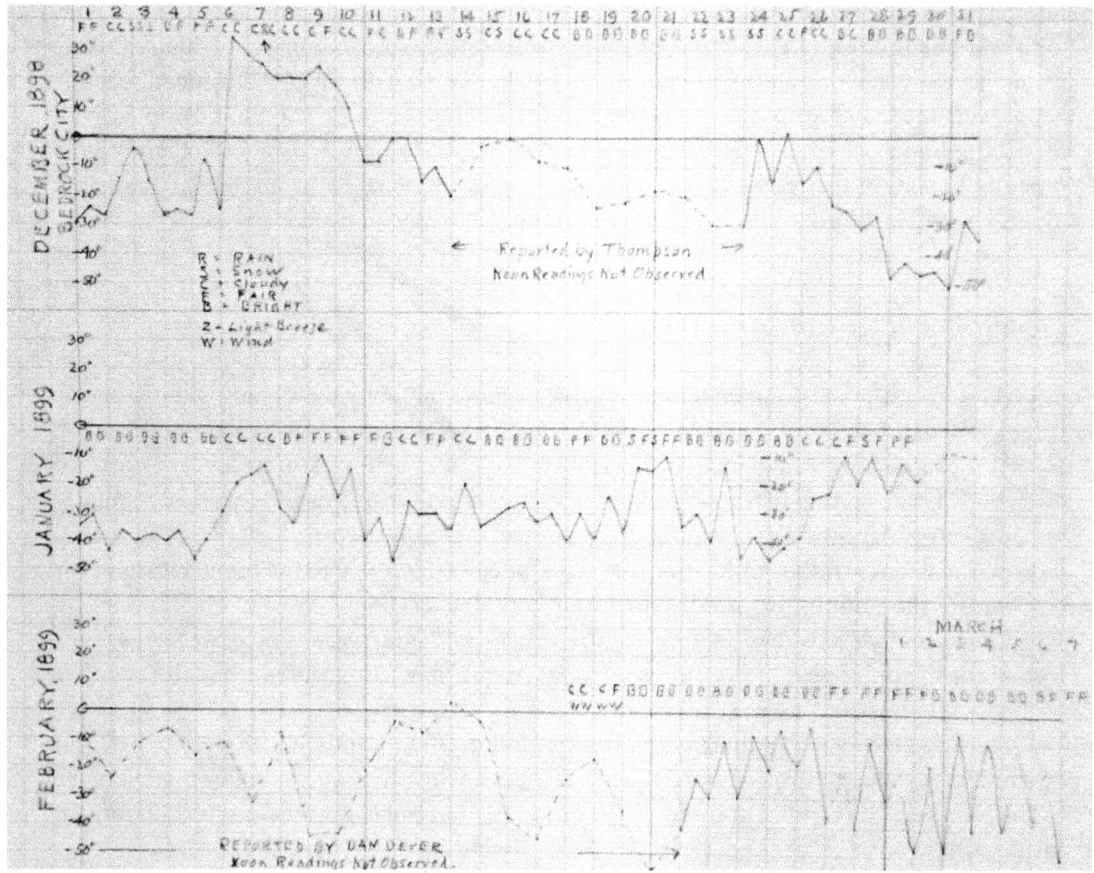

Weather report, December 1898–February 1899.

son Party and Dan and me. We knew that there would be mail waiting for us at Dawson, but Dan didn't enjoy mushing on the trail as I did, so he felt that it was wasted effort for both of us to go to Dawson. Then too, there were lots of people passing up and down the Indian River and he liked to visit with them. When we were in Dawson before Christmas I ran into an engineer named Winningstad who was interested in some railroad scheme which he hoped would develop about February 15. Above all I was interested in hunting out some good unrecorded claims which could be located. The routine of getting one of these claims was to get in with someone who had a pull at the recording office and thereby get a chance to stake and record a claim with the understanding that we deed one half of the claim to our informant.

So I had several incentives for making another trip to Dawson.

I must tell about old Thompson and his party. Telling what an old fool and old bore he is, I know that all sympathy is with him, and now Thompson's stock is way up. He's a proud conceited old rooster, organized this party at home, and wherever he went and whatever he said it was all about his, Thompson's Party, and about Thompson's Party, and about Thompson. The other three, for the first few months were content to be Thompson's Party, and then began to wish it were more of a company affair, and not so much Thompson's pet stock show. They might have given Thompson to understand that he was not the entire party, but they didn't go at it the right way. Fact is they didn't know Thompson as well as he knew them. So the other three, led by Ford Cole (who Thompson pronounces the meanest man living) began to irritate Thompson by petty little annoyances. Nothing for which a man could find grounds for a fight, but just mean little tricks. Thompson, instead of thrashing someone or getting thrashed himself, made up his mind not to notice any of their boy's play. He didn't pay any attention to them, and kept out of the cabin all he could, only eating and sleeping there. Then the other three redoubled their annoyances. The effect on outsiders is obvious. Thompson and his tales of woe were boresome, but public opinion won't stand everything.

I made up my mind early in January that the three young fools were making bigger fools of themselves than the old man could ever hope to be. After the Jorgensons moved away, Dan and I had a double dose of Thompson and finally found a happy solution. To keep him from telling stories, we got him to playing cribbage, and the scheme worked perfectly. And because he was at our cabin so much, the other three seldom dropped in, for fear he would be there. So happened the rise of Thompson.

Just before Stemple returned for his outfit, I was about ready to go to Dawson. Thompson heard Dan speak about it and wanted to go too. When Dan told me that he had put me in a box, and told me about Thompson, I surprised Dan by saying that I'd be glad of Thompson's company. Thompson makes a great many acquaintances wherever he goes. He always introduces himself, and has a great faculty for remembering people's names, a very boresome faculty when he tells a story, but a real asset when in Dawson looking for a good opening. Next day, when Thompson asked if I would like to have him go to Dawson with me, I said yes without any hesitation and we began to make our plans. We were to travel as lightly loaded as possible, just our blankets and some of the high priced grub, planning to buy cheap grub such as beans, etc., in Dawson. A Yukon sled's weight was 35 pounds, so we each made a little old-fashioned sled, weighing only six pounds.

We loaded these sleds with about 50 pounds of bedding, grub and my drawing instruments, and started before daylight on Saturday, January 28, expecting to overtake Stemple at the mouth of Indian. It was snowing when we started and the trail was full of snow, but our little sleds did good work and we made the Yukon in less than four hours, and I was able to take some necessary notes on the way, to complete my map of the 8 miles of Indian River from Arena Gulch to the Mouth.

Thompson was nearly dead when we got to McDonald's Road House, and I thought we'd never make the next ten miles to Ensley Creek. We found Stemple and Carl Jorgenson at McDonald's. Carl had a job as cook. Thompson ate lunch for seventy-five cents and I ate what I'd brought along, and we rested Thompson as long as we dared, visited old Carl and started for Ensley at 1:30. Stemple had 175 pounds in his 35 pound sled.

It soon became evident that Stemple and not Thompson would be first to play out. For the last mile I hauled Stemple's sled for him and also picked the trail. It was nearly 6:00 P.M. and dark. Picking the trail is no snap. It hadn't snowed since noon, but there had only been three or four dog teams along the trail. The main thing in picking the trail is to keep in the middle of it. Not that there is any danger of getting off and losing it. That's impossible, but if we get off the middle of the trail and drag the sled to the side, it sinks down in the loose snow at the side. And then there is a hard tug to pull it back on the hard packed trail again.

At Ensley, Poole Stemple and I cooked our grub at Richards and Hopkins' Bunk House, but Thompson sold three boxes of cigars at $5.00 each and felt rich enough to pay $1.50

A cloudy day on Indian River, January 26, 1899.

each for his supper and breakfast cooked by Mrs. Richards. For $1.00 each we slept in the bunk house on pole bunks, with only our blankets between our ribs and the poles.

Excepting the last few miles after dark, I had quite enjoyed the day. My little load of 55 pounds was nothing and I was well occupied. My survey of Indian River had interested me. I had killed and skinned a fine ermine. On the Yukon, we had gone slowly enough and rested so many times that I had a chance to enjoy every bit of landscape that presented itself. I noticed at noon that my shadow was only 35 feet long, a third as long as on December 13. The scene ahead of us was a picture such as I'd like to paint. The sky in the north was clear, and almost black when contrasted with the snow, which stood out against the sky in clear out lines. Dark rocks pierced the snow here and there, and the dark green spruce trees completed the picture, or rather, the many pictures. I had made two such sketches while at Bedrock, for Mother's birthday present, and paid Hewitt $1.00 to take them out to Seattle and mail them.

I met my old friend, Jim Forsythe, of Sheep Camp and his partner at Ensley Creek, and had a nice visit with Jim.

The second day out from Bedrock we made Dawson without very much hard work. Poole left half of his load at Ensley for McDonald's team of dogs to pick up, so was able then to keep up with us nicely. Thompson started out stiff and sore but limbered up and got along all right.

A sunny afternoon on Indian River, January 27, 1899.

Opposite Swede Creek, 7 miles above Dawson, there is a road house in a class by itself. It is the most sloppy, shiftless, inconvenient, dirty little hole I ever hope to see. We were hungry, saw the sign and followed the trail. First we went up the river bank, as smooth as a toboggan slide, and went back into the woods 100 feet. Then we encountered a small Chilkoot, whose steps were haphazard, made by chance rather than intent. At the top we could see the "Road House." It was a square affair with a flat roof. Not six feet high inside and banked half way with moss, etc., when we entered a man with a big tangled beard got off the bunk he had been lying on and said hello. Round poles, laid loose, formed the floor. There was no window, only a little hole 6 inches square in the roof, and cracks in and around the door to admit light. In one corner was a stone affair with a tin top which served as a stove. On top of the bunks and under them were bags of grub and blankets, mixed. On the floor, by the stone stove, were coffee pots and a Dutch oven. Near the door, a table, littered with dirty tin dishes, and between door and stove a long low pile of stove wood to sit on. We sat a while and then asked for lunch. His sign read "Lunch 25 cents." Our lunch was cut off a big loaf of bread, put on a plate and set under the hole in the roof, on the floor. Coffee was poured from one of the pots, after being warmed up, and likewise set down on the floor. "Gentlemen dive in, more where that came from."

I don't particularly like sour dough bread without salt. It reminds one of dried up, uncooked flour paste. I had to use the coffee to wash the bread down, and the coffee had no sugar to disguise its poverty. "Eat all you want gentlemen." But a man has to be starved to eat much dry sour dough bread and sugarless coffee.

After lunch, we met a man carrying a camera, who was out after a picture of a herd of reindeer. We had noticed the tracks of the herd at many places on the Yukon, between Indian River and Dawson, but had not seen the deer.

We were in West Dawson at 3:50. We found Alfred Jorgensen and Emil and Fred and Nel's cabin. We ate our grub and theirs in that cabin and slept in Hansen's next door.

13

Dawson's Social Life and Business Section

Monday, when we finally got up and had breakfast, Thompson and I went straight for the post office where he got a letter and I got a letter dated December 5 and magazine clippings mailed November 28 and December 5. Also four letters for Dan. Then we made the rounds of the gambling places and saloons. It doesn't sound like a very nice way to start our visit to Dawson, but there is where all Dawson hangs out and there is where everybody meets the man he is looking for, there is where all the schemes are hatched and there is where nearly all the business of the Klondike is transacted. That being the case I may as well introduce you to the various saloons.

They are all on the east side of the main street and in one long block. Any beyond that block are only of secondary importance. At the south end of the block is the Aurora which last summer was lively enough, but now most of its gambling games are closed for lack of patronage. Two or three doors north is the Pioneer, an old place, small and low and only frequented by a small crowd of regularly attendant loafers, some rich and mostly poor.

Another few doors down is the Northern. Doing the best business of any in town, and although it is an old place it is a popular old place. A jeweler had a little cage at the window on the left, and the office of the place is at the right. A long bar runs back at the right to a partition. On the left is a crowd of men and a small table or two, towards the back a big stove with its woodpile and nearby a barrel of water for those unable to buy anything else. It is a peculiar fact that all the Dawson saloons provide a big barrel of good drinking water. Passing through the big arch in the partition, we enter the gambling room which was doubled in size last summer by an addition in the rear. To the right is a crap game and then a faro table, to the left a roulette wheel, a dice game and two Blackjack tables. In the addition is a faro table and a draw poker table and three or four other tables, not in use. There also is a stove and a number of chairs.

After 8:00 P.M. the games are doing some business, a good many cappers of course, but they make a show of business anyway. In the daytime, the whole building is full of people waiting to meet a man or talking to him after meeting him, a regular public board of trade. Nowadays at 2:00 A.M., all the tables except the faro table are closed, and men lie stretched out sleeping on every table and bench. I don't know whether they are drunk or are just homeless, but from the small amount of drinking seen, I should say they are homeless. I don't know how late the faro game lasts but it seems to be the popular game, that starts first and closes last and is best patronized while open. Being such a board of trade, I have described the Northern rather in detail.

A little farther along is the Tivoli Theatre (more about it later) and then the Dominion. This is very much like the Northern only it makes a big show of architectural beauty. The saloon has an oilcloth floor, representing tile, and is papered in dark wallpaper, splashed with big wreathes of gold, enclosing a golden torch. Three big mirrors back of the bar, and the woodwork all painted and varnished. Gambling back of the saloon, and up a broad stairway on the second floor are billiard tables and poker tables and a lot of benches and chairs. In this saloon a great deal of board of trade work is also done.

Then north of the Dominion ranged on after another, though may be no in this exact order, are the Combination, the Phoenix saloon and dance hall, and the Opera House, a Swede's saloon and gambling joint, like a big barn and always dim and nobody there, except the boss and some cappers and a drunken Swede or two, in from the mines for the day. The Monte Carlo is a combined saloon, gambling house, theatre, dance hall, auction room, mining exchange and restaurant. More about it later. Next is the Oatley Sisters Dance Hall, business at times being so poor that nobody even looks in, but lively enough when the town is full of money. Then up on the corner are the faro tables of Dawson, with saloon and other games attached. There they play faro without a limit, either on the bets or the time and the two faro tables seem to be crowded day and night and the stacks of chips are so high they threaten to topple over.

There in a nutshell is the business section of Dawson. If you wish to meet any particular man in the Klondike country, you'll find him, or news of him, in one or the other of these places, most probably in the Northern, the Dominion or the Monte Carlo.

There are doctors, dentists and lawyers with offices somewhere near the saloons, and two or three hotels, and many lunch counters, and a few drug stores and clothing stores, located in the space between the saloons.

Farther north are the big barn like warehouses of the Alaska Commercial Company and of the North American Trading and Transport Company. They are very important factors in the business life of Dawson, but because of the length of frontage they occupy, the saloons have not seen fit to locate north of these warehouses, and they may be said to be the north limit of the business district.

South of the Pioneer and the Aurora there are some hotels and cafes and various minor businesses. Then farther south are the Barracks, the Recording Office and the Post Office and Dawson's famous Woodpile, in fact all those institutions that represent Government.

The Mounted Police operate the Woodpile, and they punish all manner of minor crime by condemning the culprit to the woodpile, where he and his fellows saw the wood that keeps the public offices warm, and keeps the guilty men warm while they saw.

So much for Dawson's business section.

Churches

I would not have you believe that the saloons and dance halls had an undisputed control of Dawson. The Mounted Police regulated them very well, and violent crimes were very few and far between. I have already noted that the buildings were open and heated on Sundays to serve as loafing houses for the crowd, but the games and the bars were closed.

Dawson also had its churches, and they were another factor in maintaining order.

The Roman Catholic Church was a short distance north of the Transportation Company's warehouses. St. Mary's Hospital was one of its major activities, which did very commendable service for Dawson and vicinity.

The first time Dan was in Dawson he went to church and got acquainted with the priest. On other trips to Dawson he was very generally at church on Sunday.

There was a Methodist Church and a Presbyterian Church somewhere in Dawson, but I don't remember that I ever knew just where they were. I may as well admit that churches of any denomination didn't particularly interest me in those days, although I was supposed to have some indirect connection with the Congregational Church.

On Front Street, down by the post office and the Barracks, there was the Episcopal Church. I had no more interest in that than I had in the others, but it was so situated on the main street that I frequently passed it by, and I could not help noticing what a contrast that little church was to all the other buildings on the street. How bare and unattractive all the other buildings were. The streets were rough and would have been muddy if there had been much rain. There wasn't a blade of grass the whole length of the street, except in the nicely kept little yard in front of the Episcopal Church.

The church itself was built of logs, but great care had been taken to select straight logs, all nearly of a size, and carefully jointed. The window and door frames were neatly painted and the cross which surmounted the little church boldly proclaimed its mission to the world, regardless of race or place.

The building was well back from the street, with a neat gravel walk leading from the street to the door. Along the property lines and each side of the gravel walk was a log rustic fence which harmonized with the architecture of the building. And that lawn of bright green grass completed this very pleasing and restful picture.

Anyone who passed by was bound to be impressed with this brave little church, silently but forcefully pointing out to him who cared to look, that there were better things than the bare crude buildings which housed Dawson's various kinds of games and entertainment. I didn't realize at the time what an impression it made on me. I noted the contrast, and it brought to my mind the difference in the purposes of those who comprised the church organization and those who conducted the Dawson's entertainments.

The very audacity of that little mission, presuming to combat the vices that seemed to completely overwhelm it, rather interested me as a sporting proposition, much like David and Goliath, but didn't interest me enough at that time to create any desire for a closer acquaintance.

Thompson was up bright and early, the first Sunday we were in Dawson, and invited me very cordially to attend this little church with him, but it was winter then, and we had been on a big hike the day before and I said, "No, thank you." So I never saw the inside of it, but since then I have regretted many times that I refused his invitation.

There isn't a word in my diary or my letters about that little church, except that Thompson asked me to accompany him; but it is one of the pictures that is indelibly printed upon my memory. Who knows to what extent it was responsible for my present interest in the Episcopal Church?

Breaking into Society

Monday after Thompson and I had read our mail, we went to the Northern and loafed until Thompson found an old friend of the trail named Simpson. He had a great scheme which he at once explained to Thompson. He professes (as everyone does) that he has an inside pull at the recording office. Thompson was to take dinner with him and his wife next day and hear more of it. Then we went upstairs in the Dominion and sat down and looked at the people about us. Thompson jumped up, made a dive and came back with a young fellow, tall, rather thin, with a little black straight cut mustache and a tired look about his eyes, whom he introduced as Condon of New York City. Had met him at Stewart. Of course, Thompson told him all his troubles and all about how his party had treated him and how he was in Dawson to see what he could do. Condon then told him where to buy a cabin, on the hill, and warned him about the sanitary conditions of the future and worried him about the "grafters" as they call the men professing to have a pull at the recorder's office, and about the laws of this country.

Then Condon proceeded to outline his scheme. He said the Laws of Canada are all right, but that a great many claims have not been legally staked and recorded, that the present owners are bound to lose them and someone else bound to get them when the flaw is detected. For seven months past he has made it a point to study the records and find these claims. He had just recently staked one of Alex McDonald's best claims, Number 19 Eldorado, but his claim had not yet been accepted for record. That very night he was off with a party for something good on Gold Hill, but the party was already complete, so Thompson and I could not come in this time. Next week he had something good on Dominion and Sulphur where we could get in.

He would be at home that evening and Mrs. Condon would be very glad to see Mr. Thompson again, and would I come too. We went. They live on the hill back of Dawson, 300 feet above the river, with a good spring of water near, and wood on the mountain top, a mile above them. He had not come home, but she was glad to see us, and held us until after 11:00, waiting for him. She believes in him and all his schemes, and helps him as occasion requires. When a man comes to see him, she either holds him or delivers Condon's message.

We stayed a couple of hours after Condon came, Thompson telling stories, and his Bedrock family troubles, and Condon talking about fractions and relocations, a subject that interested me greatly. As we were passing through town at 2:00 A.M. on our way to bed, we looked in the saloons, and found things very slow; a lagging dance in the Monte Carlo and a faro table here and there, was all the life to be seen,

Wednesday, Alfred and Emil went to the creeks to their lay. I went to see Olaf Winningstad, the engineer who promises to give me a job, if his railroad scheme materializes. We had a nice little chat. He is a believer in Indian River, thinks someone will make a pile there some day. Told me some of his experiences with Canadian surveyors, while building a part of the Canadian Pacific. When a friend came in, I left.

I found Thompson at the Northern, surrounded by an ever increasing crowd of trail acquaintances. It was strange how they all bunched up there, men unknown to each other, but all known to Thompson. His title at Lake Bennett had been Captain Thompson. They camped in a cove with about 500 others, and he knew them all. In Dawson, he was an entirely different person from the Thompson of Indian River. In a big crowd, all his jokes and stories seemed to be right to the point, while back at Bedrock those same stories had fallen flat. It was a pleasure to be with Thompson, when there were lots of people present.

One young fellow, Sam Taggart, wanted Thompson and me to visit him that evening and we went. Taggart boards with a New York newspaper correspondent, named Mrs. McDonnolds, whom he called in and introduced, and with whom Thompson at once began a lively conversation. Urbana, Illinois, being mentioned, Thompson told his story and she hers. The net result was that they were both born and brought up there and knew the same people and places, each confirming any statement the other made.

Then we played cards, hearts. Mrs. McDonnolds wanted to play for one cent a heart, she didn't actually propose it, but she hinted at it strongly enough. She said the liked to play poker, learned the bad habit in Kentucky. Thompson was on pins and needles until the threat of one cent a heart had passed by. It was very amusing to a spectator.

She mentioned Mike McGovern. You know Mike. One of the three who dug with Dan and Pop where we first camped on Indian River. So next morning I went to see Mike. He lives in West Dawson near where we are and was glad to see me. He gave me a lot of information and gossip about Mrs. McDonnolds and also told me about two bench claims on Lower Bonanza which were open for relocation two months ago. Said he got his information from Mrs. McDonnolds who has a stand in with Governor Ogilvie. He also had the numbers of four Dominion benches. He has an interest in two claims somewhere on Bonanza or Eldorado, but doesn't know how good they are. Jack Wamsley and a deaf man are now working one of them.

That evening Thompson, Stemple and I went to the Tivoli Theatre and it was the nearest approach to a theatre show that Dawson has yet seen. Friday we went to the Monte Carlo Theatre in the evening. That was simply flat, the worst excuse for a show that I ever saw in Dawson, and we've seen some very flat ones.

Women and Dance Halls

I was in the Klondike to make a lot of money, and not to spend money on a lot of gold-diggers. Consequently, the women of Dawson didn't mean much to me, but any story of Dawson that omitted its women would be very incomplete. There were lots of women in Dawson, and all kinds of women. A mining camp at once suggests brightly painted women who had seen better days. Of course, they were there, plenty of them, on a street by themselves, a block or two East of the main street. There were also respectable wives and almost respectable housekeepers, scattered throughout the residence district. It was a simple matter to classify these two extremes. The women who could not be classified, and therefore at once became interesting, were the women of the dance halls. They were there to make a fortune. Some didn't care how they made it and others were very particular. Many of them were as clean as wholesome looking young women as could be found anywhere. A man who danced with them was expected to buy drinks at the bar before and after each dance, and many girls scarcely tasted their many drinks.

When we were in Dawson in December, George put in a lot of time at the Opera

House and dance halls. We couldn't stand around evening after evening without noticing some of the particularly attractive girls. So when George and I were making the rounds of the saloons, we danced with some of them when our slim purses would permit. He said girls at the Oatley Sisters Dance Hall were particularly attractive and well behaved. The girls had to make conversation. We never believed a word of anything they told us about themselves, but I have always felt that there was a rich mine of human interest stories in the lives of many of these girls.

I happened to be a witness to one story that I was forced to believe. Every afternoon and evening we noticed a middle-aged man going the rounds of the saloons and dance halls, with a big tray full of candy carried by a rope across his shoulders. He was pointed out to us as a man who had left a $2000.00 a year job in San Francisco, to make his fortune in the Klondike. One cold afternoon, we noticed him, and a nice looking young woman, apparently his daughter, carrying on a rather excited conversation in front of the Combination saloon. He indicated in no uncertain terms that he was violently opposed to something, but they were making an effort to keep their conversation from being heard by passersby.

As we passed them on our way into the saloon, we heard her say, "I know it Dad, but there's no other way, if we ever expect to get back home. I'm going to do it."

"Oh Laura, to think that it could ever come to that."

That evening, we noticed a new face among the women at the Combination. It was "Laura." On days and nights that followed, we noticed the old candy man, with his tray hung to his neck, passing by the door of the Combination but never entering it, where formerly he had done a particularly good business.

When Dan and I were in Dawson in August, we were discussing the dance hall girls with a young fellow with whom we had scraped an acquaintance. He expressed his surprised at finding such a respectable looking class of girls in the dance halls. One girl had particularly attracted his interest and he had danced with her several times. He was telling us that he had asked her how she had happened to be there, so evidently out of place. She reddened, and for a moment seemed to resent his inquisitiveness. Then seeing that he was really interested, she faltered, her lip trembled, tears came to her eyes and she told him her story, which was substantially as follows:

Her home was in Oregon, where she lived with her mother and younger sister. She had been engaged to Joe for three months, when in July 1997 there came the news of the great strike in the Klondike. They were to be married in another three months, but Joe got the gold fever, and was among the first to climb Chilkoot Pass. While he was assembling his outfit, they talked it all over, and planned that Joe should send for her when he struck it rich; she would go to Dawson; they would be married there, and after Joe had gold enough they would return to the States.

Early in 1898 she received a letter from Joe in which he said "Come on, I've struck it." She came on one of the first boats up from St. Michael. She landed at Dawson with a light heart and a light purse. Joe was not there to meet here. She went to a hotel, expecting that in a day or two Joe would find her. He never came, and she was unable to find anyone who knew him, not a trace of him.

Her money didn't last long. She soon had to find a cheaper place to board, and began to look for work. Finally she had asked for a job at the dance hall and there she was, still waiting for Joe, and confident that he would soon come for her. If he didn't come by September she would have money enough saved, to take her back home.

After hearing her story, the young fellow affected a sympathy that he didn't then feel. He was rather sorry that he had given her the opportunity to spin such a fairy tale, and concluded that he had been mistaken when he believed her to be so much better than the other girls. He was inclined to be resentful, because she appeared to be so much better than she really was. As he finished telling us his story, he said "It just shows what liars people get to be after they once get into this country. She fooled me at first, and when I showed a little interest in her, she thought she could pull wool over my eyes and work me for a lot more dances."

Later, Dan and I had moved into our cabin, and when a stranger passed the door we invited him in to spend the night, and cook his grub on our stove. One evening when we had two such visitors, Dan happened to mention how foolish some women and girls were to come to the Klondike.

"Yes," said one of our guests, "I had just such a fool girl on the string back in Oregon. Last winter sometimes, just to kid her, I wrote her that I'd struck it rich and for her to come on up here. And would you believe it, the little fool packed her grip and came in on the first boat. Now she is making bushels of money down at Dawson and I haven't $10.00." It was Joe.

One evening in December, when I was dancing with one of the girls, an incident occurred that rather impressed me and greatly increased my respect for the young woman with whom I was dancing. As we leaned against the bar between dances, a drunken brute came in and began to use some particularly rough language in his conversation with one of the girls. That in itself was such a common occurrence that I paid no particular attention to what he was saying.

My partner was evidently talking to me and listening to him at the same time. She turned squarely around to me:

"Did you hear what he said?"

"What?"

"Did you hear what that fellow said?"

Her eyes blazed, and one might have thought he had addressed her instead of the other girl. "No" I answered. "I wasn't paying any attention to him."

"He called his Mother a _____."

And she said it just as though it were my own mother she was defending, instead of the mother of the drunken miner. The indignation of the girl took me so by surprise, that I'm not sure what I said by way of a reply, or whether I had time for a reply before she added "And even if she was, he ought to be the very last person ever to mention it."

The dance halls didn't put on stage shows, but it was nothing uncommon for some amateur to volunteer some sort of stunt. One evening at the Oatley Sisters Dance Hall we quite enjoyed ourselves. Business was rather slow, and as the floor was not crowded, a big rough fellow, with a drink too much, started to show the crowd that he could sing and dance. He had a good bass voice, and was amusing himself, and entertaining the spectators. He was having such a good time all by himself, that it really amused us.

Among the spectators there was a young fellow who had a daytime job as a waiter at one of Dawson's many lunch counters. He was tall and thin and had also had too many drinks. So he felt that it was up to him to show the world that he was better than the first performer. He could neither sing nor dance, but tried to do both. Alone, he would have been very tiresome, but his efforts to equal and surpass the other made him rather amusing for a little while. He greatly enjoyed singing a song with an endless number of verses. There was a great sameness to all the many verses, and the tune almost automatically suggests itself if proper regard is paid to the accented words. Here is a typical verse:

> "And so they went a hunting,
> Something more to find,
> And then they came to a jackass,
> And that they left behind.
> The Englishman said 'twas a jackass,
> The Scotchman he said nay,
> The Irishman said 'twas a beansack,
> Set up and stuffed with hay.
> And so they went a hunting…."

It was interesting to note that the first verse or two appealed to the crowd as being very funny. The next two or three got no applause, and then as the spectators began to drift toward the door, the floor manager promptly suppressed the would-be actor.

There was a big difference between the girls of the dance halls and those on Dawson's stage. The dance hall girls were interesting, and if we had had lots of money they might very possibly have been dangerous. The women on the stage can best be described in a single word, as being "tiresome." They couldn't sing nor dance, but they persisted in trying to. When they were not on the stage they would dance with the miners, and because they were less attractive than the girls of the dance halls, they were much bolder, and tiresome.

14

STAMPEDING WITH THOMPSON

Our Bonanza Stampede, February 1899

Stampeding is much like prospecting. The gold seeker knows very well that most of his stampedes will turn out to be only wild goose chases, but there is always the chance that the next stampede may develop a gold mine.

I have already explained in some detail how parts of some claims, and fractions between some claims, were open for relocation. So when Mike McGovern told me about two bench claims on Bonanza Creek, I felt that it was worth our time to investigate them especially as the information had originated with Mrs. McDonnolds.

One of my letters contains this paragraph:

> I'm just making friends and acquaintances right and left on this trip to Dawson. The Lord may help those who help themselves in the States, but not here. Here the recording office helps those that are willing to stake a claim for one half of it, and so many people want help that we have to be acquainted if we get any.

So on Saturday February 4, Thompson and I stampeded. I had told him about the Bonanza bench claims and as there were two of them, we went after them. It was only about eight miles up there, which was a matter worth considering. So we started. At one time Bonanza was supposed to be all right all the way to its mouth, but the winter of 1897–98 rather killed all the claims below Number 40 Below Discovery. Bench claims opened up in the summer of 1898, gave the lower part of the creek a better name, and now they have found pay in several good claims, as far as Number 80 Below. There is a fine trail all the way; for the first miles or so we went on the Klondike River, then traveled on the Tramway as they call the toll road or trail cut out and bridged by the toll company. Foot passengers now use it, free of charge. Cabins extended up the Klondike and the toll road, nearly to Bonanza.

Then the trails lead through the wide wooded valley of Lower Bonanza. There were few signs of work until we got to Number 66 Below. Here was one deep hole and a whole row of shallow holes, evidently the deep one had hit pay and they are opening the mine. To our right as we neared Number 61, a point of land sticks out and the creek goes around it. This point is a good paying bench and is being worked by a number of parties. Rounding the point we talked to a man who was building a fire in a tunnel which they are burning into the bench. They were making a tunnel so they might wheel the dirt out and have it handy to sluice. One of these claims 100 feet square was bought last summer by some Armenians for $100.00. It is now worth $15,000.00. At Creek Claim Number 59 we stopped to talk to the man working the windlass that hauls up the bucket of pay dirt and he showed us some coarse colors he had noticed as he dumped the buckets. Thompson saw one and asked for it and got it. Many said the pay ran as high as $3.00 per pan. They never say what it will average.

Our two claims were Numbers 53 and 54, Left Limit, which means left hand looking down stream. The creek claims by the old law are 500 feet long. The Hillside and Bench Claims by the new law are 250 feet. So they are designated as Lower Half or Upper Half, Left or Right Limit. Lower half being that 250 feet. So they are designated as Lower Half or Upper Half, Left or Right Limit. Lower Half being that 250 feet farthest downstream. I didn't know which half was open. But in looking the ground over it was evident that the upper half of Number 53 was recorded, for men were working there. And it was evident that the upper half of 54 was the better, but in my opinion not so good as 53. So I staked Number 53 Lower Left Limit, Hillside Claim 250 feet along the creek and 1000 feet up the hill. Thompson staked Number 54 Upper Left Limit, Hillside. Then back we went to Dawson, and were tired when we got there, for a 16 mile walk is something when you are not in training.

Monday morning at 8:15 Thompson and I were in line at the recorder's office. And there we waited until 9:15. Cold wait too. There were only three men ahead of us, and a big string behind us when the door finally opened. Two women behind us were given preferred attention and got to transact their business first. When I got the window his highness, Mr. Hardman, very politely informed me that my claim was a fraction and was not open for location. The law is that no bench or hillside claim can be located if it has less than 250 feet front. The 100 foot claim was recorded in 1897 and the 250 feet in 1898 thus leaving me on a fraction. Of course, I had not measured it, nobody ever does when staking. I had just made sure I had staked enough, had staked the fraction and a hundred feet or more of the 250 foot piece.

Then he told Thompson that both claims opposite 54 were already recorded. I immediately went back to Number 53 Bonanza to have a good look at the ground and see whether he told me the truth, and I found that he had. I found stakes, names, etc., as he had said. Claim Number 53 was so nearly 500 feet long that I could not stretch my fraction beyond 150 feet. So ended our Bonanza stampede and Mike McGovern's stock went down accordingly.

Our Big Stampede, February 8–11

Of course, we were disappointed in the way our Bonanza Stampede turned out, and I began to make plans of tying up with Winningstad in the engineering business. Wednesday morning, February 8, when I found Winningstad was absent from his office, I drifted over to the Northern, and there found Thompson all excited, and much relieved at having found me.

Condon had just succeeded in finding out the situation on Sulphur Creek, and needed help in putting over the biggest thing of the season. It turns out that Sulphur Creek had been staked in 500 foot claims, after the law had decreed that 250 feet was the limit. That was common knowledge. Everybody knew that, everybody had been wondering how the owners could successfully hold more than 250 feet.

The thing which was not generally known was that because of a recent court decision at Ottawa, half of each of those good claims was now open for relocation. Another thing that was being kept very quiet was that some of the higher officials in the Dawson Recording Office, proposed to have a big slice for themselves when these claims were relocated. They were not permitted to stake and record claims, therefore, they were working through Condon, and as he could only stake one claim himself, he had to find men upon whom he could depend to carry out the plan successfully. He had worked out a plan in which he assigned a particular claim to each of 20 men, covering the best claims on the creek. Thompson and I were two upon whom he depended. We were to stake the claims, and offer them for record. The recording office would refuse to accept our claims, when first presented, but when the lawyer, who was in with them quoted the recent Ottawa decision, they would be compelled to record our claims. These legal matters would all be taken care of by the men above Condon without cost to use who staked the claims. We who staked the claims had to bind ourselves to convey an undivided three-quarter interest in our claims to Condon and he in turn would divide with those above him.

Back in the United States, neither Thompson nor I would ever have been a party to any such grafting scheme, but apparently when a man is out for gold he had no conscience. We jumped at the chance, and thanked Condon for the opportunity he had given us.

That was Wednesday noon. Condon ordered us to meet him at discovery claim on Sulphur Creek on Friday at 1:00 P.M. and he would then assign us our claims. So away we went, just as we were. It was a long tramp and we would have to hurry to make it in 48 hours. I wore my coat and vest under my mackinaw coat, I'd been wise to have stopped and left them somewhere but I never thought of it. So at 12:30 we set out, not knowing where we went, or where or when we would stop. We were sure of one thing. It was no general stampede, the whole country would not be racing for the prize. We chosen few, we fellows with pulls, were going out there on a little stampede that had reserved seats attached.

We went by way of Hunker, same as I had before Christmas. The trail was good and broad and we made good time to Last Chance Road House, as far as I had gone before. It was about 4:30 then and still good day light. So on we mushed. There are road houses every mile or two but we wanted to get Number 30 Below if we could, for Thompson knew of a man there with whom we could stop. Last Chance is 16 miles from Dawson and Number 30 Below is 21 or 22 miles. The trail is not so good on that last five miles, so we made slower time. It began to get dark, and we began to get tired, so it was 6:00 P.M. before we got to Number 30 Below. Here we found that Thompson's friend Menzie was over at Number 17 Above on Sulphur. So we put up at a road house, kept by a ladylike San Francisco woman named Mrs. Moulton. A Jap cooks and a man tends the bunk house. Thompson was nearly dead and I wasn't any too lively. They provided a very good supper for $1.50, that is good for this country, but the bunks were no good. They were made of poles, same as ours at Bedrock, but were covered with coarse crooked pine branches, that stuck into us at all angles. And the blankets too thin to afford any protection from the pine branches.

Next morning, it was cold, 45 below and as we only had 14 miles to go, we took our time, and started about 9:30 up Gold Bottom Gulch. This really is a main branch of Hunker and runs nearly in a straight line with Hunker and Sulphur. We went up Gold Bottom for six miles, and there the trail takes to the mountain side and winds up the mountain for more than two miles to what is called the Dome.

The Dome is a very commonplace mountaintop 4,250 feet above sea level. It doesn't seem to be any higher than its neighbors, but there is a popular superstition that from the Dome comes all the gold of the country. I'm not superstitious, but from the Dome one trail falls down abruptly into Sulphur, another into Gold Bottom and so to Hunker, another leads along over the ridge a few miles and then falls down into Bonanza, near its head and a fourth, going over the ridge a mile or two drops down into Dominion, and all those creeks are rich. The Dome just pokes its head above the timber line, and on top where the four trails meet are a couple of road houses. I made a fair sketch showing how they looked to us as we approached them, winding along the mountainside, nearing its top.

From the Dome we had a great view of the Rocky Mountains off to the northeast of us. They don't look very far away and of course are all white, just a jagged row, like a piece of white paper torn in fancy shapes for pantry shelves. At the foot of the snow covered mountains there is a great flat plain evidently covered with trees. I suppose there are valleys and gulches there, but it looks as flat as a billiard table. We could see one fairly well defined canyon there, with snow on the side slope. Between that and the foreground is what appears to be a rolling prairie of low mountain tops.

We rolled and tumbled and slid down into Sulphur Creek and at about Number 40 Above began to see signs of work, and from there down the work was more active.

We stopped at Number 17 Above and found Bob Menzie and his partner Frazier at home. Thompson did not really know him, but had a letter from Menzie's sister, with whom

The Dome and road houses.

he is well acquainted. We were warmly received and stayed all that night, the next day and next night.

Friday morning we took a look at Menzie's claim. He staked it in 1897 and has not worked it until this year. He has it all let out in 50 foot lays. That is, he lets two men have 50 feet to work, and they get half of what they take out. His claim is good, getting $2.50 and $3.00 pans. They pick down through 20 feet to 30 feet of frozen muck and then there is about 18 inches of gravel. This gravel and 18 inches of the rotten bedrock are pay dirt. They have nearly undermined the whole claim along a pay streak some 20 feet or more broad. Here the pay streak comes close to the present creek bed, which doesn't happen in many claims.

After dinner we quit visiting and went about our business, that is, walked down the crooked creek bed to Discovery and to the road house at Number 3 Below. About 3:00 P.M. Condon arrived with three other men and first had his lunch there for $2.00. Then we went out to do our job of staking claims. Condon explained that he had studied the geography of Sulphur Creek, so that we would not be expected to stake that part of some claims where the supposed owner had sunk a shaft and was then busily mining it. Some owners were so doubtful of their rights on the 250 feet of their claim farthest from Discovery that they had confined their operations to the 250 feet nearest to Discovery. Condon had selected such claims, on that part of the creek that was known to be good.

It's a bit exciting to go boldly in and set stakes on a place claimed by another man. On the American side we would have been candidates for a valley of rifle shots. The Mounted Police made things awfully uncomfortable for anyone who lost his temper and shot anybody, so we felt that we were fairly safe from rifle shots, but the police paid no attention to black eyes or broken noses.

We didn't actually drive stakes at each end of our claims in that solidly frozen ground. We cut the tops off little pine saplings with our hand hatchet, about four feet above the ground; blazed one side of the standing pole and marked our claim thereon. Thompson and I worked together, the others had gone farther down the creek. It was almost dark, and we were rather glad that we were out of sight from the active mining operations, thanks to the brush and the many bends in the creek. Condon had also used such good judgment in selecting our claims, that we were not molested or even threatened. When we finished, it was nearly dark, and the mushing was bad as we went back to Number 17 Above, where we put up for the night.

Saturday, at 7:00 A.M. we were up and off again, bound to make Dawson before night. That was a good day's jaunt, about 35 miles, and the Dome to climb. It took us four hours and 15 minutes to go to Number 30 Below on Hunker. There we had a fifty cent lunch of 5 doughnuts and coffee and rested until 12:30. Then we set out again to make the 21 miles to Dawson. Thompson was pretty stiff, but limbered up. We made fine time to the mouth of Hunker. Rested there 15 minutes then another four miles brought us to the Cliff House near Bear Creek. Here we had a fifty cent lunch, and it was beginning to get dark. Eight miles more to Dawson, Thompson all in and I none too lively. Our luck overtook us in the shape of an empty dog team, driven by an obliging young fellow. Thompson asked him for a ride and got it. The fellow was in a hurry to get to Dawson, so he urged his dogs to a brisk trot all the way and ran after them. He was used to running after dogs, but I wasn't, but will you believe it, I ran four miles, without resting, in one half hour, after I had already walked 26 or 27 miles. There is where my surplus clothing showed up to a great disadvantage. At the end of four miles I was boiling and Thompson on the sled was half frozen. So to average things we stopped, thanked the young fellow and went into a road house there. Thompson warmed up on hot coffee while I sat and cooled off and took a bit of water, when I dared. There was a real pretty Swede girl in there who spoke English fairly well, and I for one was not at all sorry to have an excuse for waiting there a while. It seemed like home at Rockford, to see a Swede girl. It took Thompson an hour to get warm and me an hour to get cool. Then we broke away and made the rest of the trip to Dawson and over the river to West Dawson, 35 miles in 10 hours.

At West Dawson we found ourselves without a home. Fred and Nels who owned the cabin we had been using, had returned, and old Carl Jorgensen had lost his job as cook for McDonald's Road House and had come to Dawson and was staying there, so therefore, Thompson and I asked another friend of ours to invite us to sleep in his cabin on Arena Gulch, Indian River. His party has generally been called in my letters The Frenchmen. This cabin is also in West Dawson, nearer the river than the other. There are two empty bunks and they have real mattresses, brought in by way of St. Michael. Lambert is waiting here for mail. A young fellow named Kershaw from Racine, Kenosha and Tacoma, uses one bunk and owns the mattresses.

How circumstances haul and pull us about, living here, there and any old place, winter or summer. We are tramps and nothing else. Such is life in the Klondike.

The letter which I sent home the following Monday has only the following brief statement as to how our stampede ended:

> Today I had my hands full of business connected with the Sulphur Creek affair. I am by no means sure of the outcome of it. So the less said the better. If it succeeds, all right, if not, it's nothing new or unexpected.

There was a lot more to it than that. We presented our claims for record and as per schedule we were informed that the claims were not open for relocation. We noted the day and the hour when our claims were refused, and signed some papers prepared by someone and presented to us by Condon, and gave him our claim papers.

Then the legal talent who were steering the affair brought suit to compel the recording office to record the claims. That took time, so it was two or three months before we got the final chapter of the story of that stampede.

The original owners of those Sulphur Creek claims quite naturally put up a big legal fight, and that compelled them to hire some Dawson City lawyers. Those lawyers had no trouble at all in beating the lawyers who represented Condon's relocaters. The original owners quite naturally had to pay fat fees to the lawyers who had defended them so successfully and those same lawyers split their fat fees fifty-fifty with Condon's lawyers: They had rigged the entire scheme and had made cats paws of the easy marks who made the Sulphur Stampede and we thought we were so smart.

Before I leave this adventure, I want it clearly understood that I am now firmly of the opinion that the officials in the recording office were generally honest. They were most unjustly slandered by dishonest schemers, but the picture as I have painted it, shows the feeling that then prevailed in Dawson.

So that you may know that Thompson and I were not the only easy marks in the Klondike, I'll have to tell a story I heard about another easy mark.

The Old-Timer as a Gold-Digger

The Cheechaco in this story was one of those chaps, who realized that he was green, and so he spent a lot of time finding what he called a genuine Old Time Yukoner who would be his partner and teach him all the tricks of prospecting.

When he finally found the Old Time Yukoner the Cheechaco bought grub enough for two, and also other needed equipment and the two set out with heavy packs on their backs.

About 2:00 P.M. the Old Time Yukoner said, "This looks like a likely place to find gold. Shall we stop and try it?" "Guess we better," said the Cheechaco. So they pitched camp, had a good supper and a smoke. The Old Time Yukoner told a few stories and they turned in for a big sleep.

Next morning, after a good breakfast (for the Old Time Yukoner was a handy cook) the Cheechaco takes his pick and shovel, "Well, where shall we dig?" "The land don't just lay right here. Let's go up creek a bit, it looks as if we had better chances farther up," said the Old Time Yukoner. So they pack up the camp, and mush on for a few hours. Then as night approaches the Old Time Yukoner finds another place that looks good, and they camp there for the night.

Next morning, it's the same story, and so it went for a month, until grub was about gone. Then the Cheechaco got cold feet, returned to Dawson and started for the American Side, leaving a pick that was still sharp, and a shovel that was still bright, and what was left of the camp equipment, as a gift to the Old Time Yukoner.

56 Degrees Below Zero

It took us until Wednesday to turn our claim papers over to Condon's Lawyers, and deed them a three-quarter interest. We felt so good about our supposed quarter interests in good 250 foot claims that Thompson wanted to get back to Bedrock at once and cut loose from his party and bring his share of the outfit back to Dawson.

I had carried some of Dan's mail around for two weeks. I wanted to tell Dan about our Sulphur Creek Claim, and I felt that it would take the lawyers two or three months to get the claims through court, so I was about ready to return to Bedrock. But I had partly arranged with Winningstad that I would help him with engineering work of a new Water Works that was contemplated for Dawson. It was proposed to get unpolluted water from the Klondike River and pipe it around Dawson. The thing had been dragging along and I was not inclined to set around Dawson and wait for it to be started. So I took the bull by the horns and went to Governor Ogilvie's office and asked for an appointment with the governor. Greatly to my surprise I was soon ushered in, and asked him whether the Water Works was really planned or was just saloon gossip. He was very nice to me; they contemplated such an improvement, but there was no immediate prospect.

So Sunday morning, February 19, we started back to Bedrock. We had a good breakfast, and left town at 8:30 A.M. dragging our little sleds and scanty outfits. We had no sooner hit the trail, than Thompson changed back into the same old timid cranky, peevish, Bedrock City Thompson. Just like Dr. Jekyll and Mr. Hyde. It was a nasty day. A regular blizzard, blowing and drifting but the wind was on our backs. It was only 15 below zero, comparatively warm. Seven miles out from Dawson we pulled up at a road house and stopped for the day. If I had been alone I would have gone the other 12 miles to Ensley, but I was afraid the old man might freeze to death if I insisted on taking him along. The wind was shifted to our faces, and it was getting colder. He persisted in wearing a full suit of cotton next to his tender old skin, which, of course, soaked full of sweat and was always cold, and at 50 below must have been just like ice.

I could write a book about that afternoon and evening and the road house where we stopped opposite Swede Creek. It is the worst house or excuse for one in the country, kept by a man who was totally disgusted with the country and anxious only to get out. He was just about ready to go out over the ice at that time. I told you about eating lunch at this road house, on our trip to Dawson. For fifty cents the man put out a meal of boiled beans, boiled pork, sourdough bread and black coffee. Thompson asked if he might have some milk for the coffee and some butter for the bread and some vinegar for the beans. He also said he preferred fried bacon instead of boiled salt pork. However, he didn't get any of these luxuries. He told me in a terror-stricken voice that he didn't believe the man had washed the dishes. I was very well aware of that as I had seen him scrape them out and rub the plates on his coat tail and the knives and spoons between his fingers. He had no forks. I was also certain his fingers had not been washed for weeks. The conversation led around to family affairs, then the man got out a little roll of oilcloth and pulled out of it a photo of himself and two boys, nice bright little kids, and there he was a nice clean looking mechanic, a blacksmith perhaps. He had become all hair and whiskers, like a weedy garden, sloppy and dirty without any ambition except to get back to the States. He must have thought a lot of those two boys and must have had a soft spot in him where they are concerned, even though he was completely indifferent to everything about his road house. Thompson said quite unflinchingly and quite too cheerfully that if his boys were to see him then they'd probably be afraid of him and surely wouldn't know him.

For two or three hours Thompson continued to make similar insulting remarks that should make any man fight, but the man never resented it. I came near punching Thompson, when the insulted man wouldn't.

Our supper and breakfast were exactly like our dinner, and the bed was horrible, just a lot of 3 inch poles slung over two other poles and a piece of canvas laid on them. Thompson and I slept together in the bunk, which was only 3 feet wide. A late arrival slept on the floor. Our host baked more sourdough bread on the stove which was made of stone, after we went to bed. Of course, Thompson wanted to know if this couldn't be that, and that the other. He asked for a wash basin in the morning without getting it and told me most solemnly that he didn't believe the man ever washed himself. And I held my peace throughout and never boiled over, but I was boiling inside. It was so cold that morning that I kept Thompson moving after we got started.

We found when we reached Ensley Creek that afternoon that it had been 50 degrees below zero, when we started our that morning and at noon it was still 30 below. We stopped at Ensley long enough to get a good square $1.50 meal cooked by a woman and then mushed on to McDonald's Indian River Road House, about 9 miles. We reached McDonald's at 5:00 P.M. We cooked our own supper on his stove. We greatly enjoyed our evening. We found Bert Karr there and he informed us that all of our Bedrock City partners were busily moving our outfits to some mysterious place up river, beyond Nine Mile Creek. Chris Nielsen came in later, on his way to Dawson for mail and more tobacco. He told us that the Indian River trail was badly drifted and hard, slow going.

Two dog team drivers and their dogs put up for the night at McDonald's. They had left Skagway on January 25, just four weeks to make the trip. That night Thompson and I slept comfortably in two of McDonald's bunks.

Tuesday, February 21, 1899, was the coldest weather I ever saw or ever hope to see. I was up before 6:00 A.M. and bought a good breakfast, because I felt that we would need plenty of fuel for our trip to Bedrock. I took advantage of Thompson's later rising by going up the Indian River trail for half a mile to see if it really was as bad as Chris had reported it. It was bad, and it was cold, but we were much mystified by Karr's report that Dan and the others had started moving our outfits up river. That settled it. We would start anyway. We had made 21 miles the day before, so 12 miles to Bedrock didn't look like much of a trip. We had experienced 50 below zero a lot of times and we knew that it was cold when it was 50 below. It was 56 below that morning when we set out at 9:00, but as we didn't realize what that other 6 degrees meant, especially when there was a stiff breeze blowing. At 40 below we had always been quite comfortable, but we had noted a big difference between 40 and 50 below. At 40 or 50 below there had never at other times been any breeze blowing. I had seen so much 50 below weather since November that I was quite used to it and no longer covered my nose for such temperature. To be sure it always froze a little around the edges of the nostril at 50 below but that was not as unpleasant as it was to have the hood of my sweater converted into a great solid mask of ice, as it was bound to do it I covered my face with the hood. At 56 below I was quite ready to put up with the discomfort of the hood over my face. Possibly the stiff breeze intensified the cold. Thompson had one of those old-fashioned knitted mufflers that he would about his head, neck and face several times and still had a little left to hang over one shoulder trail in the breeze like a flag. When we took a full breath of that 56 degrees below zero air we thought we could feel icicles piercing the inside of our lungs. It was cold!

Thompson and I caught it on Indian River. The stiff breeze that had been blowing for the last few days seemed to reach everywhere and the trail on Indian River was drifted full of snow; just hard enough that we could step on it, break through the crust and hardly pull a foot out of it again. The six pound sled and its load rode the stuff nicely but it was hard slow walking. We figured to stop at the Scurvy cabins to get warm and have a lunch. When we reached there we found that their owners had abandoned them and taken everything with them. The doors swung open and the cabins had drifted partly full of snow. So we kept on going. About a mile beyond there, we found a little shelter on the ground and the other end was supported by a horizontal pole. The ends were filed with pine brush, but the front was entirely open. This shelter was just about big enough for two of us to squat down under. The builders had made a fire in front of it, and the cold ashes of their fire contained a considerable amount of unburned charcoal. There was also a little dry wood left there. At the risk of freezing my hands, I succeeded in getting a fire started, but as we squatted there under the shelter, we lost heat because of the wind that whipped around and through the shelter, faster than we could absorb heat from the fire.

Thompson was cold and I knew it, but he insisted that the fire was nice and comfortable. His head began to nod, and I noticed that he would close his eyes for a few moments, every little while. "Get up! Let's get going!" No. Thompson was comfortable and he wasn't going to start out again until he had rested a little longer. I don't need any diary or notes, after all these years to remind me of how I felt then. There was old Thompson slowly freezing to death, right in front of me. I dragged him to his feet, and shock him until his teeth rattled. I tied his sled so that it trailed mine. My sled was equipped with a pulling rope that went over my shoulder and left both my arms free. I put one arm around Thompson's waist and we started out. Sometimes when he broke through the crust on the snow, he couldn't lift his own foot out and I supported him with one hand and pulled his foot out with the other. I was plenty warm with 15 minutes of that sort of exercise, and by that time Thompson's circulation was restored and we had no more excitement in the two miles that brought us to the Nielsen cabin.

We reached there about 2:00 P.M., five hours to make that eight miles. Then the old fellow's nerve failed him completely. He feared that we would both want to sit down and freeze to death, that we lacked strength to go the other four miles, even though the trail was much better due to travel that there had been between Nielsen's and Bedrock. He was physically able, but mentally unable to go that four miles. He feared it might get dark before we got there and that we might wet our feet. Under such conditions there was only one thing to do. We told John and Fred that we proposed to spend the night with them. They only had three bunks but Chris was at Dawson, so Thompson slept in his bunk and I slept on the floor.

I learned a new card game that afternoon and evening. They called it solo, but I've never been able to find that particular kind of solo described in any book on card games. The queen of spades, and some card in the club suit and unusual powers, and on occasion the players would "frog." We enjoyed the game so much that I have always regretted the way in which the play of the game slipped from my memory.

I have always remembered the date of that journey up Indian River, because the next day was Washington's Birthday (February 22), and since then, I've always felt that I know just how Washington's soldiers felt at Valley Forge.

Next morning the temperature had risen to about 40 below zero, and we had a pleasant and easy trip to Bedrock, making the four miles in an hour and a half.

In our cabin everything inside was upside down, and Dan was nowhere in sight. It was dry in the cabin, but outside the glacier was piled high on three sides of the cabin. I was certainly glad that Karr had given us advance information about the exodus from Bedrock.

Dan had become anxious because we were away so long, and that very morning he had started down river seeking news about us. He was visiting with the Frenchmen when Thompson and I passed their cabin. When he found that we had missed him he hurried back to Bedrock.

Goodbye Thompson

Thompson's troubles began just the minute he got back to Bedrock. In his absence his company had met, and unanimously voted to pitch him out of the company. The company had been organized in a very formal way, with bylaws and a written contract. Thompson had put into the contract a clause that if any member dropped out the others should retain

20 percent of the share which would normally be allotted to the quitter. The others had declared Thompson to be a quitter because he had been away for nearly a month. Thompson threatened to appeal to the Mounted Police to straighten out that injustice, but his hands were tied because among his personal effects he had hidden away some 1,500 cigars that he had smuggled into Canada, to avoid the very stiff duty. The others gave him to understand that if he raised any disturbance about the 20 percent of his share which they took, they would report the smuggled cigars, and they were just mean enough to do it too. The cigars were worth more than all Thompson's share of the outfit and it wasn't advisable to get the cigars into trouble for a few beans and a little bacon. Thompson moved his stuff into Stemple and Karr's empty cabin and next day hauled his cigars down to Arena and got one of the Nielsen's to help him hide them.

Meanwhile his partners were dividing the outfit and moving a lot of it up the river preparatory for that mysterious trip. It seems they only had a little indivisible company stuff such as hardware, tents, stoves, etc. Thompson owned most of the tools and Frank Reed owned the rest, brought from New York. So they agreed fairly well on the indivisible stuff. They tried to bulldoze Thompson into paying $17.00 cash balance on this stuff, but he made a good bluff that worked. Having his cigars out of the way, he went to the Mouth and saw the police. They told him to put it in the hands of a lawyer. The other three didn't know what scant attention Thompson would get from the police, so they went upriver next day, and Thompson was out just 20 percent of his grub. I advised him to smash the cabin door down and help himself, and that is what he eventually did; only instead of the door he went down the chimney. When the population along the Indian River heard of it they chuckled and were glad. Fred, Frank and George found it out some two weeks afterwards when they returned to Bedrock for more grub.

Thompson met a colored man, mushing down Indian River a day or two after he returned from the Mouth, and hired him for $10.00 and board to pull his outfit to Dawson.

PART III

Our Second Spring and Summer, February 22 to August 16, 1899

15

Mysterious Creek

Note: If I were relating my adventures for the entertainment of the average reader, I might feel that it would be a violation of the rules of authorship to give the details of another hard winter journey. If you feel that Mysterious creek is "just another battle with the weather" you may skip this chapter. I find such a lot of pleasure in reviewing those events that I propose to relate them in whatever detail seems necessary.

It is characteristic of all works of fiction, whether romance or adventure, to describe the conflicts between various persons, and their emotions. My story describes the conflict between a well-organized little group of Cheechacos and a Klondike winter in one of its most ill-natured moods.

Possibly, I have created an impression that we had been enduring hardships at every previous step in our journey, and from my present viewpoint, as I look back 34 years, I feel that our life in the North was extremely active, to put it very mildly. However, I assure you that these adventures occurred, which I have related, and that we did not feel that they should be defined as being hardships. We enjoyed every phase of that life and if our toes were cold or our noses frozen, or we went on a fruitless stampede, it was all a part of the game.

That trip to Mysterious Creek, was an adventure which we frankly admitted at that time could well be described as hardship. We didn't see the humorous side of the trip then, as I see it now. In our impatient desire, that winter might end, so that we could begin our spring work, we jumped to a conclusion that the delightful minus 6 degrees to minus 15 degrees weather that followed our return from Dawson, was the forerunner of an early spring.

How It All Started

We found that Karr had been correct; our partners had hauled a lot of stuff somewhere up Indian River. Nobody seemed to know where they were going or why. All that Dan or anyone else knew, was that Fred Mack, who lived in a cabin at the Mouth of Nine Mile Creek had come down river and stated his case. During the summer he had spent months wandering among the hills and mountains, and late in the fall he had found what he thought was a wonderful prospect. He proposed that Dan and I, the Thompson Party and the Nielsen Party from Arena Gulch should go up there with a month's grub and plug the creek so full of holes that the pay streak could not escape us. None of us knew whither we were bound, nor what indications had convinced Fred Mack that it was so good. In our absence the others agreed to go for a month and see how they liked it and were promised a real gold field.

Dan had a knack of picking names that immediately proved popular and he had called the place Mysterious Creek long before we ever saw it. One of Fred's most persuasive points was that it would soon be March 1 and that the weather always warmed rapidly after the first of March. He proved that point by the blizzard and 56 degrees below zero that occurred in the latter part of February; winter's last struggle.

So two days after I got back to Bedrock, Dan and I hauled a load of 125 pounds each, consisting of our tent, tools, and grub, to a place we had selected about half way up to Nine Mile. Ford Cole, Frank Reed and George Trowbridge each took a load and followed us.

On Saturday, February 25, just about supper time a Swede named Dave Grassman stopped at our cabin and announced that Fred Mack had asked him to join the expedition, and had told him that Dan and I could direct him to Nine Mile. He had a heavy load, and a single dog named Jim, helped him pull the load. He had spent the previous night in the open about a mile below the Scurvy Camp. He had been so busy keeping a fire that he hadn't slept much, and was quite ready to eat his supper and sleep on our floor, without further conversation.

Sunday, February 26, 1899, was the anniversary of our start from Rockford. Dan and I celebrated, after we started Dave on his way, by mushing down to Arena Gulch to visit the Frenchmen, Dubray, Lambert and White. On the way we met John Mohlman and Fred Melby dragging a load upriver for Mysterious Creek.

Chris Nielsen joined us as we ate dinner with the Frenchmen. He had just returned from Dawson the evening before, having made the entire trip of 36 miles between 8:00 A.M. and 8:00 P.M. The weather had ranged between 20 below and 6 below, with a bright day and no breeze, and a good trail.

Monday, Dan and I and Thompson's ex-partners, made a real start for Mysterious Creek. We packed our stove, bedding, clothes, dishes, etc., and picked up our tent at the cache halfway to Nine Mile. Fred Mack and his brother Gene were delighted to see us and fed us royally on our arrival at Nine Mile. There were entirely too many of us for Mack's small cabin, so we put up Trowbridge's stove in one of the tents and cooked our meals there, and six extra lodgers slept on Mack's floor. The next night when the Nielsens arrived we had nine on the floor.

There were so many of us on that Mysterious Creek stampede that it seems rather necessary to make a detailed list of them.

First is Fred H. Mack, the discoverer of Mysterious Creek, and originator of the party. I had met him on several occasions, but knew little of him until we came up here, so I may not have a correct estimate of him. He is an ordinary sized man about 40 years old, steamboat engineer by trade. He hails from Minneapolis and has put in a long term on Mississippi River steamboats; has run a steam shovel in the Lake Superior iron ore mines, has done a bit of quartz mining around the stamp mills in the west and has worked some on Pacific Coast boats. I half believe that he tries to make out that he knows a lot more than he does. I'm sure I don't know whether he has any good prospects or not, he may have stretched that too, but it certainly looks like a good locality, with the mountain which we call Little Baldy as a possible source of gold quartz.

He has great confidence in this region and must have something back of it. He claims to have found good quartz around the headwaters of these creeks. Can't tell, may have something and may not. If he has it's worth going after. If not, I will know in another month.

I didn't expect to do more than to help Dan come up here with the grub, and then go to Dawson to work on the schemes I left there in February, but I was so pleased with the looks of the place, with Little Baldy Mountain in the background, that I just cut loose from all my other schemes and went in for this, gambling for big stakes at a long, very long chance. Time enough to look after small stuff when grub runs low, sometime in July.

Second is Gene Mack, Fred's younger brother about 22 years old. Has worked in the lumber woods of upper Wisconsin. He has seen a little of the world, up and down the Mississippi River, but that is about all. He's a pretty good worker.

Third is Bob Carroll, a fat good natured man who sings while he works. Came in here last September working for a company that brought in a big drove of cattle, who says he was fired as soon as he had safely landed the cattle in Dawson. He was on his uppers when Mack took him in for his board. He made the trip to Mysterious Creek with us but before we began to prospect Fred Mack sent him back to his cabin at Nine Mile to run a halfway house for any of the rest of us who might go to Dawson or down to Bedrock. There is not much to be said about Bob, except that the arrangement worked out very nicely, and we always found a warm cabin and good meals, as we went back and forth. Possible the fact that thirteen of us started for Mysterious Creek may have had its influence in sending Bob back, and possibly it really was because of Bob's quarrel with Jack Burns.

Note: If my story were fiction instead of biography, I am sure that I could devise a rather interesting story, about the steer that escaped from a drove, and was captured and killed at Nine Mile Creek and the little man Galvin to whom we sold our rabbits. My story would explain why it was that Bob Carroll was on his uppers, why he stayed hidden at Nine Mile Creek rather than living in Dawson, and why a mysterious quarrel subsequently developed between Bob and Jack Burns. There were lots of interesting things about the people we met that were never fully developed, and this particular train of circumstances always remained a puzzle to me.

Fourth, I list myself with whom you are quite well acquainted.

Fifth, Dan Dever needs no introduction.

Sixth, Seventh and Eighth is the Thompson Party (minus Thompson), Ford Cole, Frank Reed and George Trowbridge. When they ceased to be the Thompson Party, the boys for some unaccountable reason nicknamed them "The Chinamen," but Dan and I continued to call them the Thompson Party. The Nielsens told Frank Mack not to let them into the party. Dan was not consulted about them so he didn't say anything and Mack invited them. I'll bet he wouldn't if I'd been home. They are in bad repute. Everyone knows how they tried to skin Thompson and how he squared it. For three days at Nine Mile they sponged on the Mack brothers, taking the best of everything and not doing a lick of work. Of course, Ford got sick, invented a bad knee that always was worse when someone was looking at him. So George and Frank had to haul all the stuff from Nine Mile to Mysterious Creek. When here they set their tent off across the creek from the common herd, nothing so very wicked, but being off the beaten path, no one drops in to chat with them, unless he goes out of his way to do it. If there was any little coolness started on the trail, that was a good way to increase it. Fred Mack, as head of the party, visits their tent occasionally but only because he thinks he ought to. Only once or twice, they have visited Mack's tent of an evening. They seem to be catching a little of the dose they gave Thompson all winter.

Ninth is Dave Grassman, or "Tulie." He is a character. Swede about 40 years old. Started life as a sailor, learned his English from every nationality with whom he mixed. Tried fishing on the Pacific Coast for a number of years and for the past few years has been a fireman on Pacific steamboats. He can spin yarns "Fathoms" long. His vocabulary is immense but not such words as are commonly found in the dictionary or seen every day in print. He talks as if he were half full, but we are sure he isn't, not up here. I can't imagine his lingo nor can Dan, it is unique. He is one of the few men here who smoke cigarettes, and he pronounces the word "cigar-eat." He calls all small brush and the stunted pines that grow so thickly here "tulies." I don't know from what country the word originates. He speaks of tulies so frequently that the boys have nicknamed him Tulie. He can spin yarns about all the scrapes he has been in, and everything is either all right or all wrong with him. He says money is not good to him, and he never saw a doctor that was any good to anyone. He came here in 1897, made about $5000 that winter, gambled it all and secured a claim that he could have sold then for $7500. He still has it but nobody wants it now. Made $2000 last summer, building cabins and representing the owners on some claims; that's gone too and he is here just because he has the grub. A little money will not do him any good; he must have a big lot or it will not stick to him. His dog Jim is an oversized fox terrier. Jim knows a lot more than many men. He is the pet of the camp, and a big help to Dave while on the trail, and a nuisance to feed while we are in camp.

Tenth is Jack Burns. At eleven he left home and for six years worked at sign painter's trade at fifty cents per day. Then he came home, went away again and worked a year at blacksmithing, then back home. His uncle tried to make a butcher of him. Worked 10 weeks, left home and has never been back since. He lost three fingers of his left hand railroading on the N.P.R.R. has spent some six years as a cowboy. He knows something about Muskegon, Michigan and the lumber woods, and has a large and assorted lot of songs, all kinds, and that covers a large variety, including some that are not so nice. I believe he is a thorough deadbeat, but that doesn't worry me, it interests me. Dan thinks too that he is a deadbeat, but Dan thinks that a deadbeat is something horrible, an old prejudice arising from Dan's former business. I first met him at McDonald's Road House back in November. He is a terrible boaster, just right for a good brakeman.

Eleventh, Twelfth, and Thirteenth is the Nielsen Party, Chris, Fred and John, and they need no further introduction. They have a big wooly dog of mixed parentage, who had never done enough work on the trail to know what it was all about. They brought Jumbo to Mysterious Creek and it's hard to say whether he was an asset or a liability.

Mushing to Mysterious Creek

Wednesday, March 1, the wind of February had filled Indian River trail with snow, above Nine Mile, and as there had been nobody down from the upper river, we not only had to transport our outfits upriver from Nine Mile; we also had to break a fresh trail. Tuesday, with the help of Dave's dog Jim, Dan and I had taken a load up river four miles, breaking a fresh trail for the last two miles. The old trail had been blown full of packed snow, snow that seemed hard, but not hard enough to hold up man or sled. Dan and I and the Thompson Party hauled light loads over the trail, making about one mile an hour. It was tough work. Just as we set our feet to pull the sled out of a hole, our feet would break through the crust and give us a little shakeup. Those three sleds helped the trail a lot. As far as we had gone, the trail was fairly good when the whole party of 13 started out next morning.

On Wednesday we said goodbye to Fred Mack's comfortable log cabin, and advanced our headquarters to a point about two miles above where Dan and I cached our load on Tuesday. Dan and I broke trail again, followed by John and Chris and their dog Jumbo, and by Dave and his dog Jim. That made a rather smooth and easy trail for Ford, Frank, and George.

Dan and I cut some wood and got a mighty poor excuse for a meal, while Dave went back and helped the Macks bring their outfit up to the place where we had decided to camp for the night. Then Dan and I went back to the cache for another load. While we were gone, some of the boys erected three tents, and others broke trail beyond the place where we were to camp for that night.

Ever since our return from Dawson, we had been having such nice comfortable weather, only about 20 degrees below zero each night. But just as soon as we left Mack's comfortable cabin it began to get colder, and by the time we had our supper, it was more than 40 degrees below zero. Of course, we were comfortably warm all day for the sun was up and we were working, but the job of making camp is not done as quickly as it is described. We set up three tents, two 10 by 12 footers and a little one holding two men. We set them up roughly, right on the snow and carpeted with boughs from the spruce trees. There were six to sleep in our tent and eight to eat there.

Three of us from as many parties attended to the cooking, which was mostly beans, bacon and bread, but we always cooked a big lot of beans, just boiled them, and ate them with pepper and salt. While working like a dog, a man appreciates dog's grub, as much as a dog does.

We turned in early. We had lots of boughs under us and lots of canvas to put under and over us and we were in a tent. Some of the crowd had fur robes, some sleeping bags and Dan and I each had 30 pounds of woolen blankets. We made the sleeping bag fellows sleep next to the side of the tent. Five of us slept in the back end of the tent and one crosswise at our feet. We put a big fire in the stove and went to sleep. Besides my blankets I had, on me or under me, all the clothes I had brought along and was overwarm when I turned in. but about 1:00 A.M. I awoke, cold clear through, inside and outside, cold from my hair down to my toenails, a rather novel sensation, the first time during the winter that I really suffered from cold. I had only taken off my coats, footwear and mittens when I turned in. I explored with my bare feet and hands, felt those woolen blankets, from end to end and couldn't find a warm spot on them. I couldn't find a spot that would get warm when I kept a hand or foot there for a minute or two. I felt around for socks, German socks and mittens and put them on, thinking they would warm me. There I lay shivering for perhaps 30 minutes, when John Mohlman jumped out of his sleeping bag and started the fire. He also had been cold for an hour or more. When the air in the tent warmed a little I got up and thawed out before the fire. Then I went back to the blankets with the heat I had absorbed at the stove, and slept until morning. John kept the fire the rest of the night. It was 48 degrees below zero that night, but spring was just around the corner, and we felt certain that the following nights would be better.

Thursday, March 2, after a breakfast much the same as our supper, we organized for the day's work. Burns and Chris went back to Nine Mile to help Fred bring their last load. John and I went back to the mouth of Ophir Creek for stuff that he had cached there, and Frank and George brought the load they had cached below Ophir.

After dinner we all rested except Gene and Dave, who broke trail with a small load for the next three miles, at which point we were to leave Indian River and strike to the south.

It was 48 degrees below zero again that night, but I slept more comfortable, because I kept on all my coats and my mittens and German socks. Frank lay near the stove that night and kept the fire all night.

Friday, March 3, we took everything except the tent and stove in one load, and returned for them in the afternoon. We went up Indian River about three miles, the river keeping close to the mountains on the north. To the south there was a long stretch of apparently level country, running back to the mountains some 10 to 14 miles away. Where we left the river, we found a fair trail leading into the flat. People cutting hay on the flat had made the trail, but for a very short distance. Then the real work began, and we had to break an entirely new trail, through woods and brush, and over frozen swamp with big bunches of grass on it, and up and down hills and rough stony places. The snow was a uniform 30 inches deep and just as dry as hot sand. Its mere weight had settled it some at the bottom, but it was not packed in any way, nor was there any semblance of a crust on it. All thirteen of us left our sleds on the old trail while we wallowed along through the snow for several hours. Then we went back for the sleds. This method made a fairly hard trail with 10 or 12 inches of snow between us and the moss. A slow job, but a sure one. Thirty inches of loose snow is just enough so that it is nearly impossible to pull one leg out, to make the next step. When snow only reaches to the knees, a man can lift his leg and throw it ahead, but with 30 inches he must lift his leg and a lot of snow. Then he must put his leg straight up over his head and fall over it. It takes an acrobat. Fred Mack's skis were a big help. He led the way and would sink down in the soft snow fully twelve inches, but that enabled the rest of us to follow. After thus breaking trail without sleds, we doubled up, two men to a sled, and pulled the eight sleds over the trail, and when the last one was over it we had a fine trail, couldn't ask for better. All felt sorry we had only one more trip to make over such a fine trail. The trail we made led across what must have been a regular swamp in the summer. Then we had to climb that 150 to 200 foot terrace, which everywhere marks the old level of the Yukon and Indian Rivers. Fortunately, for us, the old terrace was greatly eroded where we encountered it, and we climbed up on a very long gentle slope. At the top of the terrace we stopped, and most of us went back to our river camp for the other loads. Fred had dinner ready at the old camp. After dinner we broke camp and left the river. The tents were not up when we reached the new camp site and part of the stuff was still at the bottom of the terrace. Dan came back to help me pull my load up the hill.

We set up a fourth tent, so there were only Dan and I, and three of the Thompson Party in our tent. Ford did most of the cooking, in order to get out of breaking trail and hauling sleds. We thought it would be warmer if we shoveled away the snow before setting up the tent. We got our tent up and plenty boughs in it. Turned in at 9:00 P.M. and at 12:30 I woke up cold, and I stayed cold until 1:30. Then I got up, lit a fire and kept it until morning. Dan also got up for a while. I put my blanket next to the stove, and kept fire and slept intermittently. Dan was not far behind me. His 200 pounds kept warm about 25 percent longer than my 160 pounds.

Saturday, March 4, we went to the flat for the balance of our outfit, while Fred got dinner. After dinner all the camp (except Ford and Bob) broke trail through brush, trees and bushes, for another two miles. Seven of us in line wallowed through the snow, following Fred Mack on skis. Dan came after us with the axe to cut the bushes. We kept at it for three hours. Then we turned back and in one hour arrived at camp. I slept well until 5:00 A.M. due partly to the additional boughs, partly to that canvas cover over and under us, partly to a very hearty supper.

Leaving the partly broken trail overnight resulted in a most surprising and most welcome phenomenon. Wherever we had disturbed the light fluffy snow on the previous day, we found next morning that it had hardened enough to carry our sled-loads very nicely. We generally camped two days at a place. The morning after camping we would bring up the grub we had left behind. That afternoon we would get out with no loads but our big feet and Fred's skis, and break a trail as far as we could, and get back for supper. Then on the second morning we would break camp and move it up to the end of our new trail, set up camp there and repeat the process. The nights were all cold, and each day our task was the same, except that in some places the little scrubby pines, willows, etc., were far more annoying than in others. We tramped the trail right over all kinds of brush, but some of it would spring up again and there were also trees as much as 3 inches in diameter, which we had to cut. Trail-breaking progressed at about half a mile per hour, and in places it took two men with axes to cut the stuff behind the wallowing party.

Sunday, March 5, I had a time steaming out the frozen rice, beans and potatoes, while the others slept. Ford drinks spruce tea for his knee, cooks and washes dishes while Frank and George mush. After breakfast everyone took a load to where we finished the trail yesterday. I cut brush. There was a squabble about what to do. The result was, we broke trail for another two and a half hours, Chris and I coming behind with axes, and clearing out the brush. This finally brought us to the great and only Mysterious Creek. Turning back, we reached our sleds in 45 minutes, unloaded them and got the sleds to camp in 45 more minutes. At 4:30 we had finished dinner and dried our wet clothes. Dan gets rather sweaty and I get wet from the snow off the trees.

Monday, March 6, we struck camp and moved ahead to a temporary location on Mysterious Creek. Rotten hard trail. We pitched the tent in a bog of bunch grass and put in two feet of small trees for a bed. Of course, they were frozen solid, as brittle as pipe stems. After dinner, Frank and George, and Dan and I went back for the last of our stuff and got it moved ahead in time for supper.

Today I turned over a brand new leaf, cut loose from the marble quarry, the railroad scheme and the Sulphur Creek business, and now I am going to work this Mysterious Creek proposition; if it is no good, I'm a loser again. I came here to mine gold; I may as well finish it that way, as long as the grub lasts.

Tuesday, March 7, what a night! Of course, it was cold when we went to bed, and the bunch grass and pine boughs were just full of frost. I froze the regulation length of time, and at 2:30 A.M. got up and started another fire. My thermometer registered 51 degrees below zero! That was the last straw. And we had all agreed when we left Nine Mile that spring was just around the corner. Even a roaring fire in the stove didn't seem to have any effect upon the temperature in the tent, or upon the temperature of my body. In desperation, and for occupation while I slowly absorbed heat, and refilled the stove from time to time, I became poetical, (or hysterical, I'm not sure which) and the result was the following verses:

The Klondiker's Soliloquy
Time: 2:30 A.M. March 7, 1899
Place: In a Tent
Condition: 51 Degrees below Zero

"A Piece of the Real Thing"
by
Wallis R. Sanborn

I.
I can do a lot of thinking
When it's 51 below,
And when I'm sleeping in a tent,
On a foot or two of snow.
Oh! How many things I think of, when I'm cold.

II.
All day yesterday I pulled,
Like a jackass on my sled,
With no grub but frozen beans,
Baked snowballs and frozen bread.
The grub gets pretty solid, when it's 51 below.

III.
When too dark to see the trail,
We stopped and pitched the tent,
Built a fire, and thawed some beans,
And straightway at them went.
We eat a lot of beans, when it's cold.

IV.
While Dan cut a pile of firewood,
And pine boughs for our bed,
I boiled another pail of beans,
And baked a loaf of bread.
Grub's the stuff that keeps us warm, when it's 51 below.

V.
Then we built a rousing fire,
For two hours the stove was red,
With a roaring fire, in a nice warm tent,
We both turned into bed,
On ice, in a tent, at 51 below.

VI.
Yes, I went to bed, with a fur cap on my head.
And my sweater hood all buttoned o'er my face;
Pants, coats and German socks, mackinaws and mucklucks,
Every stitch of clothes I owned was in its place.

And I slept like a top, spite of 51 below
On ice, in a tent, on a foot or two of snow.

VII.

In the stove the fire got lower
And at last it died away,
In our veins the blood ran slower
As we in peaceful slumber lay.
On ice, in a tent, at 51 below.

VIII.

I awoke an hour ago,
From head to foot ashiver,
Frost on my nose, frost in my toes
And in my very liver.
And I awoke that way *last* night, at 48 below.

IX.

In hope to stick it out till morn,
I curled up in a ball.
'Twas no go, I shivered still,
And out I had to crawl.
In a tent, without a fire, at 51 below.

X.

There was kindling, ready whittled,
And a pile of firewood, good and dry,
But to light those bloody matches
Forty times I had to try.
The flame freezes stiff and puts out the fire, at 51 below.

XI.

At last the fire begins to burn,
And I sit on the stove
Until my pants begin to scorch,
And *then* I hate to move.
As yet, I've not begun to thaw, at 51 below.

XII.

Now I straddle the stove awhile,
And begin to soak up heat,
And think I might be warmer,
If I had a bite to eat.
But the grub's all frozen solid, in a tent.

XIII.

And here I've sat and thought,
(What else is to be done)
Looked at my watch, but the oil's froze up,
And its stopped at half past one.
When it does that, it must be awful cold.

XIV.

The oil thawed, it starts to run,
And my thoughts run on again,
And I think of this, and think of that,
And think of now and of then.
I think of 40 things at once, at 51 below.

XV.
So here I sit and think,
At 51 below,
And I think, and think, and think,
On a foot or two of snow.
Till at last the thought comes to me, that I'm warm.

XVI.
Now I think I'll fill the stove, good and full,
Back in those frozen blankets there I'll crawl,
And before the fire goes out, and I cool off again,
I expect I'll get an hour or two of sleep.
It's a luxury—to sleep—when it's 51 below.

XVII.
Now Dan's awake, and getting up,
And as I in slumber sink,
He'll sit and think, and think,
Well, let him think.

51 Below
But I'm warm
And asleep,
At 51
Below.

We certainly did feel sorry for ourselves, and we missed the comfort of our cozy cabin at Bedrock. The lack of sleep and hard work each day had also begun to make itself felt. So it was 7:30 before we got up for the last day's mush to our destination. Mack and Company got along with their outfit before we had breakfast. Being 50 below when they got up, they waited around before starting. Then we broke trail for three and a half hours, in a reversed curve, leading to the southwest and following the creek. When we had gone nearly two miles, we turned a point and arrived at a narrower part of the creek where we decided to stop until we should determine just where we should dig our prospect holes.

Mack saw two wolves early in the morning. We also saw several moose tracks. The place appeared to be full of both. Fred Mack and Dave had dinner with us at 3:00 P.M. and then started ahead with their last load. John and Fred Melby, also went with a load.

Wednesday, March 8, up at 2:00 A.M. to thaw out, and again at 5:00 A.M. Only 43 below zero last night. Dan and I had a nice Johnny Cake for breakfast, while Ford, Frank and George had half-raw flapjacks. We packed everything except our tent, stove and bedding on our first load and went right back for them, I cutting trees along the trail on the return. Here we were at our destination, after eight days and nights of the toughest kind of hard work. In the six days that it took us to get in from Indian River, I afterwards figured that we had reached a point only six or eight miles from the river. For such work, our two dogs were a liability rather than an asset. The peculiar character of that 30 inches of feathery snow leads me to doubt whether a full team of good dogs would make any better progress without men on skis to pack the snow ahead of the dog team. It explains the secret of why the Mounted Police invariably "get their man." Whoever tries to escape into the wilderness has to break trail much as we did. The police find his trail easy traveling 12 hours after he first disturbs the fluffy snow.

We didn't propose to freeze each night after we arrived at our Mysterious Creek camp.

We had only tents to live in, but we set up five of them in fine shape, and did everything to make the tents comfortable. As usual Dan and I spent some time fixing up a comfortable home for ourselves. We believe in being comfortable even if we are in the Klondike. We selected a rather high little knob, and set our tent on top of that. We covered the floor a foot deep with boughs and built our bed of dry poles, two feet off the ground, standing on four legs. No more wet, cold, frosty beds for us.

We camped on the left bank of the creek. So did the Nielsens, Mack Brothers, and Jack Burns. The remnants of Thompson's party pitched their tent on the point just across the creek, took a big lap in the tent, so it is not so big as before, therefore much warmer. Fred and Ford went on a tramp both before and after dinner to decide where to dig, first up the right fork of the creek, then up the left fork. Both are about the same size. Had our dinner at 3:00 and supper at 8:00 and hugely enjoyed both meals. But most of all, Dan and I enjoyed being by ourselves again, with room to turn around without falling over somebody's feet or baggage.

Thursday, March 9, it took us all day to complete the work of making our tent comfortable.

Friday, March 10, Friday, thirteen of us began our hunt for gold. If that doesn't produce it, I'll quit believing in mascots. Bob Carroll is going back to Mack's cabin at Nine Mile. He and Jack Burns have some bitter quarrel that is a mystery to the rest of us, and Fred Mack doesn't seem to want any fuss. Jack, Ford, Frank and George, Dan and I go up the left fork of the creek and will crosscut it with five holes. Ford, Frank and George only count for two men and two holes. Gene, Dave, the Nielsens and Fred Mack will crosscut the right fork.

Prospecting

Our work of prospecting the creek was so much like the other holes we had burned to bedrock, that there is no need of recording our daily progress. We succeeded in sinking each of our ten holes about 18 inches per day. After working hard all day, we didn't feel much like cards after supper, so we just sat around in Mack's tent or in ours and talked and listened to our sailor members spin yarns. And I may add, I formed part of the audience at the nightly meetings. And I didn't always attend them, if I had a book or some cooking. Dan also listened more than talked, not that he couldn't talk, but it took a powerful talker to out-talk the sailor contingent.

The cold snap on the trail was really winter's last hard drawn breath. Lots of sun and daylight, nice weather, only 10 above or below at night, and everything dry, therefore comfortable. By March 15 we have discarded ear tabs, thick mittens and mackinaw coats. It almost thaws in the shade at noon, grub doesn't freeze in the tent nights, and neither do Dan and I. The sap in the trees has thawed and they are as tough as wire now. When frozen, they used to break off like glass.

On St, Patrick's Day, the season seems just as far advanced as it was a year ago when we were celebrating it at Sheep Camp. Warm and breezy and smells like rain, but I don't suppose it will rain. The snow wets right through everything. While I built a box of the boards Dan chopped yesterday, he cleaned out my hole. Great box that, boards chopped with a hatchet from dry saplings. Nails are surely more essential to civilization than schools or churches. I had a time getting enough to make that box.

We soon found that we were short of numerous other things, so on March 18 Jack Burns went to Dawson, taking my letter and bringing back tobacco and some bacon for himself. He accepted $1.00 from Dan and was to get our mail but didn't bring any, and I don't believe he tried very hard, as I am sure I had mail there.

There was the usual disagreement among the remnant of Thompson's Party. At first Ford cooked while Frank and George dug the prospect holes. Then Frank and George decided that they were doing too much hard work, so they quit working at their two holes and went down to Bedrock for more grub. Then Frank took Ford's place to cook. Ford worked two days at the hole and then he and George found business to take them to Dawson, and during the week it took them to make the trip, Frank just loafed around his tent, coming over to ours now and then. Frank is the best worker of the lot, but has no mind of his own. By voluntarily pitching in and helping some of the rest of us he might have established a place for himself but he didn't.

On March 20, Fred Melby and I, with Jumbo and Dave's dog Jim and our sled, set out for more grub. We had a nice trip down to Nine Mile. I checked notes that I had previously made for my map of Indian River and Fred rode the sled. After lunch at Nine Mile, I rode a while. We reached Bedrock at 3:00 P.M. I stayed there long enough to select the grub we wanted and at 5:30 went on to Arena. Our glacier had quit flooding our cabin. The trail was bad for a mile or more below Bedrock, due to our glacier spring and an open riffle three quarters of a mile farther down. Had a good supper of spuds, bacon, bread and peas and cocoa, but it was 9:30 before we got the dogs fed, cooking in the fire place, and 10:30 when we turned in, on a various assortment of canvas, coats, etc., and slept very well.

Thursday, we were up at 5:00, but it was 8:00 before I had cooked 6 pancakes and burned some oats, mainly because I had to melt ice for water. At 9:30 we were loaded and away. At Bedrock I packed, loaded the sled until it was full, nearly 600 pounds in our load. Bad trail to Nine Mile, so narrow that the sled slipped off into soft snow and we had to lift and tug, and the dogs wouldn't pull a bit. Got in at 5:30 and Bob got us a nice supper, and we slept well in a nice warm cabin. The Aurora Borealis was great that evening, best yet, a great big bow away down to the south, and a big splashy one overhead, and the moon nearly full.

Wednesday, was a fine day and we got started at 9:00 A.M. The trail was frozen so that we only upset twice between Nine Mile and Ophir which we made in two hours. Then a fine broad trail until we left the river, one hour, 20 minutes. We ate our lunch and then pulled in to the hill. Took just an hour to make the top of the hill, and we went nicely until we reached the creek. We thought it only a puddle, and pulled into it. Down went dogs, sled and men 8 or 10 inches to the solid ice, and it was a hard job to get the sled to a dry place, where we left it and mushed for camp, wading in water and ice for several hundred feet or through deep snow on the bank of the creek where water was too deep. Fred packed his coats into camp, and the three pairs of rubber boots.

When Dan, Chris, Fred and I went back for our sled next morning, we found ice thick enough to bear the load, so we didn't have to break trail on the creek bank as we expected to do.

Jack Burns arrived from his trip to Dawson next day, with no letters, but with a 16 page Philadelphia paper, which everyone read from front to back.

On March 27, Gene, Dave and Fred reached bedrock in their prospect holes, and we all felt that the Mysterious Creek bubble burst then and there. These were the only holes any of us had ever dug anywhere on or near Indian River that didn't produce a single color of gold. Those who had considerable previous experience pointed out that the surface of the rock when we reached it was so firm and smooth that it would not have stopped gold if it had been there in quantity. However, we were not quitters, and decided to bottom the other seven holes, even though we felt it would be wasted labor.

It was next day that Ford and George set out on their trip to Dawson.

My hole reached bedrock at 15 feet on the following day and not a color.

On March 31, all the feel of winter vanished. The snow is going away rapidly. I don't know how it goes. It seems to evaporate as much from the snow at the bottom, as from the snow at the top, where the sun strikes it. It is light and fluffy and down we go to the moss whenever we step off the beaten trail. About 40 degrees above zero in the shade, all day, and 60 to 70 degrees in the sun every day. No rain, no clouds, except a little tuft of fleecy white clouds here and there, that look like big bunches of snow. The snow is wet, soaks right through moccasins, German socks, overalls and drawers. The sun jumps up two or three feet every day, a good cooking fire makes the tent unbearably warm. I set bread at 8:00 A.M., cook it at 8:00 P.M. and things smell like spring. Spring is here, and we've pulled through a Klondike winter with all our fingers and toes, and with hardly any uncomfortable experience except our trip to Mysterious Creek.

I have that tired feeling, spring fever, laziness or what not. Hauling 250 pounds of dirt up from Dan's hole seems to be a big job, and 11 such buckets to a fire play me out. I'd feel a lot better, if I didn't know that this place is another goose-egg.

Gene is worrying about Fred and I hardly blame him for Fred did not start off in the best of health. Fred Mack has a habit of having chills up here and then getting out and at work again before he is fit, and getting another chill. That's the only case of sickness in camp and now Gene insists that Fred should go to Nine Mile and stay there in the cabin with Bob Carroll until he is all right again. This tent life will not hurt a well man but it's a poor place for a sick man to get well. There's nothing lazy about Fred Mack, or we might think he was inventing those chills.

Fred Melby made a flying trip to McDonald's Road House at the mouth of Indian for their mail. Hewitt has sold his interest to McDonald and had gone out. Fred and George returned home from Dawson on April 3 with letters for Dan.

Next day Dave announced that he was going to Dawson. I decided to go with him. Dan and Chris said they would like to run down to Bedrock and Arena for a few days. The others propose to stage a big moose hunt as soon as they bottom the few remaining prospect holes.

At Last I Stake and Record a Claim

Wednesday, April 5, up at 4:00 A.M. and away at 6:20. Had a nice trail to Nine Mile and ate dinner there. Then Dave and I started up Nine Mile, waded in water a good part of the way, and I took some notes for my map. Eldorado was wet and sloppy. My shoes hurt my heel, so I had to wear moccasins through 10 or 12 miles of water, ankle deep. Stopped at 49 Gulch, a branch of Bonanza, with Pete, a friend of Dave's. I was tired, and perhaps the 50 miles of country we had travelled would warrant being tired.

Thursday, April 6, up at 7:00 A.M. and at 8:45 we're off for Dawson. Started in my shoes but had to change to the moccasins almost immediately. The trail was frozen so the moccasins were all right, until we neared the Klondike. At the edge of Dawson I changed to shoes and there Dave left me. My shoes hurt awfully, galled the tendon of right heel. I walked about Dawson all day like a lame man. At the post office I got some 35 letters, mailed from September to February, got two for Dan and two for Chris.

I went in to say hello to Winningstad and he wanted me to go out and stake a bench claim on Hunker. I didn't know a thing about it, and he didn't know much more. But Cable, who rooms with him, thinks it is good and had already staked and recorded, as has also a friend of his. In that particular locality nobody else has yet staked bench claims. I was to stake, record and sell Winningstad a half interest for the recording fee of $15.00. Cable is an old California miner and ought to know something, and if he and Rogers were willing to stake and record and use their rights, I thought I might also. Two young fellows from California were to go with me and stake claims near mine. They were named Jack Regle and something Anderson.

Winningstad noticed that I was wearing moccasins, and made me a present of a very nice pair of Indian Mucklucks. I put them on right then and there.

I met Archie Dubray of Arena Gulch in one of the saloons and he invited me to lodge with him in West Dawson, and I was very glad to accept the invitation.

My miner's license had expired, so I had to go to the Recorder's Office and buy another, at a cost of $10.00.

I had the plat of the ground and I was to see that Regle and Anderson staked their claims properly. It is a big job to locate a claim correctly. It is hard to locate one's self, and harder to give the description of the location. It takes a surveyor to do the job.

Friday, April 7, I was up at 3:45. Had $1.00 breakfast at the Northern. At 5:15 I was a mile up the Klondike at the cabin where the other two lived. They didn't have licenses and had to get new ones. Jack said the best plan was to get the licenses at the Grand Forks and go from there into Hunker. We could do that and not lose any time. I didn't believe it, but I

Miner's certificate, April 6, 1899.

didn't think it would make more than an hour's difference if there was a trail where Jack said there was. If not, I knew it would be a big walk over the Dome. In that case we might better go to Dawson, and sit around until the Recorder's Office opened at 9:00 A.M. to get the licenses. But Jack was so certain that we adopted his plan. Above Grand Forks (Bonanza and Eldorado) there was a trail until we got to McCormack's Fork of Bonanza which leads up over the Dome. Then we had to climb up the hills without a trail, but when we arrived at the top, I wasn't a bit sorry that we had come that way. I realized that it made some 15 miles longer than via the mouth of Hunker, but the view from the Dome was well worth the extra miles.

I wish I could describe all I saw from there. We began to climb the spur that divides the two forks of Upper Bonanza. After a bit of hard climbing I looked back and could see all of Bonanza as far as Gold Hill. Gold Hill lies right at the mouth of Eldorado, northwest of the Grand Forks. From where we were, it didn't look as high as it does from the Forks. We continued to climb and when we reached the top of one hill, it was only to find another ahead of us. In two hours we had climbed two or three miles, and came to a tent called the Flag Road House, just below the top of the last uphill climb. Here we stopped an hour and waited for them to get us a lunch of bread, beans and coffee, price $1.00.

Then we mushed on, to the true summit of the Dome. The Dome is not one single peak. It is an irregular row of round-topped hills, higher than anything near it, and running along for eight or ten miles. Average elevation, 4,250 feet. Six miles east from where we were then was the place we had crossed the Dome in February, when Thompson and I stampeded to Sulphur. What a view we had from that first peak. Not a single obstruction stood between us and the Rockies to north and east. To the northwest we could mark the spot where the Yukon runs; beyond it and endless lot of round white mountain tops. Between us and Dawson the mountains near Bonanza and Eldorado bobbed up. South of us looked over into Mysterious Creek. The whole Indian River country stood out in front of me and I studied it well, and took compass bearings of all the prominent peaks for my map. East of us was the succession of hills that comprise the Dome.

We could look right down Gold Bottom and see Hunker, so we didn't realize that we had to go six miles out of our way over the Dome and then back again to get to Hunker. We saw a fair trail leading to our left, in a line for Gold Bottom and we took the trail. All the trails up there were hard and fine. This trail first led us down, then over another peak, down it and into a prospect hole at the head of Soda Creek that someone had dug there during winter. There the trail stopped, and so did we. We had seen a bit of the country. We went back to where we had turned off, and two hours after we left the main trail we were back on it again, traveling on the Dome. At one place I could look right down into Quartz Creek, and see where it emptied into Indian River. Then a little farther and we looked down into Sulphur Creek. Then I was at home again, on the trail leading down from the Dome into Gold Bottom and Hunker. At the foot of the long hill leading to Gold Bottom is a road house kept by Mr. Green, a Kansas City-Seattle lawyer. He had closed the house, but two men named Hi Boudreaux and Captain Anderson were living there, and they kept us that night. Hi was one of those jovial chaps, who always make everybody feel quite at home. When we asked if he could take care of us for the night, he replied that he would be glad to have us, if we could come to an agreement with the bed bugs and cooties, as to which was our bunk and which was theirs.

Saturday, April 8, at 6:30 we had eaten and were away, not quite so fresh after the 35 miles we traveled Friday. We went down Gold Bottom with my right knee hurting. Then up Hunker through water and slush and over glaciers to Number 2 Above, where a wood trail led up the right limit. Up we went, in snow to our knees and measured off three claims on the hillside. It was 12:30 before we completed our job. Then we ate a $2.00 dinner at a road house.

I met Kershaw and Thompson on the trail that morning: Thompson had Simpson's cabin, and Simpson had gone to Dominion.

Here is my claim. "Bench Claim, lower half of No. 3, third tier on the right limit of No. 3 Above Discovery," 250 feet by 250 feet.

I had a fine view up and down Hunker; could see the mouth and also the prominent mountain back of Dawson. My claim is a very ordinary looking piece of a side hill, covered with small cottonwood trees. I hope it is not ordinary inside. It was 1:30 before we finished our $2.00 dinners. We afterword learned that it was at this road house that Thompson got lousy. Then we started for Dawson through slush and water and over glaciers, but I didn't get there. I flunked out and stopped for the night, dead tired, when we got to Catchup Hotel at Bear Creek at 6:00 P.M. The other boys who only had 68 miles in two days, kept on and got home at 10:00 P.M. Since leaving camp four days before I had walked 110 miles and I knew when I had enough. I was too tired to eat for an hour or so, and my feet were swollen.

A Miss Lena kept the place, a straight up, flat, square German woman, but good hearted and straight I guess, but she wasn't a bit embarrassed when the men took off their pants to go to bed.

> Sunday, April 9, I gave up $2.00 for my supper and bunk and was going without breakfast to Dawson, but Miss Lena invited me to breakfast. I had $1.50 left, but I have vinegar to buy and I'll hang to that $1.50 until I get the vinegar. Sorry to lie to her.

That's what my diary says, but I may as well tell the real story. I did have $1.50 and no more, but $1.00 of that had been given to me by Fred Melby to buy them a bottle of vinegar. When I left Mysterious Creek, I had not expected to buy a Miner's License and to buy $2.00 dinners at Hunker road houses, so I had left most of my money in Dan's keeping, feeling that it was safer in his money-belt than it was in my pocket on the trip to Dawson.

The price of breakfast was $1.00, so for the only time in my life, I was in a fix where I had to confess to someone that I was broke, and I asked Miss Lena if she would feed me. To put it frankly, I begged for my breakfast. Words can't tell how it galled me and how depressed I felt. I couldn't even record the unvarnished facts in my diary.

I had dinner with Regle and Anderson, and greatly enjoyed a visit with Anderson's father who had mined gold all his life in nearly every field. I had supper and spent the night with Thompson. He had a cabin at the extreme south end of Lousetown, perched high up on an almost vertical wall, overhanging the Yukon. Of course Thompson and I had a grand visit.

Monday, April 10, downtown at 8:30 and Winningstad was in a flurry. Had a job that would pay him real money, a level survey up the Klondike for the water supply project. Claims had to wait. He was also so dead broke that he couldn't find the $15.00 needed to record our claim. We went with two of his friends and borrowed surveying instruments and made our survey for one and a quarter miles from the bridge to a point just above the tram road. On our return I had a clam chowder dinner with him, got more mail and returned to Thompson's for the night.

Tuesday, April 11, I waited at Winningstad's office all day while he tried unsuccessfully to raise $15.00. I spent my $1.50 for vinegar, dried strawberries and a 25 cent lunch and went back to Thompson's for the night.

Wednesday, April 12, Winningstad still broke and trying to raise $15.00 and I waited around idle. He knew I wanted to go back up creek, so he went out several times to try to find a man to lend him some money, but no results. No money in sight until pay comes in for that surveying job. He declared that I should sleep and board with him until he got his money, so he and I ate at the Portland where he had credit and I slept in Cable's bunk, Cable having gone up the creek.

Olaf Winningstad is a Norwegian. He comes here via St. Michael with an $18,000 steamboat, in which he and a big party are interested. One of the two men who staked just ahead of me on Hunker, a friend of Winningstad's, is named Charles S. Rogers. He is an old time civil engineer who formerly lived near Rockford. Mrs. Rogers is staying in Rockford at 414 North Church St. Strange how small this world is. Rogers is hauling grub to Hunker and he and Cable are going to work on their claims. My claim is just above Cable's.

Thursday, April 13, Winningstad finally borrowed the money, and I recorded "Bench No. 3, third tier off No. 3 Above Discovery, lower half." Then after deeding half the claim to Winningstad, I made plans to return to Mysterious Creek.

Considering my free meals at Miss Lena's and in Dawson, I get quite a laugh from the following extract from the letter I wrote home just before I set out for Mysterious:

> At 1:00 P.M. I sit at a poker table in the back room of a saloon to write this letter. You don't know how handy these poker tables are. The other games open about 10:00 A.M. or run all the time, but people don't play poker until after supper. The letter writers of Dawson appreciate that fact.
>
> Don't bother about sending me any money. I think that between us, Dan and I can raise about $500.00 when we need money. We have lots of grub, plenty of sugar and 30 pounds of fruit. We will need bacon in about a month, but we can trade rice for bacon. I am getting notes every day for a complete and accurate map of this country and that will bring money when I want it. When a man does any real work for cash, his pay piles up rapidly, so don't worry about my getting broke. The fare from here to Seattle is only $50.00, so even a busted man can get out of here when he wants to.

After mailing my letter I set out for 49 Gulch on Bonanza, where I expected to find Dave, and spend the night with his friend Pete. On arriving at Pete's I was greatly surprised and pleased to find Jack Stere, my old friend of Sheep Camp and Lake Bennett. He had spent all winter up in the Klondike, in the Flat Creek region, got some game and some money for it, but poor gold prospects. That afternoon I also met Mose Muldonald, who is mentioned previously. He had worked a lay on Eureka Creek all winter, with a partner, and they have dug out a small dump of so-called pay dirt, but Mose, like 10,000 others, is over at the Forks looking for a job, while the partner stays at Eureka to wash the dump.

Dave had tired of waiting for me and gone ahead that very morning, but I stayed over night.

Friday, April 14, I was off at 8:10 and kept a careful record of my time and direction, getting notes for my map. That day I got a lot of notes for my map and checked lots of doubtful points. The trail was fairly well frozen on Bonanza and Eldorado, but French Gulch was sloppy, the sun having thawed the snow, and the water running over the ice. My mucklucks were fully equal to the occasion and I kept my feet dry. Nine Mile was sloppy for its full length. There are two fair sized glaciers on Nine Mile, and they covered the trail, in the creek bed, with 6 to 12 inches of water, through which I walked. It was impossible to walk anywhere else, for the snow was waist deep and had only crust enough to support a man one at one step and let him down next step. At Mack's cabin at the Mouth of Nine Mile I found Ford, Frank and George going back to Bedrock for more grub and Dave Grassman, who had arrived just ahead of me. Bob Carroll was just about to leave for Dawson where he expects to get a job with Galvin, the man who bought our rabbits.

Saturday, April 15, Dave and I reached camp by dinner time, and I spent the rest of the day reading my fat bundle of letters.

Revealing the Secret of Mysterious Creek

Things had not changed much while I was away except that no one killed himself with work. I had 42 letters. I had to organize my mail, to sort out the letters, then the local news, then the newspaper and magazine articles, and to start a circulating library of the two latter. While at Mysterious Creek I didn't read anything except the letters and the local news. Saved all the rest for future use at Bedrock.

Then the boom of Mysterious Creek collapsed. With the exception of Fred Mack, we all agreed that we had been led to Mysterious Creek by a crazy man. We didn't find one single color in any of the ten holes. When it got so that they could cruise around, Fred Melby and John Mohlman went to Mack's little prospect hole a mile farther up stream, where last year Mack got colors "that you could hear drop in the pan." Fred and John were unable to find the smallest microscopic color and they were not surprised. The whole camp had begun to get the correct estimate of Fred Mack some three weeks before, but we had never considered his wild schemes as being the product of a crazy man. On the basis that he is just a bit cracked, every strange circumstance solves itself automatically, but from any other angle it is quite impossible to understand why he ever got us to Mysterious Creek.

Some of the boys were rather angry at Mack for dragging us here on such a backbreaking wild goose chase, but Dan and I had no resentment. As Dan expressed it, "We should probably have gone crazy ourselves if we had been compelled to sit idle at Bedrock during those six weeks." So we classed it as a pleasure trip. We had stampeded and dug prospect holes before with no better success so why be sore about Mysterious Creek. The trip had helped me greatly in completing notes for my map. We discovered later that Mysterious Creek did not even exist; it was only a branch of Ruby Creek.

I had suspected that there was something wrong about Mack before I made the trip to Dawson. In our evening conversations in Mack's tent, I had not felt qualified to tell tall stories that could compare with those which were told. It was hard for any man to slip a whole sentence in edgewise when Fred was around and only another talker like Chris Nielsen could do it. During one of our regular nightly confabs, many wonderful yarns had been spun, and remembering the story of that man Cary, who dreamed himself into a gold mine in Colorado, I made up my mind I'd tell that story if I had to keep Fred and Chris quiet with the axe. So I told it. Fred sat there with open mouth and a peculiar light in his eyes, and never said a word from start to finish, nor made any comment. I told Dan that night that I knew I had Fred's measure, that he had dreamed us into this Mysterious Creek expedition.

When the bubble burst shortly after I returned from Dawson, Jack Burns made plans to look for a job on Eldorado; Gene Mack surprised us all by announcing he would go with Jack. Dave Grassman really did pack and go to Eldorado at once, and the others soon followed. Jack was secretly very angry, but he squared accounts, by leaving his dog Jim with Fred Mack, and Mack agreed to feed the dog until Dave called for him.

Jim was one of those dogs we read about but seldom see. He was a rascal in every respect; he had no conscience about anything; was a perfect coward, afraid of his own shadow, but everybody liked Jim, and he liked everybody. He could steal bacon right out of the frying pan, and wag his tail to show how much he appreciated our hospitality.

The Nielsen Party didn't leave at once because they intended to keep on working in that region and I felt that they might be right, for it certainly was a good looking place to prospect, (until we reached bedrock) and the least known of any locality within 100 miles of Dawson. The creeks all lose themselves in big flat marshes before they reach the Indian River, so nobody would ever think of going back there to find a gold creek. There was one mountain just a few miles west of us that might have been a source of gold. We called it Little Baldy to distinguish it from a higher bald mountain to the south of us. I was always much interested in the lone mountain east of camp which I had named Pyramid Mountain. We could get a fine view of it from our camp, and I had also seen it from many other viewpoints. Its shape was almost that of a perfect pyramid and it stood there all by itself in what seemed to be perfectly flat country.

On April 17, an Indian and a Frenchman discovered our camp and were greatly surprised to find us there. They were hunting for moose, and killed two that afternoon within three miles of our camp. These men each wore one pair of snow shoes and each carried an extra pair on his back.

We had been there six weeks and had never seen a moose. Why didn't we? Why couldn't that Indian run a railroad curve? He didn't know how. When a civilized man gets a moose in that country he gets it by mistake. He may be hunting for a moose, but it is a mistake when he gets him, just as any man may draw a lottery prize. But those two men started from Dawson, came to Indian River and killed all the moose meat that their two dog teams could haul back to Dawson, because they knew how to hunt. Of course, our camp hunted for moose after that. One evening, John Mohlman found fresh tracks crossing the trail a mile below camp. Next morning at 3:00 A.M. John and I were off on skis after that particular moose. I have to smile when I think of it. The noise of those skis in the snow could be heard a mile. I didn't know in which direction the wind lay and I have since learned that a moose can smell a man 10 miles away if the wind is right, and when he smells he doesn't stop long. From the length of his stride as shown in the snow, I believe a moose can overtake a fast mail train. But John and I were game, we followed those tracks for eight hours and even found tracks where two other moose had joined our moose. Then the snow got so deep, and the sun had thawed it so much that we had a tough time getting back to camp. Eight hours steady up-mountain climbing on skis, over snow so soft that the skis often let us down, and no moose. But white men do get moose when they learn how to do it.

When we realized how soft it was getting, Dan and I made up our minds it was high time for us to get back to Bedrock. We had a month of grub, but by the time we could move it back into new country where we might continue to prospect, the chances were we would have eaten all that grub, and we didn't relish the idea of packing sleds and a lot of other stuff out to Indian River, after the snow had all gone. So we left Mysterious Creek and headed for Bedrock.

16

SPRING

Getting Back to Bedrock City

We were up at 5:00 and away at 7:00 A.M. on April 22, with two sleds loaded with everything except tent, stove, bedding and dishes. Three hours to get to the river where we cached our outfit in an old cache across the river and returned for the other load. It was tough going. The snow had settled so much that it left all manner of stumps, sticks, logs and bushes sticking up through the snow. Other trees and branches had been relieved of their loads of snow and frost and had sprung out across the trail. Fred Mack had followed us with his greatly overloaded sled, and had been compelled to leave it before he reached the river. So he went back to camp with us, and stayed with us that night.

Next morning we were up at 3:00 A.M. and ate breakfast at 3:40. It was 5:20 before we got away with our big top-heavy load. Took us four hours to pull to the river, over stumps and logs, with brush catching our load on each side and a sidling trail always threatening to upset it. My right knee began to trouble me, about half a mile from the river so that I was useless to Dan, but could walk after a fashion. At the cache we unloaded, left the tent and took a lot of grub and clothes, making our load even more bulky than before but as we had a broad trail on the river, we made a broad load, not easy to tip over. The trail was fine at first. It was all overflowed and frozen, so the sled pulled easily and went almost anywhere without breaking through the crust. Snow melting on the mountains had found its way to the river and the water was running along on top of the ice and under the snow that covered it. The nights were cold enough to freeze this slush and made travel fine on top of it. Later in the day when this slushy ice had melted, that also made nice going, for such open places had only 6 inches of water on the clear hard ice of the river, the best kind of trail for hauling a heavy load. The big canvas wrapped around and under our goods, kept them dry. Dan and I went swimmingly along, he in his hip boots and I in my mucklucks, until we reached our old camp site, about a mile above Ophir Creek, which comes into Indian about 5 miles above Nine Mile. There the water stopped and we had only snow on the ice and the snow was soft, even on the trail where it had been well packed all winter. One side of the sled would cut out through to the ice, and the other would stay on top, and we never knew which of our feet would break through the snow when we exerted ourselves. Of course, we finally reached Ophir, for it took more than a poor trail to stop us.

There we found Fred Mack, who had started that morning several hours ahead of us. He was putting up his little 6 by 8 foot tent and cooking some beans. Then it began to rain. So Dan and I stopped to see why he hadn't gone farther. Ophir had sent too much water to the river that there were places below us where there was 15 inches of water on the ice.

In other places the snow had absorbed just enough water so that it would pile up in front of a sled. We seemed to be hung up and it was threatening more rain. Dan and I had no cooked grub; that was all back at the cache. Mack's little tent didn't hold three very comfortably, so Dan borrowed the dog Jim from Fred, and went back for all the stuff we had left behind, while I cooked some of Mack's grub and helped him make a location for our tent. That little rain had put lots more water on the river and Dan practically floated the load all the way down, wrapped in the tent, even floated it that last hard mile. After supper we put up our tent, made the beds and had a big sleep.

It didn't rain any more, but that little raised the water level. Now I found my thermometer actually useful, and we kept a sharp eye on it. That Sunday night it was 26 degrees above; next night, 15 above, which froze a poor crust on the trail that thawed in no time. Tuesday night, 8 above, a scum of the ice froze all over the river that the sun couldn't melt during the day. Wednesday night 7 degrees above, and at 1:46 A.M. Thursday, April 27, I was up, had a fire started and breakfast going, and at 3:40 A.M. away the three of us went with half our stuff on our sleds. The snow had thawed and frozen so many times that it was a mass of big porous crystals and these were frozen into a solid mass, fine going, and the places that had been open water had a half inch of new strong ice on them, strong enough to carry a considerable load. Sometimes it held us and our loads; sometimes it didn't. It was that kind of ice known to the small boy as "rubber ice" that goes down an inch or two at every step and up somewhere else and cracks, but doesn't generally break through. When we did break through we had to keep on going, and break the ice until we came to another patch of hard snow. Of course, the solid river ice was under it, and also under 6 to 15 inches of water. But what does that amount to?

When we reached Nine Mile we threw off our stuff in a hurry and went back for the rest. On the second trip, knowing our route better, we were able to go the whole way and only broke through twice, those places being where we had to take the same trail as on the first trip, no other way being possible, on account of open water.

Those two trips brought all our stuff to Nine Mile. It was then 9:15 A.M. and we had done 15 miles of hard mushing. We were both hungry and sleepy. On the last quarter mile we had noticed that the snow had begun to soften, although the ice was as good as ever. Under such conditions we hardly felt that anyone could call us lazy if we stopped to have a square meal and a big sleep before going another ten and a half miles to Bedrock. So we ate and slept and at 6:00 P.M., we ate again. After supper Dan and I sat in Mack's cabin discussing what we should leave and what we should take with us when we started again next morning at 1:45 A.M. Fred heard a peculiar rumbling noise like distant thunder and went outside to see that the bulk of our stuff, which we had left on the sleds or near them, was properly covered. He called to us to come quickly and help him save our outfits. Fred might tell tall stories, but there was no mistaking his cry of distress. We rushed out and there coming around the bend of the river was a wall of ice, snow, slush and water fully three feet high. It was rolling along on the solid ice of the river, approaching us almost as rapidly as a freight train travels.

Our tents, stove, blankets, and all kinds of grub were down on the river on sleds, or unloaded on a little bar that lay about 6 inches above the level of the ice. That rushing wall of water and ice was a gorgeous spectacle, and under any other conditions we would have greatly enjoyed watching its progress.

We had barely time to grab our scattered outfits and throw them, or carry them beyond the reach of that resistless wave. As far as the river was concerned, there was no commotion, after that first rolling tumbling wave. The water and slush flowed along smoothly and easily and 10 minutes after Fred shouted, there flowed past us a river 18 inches deep and 90 feet wide, almost clear of ice and slush, but flowing along over the winter's ice at five or six miles per hour. The little flood didn't disturb the real ice in any way. We stayed up until 10:00 P.M. looking for more fireworks, in the shape of a bigger wave, but we were disappointed. Then for two weeks we stuck at Nine Mile, victims of circumstances and of the Klondike climate.

Saturday, April 29, Dan and I decided to try an experiment. We would go to Bedrock, get a boat and haul it up river, put our stuff in and float down. So in our rubber boots we went to Bedrock. And we hauled a boat up half a mile, and we got ourselves back to Nine Mile that night. But we didn't try to do it again. We could not cross the river, so we had to keep to the north bank and take whatever came. Luckily it was the sunny side of the river, in most places, but it also happened to be the side closest to the mountains which made a lot of perpendicular bluffs which we had to get around.

The bank upon which the pine trees grow is sometimes as little as five or ten feet above the water, but the trees and brush make it bad walking in summer, and on our trip the snow among the trees made it worse. The second type is fine. That little flat beach is of gravel, sand and grass and the best kind of trail when the sun had melted the snow, as it had done in all the exposed places. The general course of the river is to the west but many parts of the river flow north and south, and there the snow lay in deep drifts, as soft as much and almost impossible to navigate. We couldn't wade at one place, and crawled on our hands and knees for a quarter mile. There was crust enough to hold us when we used two hands and two shin bones to distribute our weight. Right across the river was the nicest going that man could ever hope to find.

On our return trip we avoided such places, and saved a lot of distance, by cutting up over the 150 foot terrace, which being exposed to the sun, was bare of snow and good going, but hard climbing. At several places we had to skin around vertical cliffs by wading on top of the ice, in water reaching nearly to the tops of our hip boots. When compelled to do this, we thought about the men we saw drown at Lake Bennett.

At Bedrock we found 6 inches of water on our floor having seeped in from the melting glacier. We took 100 feet of rope and Stemple's boat and started to haul it up river. It was dangerous, wading close to shore on the sunken ice. About a half mile upstream, we got out in the middle of the river. It looked as if we would be compelled to cross and walk on soft snow drifts. I said to Dan, "Where to now?" "Haul her on shore and leaver her." "Correct." We hauled her up, and there she stayed high and dry, a half mile up river, but nevertheless the first boat up Indian River that season. It was springtime in the Klondike, but for easy travelling, let me have the winter trail. So we decided that we would have to wait for nature to provide us a better trail. Not knowing how long that would take, we separated our pile of grub from Mack's, pitched our tent and started our own housekeeping, instead of the community housekeeping that had been in vogue since we found Fred at Ophir Creek.

We were none too soon. Next afternoon, May 1, Gene returned from Eldorado with a man named Patterson. Gene had no job, and was convinced that jobs were jobs on Eldorado.

Dave had no job, and I don't know how he was living, for he had no grub. Jack Burns had no job and not much grub. Dave has been in here two years and now knows a lot of people. Jack has the gift of gab and the ability to bum his way, but they both lack jobs. Gene reported that there were 10,000 others camped on Eldorado or Bonanza within a mile of the forks, looking for a job: "Wood is worth as much as gold, for they have to go back on the mountains for miles to get it. The water over there can't be boiled. It is so thick that it sticks to the dish and burns."

Dan and I congratulated ourselves because we had correctly estimated the situation some months before and because instead of wasting our time over there prospecting for a job, we were headed for Bedrock, where to our certain knowledge there was some gold and plenty of good water. Gene also reported that the greater part of Dawson had burned on April 26, the business part, the very heart of the town, that is to say the saloons, gambling houses and the like. It was nearly a clean sweep, but didn't get the big transportation companies and the grub. My friend Winningstad was burned out. His office was in McDonald's block over the American Consul.

Tuesday, May 2, Gene and Patterson made skis and are getting ready for some kind of an expedition. Gene and Fred told Dan and me forty different tales about why Patterson is here, but I guess it is something different from any of the forty tales. Patterson doesn't seem to be any man's fool, and I imagine that Fred and Gene will get the worst of it, if they have anything Patterson wants. Patterson is a foreman for the "French Count" as they call the man at Dawson who represents a French Syndicate there. Fred is so rattle-brained that Dan and I don't care what their scheme is, but we can't help being curious.

The two Macks and Patterson all made skis and started next day with their packs for a five days "moose hunt." Dan and I never did know what they went for, and why Patterson came over there to go with them and what they did in those five days. Did Fred have an agreement with the Count through Patterson, or was he merely talking so much that the Count had wind of it and was looking things up, or was Fred trying to sell the Count something? Not having much faith in Fred and his discoveries, we merely discussed the Patterson affair from idle curiosity and our natural feeling of being interested in Fred.

I had taken part in so many expeditions, wherein I pulled someone's chestnuts out of the fire, that I sometimes wondered if the Count had paid Fred something to get those ten prospect holes dug at Mysterious Creek!

Indian River cut one caper after another. First up and then down. But the continual stream of water began to rot the solid ice under it. Now and then a big chunk of ice would tear loose at some deep place where water had run under it all winter, and it either jambed right there or floated downstream to jamb on the first obstruction it encountered. In that way the river began to look like winter again, as the open flowing water began to be covered with drifted ice. A jamb would break and let the level of the water down, then another jamb would form a mile below and raise the water. On May 6 the water stopped going up and down. On May 7 it began to rise very slowly but steadily, and we began to look for some fun. On May 8 about noon the river rose up suddenly and took everything along with it. It was over in no time, no jamming, no noise, only about a two foot rise and in an hour the river was almost clear. Then the water went down some and a big cake of ice hung on a rock in front of the cabin. A few more cakes stopped there and soon we had a jamb of which I made a sketch that afternoon. I sent the sketch to Mother in care of a man who mailed it at Dawson. I afterwards copied that sketch, on a somewhat larger scale, and Mother framed it, and it still hangs on the wall of the guest room in which I sleep when in Rockford. About 9:00 P.M. the river rose again and the ice moved on again. Then navigation was open. That was the last of the ice, except such pieces as the receding water left lying on the low bars. But we were like the greenhorn in the opera house, who had been fooled once or twice when the curtain dropped. Now that the show was over, we still stayed there a few days, so as not to be fooled again.

We quite enjoyed our enforced visit at Nine Mile. I put in some time plotting the notes I had taken for my maps. The day the ice went out I had climbed a mountain near Nine Mile where I had a grand view of all the Indian River Country, and took compass bearings that were very useful in completing my maps. On other days, we climbed other mountains,

Ice jamb on Indian River, May 8, 1899.

Ice jamb on Indian River, May 8, 1899—detailed sketch.

sometimes to shoot a few grouse, sometimes just for the pleasure of being out-of-doors and up high above everything.

Patterson returned to the Forks or to Dawson the day the ice went out. Gene and Dan went to the Forks next day to sell Gene's grouse for $5.00 each. I think he got $5.00 for the six of them. They left at 6:00, got there at 11:00 and stayed 3 hours. Dan met Dave and Jack Burns and Lou Gorham. They all had the world by the tail but hadn't made a cent yet. Lou Gorham admitted that he hadn't made anything, but had a good thing in sight. Funny how all of us were fixed just exactly that way. Dan saw Dave Grassman looking as though he had lost all his friends. He was boosting a Blackjack game. Jack Burns had everything coming his way, but was about broke and had nearly finished his grub. Said he was offered $300.00 for a half interest in some claim or other, which he refused, with righteous indignation. Jack always had such offers Six months before he had refused an offer of $60,000.00 for the claims he had staked in Juneau. But the fact that this offer was only $300.00 instead of thousands showed that he was getting down to earth. Dan bought a side of bacon and some tobacco.

View of Indian River country to the southwest of Nine Mile Creek, May 8, 1899.

I went up on the mountain, upriver, and got a grouse, followed his drumming for a long ways. Had another fine view of the country, and got notes to finish my map of this region.

Fred also went hunting and happened to be on the same mountain. Fred was always seeing things differently than they really were. When he heard me pushing through the bushes, he knew he had a bear. I never could figure how I escaped, except that a hunter has to be very careful to shoot a vital spot when he shoots at a big bear. As I pushed through the last screen of bushes and out into the open country, there was Fred, kneeling on a little knoll, with his rifle pointing right at me.

I very carelessly broke my thermometer that afternoon. I was vexed with myself, at being so careless, but its day of real interest had passed so it was no great loss.

Among other things at Nine Mile, I read from start to finish, *Quo Vadis*, which I had half read at Bennett and which every man on Indian River, except myself, had read. That copy of *Quo Vadis* certainly earned a permanent place in my library.

I patched my socks and sweater. Just cut the holes to they had a definite shape, and cut a piece to fit and sewed it in. The socks are better than they were when new for they are not so big, and better, due to the fact that I fixed the toes by trimming off all the rags and sewing the raw edges together.

When we began to figure how we were going to get to Bedrock, Fred offered to take us down in his boat, if he could have one of the three rockers that were there. We owned one and had appropriated another and couldn't use three, so we said all right. So on May 11, nearly three weeks after leaving Mysterious Creek, we broke camp at Nine Mile, threw all our traps in Fred's boat and floated down to Bedrock in 1 hour, 55 minutes, ten and a half miles, and never an incident to lift our hair. To be sure we came through places boiling like White Horse Rapids, but we knew what was there, that it was caused by a heavy grade in the river with lots of water trying to get through it. It was a fast and pleasant trip, and we wished that some of the places were steeper, to provide more speed. It was nice of Fred and Gene to take us down and then to have to haul their boat back up that swift stream. One of my college professors used to tell us that a man never did anything that could not be traced to a selfish motive, not even a philanthropist. That day when Fred and Gene had gone and taken with them the rocker that we didn't want and which didn't belong to us, Dan and I began to wonder what Fred's real reason was for going to all that trouble. We discovered the reason later. Patterson had returned to the Forks, but Fred expected him and some others to return to Nine Mile and didn't want Dan and me to be there when Patterson returned. They arrived on May 14, were in some way connected with the Count, and immediately set out for Mysterious Creek.

Spring Activities at Bedrock

It was just like getting home again, to get back to Bedrock. We found things were about as we expected, water all over the ground, and in the moss which made bad walking. Our cabin was still wet from the glacier but our outfit was all right. Our boat had shrunk so that it was full of cracks, but we put it in the river and swelled the cracks shut. We moved into Stemple's cabin while we dried our own. While Dan started to drain our cabin, I cleared out and cleaned Stemple's. I had that nearly finished when I heard a grouse drumming in the woods. I took the gun, and went after him, and got him. Heard another and got him with two shots. By taking off one joint of our stove pipe, our stove fitted Stemple's stove pipe hole, perfectly. How we enjoyed sitting down on chairs again and eating at a table. It was just like living in a house. And Stemple's pile of cut wood would last us a month. We were soon so comfortable in Stemple's cabin that we never moved back to our own. Next morning we were visited by a French Canadian and a Parisian Frenchman, who were camped about a mile below us. They were hunting and prospecting, had killed a small caribou and a porcupine and lay in waiting for a bear every night in the gulch back of our cabin. They stayed to dinner and offered us some caribou. After dinner Dan went for it, while I rebuilt Alfred Jorgenson's rocker, made 3 pies and cooked our birds. We had a great supper and afterward Dan and I read until 10:30, enjoying our new home. Dan had killed a duck on his way home with the caribou meat. We lived high at Bedrock, caribou cutlets, caribou stew, caribou soup, grouse and partridge and duck.

We both had awful attacks of Spring Fever; there was such delightful odor of newly budded trees and plants, mixed with the moist smell of melting snow on the shady slopes. We decided that we just couldn't start hunting for gold again until Monday. We would drop anything we were doing that looked like work, whenever we heard a grouse drumming in the woods. I would start for him with the gun, but often the sun was so warm and nice that I just stopped and sat and sunned myself, or caught bugs for the collection I had started. Mosquitos were beginning to appear in quantity, at first big lazy fellows, who made no effort to devour us, then later a small double vicious variety appeared.

I suppose it is a provision of nature that wherever a man is or whatever kind of man he is, there is something with which he can occupy himself. I always took an interest in botany, and that had been renewed and redoubled during our enforced idleness at Nine Mile. As I noted winter leave and spring come, not a flower escaped me.

On Monday, May 15, when we had intended to begin rocking gold on our river bar, the river had risen so high that we couldn't work, and were glad of it. Fred Melby and John Mohlman woke us at about 9:00 A.M. They had come down on a raft bound for their cabin, for a tent and more grub. They had been prospecting on Ruby Creek and had an 18 foot hole there. The Thompson party had started toward Ruby, but had separated from the Nielsens. Fred and John got back from Arena about 6:30 and we talked until bedtime. Took them 5 hours to pull their little light boat 4 miles upstream. The Frenchmen had gone, and had taken Thompson's boat. Dan and I slept without a cover all night and were too warm. Either four men was too much for that little cabin or the weather was too warm for cabins. Next morning Fred and John left their boat and most of their outfit at Bedrock, and took with them just what they could pack on their backs.

Those were such delightful lazy days. The year before at Lake Bennett, under similar weather conditions, someone had introduced a little piece of a song that ran as follows:

> Oh! This is the day
> We give babies away
> With a half barrel of beer,
> Half a barrel of beer,
> It makes you feel so queer.

That was all of the song we ever heard, but the return of similar weather on Indian River reminded us of the song, and we sang it on all occasions. To this day that little scrap of song comes to me when winter leaves and spring really begins.

I don't know where we got the onion, radish, beet and lettuce seeds, but we had a few, and Dan found a sunny slope back of the cabin, under laid with gravel, so that it was not frozen to bedrock. There he started a little garden patch on May 15. The garden never did amount to anything, but it looked for a time as though it might.

On May 17 we took a delightful trip to the top of the mountain back of us. We are armed for bear, moose, grouse or squirrels, regular walking arsenals. We went upriver, to the place where the gulch runs down from the mountains. A short distance up the gulch we rested and I heard a grouse chirping. Saw him, shot at and missed him. He flew up father and that time I got him.

We headed for the high point, at the end of the ridge, stopping there to rest, and to chase yellow bodied grasshoppers and white-headed flies. Here we saw some, small, very dark purple shooting stars, first I had seen in the Klondike. The color was very rich. We saw signs of moose and caribou and some fresh tracks. We followed the backbone of the mountain which consisted of regular fin of rock most of the way. From one of those points I took notes for my map. Saw the whole country from Yukon around the Little Baldy, Nine Mile and back nearly to the Yukon. More helpful notes for my map. We kept going up all the time, and finally had a fair view of the Yukon, away to the south of us, too far away to tell whether the ice had gone out. We went farther hoping to see the Yukon to the northwest when we should reach the next point, but we were disappointed. However, I had a fine view of the country back of Bedrock and what I took to be the head of Ensley Creek. Then we came home via Big Bear Gulch and began to realize how far we had gone.

We had quit burning candles, even late in the evening and I noticed that day now began to break at 1:30 A.M. When I read the big batch of letters which I had received on my April trip to Dawson, I found a very considerable number of questions about things that I had evidently failed to describe to the folks in my previous letters. A few quotations from my letter may be helpful to a better understanding of my story:

> I received everything in the way of printed matter that you sent first class, but not a line of second class mail. The Dawson Post Office has a way of giving anybody that claims to be working on the creeks, a big armful of second class mail, without looking at the addresses.
>
> Does housekeeping and cooking get humdrum up here? I can't really say that it does. I rather think that after this trip, we will be a bit more patient, and cuss less when we have to stand around and wait for something or somebody. Pop should have stayed here for just that discipline.
>
> Poor old Pop. Perhaps he had more nerve than Dan and I, to go home and catch it all around for not staying. Nobody has any use for a foolish man, but if a man can only make a colossal ass of himself he becomes a hero. I expect it will eventually appear that Pop was wiser to return than we were to stay, but he'll never get any credit for it. Now that I've decided to return this fall, I rather regret that I didn't go out on the ice, but like old Mrs. Reynolds, having gotten here, I believe that I better stay the summer out and see what I can see.
>
> Possibly you sometimes wonder whether loafing and solitude is driving us crazy, but a year or two of it will not hurt us any. Dan notices in every old timer we met that he is dull, stupid and half asleep most of the time. I guess it's so. I've noticed it, but Dan and I are all right yet. I don't wonder any more why gambling is so common in mining camps. If it wasn't for gambling what on earth would a man do with his brains. If a man has any brains and wants to keep it shining, he gambles. I haven't suffered for lack of something to think about for you have kept me pretty well posted.
>
> There is no denying that I enjoy this sort of life. If Wellman or Peary or Nansen offered me good wages to go with them as an engineer, it would be a great temptation. I'd relish an exploration trip anywhere, with somebody else to pay the bills and me also.
>
> My map (see below) is a constant source of pleasure and occupation. To tell how, when and where I got the notes for it, I should have to consult a whole book of my diary, December 1898 to June 1, 1899. The net result is, that I am the proud possessor of a complete and accurate map of Indian River for 35 miles from its mouth and ranging back on both and sides of it 5 to 15 miles. In addition I have skeleton outline of a map embracing Bonanza, Eldorado, Hunker, Quartz and Sulphur Creeks and the Yukon, from Indian River to Dawson. That may sound fishy, and you may think the map pretty to look at, but not very reliable. But it's quite the contrary. I have actually measured Indian River for 35 miles. On a good level trail with no load, a man walking briskly will as a rule walk equal distances in equal times. On that assumption I took notes of the magnetic bearing of each stretch of river, and also the times required to walk it. That gave us a backbone upon which to build the surrounding country. I got notes for the river while there was a nice smooth snow trail, and plotted it all on paper. During our enforced idleness of the past month, on our slow journey from Mysterious Creek to Bedrock and then while here, I have taken the gun and gone hunting on top of some high mountain nearby, and from the top of it have taken notes and compass bearings on every recognizable land mark in sight. In this way I have checked my river course and found it to be practically correct and I have been able to get notes on every creek running into the Indian River, and the chains of mountains that determined the Indian River Basin. My larger map of all this region is more a skeleton, but it is made on a similar plan, and as far as it goes is more nearly accurate than any map yet published.
>
> Our clothes, tent and stove, that have bothered you so much, are all in fair condition. Tent as good as new, stove a little banged up, but we could do without it entirely. However, it's good for another six months. As long as we have any canvas sacks or flour sacks or gunny sacks left, the clothes problem is easy, for we have lots of thread and needles. We are pretty well fixed for grub, about 3 months' supply

of everything but beans and bacon and they are cheap. We have 10 years supply of such things as tea, yeast, split peas and matches. Split peas are a standing joke with Dan and me. We had 75 pounds of them when we left Seattle and we still have more than 60 pounds. From time to time we tried to cook some of them. No amount of soaking or boiling softened them to any appreciable extent. So I cooked some in vinegar and no better results, then I cooked some in soda and that was no good. Lots of people fed split pea mush to their dogs. We were never able to find even a hungry dog that would eat ours. Finally a couple of men stopped at our cabin and we traded 25 pounds of split peas for 5 pounds of bacon. We figured that was so much clear profit. When we tried to cook the bacon we discovered that it was very much like our split peas. It was embalmed in some mysterious way, so that we couldn't use it, no matter how we tried to cook it. So both parties were badly stung.

Once in a while I get industrious and do some fancy cooking, but all these fancy recipes call for 3 cups of sugar or two of butter. We have to be careful with our sugar. We are two of the very few people in this country who have tasted sugar regularly during the past six months. It sells at $1.00 per pound in Dawson, plenty of it, but nicely cornered. We have had all the sugar we needed for our stewed fruit that we eat three times a day, and for Dan's tea and coffee, and it now appears that we might have used it a little more freely, as we still have sugar left. But if I had made cake, pie, etc., every day all winter, we would have been out months ago. The Thompson party did that, and have gone sour ever since December 1.

We eat quantities of bacon grease on bread, in beans and in potatoes and onions. There has only been about three times this winter that there was enough bacon grease in our lard can to permit me to fry a batch of doughnuts. We've done our best to fry out more grease; we've had bacon 3 times a day for 6 months, and as for butter, hang all your cows, we don't need them.

Now comes an answer to that everlasting question that you put in each and every letter: How do you manage about your washing? A week ago I could have said with a clear conscience: 'Nothing easier than that problem, I solve it in the easiest way, by not washing very often.' Like the tramp in the advertisement, 'Three years ago I used your soap and have used no other since.' But I started to wash on Monday least and I haven't done anything since. I've washed myself and all my underclothes and both sweaters and expect to repeat the operation about every three days for an unlimited time. To put it in plain English. I'm lousy. You will think it just retribution for not being more regular heretofore; but it isn't that. It's due to eating and sleeping in lousy road houses when I went to Dawson in April. I looked for them all winter and never found one. But when I staked my claim on Hunker about one louse and his lady must have found lodging in my blue sweater hood. It is quite impossible to see or feel one louse and they are not as vicious as bed bugs. So I returned to Nine Mile Creek without suspecting that I had a boarder. While at Nine Mile, I took a bath and changed underclothes, but continued to wear the blue sweater. The clean underclothes seemed to tickle a little, here and there but that was not strange as I was not accustomed to clean skin and clean clothes. I thought of lice at the time and searched carefully for them. I didn't notice any itching during the day, only at night, when I lay still and all my clothes were loose, but soap in my underwear, or a loose thread of wool just touching the body, always itches so I thought no more of it.

Sunday afternoon I sat reading a paper when the tickling sensation occurred very perceptibly, just above one knee. I investigated and the secret was out. Where did I pick them up? At the road house on Hunker? At the road house where we had the $2.00 lunch, or was it at Thompson's cabin in Lousetown? It will always be a mystery. At first only two of them, but in time what a family.

Monday was a great day. Never such a wash day before. The stove was red hot and a big dishpan holding a pail full of water was boiling on the stove all the time. Outside in a square tub that is corked with cotton candle wicking so that it doesn't leak, I washed clothes in a sanitary, if not the most approved manner. When the water was boiling hard, I soused it onto as many garments as the panful would completely cover, and let them soak. When cold enough so that I could get my hands into them. I washed them on a washboard made of a plank, with V shaped notches sawed into it. Poured out the dirty water, waited for another pan full to boil, soused it over the clothes again, let them soak, and hung them up to dry. Shrink them? Not a particle. Since then I have thought I felt them a number of times, but I can never succeed in finding one, so I take it that I am in a fair way to recovery. But I expect one any time. Dan has not entirely escaped. He has found two good specimens that left me and went prospecting.

While I was so busy with my washing. Dan took the shotgun and went hunting grouse in Big Bear Gulch, which at that time had no name. We always joked about going out to hunt grizzly bears, but very seldom thought it worthwhile to take the rifle with us. The shotgun was so much more practical and generally produced some birds for our table. This time Dan found the bear that we had always joked about, a great big black grizzly, with a white face. He lay on his back, all four feet in the air playfully swatting bugs and mosquitos that buzzed around his nose. He didn't hear Dan, and Dan was tempted to shoot him, but he wisely decided that two or three charges of buckshot from a shotgun would spoil the bear's disposition, without any material damage to his fighting powers. So Dan watched him for some time and then decided to come back to camp and get me and the rifle and really go after the bear, but when we returned, Bruin was gone and we were none too keen on stumbling on him unexpectedly.

We had just turned in that evening when we heard voices, and two men landed a raft and came up to the cabin. They stayed all night and cooked their supper and breakfast on our stove. They proved to be a Fred Silverite who ran 50 boats through White Horse last June, and McKay, the man who rowed with Dan when our boat went through. We found out accidently that our pilot Billy Oakum, had not run many boats before he ran ours,

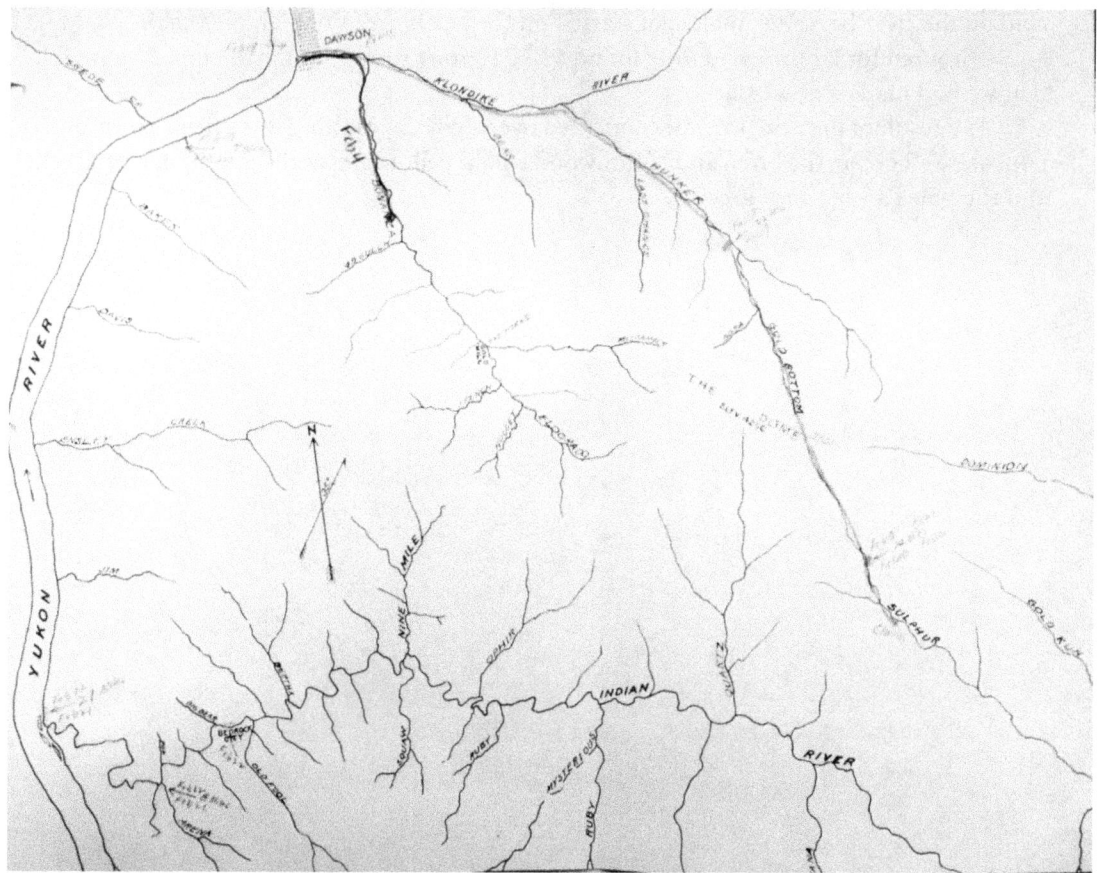

Map of the Klondike (by Wallis Sanborn).

which in fact we long suspected. The Silverites came in in 1897, got 3 claims in Quartz, went out on the ice that winter and came in again last spring without a cent, but earned a stake at White Horse. He and McKay are partners and have worked one of the Quartz claims this winter and cleaned up $65.00, which he had in a bottle, and I don't know how much more, but guess I could carry it all. They told us that the Yukon went out May 17 at night, following the day that Dan and I climbed the mountain to look at it. Indian River is falling slowly, so we can't see it from the cabin door now.

On May 23, the man and woman who ran a road house at Quartz came by in a big boat full of stuff, moving to Dawson. Women were seldom seen anywhere except at Dawson, so it was quite an event to see one on Indian River. That evening, about 6:00, when Dan was getting some water, he shouted to me, and I rushed out. He had seen a she bear and two cubs up on the mountain below Bear Gulch. We looked a bit and finally saw them again, playing around and having a fine time, black as coal, all three, and the old one was too big to meet alone on a dark night. Next morning we took our "arsenal" and went hunting for the bears, and were not really disappointed when we couldn't find them.

May 26 it rained all day, continuously, and that was about the only time since we landed at Dyea that we had encountered a real rainy day. The river had been slowly dropping to its normal summer level, and we were about ready to resume our work of rocking for gold on the river bars. We finally got started on the bar in front of Stemple's cabin, on May 31. We worked for 7 hours and only found $3.20 for our work, but for the first day, we felt that we had made a good start.

As a result of the rain, summer appeared overnight. Everything was green. The mountains were all green, the birch and cottonwood a light yellow green, the grass a darker green and the pines a very dark green.

17

Our Second Summer

June

Dan and I really worked throughout the month of June. We didn't intend to go home without taking some gold dust with us. We wanted to take the longer, more expensive route home, down the Yukon River to Bering Sea. We had about money and outfit enough to pay our way, but we couldn't afford to buy gold dust, so we had to dig it.

The bar directly in front of Stemple's cabin seemed to give the best returns, so we first concentrated our efforts there. We felt that the sluice boxes which we had used the previous summer were not as efficient as the rockers, although the latter involved more labor on our part. Rocking reminded me of my boyhood, when I had been condemned to saw a certain number of sticks of cord wood each week, if I expected to have Saturday to myself.

First we stripped off the sod and earth, until the sharp points of the bedrock were uncovered. Then we would carefully dig out all the remaining material, and especially the earth that lay in the seams of the bedrock, and dump a few shovels full into the rocker. The rocker was placed close enough to the river, so that while I rocked it with one hand, I dipped water from the river with a long handled dipper. When the water had washed all the earth off the stones in the top section of the rocker, I threw out the stones and repeated the process. The same thing, hour after hour, wondering all the while whether the cleanup at quitting time would turn out ten dollars or only one.

If the cleanup approached the lower figure, we would know that we were working away from the heart of the deposit, and would then work in the other direction for our paydirt. Only the results we got indicated whether or not we were in good paydirt, but we soon learned that the paydirt lay in a certain definite direction, which could be followed.

The summer before we had been very greatly annoyed by mosquitos (refer to our Stewart River trip). Now we found that the mosquitos were just as numerous as they had been in 1898, but their stings ceased to poison us, and we did not seem to be anywhere nearly as attractive to them as we had been. As a result, we worked in only our woolen shirts, blue jean overalls, and high topped shoes. With sleeves rolled up, or cut off, because the quantities of water handled at our rockers, we were soon tanned as black as bathers on a Florida beach.

We were often interrupted by the showers of rain, some of which raised the level of the river enough so that we could not work. There was snowfall early in June on the mountain tops, but it soon melted.

June 5 was a regular reception day that began at 10 minutes past midnight, when Fred and Gene Mack stopped their boat at Bedrock and got us out of bed. They had travelled miles in every direction hunting for moose, without success, and then they had finally shot a nice moose within 100 yards of their cabin on Nine Mile. A moose was worth money in Dawson, so they stopped long enough to take our letters and leave us a big piece of moose liver, and we went back to bed.

While Dan and I were eating breakfast, the entire Nielsen party arrived on a raft. They had ample space for a hearty breakfast of liver and bacon. They had just finished a hole 50 feet deep, with loose rock and volcanic ash all the way, and no gravel and no colors. They reported that the previous week, Ford Cole had killed two moose and had given them a quarter of one of them for cutting up and packing the two to their camp. They were 10 miles from Indian River. The Thompson Party didn't feel like backpacking the heavy quarters to the river, and the Nielsens didn't care to pack the meat unless they were paid cash for their work, so what they couldn't eat must have spoiled in due time. The Nielsens had eaten nothing but moose for 10 days, so we traded them 20 pounds of flour for a big piece of moose meat, and they continued on their way.

On June 10, the river was up again as a result of rain, so that we couldn't work. Nine Indians came down river on two rafts, with a moose they were taking to Dawson. Dan and I tried to visit with them, but our language didn't mesh properly, so the visit wasn't very satisfactory. These Indians who live near the Yukon River, below Dawson, are fine specimens, tall athletic fellows, with keen intelligent faces.

Next day, after supper we had a visit from McDonald of the Indian River Road House, and Hi Boudreau of the Gold Bottom Road House. They were out hunting for moose, with grub that had been supplied them on credit. McDonald had cleared about $600.00 from his winter's operation of the road house, and had squandered it all at Dawson in about three weeks and his partnership with Hi was the result.

Hi was as droll as ever, and told many interesting stories whose titles I recorded in my diary, but whose substance I have now forgotten. They informed us that Bert Karr had gone up river on the ice on April 5, which gave him ample time to get out before the break-up. Hewitt had made the trip in 14 days.

After they had left us, Dan and I had discussed their case at some length. Hi, the old and McDonald the young bum, both with a single aim in life, to get on a glorious jag. We wondered how long we would have to stay in Alaska before we got that way and decided that it would soon be time for us to return to the States.

Next day, Ford, Frank and George arrived just after dinner on a raft. Their supply of grub had given out. Next came a party of four from Australia Creek, who were out of grub and paid us $1.50 for 7 pounds of rice. Then at 5:30 Gene and Fred Mack arrived from Dawson, without our mail. We fed all of them that evening and next morning. Then the Macks left us and the others organized their own cabin. We sold the Thompson's our jack plane and 3 cans of baking powder for $6.50. The next day they went to Dawson in Stemple's boat that Dan and I had hauled up river half a mile a month before.

That afternoon Dan and I went to the cabin which we had built and called our own and moved everything to Stemple's cabin. (Except the nails we had driven into the logs) There wasn't room for our stuff in Stemple's cabin, so we put up our tent in good shape to hold our outfit. Then we nailed our sign "Outfit for Sale" on a tree near the river. Now the world might know where we stood. Today, I have a soft spot in my heart for our cabin, which we had built so carefully and which proved so comfortable. At that time, we abandoned our own cabin just as cheerfully as we would throw away the skin of a good banana.

On June 15 Dan went to see if the Nielsens had returned from Dawson. They had, and were in high feather. Their brother, Captain Fred, had sent them some money $150.00 to $200.00 and they again had tobacco and plenty of grub, and offered to buy part of our outfit when we went out. They had met Poole Stemple in Dawson, walking with a cane, as a result of an attack of scurvy.

Dave Grassman had secured the promise of a job on the river boat *Willie Irving*, and on the strength of that promise, had borrowed $75.00 that he was then spending all too freely.

Bob Carroll was the cashier in a Dawson meat market, the chap who weighs the gold dust when a customer pays in dust instead of coin. Such a man is called a weigher. I fear I have neglected to describe the way gold dust was used for currency. Dust was carried in a chamois skin bag called a "poke" about eight inches long and one and a half to two inches in diameter. One ounce of dust was arbitrarily valued at $16.00 regardless of its assay value, which might be a dollar less than that.

Bob had reported that both Macks went on a big spree while in Dawson, but Bob had succeeded in rescuing the money they received for their moose and returned it to them after they became sober enough to appreciate its value.

High water, which had stopped our work on the bar, had brought us most of our visitors, and when the water went down we had a chance to work again. When we had about four ounces of dust, we figured that we were getting an average of about 35 cents per hour for the time we spent in cooking and taking care of camp.

You may wonder why I was not over on Hunker, working the claim I had recorded. Some of our friends of the previous summer, White Hat, Paul and the Sea Captain, who had staked a good hillside, with real gold in it, and not far from my claim, had been compelled by the Mounted Police, to surrender it to the owner of the creek claim, because through some technicality, the hillside claim was ruled to be a part of the creek claim. Therefore, I was not spending any time or effort on my claim.

Our Indian River bar was sure, although it was rather slow, but the Nielsen's envied us what we were getting and looked upon us as being near-millionaires. On June 19 they hauled their big boat and their entire outfit up to Bedrock, and bought a considerable part of our bulky stuff at a price consistent with the amount of hard work that would be needed to transport it from Dawson to Bedrock. It was a good trade for both of us. They bought Dan's shoes right off his feet, and my blue jean jumper and overalls.

Next morning we fed and loaned them our boat to take as far as Nine Mile. In addition to what we sold them, they took two pairs of somebody's old shoes, a lot of lumber, Stemple's whip saw, and our entire supply of newspapers and magazine clippings. We promised to write to each other after Dan and I got home and they started up Indian River.

Wednesday, June 21, Dan and I set out for Nine Mile, to recover our boat and get mail that Fred Mack had again promised to get at Dawson. What a pleasure trip it was; everything was so bright and clean and a riot of flowers everywhere. The temperature was delightful, neither hot nor cold. We saw a pike or pickerel, some 18 inches long, dart out in the sunlit water, from his hiding place beneath a rock.

Once or twice we shortened the trip by cutting across where the river made a big bend, but we didn't climb the high mountains. We reached Nine Mile in three hours, and only got wet once, where we had to wade in water, three miles below Nine Mile to get around a steep wall that was too high to be climbed in a reasonable time. This time Mack had our mail, 18 pieces for me and three for Dan. The Nielsens were putting a new bottom on their boat. The stony riffles had worn the old bottom dangerously thin. The Thompsons had gone upriver that morning before we arrived.

As we were ready to return in our small boat, two men named Carden and Duggan, whom we met at Nine Mile, carrying light packs, asked to ride with us, so we took them. It made quite a load for the boat, but they earned their passage. Duggan paddled and steered all the way, and when we stuck on a riffle Carden got out in his hip boots, freed the boat and led us to deeper water. At several places three of us walked while Duggan shot the shallow rapid; sometimes all four of us rode and then I stood in the bow and kept a lookout for hidden rocks. It took us four hours to get the boat back to Bedrock, an hour longer than it took Dan and me to walk to Nine Mile. They stayed overnight with us, and next morning at breakfast we got to talking about Fred Mack, and eventually it developed that Fred had stopped at Carden's cabin, some five weeks before, and in return for food and lodging, had told Carden about the rich strike he had made on Indian River and invited him to come over and investigate. He had visited Mack at Nine Mile and was then on his way to Dawson to bring back his outfit. Needless to say we set him right, and when it developed that he was a surveyor, we parted as the best of friends. Carden offered us the use of his cabin when we should get to Dawson. All of which brought to our attention again that it pays good dividends to treat a stranger nicely, as there is no knowing how soon he may be able to return a favor.

They had hardly gone, when four men arrived and asked if they could buy dinners. That was something rather new for us, but as our outfit was for sale, I got them a good meal and they paid $2.00 each.

That evening Dan and I climbed the mountains north of us to view the Midnight Sun. We started at 10:00 P.M. and slowly climbed the slope, through and over all kinds of flowers, in a dusk not unlike a cloudy rainy day at home. Halfway up we saw the moon rising over the mountains to the south of us. It was big and round, and seemed to roll along the gently rising crest of the mountain. We could see it more and now and then a pine tree appeared to move across its lower rim.

The dusk was appreciably less when we reached the mountain top, and while we could not see any yellow from the sun at the north, yet there was a bright spot that suggest that the sun was about to rise. There were mountains some three miles north of us, and it was somewhat cloudy in the north, so we really had better daylight to the south of us.

We built a little campfire to annoy the mosquitos and waited for day break. At 12:15 it began to brighten noticeably and the clouds lifted, and at 1:00 A.M. it was fully as light as it would be at noon with the sun under a cloud. Then we rolled and tumbled down the mountain and into bed.

On June 25 Dan and I had exhausted the paydirt on the bar we had been working and moved upstream to the bar Alfred Jorgenson had worked on the previous summer and fall. Here we made a record of $1.00 per hour, so we were immediately interested.

We were interrupted by a party from Dominion, who stopped overnight in the empty Jorgenson cabin. One of them was one of two men who had sold us the moose meat the previous summer. He informed us that Alfred and Emil were making very good money on Dominion, washing dumps of poor paydirt, on shares.

That evening we also had a visit from Sweet, who had discovered our bar last year, and had unwittingly been such an influence in locating us permanently on Indian River. As an indication of the fascination the place had, he was back there with a partner, to sink prospect holes on the bench on the south side of the river, but when they inspected the many holes we had sunk, they returned to Dawson.

It was a most strange coincidence and reads like fiction, that so many of our old friends and acquaintances should reappear in those few days, or weeks, and make their farewell bow to you who read this story, while Dan and I were preparing to drop the final curtain. It was exactly like the custom that prevails in theatres today, of presenting the entire cast, as they sing the final chorus.

A few friends who did not appear at this time we soon saw in Dawson, although of course, there were a considerable number of people mentioned in my story, who missed the final chorus.

Next day the river was high, so we spent the entire day getting our two boats in good condition for the trip to Dawson. I say our boats. One was the small boat we built on Lake Bennett, the other was ours by right of salvage. Jorgenson had built it and left it on the bar, just above the normal water level, when they left Bedrock. When Dan and I set out for Mysterious Creek, we decided that there would be no boat left when the ice went out, unless we rescued it. So we hauled it up high and dry and from that time we laid to claim it.

June 27 we had radishes and lettuce from Dan's garden. We enjoyed them greatly, but it would have taken a lot of each to really make a meal. That day thirteen Canadians with four boats pulled past us, headed for Australia Creek. June 29 two men headed for Eureka bought our 9 by 9 foot tarpaulin. June 30 we did our last work on the bar, and it was a record breaker. We got nearly a half ounce in less than half a day, but the sad part of it was that we had exhausted our supply of gold bearing earth. So we weighed our dust, which amounted to about $120.00 and tied it securely in our poke. About 40 cents per hour. As I said in my diary, "Not bad for that kind of labor in the states, but not much after coming 4000 miles."

A letter I later wrote at Dawson contains the following comment:

> Rocking rough gravel and bedrock is no snap, and was not very good pay, but money's money here and we're going to bring some out with us or bust. Now everybody in the Klondike is headed for Bedrock City to rock out a grubstake. Well, if they care to work for it, we may have left something there for them. It is amusing, and at the same time pathetic, to see how men grab at straws. I am sure that Dan and I carried away 90 percent of all the gold on those bars, but we have seen a dozen parties headed for there and know of several others.

Outfit for Sale

On Saturday, July 1, we ceased to be prospectors or miners and became merchants. That day began at midnight, when the Nielsen's came down river with one moose on a raft, and another in their boat. They had killed one Monday, the other Tuesday, 10 miles back from the river, and now it was Saturday. They had a long hard trip, packing the heavy quarters to the river, 1,200 pounds in all. Had tried to rent Thompson's boat, and offered them half of all they would transport to Dawson, but the Thompson Party was on the way to Quartz Creek and wouldn't handle the moose.

The Nielsens had stopped at Bedrock because they were afraid the meat might spoil, and they wanted Dan's expert advice. Dan pronounced it in fine condition except here and there where flies had deposited a nest of eggs. Dan soon trimmed away all such defects. The Nielsens left us a big piece of moose and continued their journey and we went back to bed. On their return they were to buy more of our outfit. When they reached Dawson they received a hard blow. The meat inspector caught them. No wild meat could be landed in Dawson in July and August (health regulation) and the Nielsens had to sell the moose to the dog pound for $16.00. Wasn't that tough luck, when they should have sold it, for 20 to 30 cents a pound.

Sunday, we had a big wash day, ourselves and our clothes, and made a complete inventory of everything we owned that even appeared to have any value.

Monday, time dragged. We packed and repacked the clothes we didn't wish to sell, and a host of curios in our black canvas bags, and waited for the Nielsens to come back and buy more of our outfit. About supper time we were delighted to receive a visit from Paul White and Wallie Lambert of Arena Gulch., and a man named Barry. After supper they smoked the very last pipe full of Dan's tobacco, including the dried cuds of chewing tobacco. They were paying us a farewell visit before going to Dawson and home. When they learned that it was Dan's last pipeful of tobacco they invited him to go back to Arena with them, and gave him about a pound of T & B plug smoking tobacco and some other things, and Dan got back to Bedrock at 1:00 A.M.

Tuesday, the Fourth of July, I baked a lot of bread and we continued to wait for the Nielsens. Four Canadians from Calgary and Edmonton stopped to visit us on their way up river. Indian River was certainly popular, but we were leaving it.

Wednesday we had so little to do that I undertook to measure the height of the mountain north of Bedrock. Its height above Indian River is 46/100ths as much as the distance from the river. From my map I determined that distance, and decided that the mountain is between 1600 and 2300 feet high.

Chris Nielsen and John turned up Thursday and told us their hard luck story. They felt that they were very lucky to escape a fine, as the police had made every effort to broadcast the rule and were about ready to fine future violators.

Then we began to really move, and at 10:30 A.M. our outfit was loaded in the two boats, and we said Goodbye to Bedrock City, which had been a home to us for nearly a year, and turned our faces toward our real homes at Rockford. We had acquired a habit of saying Goodbye to the Nielsens and repeated our farewell on this occasion.

Water in Indian River was very low, and we had some hard work getting our boats over the riffles. The Yukon was very high, and that helped us as we neared the mouth of Indian. Old Hi Boudreau was in charge of the road house, so we stayed there for the night. At the road house we had a fine view of the Pyramid Mountain, that we had seen from so many angles, that we began to regard it as one of the best of our old friends. Its top was still covered with snow. We said goodbye to the friends we had made at the Mounted Police station and left them a considerable number of books and similar reading matter.

Friday morning we made a fast and easy trip to Dawson, pitched our camp on the river front, and a little above the Police Barracks and Recording Office and offered everything we had for sale. A druggist liked the sign I nailed to our tent so greatly that he paid me $1.00 to write a show-card for his window.

Saturday, I rustled around all day, saw lots of people I knew and swapped lots of gossip, and incidentally got some $50.00 for a part of the outfit. I took some stuff to a blacksmith, some to a hardware man, some to grocers and a lot of people came to us and bought.

It's pretty small business chasing around to sell something for 25 cents, but they all count, and anything that will sell at all will bring 25 cents. I made some money on my engineering instruments that I bought especially for the Klondike and have a chance to make more on a report that I am preparing for a mining broker named F.C. Liddle, a friend of Winningstad's. The report describes the lower part of the Indian River. Winningstad has a job above Quartz Creek that will take some 20 days to finish. He offered me a job, but I'm headed home and don't want to stop for a 20 day job.

Sunday, Thompson found us before we had breakfast. It was dinner time for Thompson. We had a great visit. As I was now on my way to civilization, I shaved, and dressed in store clothes, with a shirt, tie, and ordinary shoes. It was some change. Jack Stere and David Grassman spent the evening with us at a tent.

Monday, we met a man named Brown, from Cherry Valley, Illinois, who was thoroughly acquainted with everybody and everything in Rockford. He had just arrived in Dawson. It had taken him a year on the trail, to come in via Edmonton, Canada. We were particularly fortunate in the enduring quality of the mittens and gloves that my father had provided for our party and at first we had a hard time to find customers who would recognize their worth and pay a fair price for them, but we were fortunate in finding the right man hanging around an auction sale room. We spent $15.00 for gloves and mittens when we left Rockford and after 15 months of hard usage, we sold what gloves and mittens we had for $23.30.

The report of Indian River which I made for Liddle was to be submitted to Governor Ogilvie, and so it was agreed that I was to see the governor, so that he might know that Liddle had not fabricated the report. So on Tuesday, I arranged an appointment, and saw the governor on the following day. He asked me enough questions to satisfy himself that I had really been there and knew what I was talking about and to identify my report when Liddle should present the complete report. Liddle was not particularly pleased with my report, he wanted a report rosier than the truth would allow, but he paid me for it and probably added the rosie touches before he submitted it. I regret now that I made no record of some of the various amounts I received for the report, and for various other articles that were my own personal property. I just remember that I sold my Red Seal rubber hip boots for $5.00. They cost $5.50 when new and I had worn them for over a year. I sold most of my engineering equipment at a profit and sold my claim on Hunker to Winningstad for $24.50. We sold our own boat for $9.00 and we sold Jorgenson's boat for $15.00 with Carl Jorgenson a witness to the deal. It sounds a lot more cold blooded than it really was. Carl was enough a sailor to really feel that it was our boat, when we salvaged it from certain destruction, after he had abandoned it.

Following is an extract from one of the last letters I sent home:

> We have sold all our outfit except tent, blankets, dishes, and some clothing, that we shall bring home more as curios than for any intrinsic value. What we've sold provides us money enough to take us both

to Seattle and beyond. It seems strange that ever since Dan and I made up our minds to quit and go home, that is ever since we turned our backs on Mysterious Creek, we've been lucky in everything. Everything has come our way. Bears, moose, and chickens flocked around us waiting to be eaten. When we lacked the skill required to kill them, our many friends killed them for us and packed them to our very door.

When we rocked on the Bedrock City bar we couldn't find a blank. Paydirt all the time. Small pay, but the longer we worked the better it got. When we came to sell our outfit, we always found just the right people to buy the various items. I asked one man to buy my jumper and he bought it. And of everything we had in the outfit that jumper was the only thing he could use. He really needed a jumper and paid a good price. Just so with dozens of things. I could buy a duplicate of our outfit right here in Dawson in less time than it took to sell it, for about one half of what we got for it.

We used to wonder whether we should have to telegraph home for money when we got as far as Seattle. Now we make plans for seeing Frisco, Denver, Salt Lake, New Orleans, and nearly all of the U.S. We regret that we have no railroad maps, on which to trace our cruise from the Coast to Rockford. Our trip is not a financial success, but we somehow feel that we're the luckiest pair that ever ate boiled beans, and can't find anybody among our many acquaintances who is better off than we are. It may be that a fellow naturally feels that way when he is headed for home.

A rough account of what we secured for our jointly owned outfit is as follows:

Grub	$65.30
Hardware	49.35
Mittens	23.30
2 Boats	24.00
Total	**$161.95**

Our battered old stove brought $5.00 and our sled only $1.00. Our tent, shotgun, and 60 pounds of pure-wool blankets were worth much more to us than we could have sold them for, so we carried them all the way to Rockford. The tent and gun furnished a great kick to many Rockford boys. My three pairs of blankets served me and my family faithfully for fully 25 years and one of them may still be in service.

Goodbye Dawson

We finished selling our outfit on Wednesday, July 12. Then we began to figure in earnest, how we should get home. The boats had been running up river to Lake Bennett for some time, and charging all the traffic would bear. If there were several boats at the dock at one time rates were down; if only one boat, rates went up. No boats had yet come up river from St. Michael, but had been expected daily.

The *Sybil* of the British American Company arrived from St. Michael on July 15, with her regular cargo of grub, and an even bigger cargo of wild stories about the wonderful strikes made at Cape Nome. We heard about Nome indirectly for some weeks, but here was a boat right from Nome, and carrying many letters to people in Dawson, giving all the details.

Dawson went wild, and the town would have stampeded to Nome if most of the people who made the big noise had the price of steamer passage. The *Yukoner* was to leave the following Wednesday and was asking $60.00 fare. The *J.P. Light* was another upper Yukon boat that planned to run down river rather than up to White Horse. Dan and I waited for more competition.

The *Susie* of the Alaska Commercial Company arrived late that same evening. Cape Nome has been talked about ever since we came to Dawson, but everybody laughed at the talk, and accused the Steamboat Company of starting the talk, so as to get passengers for the boat. But now it looks as though all of us have taken bait. Since the *Susie* and *Sybil* came in, Cape Nome talk is very serious and everyone is in earnest about it. Everyone who talks about it is not going there, but we all discuss it, as though it might be really worth investigating.

Jack Stere's boat the *Willie Irving* had not started up river yet, so Jack came over to visit us. He was full of Cape Nome stories.

Dan and I were headed for home and proposed to be home before snow fell, and we knew that river boats would only take us to St. Michael. There we proposed to get some information about Cape Nome. If it really was good, or if there really was a big boom, we thought we might take a run over there and see what it was all about.

But, we didn't propose to prospect, to shovel and dig. We would go in style, settle down in the biggest town, and speculate. We would keep one hand hard and fast on our own pocketbook, and we use the other hand to get into other peoples' pockets. We had made up our minds that that's the way to make money in a mining camp. Let someone else work, while we loaf and sack up the dust. In other words go into some businesses that will pay well every day of the year, hire every bit of work done by someone else, and stake and buy claims whenever the opportunity presents.

But what's the use of all these air castles. We ought to know by this time that Cape Nome is no better than all the other "transportation company finds." It was doubtless gotten up by them and for their profit, and if I had made my mind up to go home via Skagway, I don't think Cape Nome would in any way influence me to change my plans.

But we do hear some remarkable tales. Jack Stere saw a letter from a son to his father here in Dawson, that it is a bona fide strike, town lots selling at $1000.00 each, wages $15.00 to $20.00 a day etc. It is a fact that the *Sybil* came up with only two deck hands and a few local Indians, because men could not be hired to come up river. We also hear, but have not seen it, that a man on the *Susie* brought up $2000.00 in Cape Nome gold, that it is red, wire gold, a quality not found either here or at Circle. We shall doubtless see some of it in Dawson saloon windows tomorrow. The *Susie* brought up a big cargo, mostly flour, but scarcely a passenger and had only a half crew. From both these boats we get the news that there are numerous other boats back at St. Michael, hung up for want of deck hands.

Dan and I decided that the *Susie* was the boat for us to take. We could get what they called Second Class passage with meals for $35.00 each, but of course, it was a gamble what expense we would have when we reached St. Michael.

We were up early Monday morning, so as to be sure of a ticket on the *Susie*. We heard that one boat was all sold. That hurried us. At 8:00 A.M. before the agent was there, Carl Jorgenson and a friend named Olsen, Dan and I lined up at the Alaska Commercial Company ticket office. But we didn't wait long. I ordered two tickets, and in payment presented Dan's old hoodoo $100.00 bill, which we had already tried to spend in Seattle, but we couldn't because of dangerous counterfeits flooding the country at the time. It had taken some time for the news of the counterfeit to reach Dawson, but it was there at that time, and the agent smiled sweetly at me and stated politely but firmly that he couldn't accept any $100.00 bills. So I paid for the tickets from the money we received from the sale of our outfit, and Dan put the hoodoo bill back in his money belt, and we both felt that we were just $100.00 poorer, than we had been five minutes before.

That reminds me that I didn't explain, in relating my adventure when I begged my breakfast, that because nobody could or would cash Dan's bill, I had spent a big part of my money for company expenses, and had thereby acquired an interest in the bill.

So now we began to have visions, or rather nightmares, about the possibility of starving to death at Nome, with the $100.00 bill unbroken, or our working our passage of firemen on a boat from St. Michael to Seattle, and taking a bill back to Rockford and framing it for a souvenir. It may read like a joke now, but it didn't feel like a joke then.

We had our tickets, so we went back to our tent, and packed everything we had left, in the fewest possible bundles, and paid 75 cents to a dog team express, with a solid wooden wheeled cart, to haul our stuff to the *Susie*'s dock.

Then we took our first peep inside the *Susie*. We rushed our bedding aboard, and we claimed bunks as soon as they left the carpenters' hands. The bunks were built three high, especially for that occasion, down between decks, between the boilers and engine room, where the freight had been on the trip up river. They were rough frames of 2 by 4 lumber with a strip of muslin run from end to end. We put our bags into a pair of lower bunks just back of the aft door, on the right side of the boat.

Then we went up town and I mailed a short letter home and ordered the post office to forward my mail to St. Michael. We fell in with Little Peterson the Tanner, half drunk and desirous of becoming so and bewailing his inability to buy passage to Nome. Next we saw Wilson, Carden's pard, and had a cigar with him. Then a last farewell poor meal for $1.00 at the Portland before we went aboard the *Susie*. The Portland was not our ideal of a place that served grub "like Mother used to cook." We ate there because it was cheap, and because we had sold our stove, frying pan, etc., and we had to eat somewhere.

After we reached Dawson and before we sold the frying pan we had lived like kings, on King Salmon. These fish are entirely different from what we find in cans. They are big fellows, maybe four feet long, and fine eating when cut into steaks, that being the ordinary way of preparing them. The season was on, and there seemed to be an inexhaustible supply of these fish, right out in front of Dawson. There were very few fishermen, as the government put a high license fee on a permit to catch these fish.

Many of our friends, and all Dawson, yes all the Klondike populace, came to see us off. We were due to leave at 7:00 P.M. but of course, did not. Those of us who were booked to go on her didn't mind waiting an hour. There was lots to be seen. Everybody shook hands with everyone else, but only because handshaking is a habit people have grown into. It was all a rather cold, business-like departure. With the exception of Thompson and Jack Stere, most of our intimate friends had already passed from the picture back to Bedrock City. Carl Jorgenson and his friend Olsen, who were headed for Nome, were the only people on the boat that we had met before.

Everyone that was going felt no regret at leaving, whether broke or rich, all were glad to get started. Those who stayed behind were glad to have us go; it made a better chance for them to get a job next winter. Many a man wished himself among the passengers as he stood on shore. And though we were nearly broke, if we couldn't break the $100.00 bill, yet we inwardly felt sorry for those left behind, even though they had dust.

Of course, somebody had to get left. Just as the gang plank had been hauled up, a fat man in a white vest and all the trimmings came running with a big grip in one hand, vainly motioning with his other. He could have stepped aboard any one of the dozen boats tied there and from that have stepped to the lower deck of the *Susie*, but he had to stop and blow and wipe his bald head, and by that time we were off.

We stood at the bow to view the scenery. One last look at the crowd left behind us, standing there like statues, with the saloons, dance houses and gambling halls for a background, and back of that the big scar on the mountain back of Dawson. Then the *Susie* turned her head downstream and we were headed for "God's Country"; and at the same time leaving behind us a country that had found a big place in our hearts, and had provided us many friends, many adventures, many pleasant memories and much strenuous exercise.

18

DOWN THE YUKON RIVER

Monday, July 17, about 9:00 P.M. the purser rounded us up, in the bunk house, and took tickets. Then we turned in. They found wire mattresses for some who had no bunks. These they put on the floor under the tables. Others had no place at all to sleep. I don't know how they made out. I fell asleep before they were provided with beds.

I had not fallen asleep when we reached Forty Mile Post. So Dan and I got up in our drawers, to see the town. We took just two looks. One look to see the town, and the second to see if that was all there was of it. Finding it was, we went back to bed.

The conditions did not encourage sleeping. I couldn't help a self-satisfied kind of a smile as I thought of being headed towards home, in good health and with money enough in my pocket to get there. People around me were talking in low tones, some quarreling about bunks, two disappointed prospectors blaming each other because they were not both rich, instead of riding second class and dead broke.

I was awakened several times in the night by a whining dog, tied out on the deck. The boat stopped some place about two or three hours to load wood. I just dimly remember hearing the bells ringing and the boat backing and starting for what seemed to me a solid hour.

Tuesday, July 18 at 5:30 A.M., just as we were landing at Eagle City, we were awakened, that we might get ready for breakfast. This awakening caused several mishaps. Our beds as before noted, had for springs and mattress a single thickness of muslin nailed by its edges to 2 by 4's. And a sorry sight some of the bunks were after heavy men or restless men had slept in them. Dan demolished his, trying to dress, and a dozen more soon ripped or split in one way or another.

We viewed Eagle City from the deck. We were back in Uncle Sam's territory once more. I felt home right away. We were in a different country altogether. As one man referring to the Mounted Police remarked, "They aint none of them damned yellow legs round here." I can't help wondering if he hasn't served a term on the Dawson Woodpile, which has been the favorite punishment for a host of misdemeanors.

The geography of the country is now totally different. The old familiar 200 foot bench has vanished. The mountains are only about two-thirds as high as in the vicinity of Dawson, but with the real American spirit, they put up a big bluff, assume sharp points and irregular breaks, with deep valleys, so that from the sketch I made of the scene at Eagle, one would imagine they were twice as high as the Klondike mountains. Timber seemed to be scarce, but those low flat bars of spruce trees are always deceptive. There may have been lots of good timber in small space. The mountains have little or no timber.

Eagle City is small potatoes compared with Dawson, but it presents a pretty good appearance, when one considers there is little or no excuse for its existence. The town was

Eagle City, July 18, 1899.

not yet awake, and we only stopped for mail, so no very definite information was obtainable.

For some time we steamed along with the sharp pointed mountains at our right, and I became so interested in looking at them, comparing their rocky saw-tooth outlines with Dawson's nicely rounded hills, that I quite forgot breakfast.

But that mattered little. We were travelling second class, and could eat almost whenever we felt like it. The boat had only 36 plates, etc., and some 150 men to use said plates, so it was necessary to set the table four times for each meal. By getting into line before the second table full had finished feeding, I was able to secure a place at the third table and when the officer in charge said, "All right boys, go at her." I accepted the invitation, stepped forward two paces and began to fill up. The table was made of three bare planed boards and was designed only to hold the plates, cups, etc., and the big pans of feed, while we animals stood up to it edgeways, with one elbow over the table and the other hanging out in space somewhere; under the handicap we helped ourselves. The grub was really good, except that the condensed milk for our oatmeal was even thinner than a prospector will make it when milk costs $1.00 a can. I filled up on good hash, good bread and good butter, with a frankfurter to help out. There was also tripe which I mistook for canned salmon, so didn't taste it. For a right-minded man, who doesn't want the earth, and who has been eating beans and bacon for a year, the meal was all that could be desired, and I'll even forgive the milk. After breakfast I went up to the main deck, to see what privileges the first class passengers enjoyed. Finding a comfortable spot and a nice view of scenery I forgot that I was on the first class deck, or imagined I belonged there. The officers of the boat were very indulgent. We could go wherever we pleased, as long as we kept out of the tiny little "First Class" cabin and dining room.

About 9:00 A.M. we landed to take coal at a point 175–200 miles below Dawson. Coaling would take some time so the gang plank was run out and a goodly number of us went ashore to investigate the mine. We didn't find the mine, but did find a host of hungry mosquitoes and a winter trail leading up a river about as big as Indian River, that I had noticed emptying into the Yukon. The mine was somewhere up this river and the coal was hauled down to the coaling station last winter on sleds. It was piled high on a platform of spruce poles, with numerous chutes of corrugated iron poked through the poles, and a neat little railroad system between the coal piles and the boat landing. The automatic spring switch, with a spruce pole for a spring, caught my eye at once. Two dump cars with end gates plied back and forth, and in due time we had taken aboard 30 tons of fluffy black power, not unlike charcoal dust, with here and there a piece as big as a walnut. Such was the coal from Uncle Sam's most northern coal mine.

Nearly all the passengers were out to see the loading, and I found opportunity to see who we had aboard. There is a funny little old Englishman, white curly hair and white whiskers, who carries a spy glass over one shoulder and wears his overcoat all day, because of the wind, really being a light breeze, due chiefly to the boat's velocity. He also wears overalls over his white flannel pants, for warmth. While we were coaling he gathered specimens of the flora which he told me he was going to press. He compared his Masonic cross with my Frat Pin and convinced himself that they were not the same.

There is one little lady (accent on the word lady) with a little girl and a boy of five or six who runs the boat's business in all departments when the Captain is too busy in other directions. This youngster has more fun than any of us and we all are enjoying ourselves.

Another little girl about 7 seems to be in charge of her father, unless the big red faced woman is the mother, which I doubt.

There is a pretty little French woman, one of the petite kind, with her hair up in curl papers. While we were coaling, she wore a veil over her face to keep off mosquitos. But the mosquitos are too wise to let that stop them. As she stood at the bow, laughing at the tricks of a Siwash [slang for Indian] and another nondescript dog, in the water, every little while she would put one foot up on the low rail, bend over and give a vigorous scratch along the ruffles of her skirts.

Three faces well known in Dawson are Ben who called dances at the Oatley Sisters Hall last winter, The Spit Box (as she is called for her ability to spit through her front teeth half across the hall) and a friend of hers.

I spent considerable time writing the account of my trip in my diary, and then rustled for a place at the second setting of the table for dinner.

After dinner I slept for about two hours, awakening to find a lot more bunks erected, solid wooden bunks, harder than our muslin bunks but better fitted for heavyweights. They had also added another tier to those already erected, where possible, making some bunks four high.

Going on deck again, I find we have made another change in geography. The river valley is from four to eight or possibly ten miles wide. Whether or not this is all filled with islands, I cannot determine. We follow the right bank. One thing is certain, there are plenty of sand and gravel bars, as the frequent slacking of speed would show, even to a blind man.

There are innumerable big islands many acres in extent, perfectly flat, rising about eight feet above the water and covered with willows. The mountains are gone. Away back behind us they are still visible, a pale misty blue outline, just rising above a tin line of low flat spruce covered benches, with a few dark spruce in the foreground. On our right shore the spruce timber slopes gently back from the river, except here and there a steep headland of hard rock shows signs of our old familiar 200 foot bench, now dwarfed about 100 feet. Ahead of us, doubtless 20 or 30 miles away, is a thin blue line of low flat country covered with spruce, and at varying distances between, are points, bars and islands varying in color from that far off blue green, to the brilliant green of spruce and cottonwood.

This is the beginning of the Yukon Flats. Circle City is not far away.

We just finished our supper as the boat landed at Circle and then we explored the town. There will be great need for a city engineer if the town ever gets bigger. It seems that everyone built a house independent of every other house, facing any and every way. There are any number of houses, stores and saloons; but the greater part are vacant, most of these deserted. A few United States soldiers loafed around, to give the place tone, and any amount of Indians, men and women and children. The women have round pleasant, rather good looking faces, and the young men and boys look just like them. High, but very round plump cheeks, and a nose that the cheeks nearly hide in profile. Upper lip short and straight, in the middle. The chin is a little, fat, well-marked round nob. Eyes set far apart. Long black hair, generally parted in the middle and done up behind. The old bucks with mustaches, have thinner cheeks and look more like Italians.

Circle City is built on a weedy sand flat. Something about it reminding me of the vacant country around Hammond, Indiana.

Its fire department is worthy of note. I found it in a corrugated iron shed. A solid wooden wheeled cart of home construction, with a gee pole and long rope carrying several homemade ladders and three strings of buckets, is the full and complete outfit. I was also interested in the blacksmith's bellows, made of a barrel set on legs, with its bottom hinged and connected to the barrel with leather of some sort.

The majority of the women I saw appeared to be respectable married women with families. Besides these I saw one lone girl, in an almost empty saloon, and we saw one homely relic with yellow hair and a blue satin jacket, black feathered leghorn hat and linen skirt. One look at her was an eloquent sermon on the subject of virtue. She was at the landing to receive us. The priest at Circle could not be distinguished from the miners, were it not for his vest and clerical collar. He wore a sack coat and striped pants and heavy shoes.

At 7:30 P.M., the *Susie* left the Circle. I went up on the top deck, and viewed the scenery of the Yukon Flats. Away to the east of us, the same color as the sunlit sky, but a shade darker, was a thin line of distant mountains. Off to the west, the color of the trousers that Uncle Sam's soldiers wear, were the mountains through which Birch Creek runs, the Circle City gold fields. Everywhere else, wherever you look, is the river with its bare bars and spruce covered islands. The river looks like a broad lake, at some points of view 6 or 8 or maybe 10 miles wide, probably much wider. Broad channels at every turn. At the foot of every island, three or four courses are open to us. But it's the depth of water that counts. Sometimes none of the three our four broad channels has more than a foot of water in it, or may lead to a labyrinth of shallow channels. Then some rather narrow channel serves us, and into it we go. Sometimes when I think we are next to the real bank of the river an old dead water channel will show up, approaching within 50 feet of the main river, then off into the woods again. The river must be even more treacherous than at present, when the water is two feet higher, for then many of the bars that now lie exposed, would be covered, and one would see a channel a mile wide, and apparently free from bars.

We passed two boats stuck on bars near Circle City. One of them high and dry, had run aground in higher water, the other looked as though she had just gone aground. This makes four stranded boats that we have seen since leaving Dawson. We have met seven upriver boats on their way to Dawson. Dan stayed up to see the mail sent off in a little rowboat to Fort Yukon at 1:00 A.M. About 3:00 A.M., I got up and dressed, not feeling a bit sleepy. We were tied up, taking on wood. I also discovered as I walked aft, that a gang of carpenters was at work on the paddle wheel. One of them informed me that the wheel had struck a snag, but another, whose word surely ought to be as good as that of the first, said that the Indian pilot, not knowing anything about the Arctic Circle, had neglected to steer clear of it, and in crossing it, the Circle had become tangled in the wheel, and caused five broken paddles, and two broken spokes. Whichever it was, the damage had to be repaired, which took about 3 hours and during that time the crew put in a big load of wood. So I spent five or six hours in the Arctic Zone. My one big reason for being up at such a time at night was that I might see for myself what the Arctic Zone looks like. One always thinks about it as a place of eternal ice, but here we are, on a big river, with green grassy bars all about us. In many places islands of older formation are densely wooded with the tallest, biggest spruce timber that I've ever seen since we left the coast. I'll never place any more reliance in statements found in all geographies.

Wednesday, July 19, Dan and I were up just in time to catch the fourth and last call to breakfast. We were even so late in rising, that we were not obliged to stand in line to use one of the two wash basins that the 150 passengers use, at the side of the engine room, and we found places at table waiting for us. But it was hard to say what we found to eat. It was cloudy and smelled of rain and so dark that we just felt for grub and our mouths.

We still seem to be among the Yukon Flats, but now, as a rule, the main channel is plainly marked and the higher banks of the sand bars indicate that the river is somewhat narrower than it was above Fort Yukon. From the top deck, just as far away as the eye can reach, so far that I have to look two or three times to make certain, are mountains on both sides of us. They are so far away that their tops seem to be floating on the atmosphere.

It soon became a raw windy cloudy day, with some occasional rain. Under such conditions one does not care much for scenery, especially when it is quite impossible to see anything beyond the nearest bar, and the country is so flat. I played whist in the cabin part of the morning and read a little. After dinner I read more, but I don't feel disposed to read; nothing that I can find to read seems to take the place of scenery I might see if the day were nice.

The Yukon Flats gradually narrowed, very slowly and almost inappreciably. The river channel became broader, with fewer islands and side channels. The three Indian pilots who so successfully guided us last night through that maze of islands and blind channels, impressed me greatly, and they had no trouble with the Arctic Circle when they crossed back into the Temperate Zone. They left us some time last night, and one has now taken their place, who is familiar with this part of the river. The boat now runs at full speed a greater part of the time, while last night she floated with the current half the time. At 4:00 P.M. when I went on deck, there ahead of us, on both sides were ranges of smooth flat mountains covered with spruce, and a fairly high bench rolling back toward them. From their shape I guess them to be the Tanana Hills.

For some miles above Rampart City, the scenery is fine. This stretch of river is called the Lower Ramparts. The river winds its way through a range of mountains and in many places is fenced in on either side by a bench some 400 to 500 feet high. We steered to the left, right under a mountain that towered away up out of sight. The river was crooked of course, with long graceful sweeping bends, and clean out gravel shores, and not an island anywhere. It was a remarkable contrast, compared with yesterday's panorama. The cold wind was a very disagreeable drawback so I retired to the cabin, where we soon organized an orchestra composed of a patent folding organ, a fiddle, two mandolins and the two guitars which we found on the cabin table. We played until the boat pulled in at Rampart City. We got off here and examined the place. Facing the river is a long line of stores, etc. Back of them a lot of cabins. To all outward appearances, it is a more bustling town than Circle; there looks to be more occupied buildings than at Circle. But I don't see what there is to make it so. The gold field near Rampart has only a very few claims. The people here give Cape Nome a bad name, probably intended to keep any more of Rampart's inhabitants from getting away. We were still at Rampart when I finally turned in.

Thursday, July 20. Breakfast was entirely over when I got up. We had passed the Mouth of the Tanana River during the night. Sorry to miss it, one of the Yukon's most important tributaries. To keep occupied while waiting for dinner, I played whist until the waiters drove us away, and began to set the table. I was the first at the table for dinner, and the last away from it. In fact they had the table cleared before I was through.

Dame Nature must have realized, when she began to fill this country with mountains and rivers, what a tremendously big patch of territory she had at her disposal. The country we passed through this afternoon is a credit to her. The river is very broad, great wide open stretches of water all around us and now the islands and bars, though big, don't seem to choke the river as they did in the Flats. The banks are clean cut, with gravel beaches, sometimes with a bluff rising up forty or fifty feet, sometimes only ten or twenty. Birch, willow and spruce grow almost to the water's edge.

To the north of us, the country slopes back very gradually to a line of low, thickly wooded mountains. Rising above these wooded mountains, there are jagged, brown mountains with black spurs sticking out all over them. They are not steep, they don't look to be so very high and they are not so very far away, yet they look tremendously big, spread out all over the country, and arranged with such nicety that they don't seem to crowd or push each other or any of their smaller neighbors, nor do they seem to crowd the river. Everything in it modest unassuming bigness seems to indicate that this is a free country, with no yellow legged policemen dogging a man at every step.

Farther along in my diary, I find the following comment, which shows how impossible it is to correctly estimate the size or extent of mountains:

> The mountains that we passed after dinner must be even bigger than I though. At 9:00 P.M. they stand out by themselves just as plain as ever, every outline clear and clean and fully 75 miles away. It rather awes me to think of it. How can I calculate the distance of one of those faint blue lines hardly discernable to the eye. The geography from which I studied limited the human range of vision to 20 miles.

Can I ever again find pleasure in the scenery of a narrow stunted little duck pond, like Delavan Lake, with its ugly hotels and brown cooked grass plots, after seeing this glorious river which right now is one and a half times as wide as Lake Delavan? The grandeur of such scenery defies description. My descriptions are just as inadequate as my sketches.

South and east of us is a great spruce covered flat with a little blue streak of mountains showing above the tops of the trees. Ahead of us and south of us are more broad smooth graceful mountains, covered with timber (the Kaiyuh Mountains).

I wonder what they will do with the crowd that got aboard at Rampart on Tuesday. To accommodate the first lot of passengers, they built a lot more bunks, built them up four stories high, to the very roof and put them in every available place, and even that wasn't enough. Yesterday they succeeded in squeezing in a few more.

They nearly all have boards under the muslin now. Dan fixed ours by nailing one of our tarpaulins across it. They are also getting the fodder trough to working more smoothly. They have made benches to seat us, which would be all right were it not for the fact that it leaves a multitude of elbows not provided for. There was some friction between the crew and the passengers last night, when we were served less bread, and hard tacks were substituted.

There is something very deceptive to the eye about a river one or two or three miles wide. I noticed this after supper. We ran along the right bank generally, but at times got out into the very middle of the stream. I noticed then that from midstream to the left shore

The gateway to the Koyukuk River, July 20, 1899.

seemed just as wide as it did from shore to shore. At times, away ahead, I could plainly see that a certain island was about in the middle of the river. Upon getting abreast of it, although half of the river had gone out of sight behind the island, yet our half of the river looked as broad as the entire river had looked a few minutes ago.

This afternoon, we traversed more flats, though not so very extensive. These bars and islands are higher out of water, than those above Rampart, looking as though sometime this part of the river was also a vast inland lake. And now that the present channel of the river has cut down to a lower level, some of the old river channels, winding in and out among the spruce trees, are left several feet above water, having the appearance of old, carefully graded railroad cuts, overgrown with bright green grass.

This afternoon, we made a stop at a coal mine, and for an hour or two the hands carried coal, in two men buckets. Everyone went ashore and examined the mines. The vein crops out of an abrupt bluff that rises up from the river, pitching at angle of 45 degrees, so that no teaming or hauling from a distance is necessary. The owner has driven two tunnels into the bluff about 125 feet. In these he runs his cars. On the upper side of each tunnel, he runs little branches in the vein from which he mines the coal. The vein is only about 2 feet deep and the coal so very soft that it crumbles, like half thawed, rotten moss. At the end of the lower tunnel, I got a specimen, that was about as solid as any that could be found. That which the steamboat bought was like a lot of wet powdered charcoal. We took on 20 tons at $20.00 per ton. It comes high. It must be quite an undertaking to run a steamboat on the Yukon. Wood costs $10.00 a cord and we use some 40 cords a day in addition to the coal. There are other peculiar things about a Yukon River boat. We have no water gauges on the boilers, so the engineer has to come to the back end of the boiler every few minutes and with a long pole he pushes down a spring valve and lets out a cloud of steam. I can't see this helping him to a knowledge of the depth of water in the boiler, but I have his word for it that it does. Firing her boiler seems to be a simple problem. Just stuff her as full as possible with wood and keep everlastingly at it. Too much is just enough.

Friday, July 21. Today they surprised us with a big bell to awaken us, and it was very successful. They have cut off our supply of sugar. For supper they substitute maple syrup, but that didn't go far. Today no sugar at all for tea or coffee, which doesn't bother me, but does bother some people greatly.

As I was up last night until after passing the Indian town of Nulato at 1:00 A.M., I was rather sleepy this morning, so after breakfast, while we loaded wood and patched the paddle wheel again, Dan and I turned in and slept until dinner time.

After dinner I sat out on the woodpile inspecting the west bank. First we passed more of mountains such as I described previously. Then came a long row of bluffs, with steep gravel beaches and trees and grass growing down to the high water mark. At intervals a creek with a saucer-like valley emptied into the Yukon. At such places there generally was an Indian village with its fish traps set along the shore every few hundred feet in both directions, from the mouth of the creek.

The village, as a rule, consists of three or four big cabins, built of a crazy mixture of logs and poles, all of those cabins huddled close together near the bank and as a rule, on the downriver side of the creek. Back of them set on poles, are several caches. These caches are permanent affairs, with sides and a roof, and a little round hole in front, serving for a door. Across he creek on the opposite point is the ever present burying ground, marked by a number of little picket fences, each enclosing a space about 2 by 3 feet, with here and there a little cross, made of a pole and a board, very much like those familiar signs, which announced "Outfit for Sale."

The fish traps are works of art, of which a white man could be proud. The quantity of salmon hung up to dry on the racks near the beach, indicate that those traps must be more effective than the white man's nets. They certainly require far less work to operate. They are set close in shore and extend out into the river about 15 feet, maybe 20. They are made of what I take to be willow switches, woven into sheets, with a mesh about two inches by four inches. These sheets are supported by poles driven into the river bottom.

Under water, somewhere near the outer end, there is attached a monstrous big long bottle, likewise made of willow. The salmon comes upstream, skirting the shore, strikes the fence, follows it until he finds the neck of the bottle, and then he cancels all his dates.

The Indians of this part of the country, judging by those I saw last night, are not as attractive as those up river; they look to be of a much lower order of intelligence, with a more open mouthed vacant expression.

At 4:00 P.M. we stopped at a sign-board labeled Grayling. The town consisted of a cabin labeled Picket Bros., a woodpile and a summer camp of Indians. The boat *Leah* was tied up there taking wood. She had two barges in charge, loaded down with soldiers and their supplies. The soldiers bear the label 7E and 7F, and are bound for upriver points.

While we took their outbound mail, and took on more wood and a barrel of what we hoped was sugar from the *Leah*, our crowd investigated the natives. They are the most depraved looking lot that I ever saw. An old woman dying of consumption and mere babies doing men's work everywhere. One blind idiot had an uncanny faculty of correctly repeating any question he was asked in English. Fish racks and a horrible smell of fish. Birch bark canoes thrown around everywhere, and the description is about complete.

The fish, which they trap, are dog salmon, not king salmon, the latter keeping farther out in the deep water of the river. I discovered here that the traps are made of pine, carefully split into rods about as big as a pencil, and trimmed by a consumptive old gray haired Indian, with an ivory handled knife, the ivory being part of the tusk of one of those prehistoric mammoths that once lived in Alaska. An old woman was washing dirty clothes, with apparently no results. Another older woman nursed a two or three day's old baby, whose mother lay with a rough pillow under her head, looking up at her audience. In this tent an old man made little birch baskets for sale to white folks. He also had two eel skin parkas, red and white striped, which he offered to sell for $10.00. A boy did the talking for him, and for ten silver half dollars he nodded all right. One Indian with two guns carefully wrapped in their covers, came in with about forty ducks, including a live duck, which a squaw put in a flour sack and threw inside the tent.

Our long cadaverous Jew who plays the fiddle, tried to show off by riding in one of the native canoes. He swamped it getting into it, but succeeded later in making a fool of himself by a more or less successful trial of it. Some of the boys, finding an old bow and arrow, tried their skill, much to the amusement of the Indians.

Recent high water in the Yukon had cut into the bank, and had exposed some two feet of mammoth tusk, which was some five or six inches in diameter. We were greatly interested in this relic of antiquity. Somebody decided that he wanted a piece of the tusk for a souvenir. He borrowed an axe from an Indian and chopped into the tusk much as one would cut into a hickory log. I described it in my diary as "an old rotten ivory tusk." It was a dark tobacco brown on the outside and had a very considerable moisture content. I hacked off a slab as big as my hand and brought it home as a relic.

When I reached home, the moisture had evaporated and my ivory slab was as hard and firm and white as a billiard ball. Then I began to feel that we had been so blinded with gold that we had let a valuable tusk of ivory slip through our fingers. I list that tusk among the things that I would do differently if had another chance.

The English doctor, he with the white curly hair, the spy glass and the overcoat, gained the reputation of being a crank, several days ago. He made a fool of himself at supper tonight. When it was nearly ready, someone said, "All right," and we stampeded the grub. The waiters stopped us, as they were not yet ready. Dan explained that it was a mistake on our part, and everyone except Doc got up and fell back. He and a waiter got into a discussion. The waiter came around the table, pulled back first one end of the bench and then the other. In some way the bench tipped over, and Doc landed in a most ungraceful heap upon the floor, adding greatly to the amusement of the crowd. No sugar at supper, even if that was a barrel of it that came aboard this afternoon. They may have used some in the stewed pears.

The vegetation is becoming more cosmopolitan than before. The spruce trees are now well mixed with poplar, willow, birch and a kind of elder. Moss seems to have given way to grass. The banks and islands now present more the appearance of those in a more southern climate.

At 6:30 P.M. we pulled into Anvik, a small settlement situated at the mouth of a river of that name. On either side are two big Indian camps and quantities of salmon drying.

View up the Yukon River from Anvik, Alaska, July 21, 1899.

South of the Anvik River, and separated from the Indian village by a small creek, is the white settlement, consisting of a big log house, five or six years old, a sawmill, a church and big cabin two years old, and a great big frame house built last year. From the size of the buildings one would take it to be a town of some importance. In front of it, a steam dredge and a steamboat were tied up, the *Wisconsin* and the *Milwaukee*, evidently mates, belonging to some Milwaukee gold dredging company. We took on some passengers and quite a bag of mail. How funny the old Indians looked as they paddled about, in their little canoes. They are so small and so cranky that the Indian has to sit on the bottom in the middle of the canoe. He can't paddle all on one side, but has to change the paddle from side to side at every other stroke.

At Anvik we picked up a man in a small boat, who has been three weeks floating and rowing down that far, from Dawson. It would doubtless take him a good ten days to do the balance of the distance, provided he didn't lose his way in the Yukon Delta. We were sleeping soundly when the boat stopped at Holy Cross Mission, another place I would like to have seen.

Saturday, July 22. It was nasty, chilly and rainy all the morning, so we all stayed inside to keep warm and read what we could find. After dinner it brightened somewhat. At 2:00 P.M. we reached a point where the Yukon split into a considerable number of comparatively narrow channels. I don't know how many channels there were. I could see several. We turned into a channel about as big as Rock River. About a mile beyond where these old channels unite again, on the north bank is the Old Russian post of Andreafski. The A.C. Company boat *Bella* was tied up here for repairs and here we got a barrel, which is sugar, if we can believe the label on the barrel. The town consists mainly of three houses of hewn logs or hewn lumber, with glass windows, whitewashed neatly and all the trimmings in red paint. Then there are two big warehouses, and up river a half mile we can see two great big red houses, to all appearances built of brick. On all sides except toward the Yukon, are great broad flat low lying hills, that might very consistently be classed as rolling prairie land. In the gulches and little gullies, and on the steeper slopes toward the river, there is a scrubby growth of brush. Here and there and everywhere to the very tops of the hills is bright green grass. What farming land, what grazing land, if it were not for the winter.

There are a few Indians loafing around here, and a tent or two full of them. The Indian graves lack the little picket fence, having only a fanciful wooden cross to mark them, evidence of civilization. I think we rather envied the little papoose who was getting his meal of milk, not Eagle Brand, either. We were getting tired of Eagle Brand.

Looking back up the Yukon from the mouth of its tributary, at one place the sky and water meet and in several places the line of blue green between them is so thin as to be almost indiscernible. How broad the Yukon is here. I cannot say. I have no way of judging. We are following its north shore in a channel about ten miles wide. South of us is a low level streak with nothing to relieve it. Islands and channels, more channels and islands, how extensive and how big I have no means of knowing.

At 5:00 P.M. looking up and down river, and as far as I could see in both directions, there was no land. The left bank was only a faint far away line. At 6:45 we reached the head of the Yukon Delta, left the main stream, and steaming into the north mouth, took a course nearly due north. The tides come up this far, as we could see by the broad stretches of wet flats, from which the water had not yet run off.

At Andreafski a very downhearted soldier boy from Evansville, Indiana boarded the *Susie*. He belonged to the crowd on the *Sarah*, a boat we met this morning, a perfect counterpart of the *Susie* in everything but the ornaments on her smokestacks. The soldier got left at Andreafski and is going back with us to St. Michael, he says, to six months guardhouse and a fine. He has reason to wish he was back in the States.

Having followed the united river channel all day, we felt rather cramped when compelled to travel one of its many mouths. That through which we passed is only about a mile or a mile and a half wide. The sun came out clear, bright and warm and all the passengers came out and sunned themselves on the forward decks. At 7:30 we passed Hamilton Landing. Here for the first time, they got out the Sounding Pole and sounded the

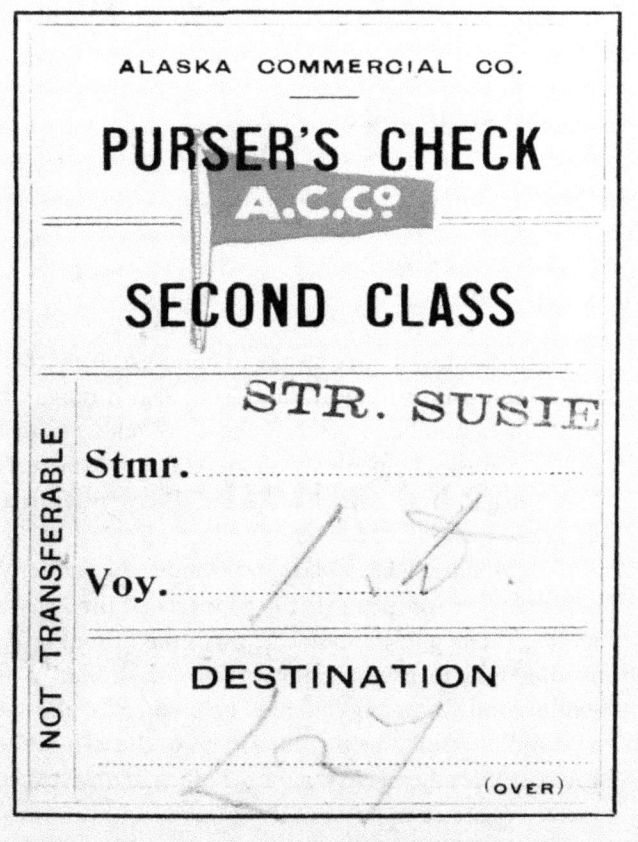

Purser's check from the *Susie*.

boat onto a sand bar, but we readily backed off, found a deep channel and went on our way, the only time on the entire trip that I felt her touch bottom.

We now have a lot of big white gulls and small gray ones flying about us. Each side of us are flats covered with grass and willows, how wide I can only imagine.

We had been going west until we entered the Delta. Then we went north aways and some of the time through this channel we were headed east, right toward a low range of mountains that we had left behind us on the main river. When I turned in, the channel had narrowed to about the size of Rock River.

Someone said that we reached the mouth of the Yukon about midnight and anchored there until high tide let us get over the bar.

19

ST. MICHAEL TO SEATTLE

St. Michael

Sunday, July 23. We awoke to find ourselves "rocked in the cradle of the deep" on Norton Sound, an offshoot of the Bering Sea. A range of mountains could be seen to the east of us, and a number of islands ahead. When we reached the islands, they proved to be vast grassy plains just such as we passed below Andreafski. We passed between two islands, Stuart Island and St. Michael Island. We went entirely around the back side of it and tied up at the town of St. Michael.

Lord, Lord, what a place, no wonder the soldier was sick at heart. One great bare grass covered, ever wet plain, is the property of the Alaska Commercial Company. Everything on it is theirs and nobody else owns anything there. South of them the North American Trading and Transport Company have a similar monopoly and north of them the Alaska Exploration Company. There is no chance for individual enterprise in any direction. Not a pound of grub to be bought except of the two big companies, not a meal or a bed unless you patronize them. No steamboat office in town except theirs, and no competition between them. We are completely at their mercy and they never heard of the word. Only one boat, the Alaska Commercial Company steam schooner *Jeanie*, lies in the harbor. She sails Wednesday, rates $75.00 and $60.00, accommodations nothing, and all tickets sold. We now know all we care to know about Cape Nome, money couldn't hire us to go there. I paid a dollar for a mighty good dinner at the Alaska Commercial Company hotel. The meal was good, extra good, but it took away my appetite when I thought about the dollar. Think of $3.00 a day until some boat picks us up. Firewood is so scarce that we can't cook for ourselves, even if we had cooking utensils. A meeting of would be passengers signed names and sent a committee out around the harbor in a small boat to see what we could do with the Wind Jammers out there, and we got no satisfaction. The wind blows all the time, a damp, raw, cold wind that cuts right into me. The thermometer showed 54 degrees above zero at noon, but it felt colder than it did last winter at 54 below. It rains almost any time, without provocation, and this is the best month of the year. Has snowed three times in the past 10 days. But we're in a free country. I caught enough fish for supper off the wharf and we set up our tent without asking and we pulled grass for a bed without a license. But what a God-forsaken place.

Monday, July 24. We had a fish breakfast with Carl Jorgenson, using his tools and bread and buying a can of milk. We also got tickets to Seattle, on the *Jeanie*, second-class $60.00 each. We got them from two men who bought them yesterday, and now don't want to go on her. We had to pay them full $60.00, but felt lucky to get them, for I know some who would pay a premium on them, and I rather imagine we should. Things also took a brighter aspect, when we found that the *Jeanie*'s sailing date is changed from Wednesday to tonight. Having our tickets and sailing tonight, we begin to get accustomed to the Alaska Commercial Company's peculiar grafting methods, and quite enjoyed hearing about the big gang that went to the Alaska Commercial Company's bunk house last night. They were plainly given to understand that by boarding at the hotel at $3.00 per day, the lodging would be free. So yesterday they very dutifully ate at the hotel and went to the bunk house to sleep. At 11:00 P.M. the boss came around and collected 50 cents a head or get out.

Dan and I killed time after we got our tickets, mostly by sitting around with other disconsolates. After dinner we explored the independent end of the island, the Alaska Exploration Company possessions, and the land beyond, in its wild natural state. It would be difficult to describe the absolute desolation of this St. Michael country, which is much the same as Cape Nome and other parts of the coast bordering on the Bering Sea. The land rises only a few feet above the sea, and extends back indefinitely in a low, perfectly flat plain.

There isn't a tree anywhere that measures two inches in diameter. The only excuse for a tree, is the occasional stunted willow shrub, a little clump of willow whips about one-half inch in diameter, and all too few of them. Grass of a coarse rank kind grows in profusion, and because of the thick grass and the flat land and the constant rain, the ground is never dry, and he who walks in it is constantly walking in a wet mass of grass that has all the characteristics of a street paved with thick wet sponges.

Add to such discomfort, the cold wet wind, which brings a fog in from the ocean, that soon changes to rain, and we have the formula for the most unpleasant climate that I ever found anywhere.

Consequently, our exploration of the afternoon did not take us very far before we were wet and chilled to the bone, and were glad to get back to our tent, change our clothes and pack our baggage for our ocean voyage. We had supper with Carl Jorgenson, and said goodbye to him. He went on his way to Nome. Then at 7:00 P.M. we checked our surplus baggage, and the little *Louise* took us out to the ocean going *Jeanie*.

Bering Sea

If you've never been seasick, words can't convey a proper understanding of what it is. If you have been seasick, you don't care to have anyone else describe it.

My diary is lamentably deficient as regards my trip across the Bering Sea.

We were interested, as soon as we boarded the *Jeanie* in looking her over, and finding our bunks. She was a great improvement, when compared with the *Susie*, built for ocean travel, of course, primarily a freighter, but provided with comfortable berths for a very considerable number of passengers. Probably she was loaded to the limit with freight on her trip north, but now she rode very high out of water, because she had practically no freight when she left St. Michael.

Dan and I turned in rather early, figuring that we would have plenty of time to explore the boat next day, but my diary makes short work of the five day trip across the Bering Sea:

Tuesday July 25. I promptly threw up all I had aboard as soon as I woke up, but the day was fair and Bering Sea was calm, so I didn't keep it at it as long as I laid on my back in my berth. Ate some dinner and some supper but not much.

Wednesday, July 26, Thursday, July 27 and Friday, July 28. Never out of my bunk except to hang my liver out to air. Never ate nor drank anything. Let's draw a curtain over this distressing topic. I had lots of company. Dan fared far better than I did, and really enjoyed the trip.

Saturday, July 29. Reached the end of Bering Sea and I finally managed to get out on deck, but the grub is so rotten I can't eat a bite yet. This old tub can't steam against a head wind, so we laid up at Unimak Pass all day.

On July 25 we sighted Cape Nome, but as we had all the passengers we could carry, there was no occasion for us to stop there. There is no harbor at Nome, consequently, no boat stops there unless compelled to.

Under great difficulties, internal difficulties, I made sketch of Cape Nome as we passed it. After two days at St. Michael, Dan and I were both very happy in the thought that we were not headed for Nome.

I really enjoyed Saturday, July 29. The waves on Bering Sea are short and choppy, so with our light boat we bounced up and down in most unexpected directions and at most unexpected moments. But I finally got my sea legs on Saturday, and came on deck prepared to enjoy the balance of the trip.

We had to get from Bering Sea to the Pacific by going through one of the many passes between the many Aleutian Islands. It was not an easy task, when there was a strong wind. Consequently, we anchored near Cape Sarichef early in the day. It was early Sunday morning, before the Captain deemed it safe to run the pass.

Cape Nome, Alaska, July 25, 1899.

Pogromni and Shishaldin volcanoes, July 29, 1899.

Unimak Pass, July 29, 1899.

We were all much interested in the Pogromni Volcano, which smoked in a lazy way some five or ten miles to the east of us, and Shishaldin Volcano, which is 9400 feet high. Shishaldin lay some 30 miles further east, and its top was entirely obscured by a dense cloud of smoke. These two volcanoes constitute about the entire area of Unimak Island, the first and largest of the Aleutians.

The Pacific

Sunday, July 30. The quiet peaceful Pacific. As soon as we really got on the Pacific, I had to turn in again and quit eating. These great long ground swells are too much for me. I try to eat a little light stuff but can't get it. These thieving Japs who cook for us, serve corn beef and cabbage when they wish to make us sick and then sell us the canned apricots, that should be served at meals, for 50 cents per can, when we begin to get our sea legs.

Monday, July 31. In spite of swells, I got on deck a while today and lost myself for an hour or so reading mother's letters. Bought some chocolate and toast from these Jap robbers, and I almost feel that they saved my life.

Tuesday, August 1. We have left the course we suppose we were to take and are now heading for Kodiak Island to shift the coal in our bunkers, and to take water. How can we ever expect to get to Seattle this season, if our captain zigzags all around the Pacific stopping at every island?

I ate some breakfast and dinner, but just before supper a wind began to blow, and the ship hauled to and I turned in to keep from getting sick again. It was the opinion of the assembled passengers that the captain was a fool, that we were lost, and that we were headed for Siberia, South Africa and the Bay of Fundy all at the same time. The blow passed over, the sun came out, with a shower right in the midst of it. The ship resumed her course North Northeast, and we renewed our confidence in the Captain and his ability. We who had missed our supper bought lunches from Mato the Jap. So I went to sleep full of chocolate and toast.

Wednesday, August 2. We have a character aboard, whom we nicknamed the Roosian Captain. He talks all the time and claims to know everything. This is a fine day and the Roosian Captain was up early telling us the whole history of Kodiak Island and the Russian occupation, its prospects and industries and geography. He has a hotel somewhere in Frisco, but seems to let someone run that for him, while he runs about the country.

Everybody went on deck to sun and to see the mainland away off to the left. Dim and hazy rough mountains could be seen, some springing up from the sea, others apparently floating and blending with the clouds, visible one instant, transformed to clouds the next. Quite impossible to adequately describe or to sketch. Just to be remembered. Snow lines running down almost to the sea and glaciers great and small.

I ate what might be called a square meal for breakfast, a lot of oatmeal and cream that I bought from the Jap with beans to fill up. Everybody ate breakfast, and as a result there was a famine, grub ran short, and we all damned the Japs behind their backs. How people will growl among themselves, and never report such things at headquarters.

We sighted and met a full rigged ship, the *Santa Clara* of San Francisco nearly 48 hours out of Kodiak, beating headwinds all the way. The ship was a beauty, three masts, each having six sails, four jibs and a sail tagging on behind the rear mast like a small boy hangs to the tailboard of a wagon.

Lice formed an interesting topic of discussion, last evening and this morning. We know one or two men are lousy and I suspect we all will be before we reach Seattle.

After dinner we all went on deck again. Kodiak Island was just visible away ahead and to the right. At our left there were three or four whales, spouting around, having a great time. We could occasionally see their big black backs and fins or tails. Their spouting looked just like smoke, looked for the world as if they were enjoying an after dinner pipe.

After we passed the whales, the point of Kodiak Island demanded all of our attention. The land all looks so misty even when within a mile or two of it. Looks as though a thin white gauze curtain were let down from the clouds, just touching the sea. The sea in front of the land, due to the sun's position at our right, is nearly black, without a suggestion of mist about it. As we get closer, what we thought were rocks, turn out to be grass covered mountains, with perpendicular furrows plowed all through them everywhere. On the side facing the ocean, they have been torn apart much as one would break an apple. Every little way is a low flat valley reaching away back into the distance. Some of these valleys are as much as a mile wide. Just before reaching Kodiak there is a big cliff of rock, a mountain broken in two, a regular Gibraltar of a rather light yellowish rock, all seemed and furrowed from the sea to the very top. What a picture it would make. I sketched it roughly.

Kodiak Island, August 2, 1899.

Kodiak is the principle town on Kodiak Island. It lies at the east end of the island. Karluk, the second town of importance on the island lies just behind a big rock on a shallow bay at the northwest corner of the island.

Karluk's harbor is bad, so bad that a number of vessels have been blown ashore there and wrecked. As a result insurance companies will not insure boats using Karluk harbor.

So all ocean boats are now compelled to anchor at Uyak Bay some 15 miles farther up the straits. Then two or three little vessels ply regular between Uyak Bay and Karluk. A lot of extra labor just to please an insurance company, but it shows how dangerous Karluk is considered to be.

Unless a man was looking for it, he would never find or even suspect the existence of Uyak Bay. It certainly must be a very safe harbor, and its entrance is plenty wide enough, if one only knew there was a harbor back of it.

The map shows Uyak Bay to run half way across the island, but even when in the harbor, there is no suggestion of any such body of water. The entrance is protected by a great lump of rock some 500–600 feet high, quite covered with grass and patches of purple flowers. The rock has that knobby appearance of popped corn or looks as if some gigantic hand had plastered huge hands full of mud one atop the other and cooked them into rock.

After supper nearly everyone went ashore, in a boat rowed by a young Russian Indian, at 50 cents per head. There we inspected the canneries of the Pacific Steam Whaling Company and Hume Brothers & Hume. The canneries are just big empty barns with a tin shop in one end and a lot of tin cans and boxes piled everywhere, and apparently that's all there is to it. But further search reveals two simple wooden machines set up somewhere, and these machines do the whole thing. The fish, after being cleaned by hand, are fed to one machine, which is also supplied with empty cans. The other machine delivers canned salmon. Quite too simple a process to be very interesting. Chinamen do all the canning business and white men catch the fish. But not in Uyak Bay. The fish are caught at Karluk or thereabouts and brought here in the company's little steamboats every evening.

According to the Roosian Captain, who five years ago spent a summer prospecting here, one of the six canneries located here has an annual output of 90,000 cases of salmon per season, four dozen cans to the case. Of course, one company owns all the canneries, and most of them are idle. Even here in the wilderness of Alaska things are business like. One canning firm buys out the opposition and shuts it down. The Captain pointed out one idle building that cost its present owners $150,000.

The reason for all these canneries is, of course, the salmon, and they in turn are attracted to this particular spot, by a river or creek some 30 miles long that empties into the Shelikof Strait at Karluk. At the head of this river is a lake or chain of lakes, very popular with the spawning salmon.

Hume Brothers & Hume's boat *Ecuador* had come in just before we arrived and thrown 4000 fish into the company's shed, which we were told would all be in cans by 9:00 A.M. tomorrow. Hume Brothers & Hume run a small store to supply the needs of their own fishermen and independent fishermen. Here I bought several cans of apricots and pears to eat on the *Jeanie* and every one had a drink of good water from the little creek that empties into the bay.

On board ship, coal was being hoisted from the hold to the bunkers. The captain offered to pay a half dozen passengers 50 cents per hour to help. But we are all too rich. We value cleanliness more than a hard dirty job at $4.00. So he got six Chinamen from shore. They earned what they got.

Thursday, August 3. Salmon for breakfast, red salmon, of course, such as they can, not the big king salmon of Dawson, and not so good. They are dryer and much like the canned fish, but much better than the salt horse that the Japs had been feeding us. The day was cloudy while small boats were bringing us a cargo of fresh water. After the subdued well blended coloring of Indian River scenery, the scenery here is a very pleasing change. Every one of the many colors, and the many shades of green, seems to be so strong and stands out distinctly.

After dinner I made a sketch looking up at Uyak Bay. A study in blue and green. Red and yellow entirely lacking.

At 2:00 P.M. after we had taken on a dozen boatloads of water, we pulled anchor and started on our home run for Seattle. The sky was fairly clear, and away across the strait, snowy mountains were visible with tops hidden in clouds. About 5:30 we turned into the narrow straight between Kodiak Island and Afognak Island and spent the evening shooting whales and looking at the myriads of jellyfish and other curious creatures of the sea.

Friday, August 4. We awoke to find all land left behind. We had a favorable wind with the sea fairly smooth. I played whilst all the morning and evening and slept all the afternoon.

Uyak Bay, August 3, 1899.

We had some fireworks after dark. Phosphorescence in the water. Looked like incandescent lights underground glass, wherever the surface was disturbed.

Saturday, August 5. Ate a big breakfast and had to hold down a reclining position in the fireroom all day to hold down the breakfast. I read magazines from breakfast until supper, and then wasn't very hungry. After supper I turned in early. Excepting the time we were in the straits back in Kodiak Island, I have been uncomfortable every minute, if not sick. There is less motion to the boat down in the fire room, so it's a popular resort.

Wallis Sanborn and Dan Dever "in costume," August 10, 1899.

Sunday, August 6. The first bright sunny day, all day, since we started, together with a most favorable breeze. We should be traveling along at a fine rate. The ship rolls and pitches as much as ever but today for the first time I have felt really at ease all over and I may say comfortable. But its mighty lazy and no variety. Read, play cards or sleep. There's the whole story.

Monday, August 7. A nice day and we did well and killed time at cards.

Tuesday, August 8. Today we expected to sight land, but didn't; encountered head winds and a heavy sea. Any boat with a normal cargo could have plowed right ahead, but the *Jeanie* rides so high out of water that she is an easy target for a stiff head wind. We held our place and gained a few miles as the wind died down towards evening.

Wednesday, August 9. More headwind and sea and a general cussing for the Captain. I almost believe that I've been lousy ever since I was aboard the *Susie* I know I've been lousy for the past week. Today Dan and I took off all our duds down in the hold. Then after sandpapering ourselves with towels, we got fresh clothes from our clothes bags and threw all of our old things overboard.

At noon it was rumored that we were 40 miles from Cape Flattery, going East Northeast. The captain had evidently overshot the mark and gone too far south of his course, which from Kodiak has been East-half-South.

At dinner we had a diversion which shows how lightly the boat is ballasted. A big swell, tipped us up on our beam ends, so that every dish, plate, etc., made a clean jump, slid the whole length of the table and landed on the floor and in Jack's bunk. The sea wasn't rough either.

All the afternoon Vancouver Island was just visible at our left, a faint shadow in the fog. From supper till 11:30 we had a big discussion as to whether the Captain knew his business, where we were and why did we shift our course so often from East Southeast to East Northeast. Some had us headed for Columbia River, others for Queen Charlotte Sound. The Roosian Captain came down at 11:30 swearing like a pirate at the "dough head captain!" At 11:31 the lookout called out "Light on port bow," and then, "Another light on port bow." The two lighthouses at the entrance of the Strait of Juan de Fuca. The Roosian Captain was relieved and turned in. Seattle couldn't escape us, if we followed the channel ahead of us.

Thursday, August 10. After breakfast I went on deck. There at the left was Vancouver Island and on our right, just visible in the dense fog that lined the shore was God's Country. I wonder where that term originated. It certainly is appropriate and doubtless everyone

Dan Dever, pre-haircut and shave, August 10, 1899.

returning to his home feels that way about it. However, barren or fertile, rough or level, the land may be. We played whist until dinner, then went on deck to watch for Seattle.

By 5:00 P.M. we had landed at Schwabacher's Wharf, run the gauntlet and taken a bus to the Diller Hotel. Then the first thing we did was to find a photograph gallery, where we had our pictures taken in costume.

Then Dan got a haircut and sacrificed his big bushy red beard, while I got a pair of shoes and looked at store windows. Then what a meal we ate. I had roast mutton, real apple sauce, raspberries and cream and how good they were. We walked around town, up and down until 10, then went back to the hotel and turned into a real bed in a real building.

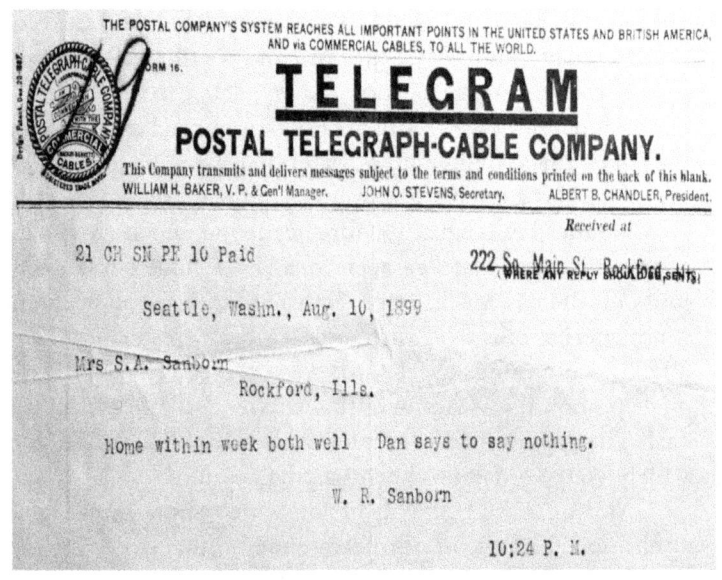

Notification of return telegram.

Friday, August 11. Sheets felt queer and the high bolster bothered me but I got a night's rest. Up at 7:30 and had breakfast of porterhouse steak at the hotel. Then we went looking at clothing store windows. Nothing in particular attracted us, but we went into MacDougall and Southwick's to see why they didn't have a show window full of clothes. The result was that we bought there and feel very well suited. We also got underclothes, shirts, collars, etc., and then we dressed in our new togs. Oh, how swell. I grew six inches when I saw myself in the glass. I got a light colored, soft hat and looked as though I had a tailor made outfit. Dan got a dark gray suit. Of course, our suits were hand me down but we felt mightily dressed in them. What a green bunch most of our *Jeanie* friends are when dressed in store clothes. Some of them are just awful, and we saw nearly all of the gang at one time or another. It was worth the price of our clothes to see them look at us in our fine togs. Most of them didn't know us.

Wallis Sanborn with gold nugget tie-pin.

The Sanborn house, Rockford, Illinois.

We had been able to pay our way without cashing the gold dust that we had dug, with the express purpose of carrying it back to Rockford. There was some fair sized nuggets in our poke. So we arranged with a Seattle jeweler, to gold plate the battered old table forks and spoons that we had carried all the way from Rockford, and to solder nuggets on them here, there and everywhere. Our idea was to show the Rockford folks, that gold in the Klondike, actually stuck to everything.

I had several tie-pins made of nuggets, as well as some other jewelry. One of the pins shows plainly in the photographs taken of me at Streator about a year later.

We went out to dinner at the Butler and then we finally changed Dan's $100.00 bill, when we bought tickets over the Great Northern Railroad to St. Paul. We met old Jim Forsythe of Sheep Camp and Lake Bennett at the station, also buying a ticket. He was to leave next day. At the post office I found a short letter from Mother. Then we collected our baggage and took it to the train. Jim Forsythe came to the depot to bid us goodbye. He had sent from Dawson for money and again at Seattle and he had waited two weeks for more money. But he was well fixed. While he was in the Klondike, one of his Pennsylvania Oil properties had built up a bank account of $30,000 for Jim. I figured that that was more than the total income of ourselves, and all of the many friends we met in that eighteen months' trip.

Moral ... It's easier to find gold close to home, than it is to dig the yellow metal in the frozen North.

20

Author's Conclusion

Here it is, almost Christmas, in the year of 1932. In these past seven months, I have enjoyed every one of the many hours that it has taken to assemble this story of my Klondike adventure. If my readers derive even a fraction of the pleasure that I have found in compiling the account, I shall feel that it was time well spent. Like many a storyteller, I can't seem to find a place to break it off. Now that the story is told, there are so many incidents that suddenly pop out of my memory and beg me to record them.

Of course, we were welcomed with open arms when we reached Rockford, and I dare say that we were both more welcome to our respective mothers, than was the assortment of curios that we brought with us.

Without counting all the miles we tramped between the first time and the last time that we were in Dawson, we had travelled some 10,500 miles. I have shown the detail of distances as follows:

Table of Distances

Rockford to St. Paul	364 (in miles)	
St. Paul to Seattle	_1904_	2268
Seattle to Skagway	1125	
Skagway to White Horse	100	
White Horse to Dawson	_450_	1675
Dawson to Eagle	100	
Eagle to Circle	175	
Circle to Rampart	350	
Rampart to Tanana	100	
Tanana to Nulato	275	
Nulato to Holy Cross	275	
Holy Cross to St. Michael	_375_	1650
St. Michael to Nome	120	
Nome to Seattle	_2500_*	2620
Seattle to Rockford		_2268_
		10481

*Probably longer via Kodiak island.

We had been gone just a few days less than eighteen months. What did it cost us? And what did we get in return? I've had some difficulty in digging out the record of what it cost. I kept an accurate record of every expense that was to be divided by us as partners, but I was careless about recording my personal receipts and expenses.

While at Dawson in February, I find that I sent a draft for $18.00 to Grandmother Wallis, which indicates that it was $300.00 that I had borrowed from her. I started with that and $500.00 that I had saved. I received $80.00 as my share from the sale of our joint outfit, and about $70.00 other personal income. I arrived at Rockford without a cent, and owing Dan 70 cents. Consequently, the trip cost me about $950.00. I have a check on all of the following items, except that defined as Expense of Various Other Trips.

Cost of Trip

Share of Original Outfit	$380.00
Rockford to Dawson	205.00
Buying Remnant of Pop's Share	100.00
At Dawson—January & February	35.00
Expense of Various Other Trips	60.00
Dawson to St. Michael	35.00
St. Michael to Seattle	60.00
At Seattle	35.00
Seattle to Rockford	<u>40.00</u>
Total	**$950.00**

I secured a short job at $150.00 per month almost immediately after arriving home and then took a permanent job at $125.00 helping to build what is now the New York Central Railroad west of Streator. That enabled me to repay Grandmother Wallis' $300.00 when the next interest came due in February 1900.

Who can say just what I derived from the trip. I treasured the $60.00 worth of gold dust that I brought home very carefully, until I was married in 1901. Then I had about a third of the dust cast into a very beautiful brooch for my very beautiful bride. When we found that two or three cannot live as cheaply as one. I cashed in all of the remaining dust, except a little sample that I still treasure as a souvenir.

For that $950.00 I had eighteen months of very novel and very enjoyable travel. How far and how long will $950.00 carry a man on a travel trip today?

I believe that trip, and my association with the various characters I met, helped in a very great measure to scrape off a crust of snobbishness that I had acquired at college along with my engineering education.

And I know that our rough outdoor life built me a body such as I never had before, which has withstood a lot of hard knocks since that time, and to all appearances is capable of withstanding a few more.

It was just too bad that I couldn't weave a thread of romance through my story. Too bad that I couldn't rescue some beautiful young girl just as she was about to plunge over the edge of Chilkoot, or as she sank for the third time in the White Horse Rapids,

Wallis Sanborn 1928.

and then have her nurse me back to life after a grizzly bear bit a big piece out of my leg, and then marry her in the last chapter. There was plenty of romance in the eighteen months following my return to Rockford, but that's another story.

And strange as it may seem, Dan and I have never met nor heard a word from any of the many friends with whom we came in contact on *The Klondike Stampede.*

The End

Index

Numbers in ***bold italics*** indicate pages with illustrations

Afognak Island, Alaska 249
Alaska Commercial Company 93, 149, 166, 226, 227, 242, 243
Alaska Exploration Company 242, 243
alcohol 132, 133, 136; beer 14, 33, 214; whiskey 33, 123, 139, 140, 141
Aleutian Islands, Alaska 244, 246
Allen, Douglas W. 7
Andreafski, Alaska 240, 241, 242
Anvik, Alaska 239, ***239***, 240
Anvik River 240
Arctic Circle 234
Arctic Express Company 147
Arena Creek 108, 117
Arena Gulch 106-07, 112, 115, 130, 146, 162, 186, 187, 199, 224
Aurora Borealis 136, 197
Australia Creek 107, 108, 220, 223
avalanche 5, 134; snow slide of April 3, 1898 50, 55, 56, 60; *see also* snow slide

bacon 5, 20, 24, 39, 59, 87, 108, 109, 113, 114, 116, 120, 123, 128, 130, 137, 145, 148, 152, 158, 180, 183, 190, 197, 202, 204, 211, 216, 220, 231
the Barracks (Dawson) 93, 149, 166, 167
beans 5, 24, 64, 87, 92, 117, 128, 137, 138, 141, 146, 148, 152, 158, 161, 180, 183, 190, 192, 193, 200, 206, 216, 226, 231, 246
bear 115, 116, 147, 159, 212, 213, 214, 217, 218, 226, 256
Bear Creek 150, 177, 201
bedrock 4, 75, 102, 106, 107, 109, 111, 112, 117, 118, 119, 120, 144, 145, 155, 177, 196, 198, 204, 214, 215, 219, 223
Bedrock City 6, 119, 120, 121, 126, 127, 130, 131, 140, 144, 145, 150, 151, 155, 156, 157, 158, 159, 160, 163, 168, 169, 175, 179, 180, 181, 182, 183, 187, 188, 195, 197, 198, 203, 205, 206, 207, 208, 209, 212, 213, 214, 215, 219, 221, 222, 223, 224, 226, 228
Bella 240
bench claim 98, 104, 111, 150, 151, 155, 156, 169, 173, 174, 199, 201

Bennett, British Columbia 56, 59, 60, ***62***, 64, 68, 69, 71, 72, 76, 77, 78, 86, 87, 92, 94, 122, 147; *see also* Lake Bennett, British Columbia
Bering Sea 219, 242, 243-46
Berton, Pierre 3, 6, 7
Big Bear Gulch 215, 217, 218
Big Salmon River 85
Big Windy, Alaska 80
billiard 166, 176, 239
Birch Creek 233
Blackjack 50, 52, 165, 211
boat number 1739 69, 78, 85
Bonanza Creek 3, 9, 91, 92, 96-100, 102, 104, 111, 125, 150, 155, 169, 173-74, 176, 199, 200, 202, 209, 215; *see also* Rabbit Creek
Bonanza Valley 97
books 6, 121, 123, 142, 157, 224; *Quo Vadis* 212
Boulder Gulch 97
boxing ***113***
British American Company 226
butter 5, 15, 24, 39, 69, 95, 108, 127, 138, 140, 180, 216, 231

cabin (Bedrock City) 109, 112, 119, 120, 121, 123-29, ***124***, 130, 131, 133, 135, 138, 144, 145, 153, 154, 155, 156, 157, 161, 171, 182, 187, 197, 213, 216, 217, 218, 220, 221
Camp Number 3 56
Canadian Pacific Railroad 168
Canyon and Rapids Tramway Company 81
Canyon City, Alaska 36, 37, ***37***
Cape Flattery, Washington 251
Cape Nome, Alaska 226, 227, 235, 242, 243, 244, ***244***
Cape Sarichef, Alaska 244
Caribou Crossing (Carocross) 77
Carmack, George Washington 3
Carmack, Kate 3
chair 127, ***127***, 128
Cheechaco 5, 93, 94, 96, 105, 111, 112, 113, 179, 186; *see also* greenhorn; tenderfoot
Chicago, Illinois 10, 14, 16, 18, 87, 97, 105
Chilkoot Pass, Alaska 4, 9, 18, 31, 36, 38, 39, 40, 41, 42, 45-48, ***46***,
50, 52, 54, 55, 56, 57, 64, 73, 80, 83, 86, 94, 154, 164, 170, 255
churches 6, 166-67, 197, 202, 240
the Circle 227, 233, 234
Circle City, Alaska 107, 122, 233, 234
City of Seattle 22-26, 27, ***27***
claim 3, 4, 7, 75, 94, 95, 97, 98, 102, 103, 104, 106, 107, 109, 111, 112, 117, 125, 150, 151, 155, 156, 161, 168, 169, 173, 174, 175, 177, 178, 179, 188, 189, 211, 216, 218, 221, 223, 225, 227, 235; stake and record 198-203; *see also* bench claim; discovery claim; fraction claim
Cliff House 177
color 4, 75, 76, 83, 88, 90, 106, 107, 108, 109, 118, 139, 155, 174, 198, 203, 214, 220, 233; *see also* gold
Colts Revolver 26, 100
Columbia River 17, 251
cost of trip 255
crap 165; *see also* dice
Crater Lake 47, 48, 54, 55
cribbage 161

dance halls 112, 150, 166, 169-72
Dawson City 3, 4, 5, 6, 7, 8, 9, 21, 24, 51, 61, 65, 87, 89, 90, 91, 92, 93, 94, 95, 96, 97, 100, 102, 104, 105, 106, 107, 108, 109, 110, 111, 112, 113, 117, 119, 121, 122, 123, 125, 127, 134, 140, 144, 145, 147, 148, 149, 150, 151, 152, 153, 154, 155, 156, 157, 158, 159, 160, 161, 163, 164, 165-72, 173, 174, 175, 177, 178, 179, 180, 181, 182, 183, 186, 187, 188, 190, 197, 198, 199, 200, 201, 202, 203, 204, 209, 210, 211, 215, 216, 218, 220, 221, 222, 223, 224, 225, 226, 227, 228, 229, 230, 231, 232, 234, 240, 249, 253, 254, 255; fire of April 26, 1899 209; fire of October 14, 1898 123; West Dawson 149, 151, 164, 169, 178, 199
Dead Horse Trail 6; *see also* White Pass Trail
Dever, Dan ***250***, **251**
dice 112, 149, 165; *see also* crap
discovery claim 106, 156, 175

257

Index

distance table 254
dog 6, 7, 29, 32, 36, 38, 40, 41, 42, 50, 54, 57, 58, 60, 61, 64, 71, 93, 106, 140, 148, 162, 163, 177, 181, 204, 216, 224, 228, 230, 232; Jim 187, 189, 190, 197, 204, 207; Jumbo 138, 189, 190, 197
the Dome 102, 175, 176, *176*, 177, 200
Dominion Creek 102, 123, 156
draw poker 165
dried fruit 5, 34, 61, 64, 123, 156, 158, 202, 216
Dyea, Alaska 3, 4, 22, 23, 26, *27*, 31, 32–35, 36, 37, *37*, 40, 41, 44, 45, 50, 51, 52, 68, 86, 96, 122, 154, 218
Dyea River 33, 34, 36, 52

Eagle City, Alaska 230, *231*
Ecuador 248
eggs 5, 16, 24, 60, 61, 95, 137
Eldorado 9, 91, 92, 96–100, 102, 104, 107, 109, 111, 112, 117, 125, 154, 155, 168, 169, 198, 200, 202, 204, 208, 209, 215
Ensley Creek 147, 148, 152, 162, 163, 180, 215
Eureka Creek 145, 202

faro 32, 34, 165, 166, 168
fire 4, 40, 42, 60, 64, 100, 106, 108, 117, 119, 120, 121, 123, 126, 135, 136, 137, 138, 140, 141, 146, 147, 148, 150, 151, 152, 153, 159, 173, 181, 187, 190, 191, 192, 193, 194, 195, 198, 207; "To Build a Fire" 5, 7
firewood 56, 77, 81, 82, 119, 121, 128, 147, 148, 149, 193, 194, 242
First Avenue (Bedrock City) 120, 137, 138
Five Fingers Rapids 85, 86
Fort Selkirk 86, 148,
Fort Wrangell, Alaska 30, 31, *31*
Fort Yukon, Alaska 234
Forty Mile Post 150, 230
fraction claim 111, 156, 168, 173, 174
"free" miner's certificate 4, 26, *28*, 29, *199*
French Gulch 98, 202

gambling houses 6, 209
glacier 36, 42, 102, 156, 157, 182, 197, 201, 203, 208, 213, 246; *see also* ice
gold 3, 4, 6, 7, 9, 10, 17, 20, 25, 75, 87, 88, 89, 92, 93, 94, 95, 96, 97, 98, 102, 105, 107, 109, 111, 112, 116, 117, 119, 121, 122, 129, 139, 140, 144, 154, 155, 156, 166, 170, 175, 176, 179, 192, 196, 198, 201, 204, 209, 213, 214, 218, 219, 221, 223, 227, 233, 235, 239, 240, *252*, 253, 255; bar 121; currency 221; dust 4, 93, 95, 96, 97, 117, 121, 140, 144, 219, 221, 253, 255; flour 121; mine 111, 112, 123, 173, 203;
nugget 4, 89, 90, 109, 129, 253; placer 102, 131; poke 221, 223; quartz 188; *see also* color
Gold Bottom Gulch 175, 176, 200, 201, 220
Gold Hill 150, 155, 156, 168, 200
Grand Forks 199, 200
gravel 4, 33, 73, 74, 75, 88, 97, 98, 99, 102, 105, 106, 107, 108, 109, 116, 117, 126, 137, 138, 139, 144, 145, 155, 167, 177, 208, 214, 220, 223, 232, 235, 237
Gray, Charlotte 4, 6, 7
Grayling, Alaska 238
Great Northern Railroad 253
Greenhorn 27, 39, 42, 87, 90, 92, 94, 95, 96, 112, 179, 210, 252; *see also* Cheechaco; tenderfoot
grouse 116, 134, 141, 143, 211, 212, 213, 214, 217

Hamilton Landing 241
Hammond's Tram 42
Hanshaw, A. Alan 1
Holy Cross Mission, Alaska 240
Hootalinqua 85
horse 6, 32, 36, 37, 39, 41, 44, 45, 50, 56, 58, 67, 69, 70, 93, 122, 140, 249
Hotel Diller 18, *19*, 252
Hume Brothers & Hume 248
Hunker Creek 102, 150–51

ice 26, 31, 34, 36, 37, 39, 40, 41, 42, 47, 48, 49, 52, 54, 57, 58, 59, 60, 61, 62, 64, 67, 69, 70, 71, 72, 74, 75, 76, 97, 99, 106, 120, 125, 127, 130, 131, 135, 139, 140, 145, 146, 147, 148, 149, 152, 153, 156, 157, 180, 193, 194, 197, 202, 206, 207, 208, 209, 210, *210*, 211, *211*, 215, 218, 220, 223; *see also* glacier
Indian 5, 33, 47, 48, 78, 84, 86, 90, 116, 122, 150, 199, 204, 220, 227, 232, 233, 234, 237, 238, 239, 240, 248
Indian River 90, 91, 92, 96, 97, 98, 99, 100, 102–84, *103*, *108*, *162*, *163*, 200, 210, *210*, *211*, 212

Jeanie 242, 243, 248, 251, 252
J.P. Light 226
Juneau, Alaska 31, 86, 211

Kaiyuh Mountains 236
Karluk, Alaska 248
Ketchikan, Alaska 30, *30*
the Klondike (locus) 1, 3–7, 9, 10, 14, 17, 36, 45, 61, 68, 69, 76, 105, 108, 109, *113*, 142, 154, 156, 158, 159, 165, 166, 169, 170, 171, 178, 196, 202, 208, 214, *217*, 223, 230, 253, 254
Klondike City 92, 96, 113; *see also* Lousetown
Klondike Creek 92
Klondike River 92, 96, 97, 102, 110, 113, 125, 150, 173, 179, 199, 201
Klondike Stampede (Gold Rush) 1, 3, 7, 256
The Klondiker's Soliloquy (poem) 193–95
Kodiak, Alaska (town) 248
Kodiak Island, Alaska 246, 247, *247*, 248, 249, 250, 251, 254
Koenig, Wolf 7
Koyukuk River *236*

Lake Bennett, British Columbia 3, 4, 24, 45–76, *62*, *63*, *67*, *70*, *73*, *74*, 77, 78, 80, 86, 110, 117, 127, 154, 168, 202, 208, 212, 214, 223, 226, 253; water route *79*; *see also* Bennett, British Columbia
Lake Laberge 83, 125
Lake Lindeman 47, 48, 50, 57, 73
Lake Marsh 78, 80
Lake Tagish 76, 77, 78, *79*, 80
laws and customs 34, 59, 90, 94, 102–04, 168, 174; Custom House 29, 47, 54, 55, 78
Leah 238
letter 1, 9, 10, 21, 29, 35, 50, 55, 56, 59, 62, 65, 67, 68–69, 76, 78, 83, 85, 87, 93, 96, 112, 116, 119–21, 123–29, 131, 132, 135, 140, 149, 154, 165, 167, 170, 173, 176, 178, 197, 198, 199, 202, 203, 215–16, 220, 223, 225–26, 227, 228, 246, 253; *see also* mail
Lewes River 85–86
lice (cooties) 200, 201, 216, 247, 251
Little Baldy Mountain 188
Little Eldorado 99
Little Salmon River Station 85
Little Windy 80
Lombard Creek 150
London, Jack 3, 5, 7
Long Lake 48
Louise 243
Lousetown 96, 110, 149, 201, 216; *see also* Klondike City
Low, Colin 7
Lower Bonanza 169, 173
Lower Ramparts 235

magazines 6, 68, 143, 250
mail 5, 6, 35, 50, 64, 68, 69, 75, 78, 87, 90, 92, 93, 96, 105, 111, 112, 113, 121, 123, 149, 161, 163, 165, 168, 178, 179, 181, 197, 198, 199, 202, 203, 204, 210, 215, 220, 221, 222, 228, 231, 234, 238, 240; *see also* letter
maps of the Klondike (Wallis Sanborn) 2, 6, 78, *90–91*, *103*, 162, 197, 198, 200, 202, 203, 210, 212, 214, 215, *217*, 224
Mason, Skookum Jim 3
McClintock River 78
McCormack's Fork 200
McDonald, Alex 168
McQuesten 89, 110
Miles Canyon 82
Milwaukee 240

Index

miner's license and certificate 4, 26, *28*, 29, 199, ***199***, 200, 201
mining 3, 4, 7, 11, 27, 31, 33, 34, 89, 93, 94, 95, 97, 98, 99, 102, 104, 111, 112, 118, 122, 123, 131, 133, 134, 139, 154, 166, 169, 173, 177, 187, 203, 215, 225, 227, 232, 237; placer mining 102, 131
Montana Creek 93
Monte Carlo Theatre 113, ***114***, 149, 166, 168, 169
moose 5, 6, 90, 115, 135, 157, 159, 195, 198, 204, 209, 214, 220, 221, 222, 223, 224, 226
Morse, Kathryn 6, 7
mosquito 24, 78, 80, 85, 86, 88, 93, 95, 99, 116, 214, 217, 219, 222, 232
mouse 6, 63, 110, 120, 128
the Mouth 90, 91, 92, 100, 109, 110, 115, 117, 123, 130, 139, 153, 157, 162, 183, 198, 224
muck 4, 98, 105, 106, 125, 138, 177
Mud Lake 48
mule 6, 32, 41, 42, 60, 97, 121, 123, 140, 142
mush 3, 5, 6, 40, 58, 64, 71, 72, 96, 98, 99, 100, 121, 139, 146, 148, 149, 152, 156, 161, 175, 177, 179, 180, 183, 187, 189, 192, 195, 197, 200, 207, 216
Mysterious Creek 186–205, 209, 213, 215, 223, 226

the Narrows 31, 78
New York Central Railroad 255
Newell, Dianne 8
newspaper 6, 45, 82, 93, 94, 113, 116, 139, 169, 203, 221; Seattle *Post Intelligencer* 80
the Nielsen Party 131, 158, 186, 189, 204, 220
Nine Mile Creek 99, 100, 102, 105, 123, 138, 140, 157, 180, 186, 187, 188, 189, 191, 193, 196, 197, 198, 203, 206, 207, 208, 210, 212, ***212***, 213, 214, 216, 220, 221, 222
the North 4, 83, 88, 186
North American Transportation and Trading Company 93
North-West Mounted Police 4, 7, 68, 78, 93, 130, 139, 147, 166, 177, 183, 195, 221, 224, 230; yellow legs 230
the Northern 149, 165, 166, 168, 174, 199
Norton Sound, Alaska 242
Nugget Gulch 99
Nulato, Alaska 237, 254
Number 20 Below Discovery 97, 107

the Oatley Sisters 149, 166, 170, 171, 232
Ogilvie (town) 90
Ogilvie, Gov. William 169, 179, 225
Old Timer 93, 96, 179, 215; *see also* Sourdough

Ophir Creek 191, 197, 206, 208
outfit 4, 14, 18, 20, 21, 22, 23, 24–26, 34, 37, 38, 41, 44, 45, 46, 47, 50, 54, 55, 56, 57, 59, 60, 61, 62, 63, 64, 65, 66, 67, 81, 82, 84, 86, 87, 88, 90, 92, 93, 94, 96, 97, 105, 110, 122, 128, 144, 156, 158, 161, 170, 179, 180, 181, 183, 189, 190, 192, 195, 206, 207, 208, 213, 214, 219, 220, 221, 222, 223, 224, 225, 226, 227, 233, 238, 255

Pacific Ocean 244, 246–53
Pacific Steam Whaling Company 248
Pelly River 86
permafrost 4
pinochle 140
Pogromni and Shishaldin Volcanoes ***245***, 246
post office 21, 32, 35, 50, 59, 68, 69, 78, 87, 93, 112, 123, 165, 166, 167, 199, 215, 228, 253
prospect 3, 4, 5, 6, 8, 24, 29, 33, 45, 47, 52, 63, 69, 75, 85, 86, 88, 89, 91, 93, 98, 102, 104, 105, 107, 108, 109, 111, 112, 125, 129, 142, 145, 155, 173, 179, 186, 187, 188, 196–98, 202, 204, 205, 209, 213, 214, 216, 223, 227, 230, 231, 246, 248
prospect hole 4, 99, 105, 106, 108, 111, 118, 133, 137, 139, 144, 145, 151, 155, 159, 195, 197, 198, 200, 203, 209, 223
purser 21, 27, *27*, 230, ***241***
Pyramid Mountain 204, 224

Quartz Creek 139, 200, 224, 225
Queen Charlotte Sound, British Columbia 29, 251
Queen Victoria 68, 94, 106, 107

rabbit 6, 106, 132, 133, 134, 138, 141, 142, 145, 146, 149, 156, 188, 203
Rabbit Creek 3; *see also* Bonanza Creek
Rampart City, Alaska 235, 236, 237, 254
Recording Office 104, 150, 161, 166, 168, 173, 175, 178, 225
Reindeer Creek 90
Reynolds, Clarence (Pop) 3, 10, 15, 18, 19, 20, 21, 22, 28, 29, 30, 34, 37, 41, 44, 45, 47, 48, 49, 50, 56, 57, 60, 62, 63, 64, 65, 66, 68, 69, 74, 75, 76, 77, 78, 80, 81, 82, 84, 85, 87, 88, 89, 90, 91, 92, 93, 94, 96, 105, 106, 107, 108, 109, 110, 111, 112, 169, 215, 255
rice 5, 24, 56, 64, 87, 92, 94, 141, 142, 158, 192, 202, 220
Rink Rapids 86
road house 3, 5, 139, 140, 141, 146, 147, 148, 150, 151, 152, 153, 162, 164, 175, 176, ***176***, 177, 178, 180, 189, 198, 200, 201, 216, 218, 220, 224
rocker 4, 25, 98, 108, 109, 117, 128, 213, 219

Rockford, Illinois 3, 4, 5, 9, 10, 14, 16, 19, 20, 24, 26, 34, 49, 109, 110, 112, 147, 149, 178, 187, 202, 210, 224, 225, 226, 228, 253, 254, 255, 256; Sanborn house ***253***
Rosebud Creek 90
roulette 112, 149, 165
Ruby Creek 203, 214

St. Michael, Alaska 3, 5, 20, 90, 170, 178, 202, 226, 227, 228, 241, 242, 243, 244, 254, 255
St. Paul, Minnesota 10, 14, 16, 26, 27, 40, 41, 253, 254
saloon 3, 6, 61, 81, 82, 93, 95, 96, 112, 149, 150, 151, 155, 165, 166, 168, 170, 179, 199, 202, 209, 227, 229, 233
Sanborn, Wallis: in costume ***250***; gold nugget tie-pin ***252***; 1928 ***255***
Santa Clara 246
Sarah 241
the Scales 39, 40, 41, 42, 43, ***43***, 44, 45, ***46***, 47, 53, ***53***, 55, 58
Schwabacher's Wharf, Seattle, Washington 252
scurvy 5, 140, 156, 181, 187, 221
Seattle, Washington 3, 4, 7, 14, 16, 17, 18–26, 33, 40, 41, 60, 68, 72, 80, 87, 93, 104, 128, 132, 150, 163, 200, 202, 216, 226, 227, 228, 242, 246, 247, 249, 251, 252, 253, 254, 255
Second Avenue (Bedrock City) 120, 138
Sheep Camp 9, 26, 34, 35, 36, 38–41, ***38***, 42, ***44***, 45, 49, 50, 51, 53, 55, 56, 57, 58, 61, 64, 86, 112, 125, 148, 154, 163, 196, 202, 253
Shelikof Strait, Alaska 248
Sixty Mile River 90
Skagway, Alaska 9, 22, 32, 34, 35, 51, 88, 140, 181, 227, 254
sluice 4, 95, 97, 98, 109, 116, 117, 118, 126, 127, 173, 219
snow 6, 25, 29, ***31***, 34, 36, 37, 38, 39, 40, 42, 45, 47, 48, 49, 50, 52, 53, ***53***, 54, 55, 56, 57, 58, 59, 60, 62, 63, 64, 67, 68, 69, 74, 75, 76, 99, 118, 120, 125, 126, 128, 130, 131, 132, 133, 134, 135, 138, 139, 140, 144, 146, 147, 148, 152, 153, 154, 156, 157, 159, 162, 163, 176, 181, 182, 189, 190, 191, 192, 193–95, 196, 197, 198, 201, 202, 204, 205, 206, 207, 208, 213, 215, 219, 224, 227, 242, 246, 249
snow slide 63, 132, 138; April 3, 1898 50, 55, 56, 60; *see also* avalanche
Soda Creek 200
solo (card game) 182
Sourdough 93; *see also* Old Timer
Squaw Gulch 107
Squaw Rapids 82
stampede 3–7, 65, 75, ***90–91***, 145, 226, 239; Arena Gulch 106–07;

Bonanza 173–74; Hunker Creek 150–51; Mysterious Creek 186–205; Stewart River 87–91; Sulphur 175–78
Stone House 42, *43*, 46, 53, 55
stove 25, 40, 47, 49, 50, 54, 56, 59, 61, 64, 77, 81, 87, 110, 119, 126, 127, *127*, 128, 135, 137, 140, 141, 142, 146, 147, 148, 150, 151, 152, 164, 165, 171, 180, 183, 187, 190, 191, 192, 193–95, 206, 207, 213, 215, 216, 217, 226, 228
Strait of Juan de Fuca 251
Stuart Island, Washington 242
stud poker 143, 149
sugar 5, 14, 24, 87, 109, 117, 120, 140, 141, 148, 158, 164, 202, 216, 237, 238, 239, 240
Sulphur and Dominion 102, 105
Sulphur Creek 139, 174, 175, 176, 177, 178, 179, 192, 200, 215
Susie 226, 227, 228, 229, 233, 241, *241*, 243, 251
Swede Creek 93, 164, 180
Sybil 226, 227

Taggart, Sam 169
Tagish Dawson Charlie 3
Tagish House 78
Tanana Hills 235
Tanana River 235
Tarzlaff, Wayne A. 8

telegram *251*
temperature 5, 58, 132, 133, 138, 152, 156, 157, 159–60, *160*, 181, 182, 193, 221; *see also* weather
Tenderfoot 5, 93, 116, *see also* Cheechaco; Greenhorn
Teslin River 85
Thirty Mile River 83, 84, 94
the Thompson Party 120, 126, 139, 144, 146, 158, 186, 188, 190, 191, 214, 216, 220, 224; the Chinamen 188
Tibbetts, John 8
tobacco 47, 120, 121, 137, 138, 158–59, 181, 197, 211, 221, 224, 239

Unimak Pass, Alaska 244, *245*, 246
Upper Bonanza 200
Upper Dominion 150, 156
Uyak Bay, Alaska 248, 249, *249*

Vancouver Island, British Columbia 29, 251
Victoria, British Columbia 29, 69
Victoria of St. Michael 89

Wallace's Maps 96
weather 4, 5, 7, 16, 40, 45, 49, 53, 56, 75, 78, 80, 95, 96, 113, 117, 118, 119, 119–20, 126, 131–36, 138, 139, 144, 148, 156, 159–60, *160*, 181, 186, 187, 190, 196, 214; *see also* temperature
Weather Report *160*
whist 15, 139, 151, 234, 235, 252,
White Horse (town) 78, *79*, 80, 83, 85, 218, 226, 254
White Horse Rapids 45, 60, 80–83, 213, 215, 255
White Pass and Yukon Railroad 75, 77
White Pass Trail 4, 6, 45, 122; *see also* Dead Horse Trail
White River 86
White's Cove 48, 49
Willie Irving 221, 227
Windy Arm 77, 80
Wisconsin 240
Woodlawn Hotel 39, 45, 51, 52
the Woodpile (Dawson) 166, 230
Working a Lay 111, 145

the Yukon (locus) 4, 5, 6, 7, 8, 17, 33, 44, 62, 151, 161, 214
Yukon Delta 240
Yukon Flats 233, 234
Yukon River 3, 4, 75, 86, 90, 92, 96, 104, 105, 113, 114, 115, 125, 130, 138, 140, 146, 147, 148, 150, 152, 162, 163, 164, 191, 200, 201, 214, 215, 218, 219, 220, 224, 226, 230–41, *239*
Yukoner 226

www.ingramcontent.com/pod-product-compliance
Lightning Source LLC
Chambersburg PA
CBHW081546300426
44116CB00015B/2779